# MODERN
# ENGLAND AND WALES

ENGLISH MILES

# OF CHAPTERS AND SUBTOPICS

| SYSTEM | THE LEGAL SYSTEM | | |
|---|---|---|---|
| LOCAL GOVERN-MENT | ORGANIZATION AND JURISDIC-TION OF COURTS | PROCEDURE AND THE LEGAL PROFESSION | SUBSTANTIVE LAW |

**PERIOD, c. 450-1066**

| II | CHAPTER III | | |
|---|---|---|---|
| Local government: the shire<br>The hundred and its organization<br>Villages and boroughs<br>The local government of the church<br>The lordship system<br>Paternalism | The Anglo-Saxon courts and their jurisdiction<br>The Witan<br>The shire courts<br>The hundred courts<br>The borough courts<br>Private courts | Procedure: initiation and process<br>Pleading and preliminary judgment<br>The trial<br>The judgment and execution<br>Methodology and legal literature | Substantive law: introduction<br>Criminal law<br>Civil law: real property<br>Personal property and contracts<br>Family law and inheritance |

**MIDDLE AGES, 1066-1307**

| CHAPTER VII | CHAPTER VIII | CHAPTER IX | CHAPTER X |
|---|---|---|---|
| The county: the sheriff<br>Reforming efforts and the coroner system<br>Hundred, manor, and town<br>The ecclesiastical side of local government | The Conquest and the new central courts of common law<br>The itinerant justices<br>The county and hundred courts<br>The feudal and other private courts<br>The ecclesiastical courts<br>Courts of special jurisdiction | The initiating step in criminal cases<br>The initiation of civil cases<br>The writs for real actions<br>The personal writs<br>Process and pleading<br>Methods of trial<br>The remaining steps<br>The legal profession and its literature | Norman ideas of law and authority<br>Real property: entail and estates<br>Conveyancing<br>Personal property and contracts<br>Inheritance<br>Family law<br>Criminal law and theories of liability |

**AGES, 1307-1485**

| XIII | CHAPTER XIV | | |
|---|---|---|---|
| Local government<br>The justices of the peace<br>General disorder: the Church | The common law courts and their rivalries<br>The development of Chancery<br>Admiralty, merchant, and church courts | Common law and Chancery procedure<br>The profession: its leaders and literature<br>The inns of court<br>Sergeants, attorneys, and solicitors | Substantive law: criminal<br>Real property and contracts |

# CONSTITUTIONAL
# AND LEGAL
# HISTORY OF ENGLAND

## M. M. KNAPPEN

MICHIGAN STATE COLLEGE

NEW YORK

HARCOURT, BRACE AND COMPANY

1942

# PREFACE

Twenty years have now elapsed since Professor G. B. Adams published his *Constitutional History of England,* and many more since the first appearance of the English manuals on this subject by T. P. Taswell-Langmead and F. C. Montague. In the intervening decades changes have taken place that seem to make a new textbook in this field desirable for American students. In addition to the progress of research and the corresponding development of new points of view there have been major alterations in the curricula of American educational institutions. Courses in general European history, or even the history of civilization, have commonly replaced those in English history at the high-school and junior-college level. The student therefore comes to the subject of English constitutional history with far less of the particular background needed than his predecessors used to have. On the other hand, the course is now frequently included in a "new plan" law curriculum which distributes what was formerly prelegal work throughout the entire program, and thus demands of constitutional history a closer integration with legal work than was hitherto necessary.

Because current curricula are crowded, this is a brief book. Many topics generally deemed important have perforce been treated in a few words or omitted altogether. If the expert reader is shocked at finding cavalier pronouncements on questions which for years have puzzled specialists, his painful sensations will be as nothing to those of the author, who has been forced so often to make use of the textbook writer's license. With what twinges of conscience I have spoken on matters still *sub judice,* or on which I ought to be better informed, the shades of earlier textbook writers may bear witness. My only justification is that I have waited in vain for the task to be undertaken by those better qualified.

To some of these doubts and uncertainties I have called as much attention in the text and the footnotes as seems fitting in a handbook of this sort. Two deserve special mention here. On the moot point of Anglo-Saxon feudalism I have eschewed the old—and to me unsatisfactory—distinction between political and economic feudalism, and by the use of the term "lordship" in speaking of the bond before 1066 and "contract" for it afterwards I have tried to suggest the difference between an undeveloped system in which personal ties predominated and the fully grown legal organism of the Norman lawyers. On the equally thorny question of the beginnings of Parliament I have associated myself with that school of thought which prefers to define the concept of that institution in terms of later developments rather than adhere to the letter of thirteenth and early fourteenth century etymological usage. In other words, I have emphasized the representative, financial, and legislative elements and paid comparatively little attention to the early judicial role played by this assembly. Whoever wishes to see the defense of this attitude set forth at length will find it in Bertie Wilkinson's *Studies in the Constitutional History of the Thirteenth and Fourteenth Centuries* (Manchester, Eng., 1937) and in M. V. Clarke's *Medieval Representation and Consent* (Longmans, Green, 1936). It may also be found in the section which T. F. T. Plucknett has devoted to Parliament in the first volume of the long-awaited series of studies on *The English Government at Work, 1327-1336*, ed. by James F. Willard and William A. Morris (Medieval Academy of America, 1940). I greatly regret that this important work appeared too late for me to make more extensive use of it.

Though avoiding lengthy justifications of the course chosen on controversial points of detail, I have felt free to introduce whatever new interpretations seemed appropriate. As political

scientists have shifted their attention from the structure of governmental machinery to the interplay of the forces that control
it, the subject of constitutional history has naturally felt the
effects of this new outlook, and the organization of the material
in this volume has been shaped accordingly. In undertaking to
suggest the causes of the developments described I have tried to
refer to geographic, military, economic, cultural, and even psychological, as well as political, forces. In addition to describing
the development of liberal nationalism—doubtless the chief theme
in any current treatment of English constitutional history—I have
endeavored not to overlook other elements in the English governmental tradition that have had an illustrious past, are not
without force today, and may be of even greater consequence in
the future.

As one who studied under Wallace Notestein, who was in turn
trained by G. B. Adams, I have obviously borrowed—consciously
and unconsciously—a great deal from many predecessors in this
field. I hope that I have profited by the careful research work
of many a monograph writer, but only on a few of the more
general works can I particularize. A. B. White's *Making of the
English Constitution, 449-1485* (2d ed. rev., Putnam, 1925) first
introduced me to the medieval portion of my subject and led
me on to the works of Bishop Stubbs and Charles Petit-Dutaillis.
W. A. Morris' *Constitutional History of England to 1216* (Macmillan, 1930) has assisted me greatly in dealing with the difficult
problems of the earlier part of that section. For the later
periods I have relied largely on D. L. Keir, *Constitutional History
of Modern Britain, 1485-1937* (Van Nostrand, 1939); M. A.
Thomson, *Constitutional History of England, 1642-1801* (London, 1938); K. B. Smellie, *A Hundred Years of English Government* (Macmillan, 1937); and A. Berriedale Keith, *The Constitution of England from Victoria to George VI* (Macmillan, 1940).
Felix Makower's *Constitutional History and Constitution of the
Church of England* (Macmillan, 1895) has been my guide in mat-

ters ecclesiastical. Like many another ordinary mortal I have been alternately charmed and awed by the genius of F. W. Maitland. From his works and the monumental opus of Professor W. S. Holdsworth I have gleaned most of what I know of English legal history. R. M. Jackson's *The Machinery of Justice in England* (Cambridge, Eng., 1940) has proved very helpful for information regarding the workings of the present court system. I am also indebted to D. J. Medley and the other handbook writers mentioned in the opening lines of this preface, whose works I have used for classroom purposes. Of W. E. Lunt's scholarly textbook in general English history a high opinion formed in some years of teaching from it has been confirmed and strengthened in the course of preparing this volume by frequent references to the recently revised version (Harper, 1938). To copy from one book, says my former teacher, Carl Becker, is plagiarism, but to copy from two is scholarship. By that standard this is a very scholarly work, since, following the illustrious practice of Homer and Kipling, what I thought I might require I went and took. In other words, this book makes no pretense of being anything but a summary of other people's work. If the experts had shown any signs of putting out a brief text in this field in the near future, I should not have attempted it. But apparently those who know more of the subject know better than to be guilty of such rashness.

There are several experts, however, who have been kind enough to go over this manuscript or a portion of it and give me the benefit of their criticisms. Professor Notestein has read nearly all of it. Three former colleagues at the University of Chicago, Sheldon Tefft, Frances Gillespie, and James L. Cate, have helped with sizable portions. On moot points I have profited greatly from consultations with one of my present colleagues, Dr. H. H. Kimber. Two anonymous publisher's readers have also given valuable assistance. But by far my greatest debt is to my friend Professor Glenn W. Gray of the University of Nebraska, who has read almost all the manuscript with great care and graciously shared with me his very extensive knowledge of the field. Without the sheaf of suggestions and corrections which he sent me this would have been a very, very much poorer book.

I wish also to express my appreciation to those who have assisted with other parts of the undertaking. Professor and Mrs. F. D. Walker of the University of Oregon made another generous contribution to a long-standing friendship by attending to the troublesome business of locating a view of Lincoln that would illustrate the points I wished to have brought out (page 30). To the kindness and artistry of Mr. and Mrs. James L. Godfrey of the University of North Carolina I owe the picture of St. Albans Cathedral tower shown on page 81. The portraits and the scenes from the two inn halls are reproduced from the original prints in the Charles B. Pike collection of the University of Chicago Law School, whose faculty has kindly consented to their use. Miss Maurine Christopher has rendered most cheerful and efficient service in typing the manuscript.

M. M. K.

# CONTENTS

## OLIGARCHIC LIBERALISM

## THE TREND TO DEMOCRATIC LIBERALISM

# ILLUSTRATIONS

# MAPS AND CHARTS

# The Anglo-Saxon Period

# 1. GENERAL HISTORY
## c. 450-1066

**The English Constitution.** The English constitution is not a written document. It is the way the English government is organized and works. This way is determined by a number of influences. These influences ultimately can be traced back to the character of the inhabitants of England, past and present, and their material and cultural environment. Some of the effects of these influences are embodied in written laws, others in court decisions, and still others only in commonly accepted customs. These laws, decisions, and customs are what we must study if we wish to understand the way the English government is organized and works—that is to say, the English constitution.

**English Constitutional History.** English constitutional history is the story of the origins and development of the English way of government. It aims to trace the workings of the different influences or causal factors from the social setting in which they began to operate to the laws, decisions, and customs that they produced. It also undertakes to describe and explain the changes in this threefold constitutional deposit which have been brought about either by the substitution of one law, decision, or custom for another or by the addition of entirely new ones.

**The Relation of Legal History to Constitutional History.** Law is a phase of government comparable to taxation or the military system. Legal history is therefore only one phase of constitutional history, a close-up of one aspect of the development of government as a whole. Accordingly, the English legal system grows directly out of the character of the English people and the

3

environment in which they have found themselves. While this volume undertakes to treat the legal side of constitutional history in greater detail than any other phase, the student should not consider this aspect necessarily any more important than, or essentially different from, those dealt with more briefly. Conceivably, students of public finance, military science, police work, or social service might have constitutional histories especially designed for them. Because it so happens, however, that this volume is intended particularly for legal and prelegal students, that portion of constitutional history which especially concerns their field of interest receives fuller treatment than any other.

**The Beginning Date.** English constitutional history begins in the middle of the fifth century A.D. when invading Germanic peoples, traditionally known as Angles, Saxons, and Jutes, secured a foothold on the island and began to overrun the country. There had been a long succession of peoples in Britain before them—paleolithic (Old Stone Age), neolithic (New Stone Age), Celt, and Roman—and each of them had some kind of a government and therefore a constitutional history. But while Romanized Celts held the country at the coming of the Anglo-Saxons, whose advance they contested, they were so completely overwhelmed that practically none of their institutions survived. The most diligent research has failed to establish any substantial connection between the Romano-Celtic civilization in Britain and the Anglo-Saxon civilization which succeeded it. We may therefore safely omit the stories of earlier tribal confederations and imperial experiments without endangering the unity or completeness of our story. For we are concerned only with the development of the government of the country after it is properly called England, the land of the Angles.

## THE PHYSICAL ENVIRONMENT

**Size and Location of the Islands.** The invading tribesmen found themselves on the southeastern coast of a long, jagged island twenty-one miles off the mainland of Europe. It was some seven hundred miles in length and varied in width from three hundred miles at its base to a hundred or less in much of its upper half. Its area was some 89,000 square miles, or a little less than the combined size of Pennsylvania and New York, or Illinois and Indiana. If today it could be superimposed on the central United States so that the modern London fell on Chicago, the northern tip of the island would not quite span Lake Superior and the westernmost part (Cornwall) would reach only to Des Moines, Iowa. In the surrounding waters of the North Atlantic—particularly to the north and west—lay numerous other islands, only one of which was of any considerable size. That was Ireland, lying eighty miles to the west, with an area of 33,000 square miles.

**Topography and Natural Resources.** For the time being, however, the invaders did not concern themselves with Ireland, because they found their attention fully absorbed by the major island. This was known to the people of that day as Britain—a name whose origin we are unable to determine with certainty. The southeastern portion of Britain was a green and pleasant land, sloping gently down to the sea, where numerous river mouths afforded good harbors. Though heavily wooded in many sections, it was a good agricultural country broken here and there by hills which rarely rose more than seven or eight hundred feet above sea level. To the west and north the land became rougher and less productive, rising in one "mountainous" section to an elevation of forty-four hundred feet and in several others to over three thousand. In this area were considerable deposits of lead, tin, iron, and coal.

**Climate.** All the country was well watered, and the rainfall was of such a gentle and intermittent variety as to make the climate much damper than the thirty to forty inches of annual precipitation would seem to indicate. Although the island lay well to the north—in the same latitude as the modern Labrador—the prevailing winds and ocean currents provided a surprisingly moderate mixture of heat and cold. At the present time the average temperature is 39° Fahrenheit in January and 63° during July. Probably there has not been a great deal of climatic change in the last fifteen hundred years. Farming operations could be carried on nearly the year round. Snow rarely lay on the ground for more than a day or two, and when a river was frozen over it was considered a great event. Yet these facts are somewhat deceptive, for the gradual precipitation and the winds regularly blowing off the ocean gave the island a great deal of raw, damp weather. The possible effect of this damp climate on the development of the English constitution must not be overlooked. Many other factors have played a part in shaping the character of the modern Englishman, but since warm, dry, continental climates tend to make people excitable if not irritable, it seems reasonable to suppose that the cool, damp climate of England may have had an opposite effect. The men and women who have lived in this climate day after day have tended to become not only hardy and persistent, but patient and even-tempered, if not phlegmatic. A flexible and somewhat vague constitution has perhaps suited such a people. Street revolutions have never been popular in England. Enthusiastic parades and the manning of barricades, which may be practicable in a continental climate, do not go with an environment where steady drizzles and "Scotch mists" are frequent. It is true that the Irish also have a damp climate, but in their case there are many counteracting factors.

## THE ANGLO-SAXONS AND THE CONQUEST

**Racial Origin of the Invaders.** The invading peoples were Germanic, coming from the area that is now Denmark and northern Germany. As we have already indicated, they are known in history as Angles, Saxons, and Jutes. The best available evidence, however—especially that collected by archaeologists who have studied the burial remains in England and the continental regions across the Channel and the North Sea—suggests that probably only the Angles, who originally inhabited the territory of the modern Schleswig, were a genuine historical tribe. It would seem that the other two names were applied to alliances of tribes or mixtures of peoples which developed comparatively late in historical times. It is now generally agreed that the Saxons, whom we first meet in the region south of Schleswig that is now Holstein, were so called because they were the users of the seax or sahs, a short one-handed sword. Since their name does not appear in early lists of German tribes compiled by the Roman writer Tacitus, it is probable that "Saxon" was a group name for an alliance of tribes, just as was the term "Frank," which means a spearman. While the Jutes may have been so named because their first leaders came from Jutland in northern Denmark, this band of invaders seems to have recruited its ranks largely from the Frisian and Frankish peoples living to the southwest of the Saxons. Probably all the invaders were racially very much alike. Between the Angles and Saxons, certainly, there was little marked difference after they came to England, for the Angles were frequently called Saxons by strangers and the Saxons in time came to call themselves Angles, and their country England (Angleland).

**Material and Cultural Background of the Invaders.** These three invading peoples, whom we may call Anglo-Saxons for the sake of convenience, were typically Germanic, tall, longheaded,

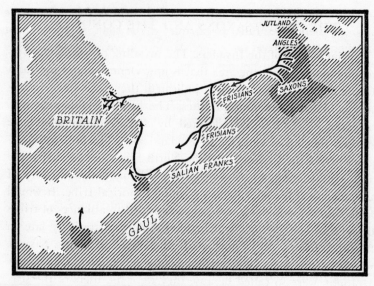

THE ANGLO-SAXON INVASIONS

and fair-haired. Originally they must have depended largely on hunting for their livelihood, but in time they had learned the less exciting but more certain art of cultivating the soil. They had also acquired other skills. They could weave cloth and even put into it various patterns, such as the diamond-shaped one. In their long open boats, which they commonly rowed rather than sailed, they proved themselves expert seamen. Round wooden shields, swords, spears, bows and arrows, were their chief weapons. They worshiped gods of nature and war, and seem to have had some vague belief in a future life. Human sacrifices were apparently offered in some cases; prisoners taken in war probably provided the victims for these sacrificial rites. There is nothing to indicate that the Anglo-Saxons, or the Germanic peoples in general, had any special aptitude for democracy or any other type of governmental development, aside from that which can be explained by their environment. Celtic peoples, such as the Welsh, and mixed stocks, such as the Scots, have proved themselves fully as capable in the field of government as their Anglo-Saxon neighbors. Modern scholarship is not only breaking down old notions of the purity of any given race, but also dissipating ideas of the natural superiority of one over another.[1] Governmental pre-eminence is not a racial prerogative.

**The Beginning of the Invasion of England.** At the beginning of the Christian era the homeland of the Anglo-Saxon peoples seems to have provided ample room for their hunting and farming activities. But in the following centuries they increased rapidly in numbers. At first they relieved the pressure by spreading out along the Atlantic coast to the southward, into the region in the eastern part of the modern Holland known as Frisia. But their numbers continued to increase, and the encroachment of the ocean on the sandy Frisian coast took away some of their "living room" and forced them to build their homes on terps—mounds of clay, sod, and reedy manure. Consequently, from the third century onward they frequently attacked Britain, though until the fifth century the southern half of the island was a province of the Roman Empire. For protection against these assaults the Romans in Britain constructed a system of fortifications along the eastern coast of the province, which came to be known as the Saxon shore. With the breakdown of the Western Roman Empire the Germanic invaders poured in all along its northern frontier. Some of the Saxons then made their way farther along the Continental coast into what had been the Roman province of Gaul (modern Belgium and France). About the middle of the fifth century the Anglo-Saxons began moving from the new bases thus obtained and also from the old ones into Britain, the province that they had marked for their own.

[1] "We regard it as practically certain that there is no necessary biological relation between the criteria of race and the capacity for mental growth."— Gardner Murphy, L. B. Murphy, and T. M. Newcomb, *Experimental Social Psychology*, Harper, 1937, p. 68.

ENGLAND IN THE PERIOD OF THE HEPTARCHY

**The Method of the Invasion.** The invaders did not come to Britain as a national army, but as separate warrior bands. Each of these found what foothold it could on the coast and slowly worked its way inland. The Romanized Celtic inhabitants, called Britons, resisted as well as they could. One of their most stubborn and gallant leaders was the chieftain known in legend as King Arthur. Slowly, however, the Britons were overcome. Those who were not killed were either enslaved or driven westward into the rougher section of the island. The ratio of surviving Britons to Anglo-Saxons in the areas overrun by the invaders varied from a negligible percentage on the eastern coast to a large minority in the west and in the southern midland region of the upper Thames Valley. Though the social and political institutions of the Britons were almost completely destroyed, the survival in the Anglo-Saxon language of such Celtic words for domestic objects as "rug" indicates that the Britons did household and agricultural service for their conquerors. Their blood was soon mixed with the Anglo-Saxon, and thus whatever racial purity the invaders may have had at the beginning of the invasion did not long survive the conquest.

**The Area Conquered.** The struggle between Celt and Saxon lasted about a century and a half. By a victory at Deorham, in the southwest, in 577 the intruders succeeded in establishing themselves on the Bristol Channel, and by a similar success at Chester in 616 they reached the western coast to the north of Wales. The Celtic opposition in the southern part of the island was thus divided into three separate geographical sections. Of these the northern and southern were overrun in the two succeeding centuries, though the Cornishmen in the southwestern tip of Britain remained so predominantly Celtic that even today they consider themselves different from the average Englishman. ("Fee fi fo fum," says Jack's Cornish giant. "I smell the blood of an *Englishman*.") Mountainous Wales alone was left as an independent Celtic area in the west, owing not only to its rugged terrain but also to the fact that the river Severn provided it with a natural boundary. The Celtic opposition in the northern part of the island was handicapped by the lack of any such natural boundary, and the Saxon power at times extended beyond the Forth River, well into the modern Scotland. But the Highlands lying to the north of the Forth Valley were never subdued, and the Celtic peoples preserved there a base of operations which later grew into an independent kingdom (page 90).

## THE HEPTARCHY AND THE ANGLO-SAXON ECONOMY

**The Kingdoms Established.** Since the invaders came in scattered bands, they did not organize their gains into one large state but into many smaller ones, each under its own warrior-chief. The mixed people known as Jutes settled the southeastern tip of England and established in it a kingdom called Kent. West and north of them came the South, West, Middle, and East Saxons, whose kingdoms bore the contracted names of Sussex, Wessex, Middlesex, and Essex. Three groups of Angles occupied the rest of the conquered territory. Of this, the midland section, bordering on Wales, was called Mercia (the march, or borderland), the peninsula north of Essex was known as East Anglia (the country of the East Angles), and the territory north of the Humber River became, by another contraction, Northumbria. At times there were even further subdivisions. A section on the border of Wessex and Mercia known as Hwicce was for a long time independent, though at other periods a dependency of one of its neighbors. East Anglia was divided into the territory of the North and South Folk (whence the modern Norfolk and Suffolk) and Northumbria was sometimes separated into Bernicia and Deira. There were thus usually ten or a dozen different kingdoms during early Saxon times, but the first modern historians to write about this period distinguished only seven

of the larger and more important. As a result the arrangement
is frequently referred to as a heptarchy, a system of rulership by
seven powers.

**Saxon Economic Life.** The Anglo-Saxons preferred the country to the town, and agriculture to trade. It is true that they kept
up more intercourse with the Continent than is commonly supposed, and by the end of their period of domination on the island
there was notable mercantile activity among them. But they fell
far short of the Roman standard. In most parts of the island,
the fine roads that their imperial predecessors had built were
neglected and allowed to deteriorate, until in many places only
the merest tracks remained, impassable even in dry weather for
all but pedestrians and men on horseback. Though the survival to the present day of some vestiges of the classical names
for such towns as London (called *Londinium* by the Romans),
Lincoln *(Lindum colonia,* colony), York *(Eburacum,* later modified into *Eofer-wic*), and all those ending in -chester *(castra,*
camp) shows that the sites were not altogether abandoned at
this time, their population suffered a sharp drop. In the rural
areas, for the most part the Anglo-Saxons tended to leave the
village sites on the hills, which the Celts had preferred, and to
settle in the valleys, where water was more easily obtained. More
important, they usually concentrated the rural population in
compact villages, and thus abandoned the isolated homesteads
that had been common among the Celts. The land surrounding
the villages was divided up into two large open (unenclosed,
unfenced) fields, which were in turn subdivided into strips owned
privately by the different villagers.[2] A system of crop rotation
was practiced; that is, one field was allowed to lie idle or fallow
each year, and thus its fertility was in large part restored. In

[2] Toward the end of the Anglo-Saxon period the practice was introduced
of dividing the cultivated lands around the typical village into three instead
of two fields. It was thus possible to raise two different crops in a given year
and have only one-third of the land fallow at any one time. There were
other types of field systems, notably in the semi-Celtic west and in Kent.

addition to the two fields, a separate tract was set aside for a meadow to be used in common, and the woodland and wasteland in the neighborhood were similarly shared. Since the great majority of the Anglo-Saxon peoples—as indeed of all the English down to the eighteenth century—made their living by agriculture, it must be remembered that the governmental institutions which they developed were originally designed for a civilization predominantly rural and agrarian rather than urban or industrial.

**Standards of Living.** Because standards of living are dependent on economic conditions, it is not to be expected that in such a simple economy as the Anglo-Saxon one housing arrangements would be very advanced. The bulk of the people lived in rude huts of a room or two, usually sunk two feet or more in the earth. By digging out the floor the builder could make the surrounding dirt serve as low walls, on which rested a sloping roof of mud and straw laid on a framework of poles. In another type of dwelling the walls were apparently made of wattle and daub—clay plastered on a network of willow withes fastened to corner timbers—and the roof was thatched with straw. More prosperous individuals lived in houses built of logs set upright in the ground and surrounded by palisades similarly constructed. Toward the end of the Anglo-Saxon period a few of the more important buildings—such as churches and monasteries—had moderate-sized portions built of stone, usually the towers. The costume of the Anglo-Saxons consisted of rough cloth tunics and trousers or puttees for the men, and long flowing tunics and mantles for the women. Food was rough and simple—meat when it could be had, but more often bread, cheese, and a soup of peas and beans called pottage. The favorite drink was mead, a fermented mixture of honey and water, but in the poorer homes beer was more often used. A somewhat better impression of the period is given by the jewelry that has survived, especially the safety-pin type of brooches by whose curiously different styles, as revealed in excavations of Saxon cemeteries, archaeologists are enabled to follow the trail of the different tribes. Some of these brooches are embellished with garnets, very fine cloisonné (cell work) settings, and filigree decorations. In the opinion of experts they show a fineness of craftsmanship which can bear comparison with the best of modern times. On the whole the standards of living of the Anglo-Saxons after they reached England, while very low when judged by Roman or modern standards, represent a considerable improvement over the living-conditions they had known in their Continental homelands. Furthermore, there was a definite, though by no means continuous, tendency for these to rise as the invaders became more settled in their new homes.

## THE ESTABLISHMENT OF CHRISTIANITY

**The Introduction of Christianity.** About the time the Celtic front was finally broken at Bristol and Chester, the cultural side of Anglo-Saxon civilization was greatly affected by the introduction of Christianity. This religion had established itself in Britain in Roman times, but as a result of the Anglo-Saxon conquest it had been destroyed or pushed westward along with most of the other elements of the Romanized Celtic culture. In 596 Pope Gregory the Great determined to re-establish Christianity in its old location. He sent a missionary monk named Augustine (not the great theologian, who lived two centuries earlier) with a band of fellow monks to convert Ethelbert, King of Kent. This ruler was obviously susceptible, because his domain was close to the Continent, and he had already taken a Christian wife from across the Channel. A pagan priesthood existed among the Anglo-Saxons, but since little is known of its duties or activities, it must have been very weak. The prestige of Rome, the superior cultural attainments of Augustine and his fellow monks, and their confidence on the question of the future life soon carried the day. In 597 the King accepted the new religion, and his subjects promptly followed his example. During the next century the Christian influence slowly spread itself over the kingdoms to the north and west. Because Canterbury—the bury or town of Kent—was its first English center, this city has remained ever since the ecclesiastical capital of England.

**Rivalry with Irish Christianity.** In the north the Roman missionaries met with more than the usual difficulties, for there they found that Celtic emissaries, coming in from Ireland by way of Scotland, were preaching a slightly different variety of Christianity. The only important difference between the two was that Celtic Christianity was organized around monasteries while the government of the Roman one was through bishops. But the issues on which the two clashed were such minor matters as the dating of Easter and the style of tonsure (haircut) to be adopted by the clergy. For a time it seemed that a Christian frontier was to be established somewhere inside the heptarchic system. But in 664 at the Synod (Council) of Whitby, on the Northumbrian coast, the points of controversy were decided in favor of the Roman Catholics by Oswy, the ruler of Northumbria. The result was to establish one religion for England as a whole, and to open the way for Continental religious and cultural influences to spread throughout the island.

**The Work of Theodore.** Five years later, in 669, Pope Vitalian sent out a Greek named Theodore of Tarsus to be Archbishop of Canterbury and to organize the victorious Church. When he arrived he found the Church hampered by the fact that there was only one bishop to each kingdom, which in the larger kingdoms gave the bishops too great an area to supervise. He proceeded at once to set up additional bishoprics and to facilitate the establishment of parishes—the areas around the churches in charge of individual priests (page 43). So well did he do his work that in 673 it was possible to hold at Hertford, twenty-four miles north of London, a synod of churchmen gathered from all the English kingdoms. The importance of this for our purpose is that it gave to the Anglo-Saxon part of the island a model of unity which the secular rulers eventually followed. Since political unity was not secured for almost a century and a half, it is clear that the ecclesiastical example was not all-compelling. But it did exert some influence.

## THE BEGINNING OF POLITICAL UNIFICATION

**Rivalries of the Bretwaldas.** The ambitions of the rival kings made another important contribution to the cause of political unification. Not content with ruling their own territories, they sought to extend their power over their neighbors. Sometimes this was done by conquest and absorption, but more often these ambitious rulers extorted from weaker neighbors an acknowledgment of suzerainty (overlordship). This acknowledgment gave the overlord an uncertain and fluctuating kind of power of which the most definite feature was the right to collect tribute from the underkings. Also the overlords (bretwaldas, rulers of Britain) frequently secured personal estates in the subject kingdoms, and sometimes seem to have exercised a kind of supervision over all important grants of land within them. But the power varied greatly from bretwalda to bretwalda, and in spite of the name, until the ninth century the bretwalda's power did not approach that of a monarch of a genuinely unified state. Ethelbert of Kent, Augustine's convert, first built up this vague kind of overlordship toward the close of the sixth century. In the seventh the power passed to the kings of Northumbria—hence the importance of the decision at Whitby—and in the eighth century Mercia was supreme under two kings, Ethelbald and Offa. Finally, in the ninth century the predominant power was claimed and won by Wessex, under a king named Egbert.

**Egbert's New System.** Before Egbert came to the throne of his native Wessex in 802 he had been involved in a dynastic quarrel

and had spent some time in exile on the Continent at the court
of Charlemagne, who was trying to revive the Western Roman
Empire. There he had seen in operation a system of government
controlling a wide area in which no underkings were permitted.
All the imperial possessions were managed by the one central
government and its agents. Once back in England, Egbert enjoyed great success in his military operations and thereafter
undertook to institute something of the Continental system in
his enlarged sphere of influence. Even he, however, was not able
to destroy the power of the underkings completely, and while
later representatives of his line were eventually successful in this
effort, this success was only made possible by a kind of left-
handed "assistance" from outside.

## THE DANISH INVASIONS

**The First Invasions.** The new element in the situation was
the coming of the Northmen (Vikings), whom the English called
Danes. These Scandinavian raiders and invaders were actuated
by much the same motives as the Anglo-Saxon invaders of the
fifth century—the desire for plunder and new homesteads. In
the early ninth century they began to secure footholds on the
eastern coast of England. As they advanced they overran and
destroyed the petty subkingdoms with which they first came in
contact. Wessex proper had to struggle hard for its existence,
but under the leadership of a grandson of Egbert named Alfred
it at last stopped the Danish advance. When Alfred, whose remarkable abilities caused him to be known as "the Great," came
to the throne in 871 he was only twenty-three. His health was
not good, and the Danes had already begun the attack on his
country. But after fifteen years of difficulty and danger, careful
planning, and hard fighting, Alfred forced his adversaries to accept an agreement called (from the name of the Danish leader)
Guthrum's Treaty (886). This gave to Wessex all that terri-

tory southwest of a line drawn from Chester in the northwest southeastward through Bedford and to the Thames east of London. The remainder of England was given to the Danes and came to be known as the Danelaw (the area in which the law of the Danes prevailed). Alfred's children and grandchildren undertook to reconquer this Danish territory. After more hard fighting, in which Alfred's daughter Ethelfleda distinguished herself as a strategist, the task was accomplished. By 954 Alfred's grandson Edred could be called the king of a genuinely unified England. The Danish invasions, which had almost completely destroyed the smaller kingdoms of the northeast, had made this possible.

**Dunstan's Reforms.** In the last years of the struggle with the Danes a churchman named Dunstan exerted great influence at the royal court. Afterward, as Archbishop of Canterbury, he continued to do so for nearly thirty years, until his death in 988. During this time he was the chief power in the Saxon state. He was of noble birth and had early braved the scorn of his aristocratic friends by becoming a monk. Largely through his efforts a monastic reform that had started in the Benedictine monastery at Cluny in France (page 107) was introduced into England. Under the influence of this reform, monks kept their vows more strictly and devoted themselves to study and teaching, as well as to religious activities. Stimulated by this example, the secular clergy (page 42) became more attentive to their duties. The reform also affected the laymen, for higher standards of morality were enforced by ecclesiastical discipline. Where divorce had once been a matter of mutual consent, the marriage tie was now made more binding, under threat of excommunication—barring the offender from the Christian sacraments and even social intercourse with the faithful. The Saxon vice of drunkenness was also attacked. Excess of this sort had formerly been so common that it passed almost without notice. A monastic chronicler of the earlier period reported in a matter-of-fact

way that during a daylong drinking bout the monks' barrel of
mead was miraculously kept to within a handbreadth of its original level until visiting noblemen were "drunk as hogs." But
Dunstan frowned on such dissipation and had marks put in the
cups so that the drinkers would be aware of how much they
were taking.

**The Second Danish Invasions.** During the period of Dunstan's
influence the House of Wessex continued to rule, and held its
position without serious difficulty until 980. In that year, however, the Danish raids were resumed. These raids were organized on a larger scale than those of the ninth century had been,
and after a time they received the definite support of the rulers
of Denmark. The reigning King of England, called Ethelred the
Redeless, or Unready (counsel-less, "rede" meaning "counsel")
because of his weak policy, attempted at first to buy the invaders
off. To that end he levied a land tax called a Danegeld (Danes'
money), the first direct money tax in English history to be levied
for the benefit of the secular government. This policy of paying
blackmail to the invaders naturally brought about further and
more serious invasions. Eventually, in 1017, Canute, or Cnut,
son of the Danish king who had given government support to
the invasions, became King of England. Later he succeeded his
brother as King of Denmark also. Surprisingly enough, he gave
his conquered realm a comparatively peaceful rule. There were
no great confiscations of property and there were comparatively
few innovations in government. Had Canute's sons, who followed him on the English throne after his death in 1035, been
as capable rulers as their father, the Danish line might have
lasted indefinitely. The sons, however, were grossly incompetent, and in 1042 the English called to the throne a representative of the old Wessex line, a son of Ethelred known as Edward
the Confessor because of his religious zeal.

## THE LAST ANGLO-SAXON KING: SUMMARY

**Edward the Confessor's Reign (1042-66).** Edward had spent the years of the Danish rule in exile at the court of Richard of Normandy, his mother's brother. Normandy (the land of the Northmen) was a kind of Viking Danelaw on the north coast of France, which had been conquered by the Northmen at the beginning of the tenth century. On Edward's return to England he brought with him a good many Norman customs, and also Norman friends whom he appointed to important offices. His reign of twenty-four years was therefore something of a preparation for the Norman Conquest that was to follow.

**Forces at Work during This Period.** In this chapter we have tried to suggest some of the main forces that were at work in Anglo-Saxon society. (1) The first and most important of these was the rising tide of civilization, that is to say, a combination of a desire for greater creature comforts and an increased interest in the finer things of life—the true, the beautiful, and the good. The ebbings and flowings of this tide of civilization are more easily noted than explained. Why the Anglo-Saxons should suddenly find new vigor when the Romans, with all their advantages, were losing theirs is a fascinating puzzle to which many solutions have been proposed but none found entirely satisfactory. Perhaps the theories based on the phenomena of social fatigue and the stimulus of novelty are as good as any. For as one people seems to tire of the effort needed to develop and maintain a civilized existence, a new race begins to find it interesting. (2) Closely related to this general force of civilization was the introduction of the Christian Church, with its moral, intellectual, and political influence. (3) There was also the ever present desire among the Anglo-Saxon kings for an enlargement of boundaries and for the political unification of the land. (4) Another important force was land hunger. As we have seen, this was influential in bringing about the original Anglo-Saxon invasions. As the Saxon period drew to a close it again became important, for land was becoming relatively difficult to secure and the economic opportunities open to the rank and file of the Anglo-Saxon people declined accordingly. (5) The working of all these forces was complicated by a system of communications that was decidedly primitive. With the exception of a few prearranged beacon signals, no message traveled more rapidly than human or animal foot could carry it, and the transportation of bulky commodities by wheeled vehicles was carried on only under the greatest of difficulties.

**A Time of Violence for the Great.** (6) One factor, however, has necessarily been slighted in this brief summary. That is the element of violence, which is often forgotten in any short sketch of events covering centuries. It is easy to say that in spite of the slowly rising tide of civilization there were many wars. It is hard to suggest in a few words what these wars meant to the people of that time. Yet if one reckons up the number of invasions and border conflicts to which we have referred in this brief account of the Anglo-Saxon period, it should be apparent that during this time life was a very uncertain thing. A few illustrations must suffice on this point. The succession to the throne was frequently disputed, even after the time of Egbert. There were innumerable palace plots. One ruler, who has come down in history as King Edward the Martyr (reigned 975-78) was fatally stabbed by partisans of his half-brother, Ethelred the Unready, while on a visit to his stepmother, Ethelred's mother. On the death of Canute, Edward the Confessor's older brother was considered by Canute's son Harold Harefoot a dangerous rival for the crown. By Harold's order he was enticed back to England by a forged letter, seized, and blinded. A captured Archbishop of Canterbury had his skull split by drunken Danish sailors. Even Canute's reign was peaceful only in a relative sense. When his own brother-in-law Ulf, who had recently saved his life in battle, refused to take back a clever chess move that his royal opponent had not anticipated, Canute flew into a rage and broke up the game. The next morning, still nursing his grievance, the King ordered Ulf slain. The command was obeyed, even though the unfortunate nobleman took refuge in sanctuary and had to be killed in the church.

**And for the Small.** With the great men of the realm faring thus, it is obvious that lesser men could expect to fare no better. When Edward the Confessor's brother was captured, his followers, who made no resistance, were nearly all killed in cold blood. It is recorded that on a certain day in the reign of Ethelred an attempt was made to massacre every Danish man in his realm. With all too good reason many an unknown soldier feared the worst as he took his place in the shield-wall (battle line). Too frequently the defenders' bodies were hacked to pieces when the enemy "held the place of slaughter." Other stout fighters perished even more obscurely, struck down at dead of night in some forgotten cattle-stealing fray. Neither life nor property was safe in those tumultuous times.

# 2. ANGLO-SAXON GOVERNMENT

## THE GERMANIC INHERITANCE

**The Anglo-Saxon Pattern of Government.** In choosing a way of governing themselves in their new island environment the victorious invaders adapted and continued the practices with which they were familiar at home. It is not hard to imagine why the ways of their Celtic adversaries did not appeal to them. On the other hand, the complicated Roman procedure, of which they probably learned something in the course of their migrations, though doubtless somewhat awe-inspiring even to the invaders, was beyond the level of civilization to which they had attained. They might vaguely admire the imperial tradition, but they could not abide town life nor cope with the other problems which the Roman type of government involved. So they followed the line of least resistance and, like the early American settlers, relied upon the methods with which they had been familiar in their former homes, modifying them only enough to fit the new conditions.

**Sources of Information.** In trying to determine just what constitutional system the Anglo-Saxons had been accustomed to on the Continent we must rely on several different kinds of evidence, no one of which is as good as we should like. There are general descriptions of the Germanic tribes given by the Roman writers Caesar and Tacitus, about the beginning of the Christian era. There are hints to be gleaned from Anglo-Saxon writings of a later date, such as the poem *Beowulf*. The finds of arms and similar equipment in burial mounds give us some idea of Saxon military arrangements. Lastly, we are helped by our knowledge of the habits of other primitive peoples. While all tribes with a low level of civilization do not fully conform to a standard pattern, there are many striking points of similarity about their cultures. Where better evidence is lacking, the historian is often guided by these general similarities when he must picture the culture of a primitive people about whom he has inadequate information.

**Factors in the Early Anglo-Saxon Constitution.** In the Continental Germanic constitutions there were a number of different and (to some extent) competing factors. In this respect the Anglo-Saxons were like any other people who have had a working constitution, for normally these same factors are present to some degree in all governmental structures. The varying emphasis on one or another, or some combination of them, is what commonly distinguishes one constitutional system from another. (1) There was an element of rulership or leadership. The Anglo-Saxons, to judge by the scanty evidence available, recognized that, at least in emergencies, efficiency demanded the concentration of power in the hands of one man. The most loosely organized of the Germanic tribes elected chiefs to lead them in time of war. Others had rulers who held office for life, and we know that the Angles had had at least one powerful king, Offa, before they left their Continental home. (2) There was an element of aristocracy. The abler fighters and counselors were given more land, and positions of greater influence in the government, than those enjoyed by the average man. (3) There was a hierarchical or priestly element. Those who were the religious and moral leaders of the community also enjoyed special privileges, and were influential out of all proportion to their numbers. They were not required to work with their hands, and in council their advice was respected. (4) There was also a democratic element. Tribal assemblies were consulted on important matters, such as those of peace and war. Men came to these primitive legislatures fully armed, and clashed their spears against their shields to show approval of a proposition. Murmurings indicated opposition. (5) There was an element of community sharing. Lands originally appear to have been held by the tribe (kindred group) in common and allocated from year to year according to considerations of fairness and individual need.

**The Universal Nature of These Elements.** Ever since this primitive period the main lines of the English constitution have developed according to the way one or more of these elements have been emphasized and others minimized. But none of them has ever completely disappeared, any more than it has in other constitutions. Though we speak loosely of states as being monarchies, oligarchies, theocracies, democracies, or socialistic commonwealths, what we really mean is that one or the other of these factors predominates. No monarchy or fascist dictatorship could long endure without considerable support from the other political elements in society. Theocracies must have their secular arms. Democracies need executive officers with extensive powers. Communistic states have their leaders and even priests, though these public servants may be known by other names.

**Social Classes and Their Constitutional Interests.** It will be noticed that to each of the five factors mentioned there corresponds an individual or social class whose political interests are best served by an emphasis on that particular factor. Kings wish to expand the powers of the executive. The nobility flourishes in an aristocratic system, and the clergy where the hierarchy is strong. The middle class normally prefers a democracy, and the working class tends to play its largest role in a socialistic society.

**The Position of Classes in the Primitive Germanic Constitution.** When we first hear of the Anglo-Saxons, on the Continent, their constitution seems to have been in a kind of primitive balance. As we have seen, all of the five elements mentioned had a considerable share in the governmental arrangements, though we must except that part of the working class which consisted of slaves and freedmen, or semifreemen. These members of the lowest class were definitely underprivileged in the matter of governmental influence. We are, however, unfortunately ignorant of the size and importance of this element.

## THE EFFECTS OF THE ANGLO-SAXON CONQUEST

**The Change in the Royal Status after the Invasion.** Since the Anglo-Saxons endeavored only to transplant their old institutions to the new country, this general pattern of government was followed for some time after the invasion. There were, however, some minor modifications in the first two or three centuries after the occupation of Britain. The position of the king was strengthened by the events of the invasion. For in the hundred and fifty years of the conquest struggle the Anglo-Saxons found it inconvenient to depend on temporary war chiefs. Instead they came to rely on leaders who held office for life and passed the position on to one of their children. There is an old saying which reflects this development—that war begat the king. Since we have already seen that there was a powerful king of the Angles before the invasion, it is obvious that there is some exaggeration in this proverb when it is applied only to the period of the conquest. Nevertheless, there is enough truth in it so that we shall let it stand. It is an axiom of political science that society nearly always sanctions an increase in the power of the executive in times of great stress, and the developments during this period of Anglo-Saxon history illustrate this principle. For although the institution of monarchy was not entirely unknown to the invaders before their emigration, it was certainly much strengthened by the events of those strenuous years.

**The Weakening of the Power of the Common People.** At the bottom of the social scale, on the other hand, in the sections of the conquered country that were long held peacefully the power of the rank and file in time declined. Because the supply of land was now seen to be limited, there was less disposition to relocate and redistribute the tribal holdings in accordance with individual needs. As there was less and less demand for his services as a fighting man the average member of a tribe found less opportunity to claim an economic reward for his military activity or to insist on a general redistribution of the available land. Early in the course of the invasion, if not even before, the strips of land in the great arable fields surrounding the villages came to be considered private property, and little or no effort was made to provide for redistribution according to need. Consequently the members of the larger families tended to inherit less and less land, since there were so many to share the ancestral estate. Only in Kent, East Anglia, and one section of the west (Dorset) can we find some traces of the earlier system. The member of the community, as such, was losing out economically. A decline in political power naturally accompanied this decline in economic power, since the two are nearly always closely related.

**Family Spirit Lingers at First.** Yet, on the whole, the chief characteristics of the older society are still visible. The political units of the heptarchic period were small enough to retain much of the family spirit that had permeated the small tribes on the Continent. If a king was not actually considered the head of the clan or family composing the kingdom, he was still regarded as the leader of a small war band, in which the spirit of fraternity and comradeship remained strong. Assemblies of all the fighting men of a kingdom were yet possible and desirable. Normally a man was still viewed in the eyes of the law as a member of a family, whose other members were to some extent responsible for his protection and also for any misconduct of which he might be guilty. Where the family had been broken up by the journey across the sea, or for other reasons, lordships modeled on family relationships did duty as a substitute. Here the lord acted as head of his followers and gave them the discipline and protection that the family was expected to supply. There was still another evidence of the survival of the old clan spirit, for if the individual tribesman had lost his privilege of sharing in the division of arable land, there were still extensive rights of common (community sharing), in the meadow and wastelands.

## THE DISTRIBUTION OF POWER IN THE MEDIEVAL SYSTEM OF GOVERNMENT

**The General Effect of the Changes after 800.** As the process of political unification progressed, however, this family or clan system, admirably adapted to small areas, necessarily gave way— under the influence of the forces described at the close of the last chapter—to one better adapted to larger governmental units. No longer was it possible to gather all the soldiers of a kingdom together for consultation. Nor did it seem natural for the king to consider his people one big family. They were now regarded rather as the dwellers on his estate. Territorial sovereignty tended to replace personal ties. The effect of this change was, as we shall see in detail later, to shift the control of Anglo-Saxon society into the hands of the three upper elements, the king, the nobles, and the Church. Society became organized with a coalition of monarch, nobility, and priests at the top, sharing the rule of the middle and lower classes. There was a division of labor among the allied groups. Each was given a particular sphere of influence on which the others made no effort to intrude. Each profited by the co-operation and support of the others. The nobility were granted offices, titles, and land by the crown. The Church was given land and protection by the king and the nobles. The churchmen ingratiated themselves with their secular colleagues by offering prayers for their temporal and spiritual welfare, and also by supplying religious sanctions for the superior political positions of their associates as well as themselves. In other words, they explained to the middle and lower classes that it was right that the nobility, the king, and the clergy should be the ruling elements in society. The king was pleased to have powerful nobles to assist him in military operations and also to grace his court. He enjoyed having his important subjects attend the great feasts in his hall when he held meetings of his Council. There was a good deal of deep drinking as well as deep speech on such occasions. Government and social life were very closely connected then, as they are today at party banquets, parades, and ward picnics.

**General Co-operation, Though Variations of Power.** Thus each of the ruling elements was willing to share the control of society, and to co-operate with the others in the work of government. Now and then, they might be uncertain about the boundaries of their jurisdiction and have a dispute on that issue. Just where the line would be drawn at a given time depended largely on the personalities of those who held the different positions of influence. When the king was a vigorous person, his share of governmental power and responsibility would be larger than that of his associates. When the monarch was weak, however, one or more nobles, or a capable churchman such as Dunstan, would be the most important cog in the governmental machine. But though the relative proportions might thus vary and vary greatly, rarely did any of the ruling elements think of eliminating entirely the political power of its associates. Occasionally we shall see that one or another of them made exaggerated claims, but these excessive demands were soon withdrawn and were not typical of the general medieval attitude.

**Sovereignty in the Medieval State.** The modern political scientist would call the system that we have been describing one of divided sovereignty, but this arrangement was not made by any written agreements or even by conscious thought. The Anglo-Saxon had few if any ideas of political theory. He did not

## VIEW OF LINCOLN

The city of Lincoln typifies the medieval theory of government. Crowning the ridge, side by side, are the cathedral and the castle (left foreground), representing the spiritual and temporal arms of the body politic. The castle was a royal stronghold, but was commonly held in the king's name by a nobleman, and thus typifies both of the co-operating secular elements in the dominating coalition. Down the hill, below these two imposing symbols of authority, straggle the homes of the shopkeeper-merchants and their less prosperous employees, suggesting the inferior positions of the middle and lower classes in medieval governmental arrangements.

think in the terms that are now so familiar to students. It would, in fact, have been very difficult for him to grasp the concept of sovereignty—that is to say, absolute, or unrestricted, authority in the national state—for the Church was an international organization, owing allegiance to Rome, and it would therefore have

THE DISTRIBUTION OF POWER IN MEDIEVAL SOCIETY

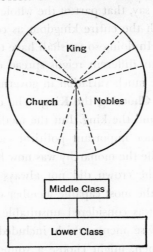

The dotted lines indicate the uncertain boundaries between the spheres of influence of the ruling elements.

been impossible to discover within the boundaries of the Anglo-Saxon state any one power or group of powers which enjoyed what we now mean by that word. In practice, however, the Anglo-Saxons, and their Norman successors as well, found this sharing of authority among monarch, nobles, and churchmen a very convenient way to arrange their governmental responsibilities, and so it may be called the general theory of the medieval English constitution in the sense that it describes the general outline of that constitution.

## THE CENTRAL GOVERNMENT: THE KINGSHIP

**Details of the System.** We turn now to a closer examination of the governmental machinery that in the Anglo-Saxon period implemented (made effective) this general constitutional theory. We shall begin by describing the mechanism of the central government, that is to say, that part of the whole government which was concerned with the entire kingdom as contrasted with one of its subdivisions. In doing so we shall have to generalize a good deal, for in so many different reigns spread over so many years there was of course much variation in governmental customs.

**The Method of Choosing the King.** The central government was organized around the king. But the method of his selection shows how the other important political elements made their power felt. For while the monarchy was now hereditary, as noted above (page 27), the crown did not always pass to the eldest son, but rather to the most capable member of the royal family. If the oldest boy was considered unsuitable for the office, the Council (Witan, wise men), which included both nobles and important churchmen, might choose a younger member of the family. Or if the deceased king left only minor children, one of his brothers or cousins might be selected. When Alfred was chosen king to succeed his brother Ethelred in 871, for example, two young sons of his predecessor were quietly passed over. If a ruler proved incompetent, he might be deposed by the same group that had chosen him. It must be admitted, however, that violence frequently played a part in these changes which sound so quietly legal when we read of them in books. Once the decision was made, in whatever fashion, the new king was inducted into office with religious ceremonies of anointing and crowning, conducted, of course, by a churchman. The new monarch took a coronation oath [1] in which he promised to protect the Church, punish wrongdoing, and rule with justice and mercy. These ceremonies are a further indication of the power of the Church, for the king's authority lapsed on the death of the ruler and the chosen successor was not legally king until he was crowned. Since the churchmen might refuse to crown a candidate of whom they disapproved or one who refused to take the oath, this gave them a considerable voice in the election and to some extent bound the successful candidate to respect clerical interests.

**Powers of the Crown.** Once installed, the king was, in theory at least, a very powerful person, especially in the later centuries, when he came to be considered the ruler of a territorial state instead of merely the leader of a small war band. He was supposed to enjoy many particular powers, though in practice he was not always able to exercise them. He was entitled to large royal estates, and he supplemented his income by a percentage of the fines assessed for criminal offenses. In the earlier part of the Anglo-Saxon period there seems also to have been a levy in kind laid upon the agricultural produce of his subjects, which later gave way to the money tax called the Danegeld, whose original purpose we have already described (page 20). The monarch commanded the armed forces of the kingdom, and appointed most of the important officials in the government. A special protection, called the king's peace, was extended to certain individuals, seasons of the year—such as Christmas—and parts of the realm in which he had a particular interest. The king also possessed certain vague residual powers, which were never properly defined in that untheoretical age. It was taken for granted that he would supervise all the other agencies of government and be the individual chiefly concerned with the

---

[1] For a sample of such an oath, see Carl Stephenson and F. G. Marcham, *Sources of English Constitutional History*, Harper, 1937, No. 10, p. 18. The book is cited hereafter as S-M.

welfare of his domain. Accordingly he often exercised powers, such as those involved in furthering the introduction of Christianity into his realm, for which there was neither law nor precedent. After all, he was the king. Possibly he had won his position in battle. If he was a great military leader, who was to question his authority?

## HOUSEHOLD, WITAN, AND FYRD

**The Household.** Obviously the king could not perform all the necessary executive functions of government in his own person. In the early days, when the rulers had only small areas to deal with, they depended on their own household servants to help them. By the close of the Anglo-Saxon period four of these household positions—now filled by great men of the realm who deputized others to do the menial service—had developed into important administrative offices of the government. The Steward (Seneschal) supervised the arrangements for the royal food and at times probably collected the levies in kind to which the king was entitled in the earlier centuries. The Chamberlain—whose original status is indicated by his Saxon title of *Hraegel-Weard* (Keeper of the Wardrobe)—was in charge of court ceremonial and the royal treasure, for the king's money was at first kept in his bedroom. The Staller, later called the Constable, originally had charge of the royal stalls or stables. From looking after the horses he developed into the king's chief assistant in military affairs. For most of the Anglo-Saxon period no special attention was paid to the royal records, but by the time of Edward the Confessor an official called the Chancellor was appointed to look after them. Originally he was the chief royal priest (chaplain), a man who could write and also be trusted to keep sober at a feast and record accurately the king's promises. He kept the great royal seal, which he used to authenticate documents drawn up by the clerks under his supervision. This kind of authentication was necessary in a period of general illiteracy. There were many other household officers, such as butlers, doorkeepers, and huntsmen, but they were of minor importance and never developed administrative duties of constitutional importance. The four officials mentioned, however, were major figures in English governmental administration for many centuries, and most of the modern executive posts in the British government have developed from a subdivision of the offices of one or another of them, as we shall note from time to time (pages 137, 273, 380, 498, 562). In the Saxon period the king had absolute control of all his household officers, appointing and dismissing them at pleasure.

**The Witan.** He had, however, no such control of the Witan, to which we have already alluded (page 32). This was a body of between fifty and one hundred of the leading men of the realm. Since it was all that remained (in the central government) of the old tribal assembly of the Germans, it can be seen how the ordinary fighting man had declined in political importance. The Witan included the king's immediate relatives—not omitting the feminine ones in many instances—and the important household officials, usually as many of the four main ones already mentioned as had developed at the time. But in it were also the leading nobles of the country and important churchmen, such as the archbishops, the bishops, prominent abbots, and the royal chaplains. While the king seems to have summoned the members of the Witan to their meeting and while we have no definite information about how they were chosen, it seems highly probable that by established custom holders of prominent positions regularly came, whether they were on friendly terms with the king or not. The Witan met at least once a year, usually at the season of one of the great Church festivals, such as Christmas, Easter, or Whitsunday (Pentecost).

**The Powers of the Witan.** The Witan had various powers besides that of electing the king, to which we have already referred (page 32). It performed what we should call legislative functions.

That is, it approved statements of the law of the land that were to be in force in the future. According to the Saxon theory this was not a making of new law, but merely a formulation of principles of justice already latent in the English consciousness and in English custom. It was a declaration of law, not a creation or manufacture of it. The Witan had certain judicial powers, which will be described in the next chapter (page 55). It was also a council that discussed matters of state policy, such as peace, war, and the making of treaties. After the introduction of the Danegeld it authorized the collection of this tax. Furthermore, it ratified royal appointments and grants of land and privileges. On some occasions there is evidence of opposition to the royal will in such matters. Consequently it is clear that the Witan was often more than a rubber stamp for the ruler. In general the power of the Witan fluctuated, as has been already suggested (page 30), with the variations in the personal qualities of its members and the successive monarchs.

**The Fyrd.** The military system of the Anglo-Saxons was originally based on the idea that it was the duty of every able-bodied freeman to serve in the army in times of emergency. The royal officials in the different spheres of local government that we shall describe (pages 39-41) were charged with the responsibility of summoning and marshaling the popular army whenever the need arose. This military levy (militia) was known as the fyrd. Since it represented the sum total of all the available military forces in the country, in theory the fyrd should have proved equal to any crisis. But as we shall see (page 45), in practice it did not work very well, and other means were devised to deal with the problem of securing military forces that would be more nearly capable of meeting the needs of the time.

## THE ECCLESIASTICAL ELEMENTS

**The Church an Integral Part of the Central Government.** In addition to being represented in the Witan, the Church exercised its power through other agencies. These ecclesiastical agencies were as much a part of the Anglo-Saxon central government as the king and the Witan, though they are more difficult to explain because at the same time they were a part of an international organization. Nevertheless, it must not be forgotten that the Church was an integral part of the medieval state. It is an error to speak of Church and State in this period as though they were two separate entities. There were spiritual and temporal arms, but only one body politic; religious and secular rulers, but only one state. The concepts of Church and State as mutually exclusive bodies date from post-Reformation times.

**The Continental Authorities and the Archbishops.** The head of the medieval Church was, of course, the pope, assisted by the Roman curia (court) and an occasional general council. He exercised supervision over all western Christendom. Now and then he exerted his influence in England directly by issuing communications—called either briefs or bulls (from the *bullum* or leaden seal attached to them), depending on their formality—and also by sending agents called legates, whose authority superseded that of any resident English clergyman. But ordinarily the English Church was dominated by the archbishops, with the assistance of local councils (synods), which were assembled at infrequent intervals. There were two of these archbishops, one at Canterbury and one at York. The choice of Canterbury for one location has already been explained (page 16). The second archbishopric was located at York in the seventh century because it was the capital of Northumbria—then the predominant Anglo-Saxon power—and the largest town in the north. (When Mercia became supreme in the eighth century, there was a short-lived effort to establish a

third archbishopric at Lichfield in that kingdom.) The archbishops were theoretically elected by the clergy of their areas, but
actually in the late Anglo-Saxon period they were chosen by the
king and the Witan. However, just as the monarch named by the
Witan could not rule unless the Church consented to crown him,
so the prospective archbishop could not assume office until the
pope had conferred upon him a wool shoulder piece (pallium),
and this gave the Church some check on the filling of these
vacancies. Once installed, the archbishops exercised a general
supervision over the surrounding bishoprics in their provinces,
as the areas under the archbishops were called. Since these archbishops and the other leading clergymen of the realm were members of the Witan also, religious matters were often discussed in
the sessions of that body, and after the time of the Danish invasions there were few purely ecclesiastical councils. The Witan,
because of this clerical representation in its membership, acted
as a connecting link between the temporal and spiritual arms
of the government, and as a unifying factor in co-ordinating
spiritual and temporal policy.

## LOCAL GOVERNMENT: THE SHIRE

**Local Government in the Early Saxon Period.** Before the unification of England, local government seems to have been largely
in the hands of royal reeves (agents), who were assigned to the
different districts into which the petty kingdoms of that day were
subdivided. The reeve was the king's representative and exercised
the royal authority in his particular district. Each made his headquarters in a royal burh (fortification), and had at least military
supervision of the surrounding area. Probably they had judicial
and financial functions also. They must have had informal consultations with the important men of their district, but we have
no record of their being assisted by a formal council.

**Later Local Government: The Shires.** Anglo-Saxon local government after the unification may best be described by taking the various subdivisions in order of size. Of these the largest was the shire, or county, as it came to be called later. Some of these shires were originally subsections of Wessex, which, like the other heptarchic kingdoms, was arbitrarily divided for administrative convenience. Others had been separate kingdoms—such as Kent, Sussex, and Essex—which were assimilated after their conquest into the West Saxon system. Those in the Midlands were carved out of the Danelaw and its border territory after the reconquest. They usually consisted of the territory around a fortress town that gave its name to the shire, as, for example, Derbyshire and Nottinghamshire. The county organization in the north was not completed until after the Norman Conquest. By the time of the Reformation there were forty English counties, which have had roughly the same importance—though not the same constitutional organization and relationship to the central government—in England as the states in the United States of America.

**Shire Officials.** Over each of these shires—so far as they were constituted in the ninth and tenth centuries—was set an ealdorman (chief man) appointed by the king. He was chosen from the noble class and had both judicial and military functions. After the tenth century the ealdorman was frequently given more than one county to rule, and became virtually a viceroy, or underking. In the time of Canute the title was changed to the Danish *iarl* (pronounced *yarl*), which was the equivalent of the Saxon *eorl* or *earl*, the general term for any nobleman. Subsequently the Saxons used *earl* to designate this official. As the earls came to have more and more territory under their supervision, they also became a hereditary group, passing their territories and offices down from father to son. To meet the menace to the central government which this development presented, a new officer was appointed to give closer supervision to the individual shires, and to protect the king's interests in them. He was called the shire

reeve (sheriff), and represented a development from the old system of royal reeves who had carried the chief burden of local
administration in the earlier period. Now, however, one was commissioned to act for an entire county. He also served as deputy
for the earl in military and judicial matters. As the earl took less
and less interest in shire affairs the sheriff became the chief administrative officer in the county. The sheriff's office was not
hereditary, but was entrusted to any suitable person in whom
the king had confidence.

**The Shire Court.** Whether the conduct of shire affairs was in
the hands of the earl or the sheriff, however, to assist him there
was always a court or a council—the terms are interchangeable
in medieval times. This county court met at least twice a year
and sometimes oftener. It was composed of those landholders of
the shire who possessed some degree of economic independence.
Probably it was the direct descendant of the old popular assembly
of the Germans, which the poorer classes had now ceased to attend—another sign of their loss of political power. The local
bishop was usually present, since the court dealt with both ecclesiastical and temporal affairs, and he shared the duty of presiding
with the earl and the sheriff, especially when the business was of
a religious nature. Occasionally separate villages were represented
by their reeve and four men when matters were to be discussed
which particularly concerned their locality. The court performed
certain judicial functions, which will be described later (pages
55-64), and also acted as a medium for the publication of royal
decrees and new legislation. Wills and land transfers were witnessed by it, and taxes assessed.

## THE HUNDRED AND ITS ORGANIZATION

**The Hundred.** The largest subdivision of the county was the
hundred. The number of these hundreds in a county varied from
four to sixty-one, depending on the size and population of the

shire. It is probable that originally the term was applied after the conquest of the Danelaw to an area which could furnish one hundred men for police and military purposes, but soon it came to mean a territorial unit without regard to the population. In some parts of the country it appears to have been used also as a unit of taxation, to designate an area of one hundred hides (sections of one hundred and twenty acres each). In the northern part of the Danelaw the hundreds were called wapentakes, but their governmental structure was the same as that of the hundred.

**Hundred Organization.** This consisted of a hundredman, or hundred reeve, who was usually the agent of the earl or the sheriff, and performed the same functions on a smaller scale. Doubtless he was, in origin, the king's local reeve who, as already noted (page 38), played such a big role in local government before the development of the shire system. To assist him he had a hundred court, or council, which met every four weeks, or even oftener. Attendance seems to have been required of those who held certain amounts of land, but in time this obligation came to be fixed on certain holdings only, and some owners escaped this burden. Even in these small units, therefore, it will be seen that the early German practice of holding popular assemblies (page 25) had broken down. Sometimes the sheriff attended the court and presided in place of the hundredman. The gathering probably had administrative duties in addition to its judicial ones (page 55), but the records are too scanty to enable us to speak with certainty.

## VILLAGES AND BOROUGHS

**Villages.** Lowest in the scale of local governmental units came the tun (vill, village). This was rather an economic than a political division, but it is probable that an annual meeting was held to determine agricultural policy for the next season. Certainly by the end of our period the villages had reeves, either elected in such a meeting or appointed by the hundredman or some local lord. As we have seen, this reeve, with four men of the community, occasionally represented the village interests at meetings of the hundred and county courts.

**Boroughs.** Some of the villages, however, were important for military, administrative, or economic reasons, and so came to enjoy special governmental privileges. The king's tuns—those in which royal reeves were located and from which, in the early days, they administered the surrounding country—came in time to be called boroughs, because they were usually fortified (burh, fortification). As the hundred organization took over the government of the rural areas, the royal reeves, or port reeves, as the heads of boroughs were called, confined their attention to the towns themselves. These were provided with special courts or councils, which met three times a year or oftener. But the economic importance of the boroughs was still small, and the increase of wealth that enabled them to secure autonomous privileges for themselves (page 161) did not begin until the very end of our period. During Saxon times they were still largely under the control of the crown or some intermediate overlord.

## THE LOCAL GOVERNMENT OF THE CHURCH

**Secular.** The ecclesiastical arm of the state also had its local government. In each of the two archiepiscopal provinces there were subordinate bishoprics—only one in addition to York in the north, but thirteen besides Canterbury in the south. Since there were over thirty shires, it can be seen that one bishop usually had charge of church affairs in more than one county. The bishop at this time, like the archbishop, was commonly elected by the king and the Witan, though some sort of approval was usually secured from the clergy of the diocese, or a part of them. He was aided in his work by a staff of assistants called canons, who conducted the services in the cathedral church. In this period the canons were almost entirely under the control of the bishop and had no independent authority. Within each diocese were churches (called minster churches) that were directly under the bishop's authority. Their priests exercised a general supervision over their neighbors. The ordinary parishes were supplied by priests who were normally appointed by some neighboring lord who was the patron, and at this time virtually the owner, of the church. This right of individual laymen to fill vacancies in church livings, as the priests' places were called, was known as an advowson. It could be bought and sold, like any other piece of property. The bishops and the more important church officials were supported by endowments consisting of lands donated by generous patrons and thereafter attached to the ecclesiastical positions. The village priest received part of his income from parish endowments of a similar sort, called glebe land, usually amounting to fifty or sixty acres, but for the most part he was supported by the tithe. This originally was a 10 per cent income tax on all the parishioners, though time brought various reductions in the size of the fraction.

**And Regular.** Another type of ecclesiastical organization was the monastery or nunnery, which attracted men or women, respectively, who wished to be freed from the cares of ordinary life that they might devote themselves to religious activities. These people followed strict rules, of which the Benedictine, the one devised by St. Benedict, was the oldest in western Christendom. The rules bound each member of the order to poverty, chastity, and obedience, as well as to other obligations. Because these churchmen followed a rule they were known as the regular clergy, from the Latin word *regula*, meaning "rule." As regulars they were contrasted with the secular clergy—those whom we have already described, who remained outside monastic walls in the secular world. Each monastery was headed by an abbot elected by the group. He was assisted by a prior and other officials whom he appointed. Normally each monastery was subject to the supervision of the bishop in whose diocese it was located, though such control was often evaded. The monks were supported by landed endowments, which were originally contributed by lay supporters and which were the property of the monastery.

## THE LORDSHIP SYSTEM

**Lordships and Their Origin.** Like the churchmen, the nobles, though represented in the county and hundred courts, had their own special institutions of local government. As we have seen, the more prosperous landlords not only dominated the membership of the shire court, but also enjoyed certain rights over hundreds, boroughs, villages, and even the parish churches. These powers grew out of a lordship system that is very important for subsequent constitutional history because it is the background of later feudalism.

**From War.** It is often suggested that the lords, like the kings, were the direct outgrowth of the wars of the period. This again is partly true, but not the whole truth. Men did find it essential to have leaders in time of war, and they had brought from the Continent a traditional code of conduct governing their attitude toward them. Among the early Germans it was customary for a band of fighting men to choose a chief and swear loyalty to him. They vowed to accept his leadership and not to come out of battle alive without avenging him if he were killed. This bodyguard was known as a comitatus (comradeship). There was thus created a relationship of personal dependence known as vassalage. The lord gave directions to his followers and kept order among them in much the same way as the leader of a criminal "gang" may today. In time this right to keep order among his followers led to the development of private courts, which were sometimes known as seignorial (lords') or manorial (from the manor or village area over which the lord had jurisdiction) courts. Men who voluntarily placed themselves under such personal leadership were said to commend themselves, and the process was known as commendation. The lordship system was doubtless further strengthened by the Danish invasions, which emphasized the need of capable local leadership. While there was a fyrd (militia system) which, in theory, should have furnished proper protection to the individual, in practice news traveled slowly, sheriffs were hard to reach, and commonly far too slow in arriving on the scene of difficulties. Men learned to look for help where they could find it, in their local lords.

**And Peace.** Yet it is quite improbable that in a period of continuous warfare the average Saxon tribesman (ceorl) would have fallen as low as he did in the political and social scale. If warfare glorifies the chieftain, it also lends some importance to the man in the ranks. It is very likely that the status of the common man declined more in the periods of relative peace between wars than during the hostilities themselves. Men who lost touch with the arts of war were more at the mercy of occasional raiders or neighborhood bullies than were practiced warriors. Consequently, if royal assistance was not forthcoming, they were even more likely to commend themselves to a lord in time of sudden stress than people who were living on the western frontiers where hostilities were more frequent. As the kingdom grew larger and the kings more remote, the peace-loving tiller of the soil was more and more inclined to seek such a local tie rather than to trust to his own resources or the royal protection.[2]

**Economic Roots.** These lordships also had an economic aspect, to which times of peace certainly contributed as much as did the wars. For every small landholder who hastily donated his property to a neighboring magnate when the smoke of the next village told him that the Danes were at hand there must have been many who gradually lost their holdings in less dramatic ways. The supply of land was limited. As previously explained (page

[2] For a typical Anglo-Saxon oath of fealty (faithfulness) to the lord see S-M, No. 14A, p. 25.

13), the Saxons had adopted a system of private ownership of most of this natural resource, and had abandoned earlier provisions for redistribution according to need. Under such circumstances time inevitably brought the greater share of the available wealth into a few hands. The hard work, cleverness, unscrupulous tactics, or good fortune of some combined with the idleness, dullness, scrupulousness, or misfortune of others produced this result in a few generations. Many mouths to feed, a succession of bad crops, a maiming injury, and a man had to come to terms with his more prosperous neighbor.

**The Establishment of the Lordship System.** By war and even more by peace, therefore, the economic power of the lord grew, until frequently he held the title to a whole village and the surrounding land. Obviously he could not work all this himself, so normally he permitted his new dependents to go on working their old holdings, but required them to give him a third or more of the produce. In many cases this was done by putting one large field, or a good fraction of the strips in all the fields, into what was called the lord's domain and forcing the villagers to work a certain number of days per week (usually two or three) on this domain. No written contracts were drawn up in these early days, and there is a good deal of variation in the arrangements, but much concentration of wealth was brought about in something like this fashion. So the old free villages became dependent ones of the sort that were later called manors, and the free villager (ceorl) sank to a level approximately that of the later villein (dweller in the manorial village). Normally he worked about thirty acres of his "own," besides the lord's domain. There were subclasses of geburs and cotars, who held even smaller units. Below them were some individuals who were slaves—usually criminals or prisoners of war, but this class also included some completely destitute who "in evil days had bowed their heads for bread." The lords, as we have seen (page 39), were called earls at first.[3] Later another class developed called thegns (thanes). These originally owed their position not to birth, but to some special service, often of an economic nature. Any merchant who made three trips across the sea, for example, became a thegn. As the word *eorl* or "earl" came to be used in an official sense, the term "thegn" became the general title for all the landlord class except those lords with special offices. Anyone who held five hides of land (six hundred acres in all) was considered thegnworthy and therefore a thegn.

**Royal Contributions to the Lordship System.** The Anglo-Saxon kings, far from interfering with the development of these lordships, strongly approved of them, and strengthened them further by royal grants. Perhaps this was partly because the monarchs were related to many of the lords and on good personal terms with many others. But it was also because these lords were able to help the rulers with their governmental problems. The kings were now masters of large territories, remote from the average subject, and generally unmindful of their original duties as the fathers of their people. As suggested above (page 45), they were much more concerned with extending the area over which they held some kind of sway than in strengthening the democratic features of their form of government, or even in suppressing internal disorders. Instead of continuing to keep close check on their local reeves they were quite content to grant considerable powers to the lords, in exchange for help with the problem of local government. On the thegns could be put the burden of guaranteeing the payment of royal taxes and church dues. The lords were also expected to see that the freemen in each community did their duty in keeping up roads, bridges, and fortresses in their neighborhood, an obligation known as the *trimoda necessitas* (three-formed necessity). The thegns could also be use-

[3] "Gesith" is sometimes used as an alternative term for these lords by birth, but gesiths seem more often to have been royal attendants somewhat similar to thegns, and therefore should be distinguished from the more independent nobles.

ful in keeping peace in the land by holding their followers in check. To this end Alfred's grandson Athelstan went so far as to ordain that every landless man must find a lord.[4] Most important of all, large landholders could be expected to do mounted military service, particularly against the Danes, and royal grants of land were frequently made to them on such a condition. In many cases the lords delegated this duty to armed household retainers, called *cnihts*. Originally these *cnihts* were little better than servants, but in time they developed into the later knights. Sometimes churchmen made grants of land similar to the royal ones, or loaned a tract for a given period, on condition that the recipient should do such military service in protecting the Church or aiding the king.

**Franchises.** So convenient did the kings find it to rely on the great men of the realm for such governmental service that they went even further in many cases and granted them not only lands but franchises involving jurisdictional rights over the lords' dependents, and even over others in the neighborhood who were not otherwise under their lordship. Whole hundreds might thus be given to certain lords. The king's sheriff no longer visited them, and all profits from the court went to the local magnate. This court right was called sac and soc, or sake and soke, though historians have never quite been able to agree on the explanation of this terminology.[5] Sometimes the lord went so far as to amalgamate this hundred court with the seignorial (manorial) court which he held for his own tenants. Thus many of the nobles, though from the modern point of view private citizens, came to hold and exercise authority that to us is an integral and indivisible part of the state. Not only laymen but also powerful churchmen were able to secure such positions of pre-eminence. For

[4] S-M, No. 7, Sec. 2, pp. 13-14.
[5] Julius Goebel, Jr., in his *Felony and Misdemeanor*, 3 vols., Commonwealth Fund, 1937, Vol. I, pp. 339-78, challenges the theory that these private franchises conveyed more than fiscal (financial) rights over the public courts. But he grants (pp. 360-61) that there were considerable extralegal encroachments of private individuals on public jurisdiction in this period.

though the churchmen could not fight themselves, they could exact military service from their dependents, and, as we have seen, their moral and intellectual leadership was felt also to entitle them to such special privileges.

**The Lordship System Not Fully Developed Feudalism.** This concentration of economic and governmental power in the hands of the clerical and aristocratic classes is similar to that which is known as feudalism. In feudalism, however—which, strictly speaking, only existed on the Continent from the tenth to the thirteenth century and in England in a modified form after 1066— the legal and political powers of the lords were even greater than those we have described. No free villages survived in their territories. They enjoyed the right to wage private war against their neighbors and even against the king. Their subordinates were bound to one lord, and could not change their allegiance or refuse to do service for their lord against the royal overlord. In Anglo-Saxon England, on the other hand, some free villages remained, and not every man was subordinated to some lord. Military or other governmental service was not regularly exacted in exchange for all grants of land, and royal vassals might not indulge in private warfare or attack their monarch. The better classes of men might change lords and even transfer their land at the same time. Nor were landlordship and lordship necessarily united. That is, a man might hold land from one lord and be under the legal jurisdiction and military leadership of another. Legally and technically, therefore, the Anglo-Saxon conditions we have been describing do not amount to fully developed feudalism. At the most they constitute a preliminary stage in its growth, a rudimentary feudalism. But this incomplete growth affords not only a suggestion of what was to come after the Norman Conquest, but an indication of how far the Anglo-Saxons had departed from even that measure of tribal democracy and social equality which they seem to have enjoyed on the Continent. War, peace, and a limited supply of land had begotten not only the king but the lord.

## PATERNALISM

**Safeguards for the Lower Classes.** The concentration of political power in the hands of a comparatively few individuals was not, however, an unmixed evil for the others. Not only did the lower clasess enjoy certain rights to protection and property as a result of these arrangements, but those in power did not always insist on the full measure of their own legal rights. There was a certain sense of obligation to the lower classes, of noblesse oblige, which shows that the primitive sentiment for community sharing was not entirely dead. Individual lords strove so hard to protect some of their dependents, even when they were in the wrong, that laws restraining them had to be drawn up. The kings also were not altogether unmindful of their original obligations, and there are some traces of paternalism in their laws. In Canute's code we read this philosophic warning to his lords:

He who pronounces a more severe judgment upon one who is friendless or come from afar than upon one of his own acquaintances injures himself.

And again:

In all cases the greater a man is and the higher his rank, the more stringent shall be the amends which he shall be required to make to God and to men for lawless behavior.

Also this:

Henceforth all men, both rich and poor, shall be regarded as entitled to the benefit of the law.

**The Contribution of the Church to This End.** The Church was equally active in furthering this paternalistic attitude, because of its belief in the importance of each human soul. It was not sufficiently in advance of its time to condemn slavery, but it recommended various alleviating measures that we find in the royal laws:

> We forbid the all too prevalent practice of selling Christian people out of the country, and especially of conveying them into heathen lands, but care shall be zealously taken that the souls which Christ bought with his own life be not destroyed.

Most sweeping of all were the charitable ordinances that Athelstan issued on the advice of his bishops. Each of his reeves was told that he must always provide a destitute Englishman with food:

> He shall be supplied with an amber [a measure whose size at this time cannot be determined] of meal, a shank of bacon or a ram worth four pence every month, and clothes for twelve months annually.

> [And I desire you] to make free annually one man who has been reduced to penal slavery.

Thus some official provision was made for those at the lower end of the social scale, and so the authorities kept alive a few sparks of the attitude which in time was to restore something of the strength of the original fraternal spirit of the Anglo-Saxon tribes. But these were very small survivals, and their ultimate fruition was as yet a long way off.

**Anglo-Saxon England Not Democratic.** Historians who have wished to give democracy an ancestry of respectable antiquity on English soil have often yielded to the temptation to exaggerate the amount and importance of popular participation in the government in Anglo-Saxon times. But as we have noted in this chapter, further research is proving that the natural inclinations of a primitive people to a considerable measure of political and economic equality were not strong enough to endure the strain put upon them by war and by their efforts to attain a higher state of civilization in an area where economic opportunities were restricted. Centuries of discipline, under the direction of lay and spiritual leaders, were necessary, as the great historian Maitland has pointed out,[6] before the new settlers could hope to redress the balance and restore a large measure of popular power and freedom. In the meantime the tragedy of the Saxon period is not that the people had strong leaders, but that they were not strong enough. What was needed was more military and political skill in a few men and less factional jealousy—more Alfreds and fewer Ethelreds. To Anglo-Saxon society, therefore, the Norman Conquest, which to a considerable extent was to remedy this deficiency in the succeeding period, was a real blessing, albeit very much disguised at the time.

[6] *Domesday Book and Beyond*, Little, Brown, 1897, pp. 222-26.

# 3. ANGLO-SAXON LAW

**Law and Government Products of the Same Forces.** We have seen that the chief problems of Anglo-Saxon government grew out of the efforts of the people to raise themselves from a primitive tribal stage of civilization to something higher. We have noted the difficulties and disorders produced by the struggles to unite a large area under one political rule, by the decline in the amount of available land, and by the poor communications of the time. The problems of that aspect of government which we call the judicial, or legal, were, as may be imagined, much the same, except on a smaller scale. The courts were concerned with conflicts of an individual rather than a community or national sort, but since society is made up of individuals, the same motives and forces operated in private as well as public affairs. Just as the state was developing painfully and slowly from a familial organization to a territorial affair in which blood ties would play no great part, so society was striving to persuade individuals to settle their disputes by peaceful means under community supervision rather than by having recourse to personal and clan violence.

**Violence and the Blood Feud.** It was a difficult business, for a people accustomed to settle public disputes by violent means naturally applied the same tactics to their private affairs. They tended to follow

> the simple plan,
> That they should take who have the power,
> And they should keep who can.

53

Cattle constituted the chief form of movable wealth in those days. A dark night commonly meant a rustling expedition, and if the raiders were detected it went hard with them. Blood was very much thicker than water, and such violent tactics frequently led to the development of what was called the blood feud, in which the relatives of a man slain in a private fray avenged his blood on the killer. The original killer's kinsmen then retaliated in kind, and so on ad infinitum, after the manner of those feuds for which American mountaineers are famous. These feuds were very much easier to start than to stop. Frequently society could do no more than moderate them by imposing rules for their conduct. To substitute for the feud any kind of legal means at all for settling disputes was a real achievement. If, therefore, Anglo-Saxon law on first acquaintance seems to the modern reader crude and incomplete, he must remember the difficulties with which it had to deal. Rough-and-ready times demand rough-and-ready justice, as the history of the American frontier indicates; and the student must keep in mind the fact that the members of Anglo-Saxon courts were often little more than armed vigilantes.

**The Outline to Be Used in Legal History.** In our analysis of the legal side of the government in this and succeeding periods we shall describe (1) the organization and jurisdiction of the courts, (2) the legal procedure used and the professional means, if any, employed to operate it, and (3) the legal principles that the courts and their procedure were designed to enforce. Lawyers call the rules embodying the legal principles themselves the substantive law, because they have to do with the very substance or essence of the law. On the other hand, regulations concerning the structure and procedure of the courts are called adjective law, because they have to do with agencies which, like an adjective modifying a noun, are merely auxiliary to the substance of the law itself. In some ways it might be more logical to explain the principles of the law before describing the devices employed to make them effective; but there is an old legal proverb to the effect that adjective law comes before substantive, which means that procedural questions often determine the doctrine to be applied in a particular case. Some of the reasons for this we shall see as we go along, but for the moment it is sufficient to point out that the story of the organization and jurisdiction of the courts is the aspect of legal history that best shows the close relationship between the wider constitutional aspects of government and the narrowly legal questions which students too often seem to consider quite unconnected with them. The structure and powers of the English courts have at all times been very closely related to those of other governmental agencies, and this subject of the organization and jurisdiction of the courts therefore affords a good transition from constitutional history in general to legal history in particular.

## THE ANGLO-SAXON COURTS AND THEIR JURISDICTION

**Organization of the Courts.** We have already described the organization of the Anglo-Saxon courts (pages 35, 40, 41, 42) because, as was said (page 40), court and council were the same in those times. The sharp distinction between the executive, legislative, and judicial aspects of government was unknown before the eighteenth century, and our ancestors prior to that time saw nothing anomalous in having one official body perform two or more of these functions. The Witan and the shire, the hundred (both public and private), the borough, and the seignorial (manorial) courts were the judicial tribunals of the time as well as the administrative agencies.

**The Jurisdiction of Anglo-Saxon Courts.** The jurisdiction of these courts was determined partly by geographical considerations, but mostly by the importance of the case and the parties to it. The hundred court was the court for the ordinary cases of ordinary people. After the development of the lordship system the case of a dependent tiller of the soil was tried in the lord's private seignorial (manorial) court. Where towns were granted the right to have their own courts, in ordinary circumstances the case of a burgess would be heard in the borough court. People who were important enough to attend the county court, however, had their hearings there, while the Witan served the same purpose for the men and women of first rank. Specially difficult or important cases involving people of lower status might be transferred at the commencement of legal proceedings to one or the other of the higher courts. All of the courts heard what we should call both civil and criminal (page 66) cases, and the Witan and the county courts also heard cases involving ecclesiastical matters.

**Appeals.** Once a case was tried in one place, however, there was, in strict legal theory, no appeal. A case could be tried only once. All jurisdiction was therefore original—or first, as opposed to appellate, as we use the term—and all courts were thus theoretically courts of first instance where a case would be heard for the first time. But actually the higher courts exercised some supervision over the lower. Where justice was unobtainable in the hundred court because a hearing was refused or an opponent could not be compelled to appear, the county court either heard the case or outlawed the recalcitrant party, as the occasion demanded. Similarly, the king and the Witan heard the petitions of those who alleged that they had been unable to secure justice in the county courts. In some cases the king, with or without his council, settled the matter himself. In others he put pressure on the county courts by sending a royal writ (message). In all cases he enjoyed a pardoning power and might intervene to moderate or remit the penalty imposed by the local courts.

## PROCEDURE: INITIATION AND PROCESS

**Complexity of Procedure.** In order to make clear the procedure employed in Anglo-Saxon courts we must first point out that there were a good many different steps in the conduct of a case, of which the actual trial was only one. Most of these steps are still a part of the procedure in a modern suit, though the means employed at each stage has in most instances been greatly modified. (1) First came the initiation of the case. Formal notification had to be given by the plaintiff to the defendant. The aggrieved party was required to take witnesses with him and go to his adversary's home in broad daylight—this to remove all suspicion of foul play and all justification for an attack by the defendant—and summon his rival to attend court on a particular day to answer such and such a charge.

**Distress and Outlawry.** (2) Second came the process, the step of compelling appearance if the defendant proved recalcitrant. One's adversary frequently refused to come to court in Saxon times, and the law made many different attempts to solve the problem presented by this difficulty. Most commonly during this period the defendant was summoned twice more and then repeatedly fined for nonappearance. In collecting these fines the plaintiff was allowed to use the process of distress. He did this by going once more, with witnesses, and seizing some of his opponent's goods—most likely cattle. Sometimes the goods were merely held as a pledge of the defendant's appearance and returned to him when the case was ended. Should the defendant still refuse to come in spite of the distress, however, the court would allow the plaintiff to satisfy his claim from the goods already seized if the grievance was a minor one. But if the charge was more serious, the defendant would be outlawed by the county court. Outlaws were put beyond the protection of the law they had flouted, and in the Anglo-Saxon period might without penalty be slain on sight by anyone who could find them and cared to take the risk of combat.

**Other Devices.** Since, however, there were many offenders who had no property to be seized, and since outlawry was a slow and dangerous way of obtaining satisfaction, other experiments were also tried. In the early days a man's relatives were required to produce him in court when required. This was doubtless a survival of primitive Germanic custom. But as family solidarity declined this obligation ceased to be very binding. Pressure was consequently put on the lords to produce their dependents when required, and this was one of the reasons back of the injunction that every landless man should have a lord (page 48). Finally, recourse was had to artificial families. Groups of ten men, called tithings, were organized under the supervision of the sheriff when he visited the hundred courts. Thereafter these tithings were fined in the event of their inability to compel the appearance of one of their number when his day in court came.[1] It must be admitted, however, that no matter what devices were employed, process was frequently all too ineffective in this period.

**Criminal Process.** In some of what we should call criminal cases provision was made for pursuit and arrest. Persons discovering murder, theft, or assault were supposed to raise the hue and cry, and all able-bodied citizens were expected to join the local reeve in searching any likely hiding-places or following the trail, if one existed. Should the trail lead into another area, its inhabitants were expected to carry on the pursuit until the fugitive was apprehended.


## PLEADING AND PRELIMINARY JUDGMENT

**Pleading.** (3) In those cases where the defendant was induced by some means or other to put in an appearance in court, the

[1] S-M, No. 13, Sec. 20, p. 23.

next step was the pleading. This was a kind of formal dispute, designed to enlighten the court on the points of difference between the two adversaries, in other words, on the issue involved. The plaintiff usually began this with a foreoath, or sworn statement that he was making his claim or accusation in good faith:

"By the Lord," said the plaintiff in a typical case, "I accuse not A either for hatred or for envy, or for unlawful lust of gain; nor know I anything soother; but as my informant to me said and I myself in sooth believe, that he was the thief of my property."

He then proceeded to make his charge in detail and in the appropriate formal language. The plaintiff was also required to give sureties to guarantee that he would properly prosecute the action and be responsible for damages in case it should be decided that he had made a false claim. Furthermore, he produced a group of friends, called a *secta* (suit),[2] to prove that he was bringing a serious case and not troubling the court unnecessarily. In case the plaintiff could produce an open wound in court, or show a fresh cattle trail leading into the accused's land but not out of it, this was considered an acceptable substitute and the foreoath and suit were not required. Once the accusation was properly made and thus substantiated, the defendant had to counter it with a sworn denial.

"By the Lord," said the defendant, "I am guiltless both in deed and counsel of the charge of which B accuses me."[3]

It was required that the statements be delivered in set form with verbal accuracy and without correction or stammering. He who failed in a syllable failed in everything, said a legal proverb. The point of this was that the religious-minded Anglo-Saxons

[2] Hence the modern phrase at the conclusion of the count, or initial pleading, "and therefore the plaintiff brings his suit."
[3] For these and similar formal charges and denials see S-M, No. 14B-E, p. 25.

put great faith in the supernatural, and they felt that if a man was about to swear falsely, God, by whom he swore, would cause him to falter in his speech.

**Preliminary Judgment.** (4) There then followed a preliminary judgment by the court. This took the form of an award of proof, normally to one side or the other, but not to both. Either the plaintiff or the defendant was allowed to substantiate his statement in the particular manner which the court stipulated. This award was doubtless made on the basis of the judges' opinion of the character of the contending parties, their behavior in court, and the nature of the charge. Since it seems generally to have been possible to produce enough compurgators (page 61) to satisfy the court, the award of this most common kind of proof amounted to a distinct advantage rather than a burden for the party awarded proof.

## THE TRIAL

**Witnesses.** (5) The trial stage consisted in the offering of proof by one party, normally in one of three ways. (a) Where something approaching impartial evidence was available, the party awarded proof might be asked to produce it. Our ancestors were not quite as slow to make use of common-sense methods of trial as is sometimes supposed. We have several records of land cases in which the matter in dispute was settled by the production of written grants. Since there were so many disputes about cattle, it was provided that the sales of such property should take place only before witnesses, and these were to be produced in court in case of dispute. This is one of their typical oaths:

In the name of Almighty God, as I here for N in true witness stand, unbidden and unbought, so I with my eyes oversaw and with my ears overheard that which I with him say.

This same principle was later extended to sales of all other movable property of any value.[4]

**Compurgation.** Where trustworthy human means seemed to be lacking, however, recourse was had to devices that called in the all-seeing Deity. (b) If the party who had been given the privilege of making proof, or waging his law, as it was called, were of good reputation, he was commonly asked to produce at the next session of court a certain number of compurgators (oath-helpers)—often from a designated group, his own family or leading men of the community—who would swear that his story was true. In this period they did not swear that they believed his story, but that it was actually true.[5] Fear of damnation for taking God's name in vain was supposed to make people reluctant to assist a man of bad character in this fashion, and so he would be unable to wage his law. Usually the man making proof in this fashion was asked to bring in six, twelve, or twenty-four oath-helpers, depending on the seriousness of the charge. On such occasions the oath of a thegn counted as the equivalent of six from ceorls (ordinary men).

**Ordeal.** (c) Men accused of serious offenses were usually asked to submit to the ordeal. Sometimes this was also allowed as an unpleasant alternative if the required number of oath-helpers could not be found. This was an appeal to the God of nature to show whether there was corruption in the suspect. After solemn religious services the accused might be wounded in some way, either by having to carry a piece of hot iron in his hand for a certain number of steps, or by being required to pick a stone out of boiling water. The distance to be traversed with the iron, or the depth of the water, usually varied with the seriousness of the charge. It would appear from this and the

[4] S-M, No. 4, Sec. 25, p. 8; No. 6, Sec. 1, p. 12; No. 7, Secs. 10, 12, p. 14; No. 11, Sec. 8, p. 20; No. 13, Sec. 24, p. 23.

[5] S-M, No. 14F, p. 25.

fact that the ordeal was sometimes prescribed when compurgation failed that the ordeal itself was regarded as somewhat in
the nature of a punishment as well as a means of trial. Immediately after the wound was inflicted the priest bound up the
injured arm. After three days he inspected it. If it was healing
cleanly, the man was innocent. If not, he was guilty. Another
type of ordeal was that by cold water. The suspect was thrown
into a pond or other still water that had been blessed by a priest.
If the consecrated water accepted him to the length of two yards
on the rope by which he was held, he was innocent. If he floated,
he was guilty. In many cases the complaining witness was allowed to choose the type of ordeal to which the accused should
be subjected.[6]

## THE JUDGMENT AND EXECUTION

**Types of Judgment.** (6) The result of the trial was then made
known to the court, and on the basis of it judgment was pronounced. If the defendant had been successful, the plaintiff
might be fined for having made a false charge. When the charge
was considered proved, however, the defendant might be imprisoned, corporally punished, ordered to restore the property
in question, or required to pay a sum of money. Imprisonment
was comparatively rare all through medieval times because of
the scarcity of substantial buildings that could be used for jails.
Excepting churches, which could not be employed for this purpose, only castles and mills were built substantially enough—
for a prisoner could easily break out of a wattle-and-daub house
—and millers found prisoners in their storeroom basements a
great nuisance. Corporal punishment was reserved for the most
serious cases. Men lost hands, or feet, or tongues for such offenses as counterfeiting, and suffered death for plotting against
their lords and sometimes for theft. In the latter type of case the

[6] S-M, No. 7, Sec. 23, p. 15; No. 8, pp. 15-16.

thief caught in the act with the goods in his hands (the hand-having thief) might be slain on the spot without trial.

**Wergeld and Wite.** A money payment, however, was the type of compensation most frequently exacted. This had the advantage of providing a financial satisfaction for the injured party or his relatives as well as—in most of the later cases—a fine called a wite for the king or whoever owned the court. The compensation to the relatives in case of death was called the wergeld (man payment of the deceased). This was supposed to represent the full value of the man's life. For an ordinary ceorl this was usually two hundred shillings [7] and for a thegn six times as much, a ratio which explains their relative values as oath-helpers in compurgation. The advantage of the wergeld system was that in theory it enabled the offended relatives to secure full satisfaction without having recourse to the blood feud, though in fact tempers did not always cool so easily.[8]

**The Bot.** The compensation for injuries less than death was called a bot. The care with which these bots were calculated will show something of the esthetic ideas and social amenities of the time and also afford an indication of the anxiety of the lawgivers to provide just and adequate substitutes for violence.

For seizing a man by the hair fifty sceattas [2½ shillings] shall be paid as compensation.

[7] At this time a shilling was worth five pennies. The later scale of English money in American money is as follows:

1 penny (abbreviation, d. from Latin *denarius*, penny) = 2¢
12 d. = 1 shilling (s.) = 24¢
20 s. = 1 pound (£ from the capital L of the Latin *libra*, pound) = about $4.85 at par

Because of changes in purchasing power, which is not uniform in the case of different commodities, such as sugar, which was once very scarce but now is relatively cheap, and wheat, for which the prices have changed in different proportions, it is almost impossible to estimate the value of medieval money in modern terms, but for early medieval times the sum should be multiplied by at least fifty. There has been an almost continuous, though irregular, inflation throughout English history.

[8] For examples of different wergelds and the relation of wergeld to blood feud see S-M, No. 4, p. 8; No. 9, p. 17.

If a bone is laid bare, three shillings shall be paid as compensation. For each of the four front teeth, six shillings [shall be paid as compensation]. For each of the teeth which stand next to these, four shillings; then for each tooth which stands next to them, three shillings and beyond that one shilling for each tooth.

If one man strikes another on the nose with his fist, three shillings. If it leaves a bruise, one shilling.

If it leaves a black bruise [showing] outside the clothes, thirty sceattas shall be paid as compensation.

If it is under the clothes, twenty sceattas.[9]

**Appeals and New Trials Rare.** Normally there was no appeal from these judgments (page 56), though there are a few unusual instances in which the original decisions appear to have been reversed. In one case it is suggested that one who had successfully waged his law by compurgation might later be outsworn by a greater accumulation of oath-helpers on the other side.

**Execution.** The execution of the judgment seems to have been committed to the local reeve, though in some cases the successful party himself was required to exact his satisfaction, just as he served the original notice.

## METHODOLOGY AND LEGAL LITERATURE

**No Legal Profession.** There were no professional lawyers or judges in Anglo-Saxon times. Since the law was supposedly buried in the breast of every Englishman (page 36), everyone was considered competent to conduct his own case or serve as a member of a court. Though the reeves, sheriffs, earls, and others who headed up the courts doubtless exercised a good deal of influence on the decisions rendered, theoretically these dignitaries were merely presiding officers, and could be outvoted by their colleagues. In any case, they had no formal legal training for their positions. In one or two instances we find traces of a committee of the entire court which seems to have been specially charged

[9] For other examples of bots see S-M, No. 1, pp. 3-4.

with legal matters, but its members were not professional lawyers.

**Legal Literature: Law Codes.** Because of the lack of professional lawyers in Anglo-Saxon times there is also a dearth of legal literature. No systematic treatises on the law of the time have come down to us from this period. Short codes, issued by various rulers, and documents conveying land or privileges over land are the chief sources of our knowledge of Anglo-Saxon law. The earliest codes were issued by the kings of Kent, the first kingdom to exercise suzerainty over its neighbors. The oldest code we have is from Ethelbert, Augustine's convert, and was issued at the end of the sixth century.[10] Two others were put out in the following century.[11] The House of Wessex, beginning with Ine (reigned 688-725) and continuing through Alfred, Athelstan (reigned 925-40), and several others, has also left codes.[12] The Danish king Canute issued two sets of laws that have survived.[13] Though there are some striking differences between the Kentish codes and those of Wessex, there was a marked tendency for the later sets to borrow largely from their predecessors rather than begin afresh. Alfred tells us clearly that he was choosing the best from his ancestors. He was thus adhering to the principle that law is not so much a new creation as an application to current needs of already accepted principles (page 36).

**Charters.** The land grants were recorded in charters—the usual name for any formal document in medieval times. These not only described the granted land or privileges—jurisdictional, fiscal, or both—but contained the date, invocations of God, religious observations on the transitory nature of this world, and a curse on all who might endeavor to upset the arrangements made.[14] From these land charters we are able to discover something of Anglo-Saxon notions of real property (page 69). Some

10 S-M, No. 1, pp. 2-4.
11 S-M, Nos. 2-3, pp. 4-6.
12 S-M, Nos. 4-12, pp. 6-22.
13 S-M, No. 13, pp. 22-24.
14 S-M, No. 15, pp. 25-32.

help on the problems of this period is also obtainable from a study of the codes of neighboring peoples, such as Celts, Franks, and Scandinavians. Literary works, such as *Beowulf* and the Norse sagas, are also of value in reflecting current legal concepts.

## SUBSTANTIVE LAW: INTRODUCTION

**The Theory of Authority.** Although codes were issued from time to time by the various kings, it must be repeated that in the vague theory of the time these did not make law, but merely declared it. Justice remained the product of the collective English conscience, to which appeal could be made from time to time through duly constituted authorities. These might be the men of the hundred or county court who applied the inherited principles to a particular case in hand, or they might be the men of the Witan who expanded this precious heritage into formal statements of general principles. This concept of justice accounts for the very considerable similarity among the codes, to which we have already referred. It might be expected that courts acting on such a theory would consider themselves bound by precedents, that is to say, the decisions of similar courts in similar cases. This is the legal principle known as *stare decisis* (to stand by the decisions; page 208). But though the generally accepted theory of justice tended to support this principle, it had not yet been clearly worked out. Thus courts at this time might feel free to interpret their sense of justice in a fashion differing from that of an earlier court without thinking that they had done anything out of the way. They would still be applying the community store of fairness to the matter in hand. But in practice they did tend to make similar decisions in similar cases.

**Civil and Criminal Law.** The substantive law of the Anglo-Saxons had not yet developed to the point of recognizing legal distinctions that are commonplaces today. Because what we know as criminal actions were commonly begun by the complaining witness, and because of the amount of self-help involved throughout the conduct of these cases, such actions in this period (pages 59, 64) were not definitely considered a class apart, as they came to be later when the state shouldered the burden of prosecution and thus gave them a special status.[15] Because of their primitive arrangements about prosecution the Anglo-Saxons did not recognize—as distinct from crimes—any separate class of torts (wrongs), which we now define as injuries to one's person or property that give grounds for a civil action, one which the individual himself must institute if anyone is to do it. Yet because we are trying to trace the roots of modern legal notions, we shall discuss the subject of substantive law in this period under the headings of criminal and civil doctrines. In this chapter we shall take the criminal topic first because in the troubled times with which we are dealing slayings, woundings, and theft bulk largest in the codes. Society was so preoccupied with the effort to substitute for the unending blood feuds some method of securing rough justice in such cases that it did not develop much detailed theory on other subjects.

## CRIMINAL LAW

**Influence of the Blood Feud.** The doctrines of Anglo-Saxon criminal law are dominated by the institution of the blood feud and the idea of supplanting it by some acceptable legal device. For the old ways died hard. The Anglo-Saxons, like modern nations, clung stubbornly to the theory that they might fight if they did not choose to submit to a court of arbitration. Alfred's code so far recognized this as to lay down rules for the conduct of the feud, and in Canute's time it had not yet died out com-

---

[15] The writer knows no better definition of a criminal case today than that it is one which, for some reason or other, the state has decided to be responsible for prosecuting.

pletely. The system of bots and wers (wergelds) already described was the alternative which the law undertook to substitute so far as possible. Since it was actually considered a substitute, the relatives of the offending party were often required to help pay the money, just as they would have been required to take part in the feud. And if the money was not forthcoming, the feud was waged. "Buy off the spear or bear it," said the legal proverb.

**Criminal Liability.** For the same reason the principle of legal liability on which the law proceeded was based on the effects of a man's actions rather than the intent which prompted them. If a person was killed, even though accidentally, his relatives supposedly would be displeased and would wish for satisfaction. To prevent the development of the feud, the law provided for the money payment in such cases. "Whoever offends unknowingly shall correct the fault [pay] knowingly," said the legal proverb. A man acted at his peril. If he rode down a dark lane with an exposed spear he was responsible for any accident which might occur. Only if he were holding the weapon in a supposedly safe fashion and standing still could he clear himself, for he must swear that he had done nothing to bring the deceased "nearer to death or further from life." The law was regarding not so much the culpability of the actor as the feelings of the injured person or his relatives, who might be moved to start a blood feud. Even when a man killed in self-defense the wergeld was commonly exacted.

**Foreshadowings of Modern Ideas.** Yet there were some elements in the criminal law that point forward rather than backward. The addition of the wite (page 63) to the bot or wer suggests the dawning of the idea that the user of violence owes something to society in general as well as to his injured neighbor. The growth of the idea of the king's peace (page 33), and the imposition of fines for neglecting militia (fyrd) service, or for failure to attend county court, show the development of the notion that the state can be offended and that it also can and should punish. In the later laws we find that only the wer and not the wite was exacted from the unfortunate agent in cases of accidental death, and this indicates a tendency to modify the harsh original theory of criminal liability in cases of accident.

## CIVIL LAW: REAL PROPERTY

**Real Property and Its Importance.** Among the civil topics we take first that of real property. Here again we are dealing with a concept strange to the Anglo-Saxons, for all property actions at this time were real in the sense that the plaintiff wished to recover the thing (*res*) in dispute itself, rather than its money value. Only later was this type of suit confined to land cases. But for the sake of convenience we use the later term when talking about land law, and we put it first under the civil heading because then, as for many centuries to come, land, as we have seen (page 14), was the chief form of wealth in England. We have already noted how the land was worked, and how the title to most of it fell into the hands of the well-to-do (page 45).

**Alienation.** Lands were alienated (transferred from one person to another) by a public ceremony known as livery of seisin (delivery of possession), by which the seller (vendor) formally put the purchaser in possession of the property before witnesses and at the same time gave him some symbol of the transaction. This might take the form of a lump of earth, a twig, or the key to a door. Thereafter, should there be any dispute about the matter, the original witnesses to the transfer could be produced to settle the controversy. After the development of the lordship system (page 44) grants made by the lords and their dependents were commonly accompanied by a written document, such as we have already described, which the Saxons called a land book. All land conveyed in this fashion—property over which a book had passed —was subsequently known as bookland. If it was not granted permanently, but merely for a term of years or lives, it was called laenland (loan land). There was another type of land called folkland, about which we have little evidence. It is possible that this term was used to designate the holdings of the crown—the public domain, pieces of which might be temporarily granted to the king's servants and from which future grants might be made to lords who could convert it into bookland. Both bookland and folkland appear to have been freely salable, and could be disposed of by will in any way the owner might desire.[16] This freedom of disposal by will is in marked contrast to the prohibition imposed in the period of fully developed feudalism (page 181).

## PERSONAL PROPERTY AND CONTRACTS

**Personal Property.** The law of movable property—later called personal property because actions concerned with it recovered not the thing itself but only its money value from the defendant personally—was concerned almost exclusively with sales and possession. The law did not distinguish between ownership and possession, and undertook to protect only the involuntary loss of possession. That is, if one had entrusted (bailed) his horse voluntarily to another man and it was taken from the person to whom he had entrusted it (the bailee) against the bailee's will, the law would help the bailee and only the bailee to recover it. In other words, it was as much as society could do to devise rough-and-ready means of dealing with outright theft without bothering about subtle frauds that might arise from the

---

[16] On this point see G. J. Turner, "Bookland and Folkland," *Historical Essays in Honour of James Tait*, Manchester, Eng., 1933, pp. 356-85. For a contrary view on folkland see J. E. Jolliffe, *Constitutional History of Medieval England*, Macmillan, 1937, pp. 73-74. He agrees that folkland could be freely sold and willed—at least at the end of the Saxon period—but still maintains, with Vinogradoff, that folkland was private property and to be distinguished from bookland only by the fact that it was held by customary right, or the custom of the folk, instead of by bookright. There are only three references to folkland in Anglo-Saxon legal documents. Hence the difficulty of determining its exact nature.

bailee's being in collusion with the thief. Hence the elaborate provision for public sales before witnesses, to which we have already referred. These were designed to secure the greatest possible publicity for agreements legally transferring possession of cattle. A law of the tenth century provides a further amplification of this principle:

> He who rides in quest of any cattle, let him declare to his neighbors about what he rides; and when he comes home let him also declare with whose witness he bought the cattle. But if he, being on any journey, unintentionally make a bargain without having declared it when he rode out, let him declare it when he comes home; and if it be live stock, let him, with the witness of his township [tun, or vill] bring it to the common pasture.

If, after a sale, a question was raised as to the ownership of movables, the purchaser was entitled to summon the seller and the witnesses before whom the original bargain had been made and demand that the seller validate the title. This process was called vouching to warranty, because the seller was called on to warrant (guarantee) the title. If he could disprove his responsibility, the one who had summoned him was held guilty of theft; otherwise the seller was required to take the defendant's place in the suit. He might then vouch another person to warranty, and so on until the question of ownership was properly cleared up. But by Canute's time, to avoid interminable proceedings it was provided that the case should be ended and the defendant discharged after three successful vouchings.

**Contracts.** Anglo-Saxon society had not yet devised any satisfactory way of enforcing promises to do something in the future. In other words, no law of contract had developed. But the custom of exacting promises to pay wergeld, and the practice of having one man stand surety for the good conduct of another in the future, suggested the later line of advance in this field.

## FAMILY LAW AND INHERITANCE

**Marriage.** Marriages were originally contracted among the Anglo-Saxons by means of bride purchase, the payment of a sum of money to the bride's parents for having broken the unity of their family. Just as the king had his sphere of authority (mund) that could not be violated without penalty, so every lesser citizen had his own sphere of authority on which one might not trespass with impunity. Hence the marriage payment was called a mundbryce (sum for the breaking of the mund) and compensated the parents for the loss suffered in the removal of the child from their power and authority. In later Anglo-Saxon times this payment was transferred to the bride, becoming part of her dowry, while the consent of the parents was supposedly obtained by the promise of the groom to keep his bride "according to God's law, as a man should his wife." The wedding ring became the pledge of these agreements, and ecclesiastical custom added the blessing of the priest, though this was not considered legally necessary until long after this period.

**The Status of Women.** Once married, the woman passed into her husband's control (mund), and was expected to obey him. She retained, however, legal independence to the extent of being able to hold her own property, and this was not liable for wrongful acts of her husband. She could prosecute a legal action, act as a witness, and make her own will. Divorce was permissible by mutual consent, or on account of the wife's infidelity or desertion.

**And Children.** Children were in the father's mund until they reached the age of majority, which varied from ten to seventeen years at different periods and for different purposes. Marriages could be forbidden during this time of minority, but an unwelcome alliance could not be forced upon an unwilling child. Before the age of seven children could be sold as slaves by their parents, but only in case of absolute necessity.

**Inheritance.** If a man died intestate, that is, left no will, his property was divided in various ways, according to local custom. In Kent the sons all shared alike, according to a practice known as gavelkind. Elsewhere the tendency was for the oldest son to inherit at least the lion's share, in order that the family holdings might be kept of reasonable size. This custom was known as primogeniture, the right of the firstborn (son) to succeed to his father's property. In some cases the widows seem to have been entitled to one-third of the estate. Sometimes there were different rules for different types of property, such as land, armor, and money. The Church strongly urged the making of wills, largely because the priests, who alone were able to write them, often found it possible to have the Church included among the beneficiaries. Nuncupative (oral) wills, and gifts to take effect after death were also known. The legal position of executor had not yet been devised, but one of a man's relatives, a churchman, or the king was frequently requested to carry out the wishes of the testator (maker of the will).

**Anglo-Saxon Law Primitive, but Sound in Principle.** Some idea of the rudimentary character of Anglo-Saxon law may be obtained from this summary. Not only were large sections of modern business law wholly unknown in this period, but the problems dealt with, as in the case of legal liability, were frequently handled in what we should consider a most unfair manner. Many provisions of the law that today we regard as axiomatic were unknown to the Englishman before the Norman Conquest. The attention paid to the reputation of the accused and the employment of the ordeal as a form of semipunishment show that the idea had not yet developed that a man was innocent until proved guilty. Even the famous principle of the first bite— by which for centuries the owner of a dog has not been held responsible for the animal's first offense—was not followed in this period. According to Alfred's code the very first bit of canine delinquency cost six shillings. Yet the germ of the later development was there, for the second and third offenses were punished with correspondingly heavier fines. So also, as we have seen, the beginnings of modern principles are to be found in such other fields as criminal law, and even contracts. If the Saxon methods were often rough-and-ready solutions of the problems of rough-and-ready times, they were solutions worked out by real people for real people, and so were founded on essentially sound psychological principles. For, fundamentally, human nature does not change, however much it may be refined. In the modern lie-detector we see merely a more skillful adaptation of the Saxon principle that the foreoath and denial had to be taken without slip. Furthermore, time was to show that—properly interpreted and expanded—the basic theory of a sense of justice reposing in the breast of every Englishman was adequate to the needs of the more complicated society of the ages that were to follow.

# The Height
# of the Middle Ages

# 4. GENERAL HISTORY
## 1066-1307

### THE NORMAN CONQUEST AND ITS RESULTS

**Exhaustion of the Saxon Civilization.** In 1066 the reign of Edward the Confessor ended in a haze of weakness and uncertainty. The Anglo-Saxons, who had now been masters of Britain during most of five or six centuries, like the Romans before them had begun to lose their vigor. They had risen considerably in the scale of civilization, but appear to have been tired out by the end of this period. Evidence of this exhaustion may perhaps be seen even in the physical history of the royal family during the late Saxon era. Alfred himself was none too strong (page 18). After his son's time none of his Saxon successors except the last lived to be fifty, and at least one was a chronic invalid. While Edward the Confessor survived to the age of sixty-two, he showed the typical weakness of his line by his anemic saintliness. But whether the decline was really a physical one or not, there is certainly evidence of social fatigue among the late Anglo-Saxons. No longer did their state show itself capable of rising to emergencies or adapting itself to changing conditions.

**Edward the Confessor as an Example.** The good private morals of an administrator do not necessarily make for governmental efficiency. The student must never forget this difference between private and public morality. While it is reprehensible for an individual to repudiate his debts, governments from time immemorial have found this policy the only alternative to far greater social disasters. A spirit of forbearance and forgiveness may make a man a good citizen, but the same spirit in a responsible execu-

77

tive leads to widespread contempt of authority and resulting disorder. W. S. Gilbert's pirate king has explained this principle very well:

> But many a king on a first-class throne,
> If he wants to call his crown his own,
> Must manage somehow to get through
> More dirty work than ever *I* do,
> Though I am a Pirate King.

Edward the Confessor did not get through his stint of this kind of work, and as a ruler the very religious monarch fell far short of meeting his country's needs. He put Norman friends in English offices and so antagonized his Saxon subjects. When the resentful natives combined to expel the foreigners, Edward allowed himself to be dominated by the Saxon faction, led by an earl named Godwin. As a result, the pious King soon found himself at odds with the Pope, for one of the ejected Normans had been Archbishop of Canterbury, and the Roman pontiff would not send the pallium (page 38) to the Saxon nominee. Worst of all, Edward had no children, and in the Wessex line there was no acceptable candidate of royal blood to succeed him.

**The Resulting Struggle for the Crown.** Ambitious men were not slow in trying to take advantage of this situation. Harold, Godwin's son and successor as Earl of Wessex and chief adviser to Edward, had himself elected king the day after his predecessor's death. From Norway came its ruler, Harold Hardrada, at the head of an army, hoping to restore the Anglo-Scandinavian empire of Canute. The Saxon claimant met this challenge by defeating the Norwegians at Stamford Bridge (near York) and leaving Harold Hardrada dead on the battlefield. But a second rival, William of Normandy, proved too much for the Saxon king. For William had at his back men who had the double advantage of coming fresh to the struggle to raise their level of civilization and also of being in touch with the fruits of the great Roman achievement in this field.

**The Normans and Their Viking-Roman Heritage.** Normandy, as already indicated (page 21), was a ninth- and tenth-century Viking settlement made by the Northmen—hence the name—on the north coast of the modern France, opposite Hampshire in southern England. With the breakup of Charlemagne's empire individual local lords established themselves as the virtual rulers of their particular areas in the old Frankish territory. These men owed only slight allegiance to any higher authority. In this feudal system the dukes of Normandy became vassals of the kings of France, who exercised nominal sway from Paris but commonly left their powerful subordinates to follow their own devices. Some traditions of the imperial Roman rule that Charlemagne had endeavored to copy lingered on in his former domains, however, and as the Normans intermarried with the native French—themselves a mixture of Romanized Gaul and Teutonic Frank—they absorbed some of these governmental principles. The vigorous Norman dukes soon built up a highly centralized feudal state, and Edward's second cousin William—the grandson of the Confessor's Norman mother's brother—held it at Edward's death. He had laid careful plans for profiting by his kinsman's childlessness.

**William's Rationalization of His Invasion.** William had some justification, of a sort, for claiming the English crown. He himself had no Saxon royal blood, but he shared Edward's Norman strain, and his wife—whom he married quite possibly on this account—was a descendant of Alfred the Great. Harold had once been shipwrecked on the Norman coast, and before releasing him the Duke had exacted an oath to support William's claim. It was also asserted that Edward had promised that his cousin should succeed. But since the Witan had the right of election, these arguments were of no great strength. More important was the fact that Pope Alexander II had sanctioned the projected invasion, on the understanding that his claims would be recognized in the matter of the disputed archbishopric of Canterbury.

**The Argument of the Sword.** Most important, however, was the fact that William had a good army. His feudal dependents could not be compelled to do military service across the Channel, but there was no shortage of volunteers. Some of these supporters came because of the papal endorsement, but many more because of the prospect of plunder and profit. For William already had a reputation as a successful fighter and a capable ruler. Starting with the double handicap of illegitimate birth and of having succeeded to the dukedom as a minor, he had ruthlessly beaten down all opposition. Twice he had defeated his feudal lord, the King of France, in pitched battles. Grimly he had suppressed rebellions at home. After an unsuccessful resistance to one of his sieges, during which certain of the defenders had taunted him with his base birth, he lopped off the hands and feet of thirty-two of them to discourage such comments in the future. He had even awed the churchmen who, for some unknown reason, had presumed to forbid his projected marriage. When their lands were savagely laid waste, they hastily came to terms. It was generally supposed that no Englishman would be able to stand against him.

**The Conquest.** The event proved the correctness of this assumption. On October 14, 1066, less than three weeks after the victory at Stamford Bridge, the tired Saxon army was beaten at Hastings on the Sussex coast, and Harold was killed by an arrow that pierced his eye. William moved north, burned the town of Southwark, opposite London on the south side of the Thames, crossed the river farther west, and terrorized the surviving members of the Witan into electing him king. For several years, however, there was still opposition in many parts of the country, notably in the north, and also in the west, where Harold's mother stood a long siege at Exeter in Devonshire. William dealt with these areas as he had already dealt with troublesome districts at home. After the suppression of the disorders in the west, the northern counties were mercilessly harried until there

## ST. ALBANS CATHEDRAL TOWER

Located twenty miles northwest of London, this structure, approximately 150 feet high, gives some suggestion of the mixture of types of institutions in medieval England after the Norman Conquest. It is largely made of bricks collected by a Saxon abbot from near-by Roman ruins. When the Normans took over the project, they built the tower out of the materials ready at hand, but in their own characteristically solid and rugged style. The portion of the cathedral to the left of the base of the tower is in the Gothic style of the period after 1180.

was no resistance left in the burned villages and desolate fields. By 1071 William was undisputed lord of England.

**The Results of the Norman Conquest.** The chief and most general effect of the Norman Conquest was to give the control of England to a more vigorous and capable people than the Anglo-Saxons had been in their later years. This superiority was not the result of any essential difference in race, for the invaders were also largely Teutonic in origin. Rather it was the result of those traits to which we have already alluded (page 78), their freshness and their contact with the Roman tradition. No impartial observer who studies the history of English architecture, and notices how soon after the Conquest great and attractive structures sprang up to take the place of the humble Saxon buildings, can fail to be impressed by the superior mechanical and cultural abilities of the Normans.[1] These traits manifested themselves in a variety of particular ways. The Conquest opened up a few more avenues of trade, though by no means as many as are commonly supposed.[2] It greatly speeded up the process by which Continental ideas—constitutional, religious, and artistic—were already being introduced into England. Furthermore, the French language, which was spoken by the conquerors, eventually produced a marked change in the native English tongue.

**The Effect on the English Monarchy.** But the most important particular effect, for our purposes, was that the island kingdom now received a line of rulers who for nearly two centuries and a half were, on the average, far more able and energetic than their Saxon predecessors. As a result of William's genius and the

[1] Much of the past reluctance to grant this Norman superiority has sprung from the feeling of English historians and critics that the Normans were foreigners, while the Saxons were truly English. The achievements of the two peoples have therefore been judged accordingly. The student must beware of nationalism in the interpretation of history, even that of the Middle Ages.

[2] On the disproof of the sweeping assertion that the Conquest revolutionized English foreign-trade relations see J. L. Cate, "The Norman Conquest and Anglo-Continental Trade," University of Chicago Ph.D. thesis, 1935.

accidents of subsequent heredity they stood out against the background of the generally capable Norman nobles and churchmen much more than had the Saxon kings from their comparatively weak associates. There were three important consequences of this superiority. The kings assumed a predominant position in the three-sided coalition that controlled the state (page 30), the government of England was highly centralized at an early date, and the country (helped also by its fortunate geographical situation and natural boundaries) developed a national spirit long before most of its rivals. Because of this greatly enhanced importance of the monarch—which is further indicated by the fact that the system of numbering the English kings begins with this date —it is essential to keep the personalities of the individual rulers and the order of their succession in mind from this time on. English history was so greatly influenced by these men and women, and so many important institutions and laws are dated from their reigns, that the subject becomes hopelessly confused unless this list is kept in mind.[3]

## THE SUCCESSION TO THE CROWN: EARLY RULERS

**The Reign of William the Conqueror (1066-87).** William ruled for sixteen years after the completion of the Conquest. It was a period not entirely free from revolts, but the Conqueror showed his great power in many ways besides putting them down. He reserved great tracts of land for hunting and enforced strict game

[3] See the table in the back of the book. It may also be useful to append a modified version of one of the mnemonics which are frequently used in English schools for this purpose. This is the shortest, though the worst doggerel.

Willie, Willie, Harry, Ste,
Harry, Dick, John, Harry Three,
Edwards three and Richard Two,
Harry Four, Five, Six, then who?
Edward Four, Five, Dick the Bad,
Harry, Harry, Ned the Lad,

Mary, Bessie, James the Vain,
Charlie, Charlie, James again,
Will and Mary, Anna gloria,
Four Georges, William and Victoria,
Edward, George and Edward again,
Another George and now, Amen!

laws in them. "He loved the tall stags as if he were their father," said the Anglo-Saxon chronicler. "The rich complained and the poor murmured, but he was so sturdy that he recked not of them." In 1086 he ordered something like a national census, which resulted in the compilation of a record of the country's financial resources and the royal rights over them. This record was called the Domesday Book (the early spelling of the Dooms-day Book of the recording angel).[4] Probably no other ruler of his time could have extorted such information from his people, but reluctant men produced it under oath for the "stark, stern, and wrathful" Norman. On the Continent he forcibly annexed Maine, a county lying just south of his ancestral territory.

**The Succession of William Rufus (1087-1100).** The Conqueror's disposition of the English crown on his deathbed in 1087 further illustrates the predominant position he had come to occupy. Virtually disregarding the Saxon custom of leaving such matters to the Council, he partitioned his domains as though they were his private property.[5] He had three sons, Robert, William, and Henry. There was also a daughter named Adela, who had married Stephen Henry, Count of Blois, a neighboring territory on the Continent. Robert, who was known as the Sleepy, the old monarch deemed too weak to rule a large conquered country, so he gave him the Continental possessions. William, called the Red (Rufus in Latin), was given England, and Henry, known as Beauclerk (the well-educated) was left only a grant of money. Adela received nothing. Many of the Conqueror's nobles who held lands in both Normandy and England would have preferred Robert as King of England as well as Duke of Normandy—possibly because they wanted a weak overlord in England as well as across the Channel. But the Conqueror's

---

[4] S-M, Nos. 21-22, pp. 40-46.
[5] He went through the form of requesting the Archbishop of Canterbury to make William king "if he deemed it might justly be done," but we have no record of any election having been held.

arrangement was accepted for the time being, and the Red King
showed that he had something of his father's fire by suppressing
a revolt of the dissatisfied a little later.

**His Rule and Death.** William Rufus did not, however, have
his father's administrative ability. He understood military tactics and terrorism, but little else. He used his position as king
and head of the feudal system largely for the purpose of exacting huge sums of money from those who wished to succeed to
their ancestral estates or to vacant bishoprics. One day in 1100,
while hunting with his brother Henry and a party of his nobles
in the New Forest outside of Winchester—the Hampshire town
which from the time of the Wessex supremacy had been the capital of England—he was shot through the heart with an arrow.
It may have been by accident, or possibly by design. So many
people wished him dead that historians have had their suspicions, but the hunting-field mystery cannot be solved. In those
days it was dangerous to be too curious about such a matter,
and if there was any incriminating evidence it was almost entirely suppressed.

**The Succession of Henry I (1100-35).** At all events, when notified of the shooting Henry was in another part of the forest. He
then rode hard for Winchester and the royal treasure. William
Rufus, a bachelor, had left no issue, and Sleepy Robert was then
in Sicily—on his way back from the First Crusade, in which he
had participated, usually at a safe distance behind the leaders.
Henry, with the treasure and the crown in his possession,
promptly issued a charter in which he promised to remedy
the abuses of his brother's reign,[6] and thus managed to secure
the kingdom. When Robert finally returned and invaded England, Henry persuaded his lethargic rival to withdraw. A few
years later the English King crossed the Channel, defeated his
brother in battle, imprisoned him for life, and took over his

---

[6] S-M, No. 23, pp. 46-48.

domains. So the son who was left none of his father's territory obtained all of it.

**Henry's Rule and the Succession of Stephen.** Henry's reign lasted until 1135, and he gave England a firm rule on his father's model, the constitutional effects of which we shall see later. His only son, however, was drowned while trying to cross the English Channel one stormy night, and this raised a problem about the succession to the throne. To perpetuate his family's hold on the crown, Henry tried to persuade the nobles to accept as his successor his daughter Matilda, who was married to Geoffrey of Anjou, a powerful French count who ruled a territory south of Maine. The promises were easily given during the father's lifetime, but as easily broken when he was safely buried, for there was no precedent in the Norman tradition for a feminine ruler. A son of Adela, Stephen of Blois, came over from the Continent and succeeded in securing election as monarch.[7]

**The Anarchy of Stephen's Reign (1135-54).** Matilda, however, proceeded to show that a woman might not be as negligible a factor as was supposed. Though she did not come to England immediately, she soon made trouble in Normandy—without much help from her husband—and in 1138 she crossed the Channel. She was vigorous enough to capture London, and even Stephen himself at one time. But she overplayed her hand by being too arrogant, and unwilling to make concessions to her prospective subjects. Public opinion veered around, and within two years of the time of her early successes she was hard pressed to avoid capture. Only by a clever ruse did she escape from Oxford Castle, in which she was besieged. One snowy night just before Christmas of 1142 she and three companions dressed themselves in white and slipped through the enemy's lines. At length, in 1148, Ste-

[7] Whenever the claim to the throne passes through a woman, the surname of the ruling family naturally changes (thus Adela Norman became Mrs. Blois, so to speak), and therefore historians call the new rulers a new dynasty (line of monarchs). Stephen is therefore the first (and last) of the Blois dynasty.

phen—whom Matilda had exchanged for her half-brother, who had been captured by her rival's supporters—succeeded in expelling her from the country. In the course of all these troubles robber barons built themselves private fortresses and preyed on the surrounding territory. The land thus fell into a state of feudal anarchy, from which Stephen was unable to rescue it. His failing was the exact opposite of Matilda's. "A mild man, and soft and good—and did no justice," in the words of a contemporary chronicle, he was far too willing to make concessions, and though a brave fighter, he showed a lamentable lack of decision in political crises. At long last the oldest child of Matilda—fortunately a son—called Henry, grew to young manhood and delivered the country from the extortionate "devils and evil men" in the stone castles. In 1153 he came to England with an army, and soon persuaded Stephen, who had lost the son whom he had chosen as his successor, to recognize him as his heir. A year later Stephen, like many another politician soon after a defeat, died, and Henry II became the first Angevin king of England.[8]

**The Character of Henry II (1154-89).** Red-haired, freckled, short, stout, and bowlegged, Henry did not look the part of a king. But in training, ambition, tact, tireless attention to detail, and, above all, in energy he more than made up for any physical shortcomings. After a day in the hunting-field he could transact business half the night, pacing restlessly back and forth. Dismayed courtiers, who were not permitted to sit while the King stood, noted that even sores on the royal legs would not keep the monarch off his feet. Though a master diplomatist, when necessary he could employ all his great-grandfather's grimness in suppressing revolts. He was, in fact, along with William the Conqueror and Edward I, with whom we shall end this chapter,

---

[8] The first of the House of Anjou. Because Geoffrey of Anjou frequently wore in his cap a sprig of the broom (genet) plant, he was nicknamed "Plantagenet," and this term has come to be used by historians as the equivalent of "Angevin."

one of the three great dominating figures in a period of powerful rulers.

**Restoration of Order.** Henry had need of all his strong qualities to bring order out of Stephen's chaos. It was not enough to secure the consent of the council to an edict that all castles built without the royal license—adulterine castles, they were called—should be destroyed. It was necessary to have the sheriff's report whether the order had been obeyed, and to make some horrible examples of the disobedient. When the second lord's castle had been reduced to a smoke-blackened stub of stones littered with various unpleasant bits of human debris, the others thought it the better part of valor to bow to the royal will.

## THE ANGEVIN EMPIRE AND ITS PROBLEMS

**The Angevin Empire.** England and Henry's Continental inheritance—which included Anjou and its dependency Touraine as well as the Norman dominions—were not, however, capable of fully holding Henry's attention. In 1152—before Henry's accession to the English throne—Louis VII of France tired of his wife, Eleanor of Aquitaine, and obtained an annulment of their marriage. She was, however, heiress to Aquitaine and the neighboring territories of Gascony and Poitou—most of southwestern France. Henry quickly secured the discarded lady's hand and her territories. Shortly after he became King of England he aided the Count of Brittany, whose territory lay west of Normandy, in suppressing a revolt, and in the process obtained suzerainty over that area also. He was therefore not only King of England but the feudal ruler of half of France. Consequently his domains are sometimes referred to as the Angevin Empire, though there was no system of central government for them all and though the French territories, furthermore, were held by a variety of separate claims.

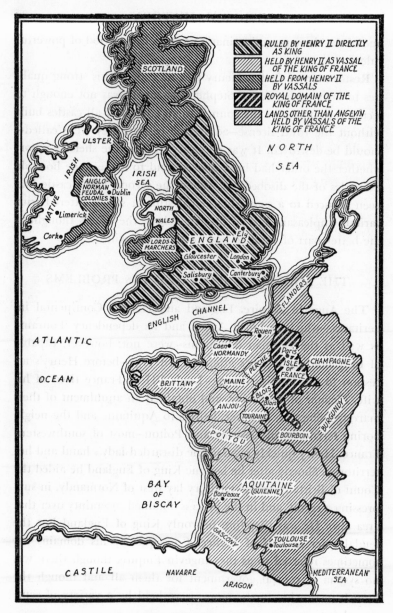

Legend:

- RULED BY HENRY II DIRECTLY AS KING
- HELD BY HENRY II AS VASSAL OF THE KING OF FRANCE
- HELD FROM HENRY II BY VASSALS
- ROYAL DOMAIN OF THE KING OF FRANCE
- LANDS OTHER THAN ANGEVIN HELD BY VASSALS OF THE KING OF FRANCE

SCOTLAND

NORTH SEA

ULSTER

IRISH

NATIVE IRISH

Limerick

Cork

ANGLO-NORMAN FEUDAL COLONIES • Dublin

IRISH SEA

NORTH WALES

LORDS MARCHERS

ENGLAND

Ely

Gloucester    London

Salisbury    Canterbury

FLANDERS

ENGLISH CHANNEL

ATLANTIC OCEAN

Rouen •

Caen • NORMANDY

Paris •

ISLE OF FRANCE

CHAMPAGNE

PERCHE

BRITTANY

MAINE

BLOIS

Blois •

ANJOU

TOURAINE

BOURBON

BURGUNDY

POITOU

BAY OF BISCAY

Bordeaux •

AQUITAINE (GUIENNE)

GASCONY

TOULOUSE • Toulouse

CASTILE    NAVARRE

ARAGON

MEDITERRANEAN SEA

**THE ANGEVIN EMPIRE**

**Wales.** After 1158 Henry began to extend his influence to the north and west also. The Celtic region of Wales, which the Saxons had not conquered, attracted the attention of the land-hungry Norman lords as early as the time of William II. Like the American pioneers, they began moving westward, carving out new estates for themselves on the frontier. The Celts, still organized in tribal units, could put up no very effective resistance in southern and eastern Wales, and many of the Normans succeeded in establishing for themselves marcher lordships, so called from the word "march" (*cf.* Mercia), meaning "border." As holders of borderlands in especially dangerous positions they claimed and exercised special powers, though William Rufus and Henry I made expeditions to this area to assert their feudal overlordship. Under pressure, the Welsh had been driven to establish a more unified form of government, and in Stephen's time they had regained a considerable measure of power, especially in the mountainous northern region. Henry II now began a series of campaigns that re-established English power in the south and extorted a nominal acknowledgment of vassalship from the chieftain who was now known as the Prince of North Wales.

**Ireland.** Ireland, lying as it did farther to the west, constituted in Norman English eyes merely an extension of their Celtic frontier. As soon as Henry II established his authority in southern Wales his marcher lords began to repeat in Ireland the process their grandfathers had begun northwest of the Bristol Channel. Taking advantage of a dynastic quarrel in one of the several clan kingdoms into which Ireland was divided, Richard Clare, Earl of Pembroke—generally known as Strongbow—led a Norman force to the smaller island in 1169. In two years the southeastern coast of Ireland, from Dublin to Cork, was conquered, and Henry found it advisable as well as convenient (page 112) to hurry over to assert his overlordship and prevent the establishment of a separate Norman kingdom. He did not, however, remain long enough in the Pale, as the English sphere of influence came to be called, to complete the work of setting up an administrative organization, and after his departure the Norman lords regained a considerable measure of independence. In 1177 Henry designated his son John as Lord of Ireland and in 1185 sent him to restore order and finish the conquest. John, however, found it more amusing to pull the beards of his Irish subjects than to tend to the serious business in hand. He soon returned, leaving the Norman lords to spread their influence as best they could from the Pale out into the areas still held by the native Celts. Years of petty border warfare followed, in which the Irish began to learn that lesson of hatred for the English which eventually they came to know all too well.

**Scotland.** With Scotland Henry inherited an old, old quarrel. That territory had once stood in much the same relation to Anglo-Saxon England as Wales had, and, as already noted (page 12), there had been a considerable infiltration of Northumbrian Angles into the Lowlands, the southern part of Scotland. Three separate Celtic kingdoms in the north and west had, however, succeeded in unifying themselves as their southern neighbors had done, and in the process they took over the Anglo-Saxon lowland territory as well. Shakespeare's Macbeth was one of the first and, in real history, one of the best of the rulers of united Scotland. From the time of Athelstan (reigned 925-40) the kings of England had claimed suzerainty over Scotland. When they had a strong army in the north they were able to secure acknowledgments of it from the reluctant Scots, who subsequently always disputed the significance of their act. William the Conqueror and William Rufus kept up the tradition, but there was no effective English control, and during the anarchy under Stephen the Scots not only asserted their independence but secured the three border counties of Northumberland, Cumberland, and Westmoreland, which had formerly belonged to England. While negotiating for the English throne Henry of Anjou had agreed to accept this settlement, but once in power he disregarded his pledge. In 1173 the King of Scotland was captured while aiding

English rebels. To obtain his freedom he was compelled to agree to hold Scotland as a vassal of the English, and to permit his own vassals to acknowledge Henry as their suzerain. Legally, this settled the old argument. There was a considerable influx of Norman lords into Scotland, and a real amalgamation might have been possible in the next decades had Henry's successors been wise enough to work toward that end.

**France and the Revolts of the Royal Family.** With France Henry also inherited an old quarrel. This dated back to the time of the Conqueror's wars with his feudal lord, the French King, and had been growing in intensity with the passing of the years. Friction inevitably resulted from a situation in which one king, as a nominal vassal, held half the territory of another. Yet in spite of his widespread interests elsewhere, Henry more than held his own in this strife until his children became old enough to take part. Then Louis VII and his successor, Philip (Augustus) II, found Henry's one weakness. Though Henry was too busy to finish his work in Wales and Ireland, and though he did not gain all his objectives in a controversy with the Church to which we shall return later (pages 110-3), in general it is fair to say that the florid Angevin was master everywhere except at home. At one time or another his wife and all his four sons— Henry, who predeceased his father, Richard, Geoffrey, and John —leagued with the King of France and conspired against him. Contemporaries called the family a lion's brood, and the boys gloried in their reputation for unruliness. One revolt was put down in 1173 by the doughty father, who was aided by the mercantile elements in the towns rallying to the cause of law and order. Sixteen years later an uprising led by the belligerent Richard was more successful. In Anjou the broken monarch made terms with his son and Philip, the French ally, and then took to his deathbed muttering, "Shame, shame on a beaten king." The lion's brood was left in possession of the spoils.

**Richard I, the Lion-Hearted (1189-99).** The more peaceful arts of government made little appeal to Richard, who was interested in almost nothing but warfare. Now suddenly transformed from rebel to king, he was forced to look abroad for pretexts on which to fight. Fortunately he was pledged to go on a Crusade, and for several years that spared him the drudgery of administration. On his way home in 1193, after having won glory but not Jerusalem, he was captured by a vassal of the Duke of Austria and held for ransom by the German Emperor, to whom the Duke virtually sold his royal prisoner. Richard's brother John, who had profited by Richard's absence to seize power in England, did his best to prolong the imprisonment. Loyal subjects, however, thwarted John's schemes, and after much straining of the country's financial machinery found enough money to make a substantial down-payment on Richard's huge ransom and thus obtained their lord's release. Richard showed his gratitude by a few months' visit to his generous island kingdom and by a demand for more money so that he might fight his former ally, Philip of France. Then he returned to the Continent, where he spent the remainder of his reign in what wars he could find. During a minor siege in 1199 a keen-eyed crossbowman avenged a slaughtered family by a bit of clever maneuvering that culminated with a mortal wound in the royal armpit. So ended the career of Richard, called the Lion-Hearted, who was subsequently to be honored with a statue before the Houses of Parliament, while the popular mind has long since forgotten his less romantic but far greater father.

## JOHN AND THE LOSS OF NORMANDY

**The Succession of John (1199-1216).** Richard had no issue. Geoffrey, the next brother, was dead, but he had left a son named Arthur, who had been brought up in Brittany as the prospective ruler of that territory. Judged by some Continental practice, his claim to succeed Richard was better than John's. But the grown man was preferred in England, and secured the throne. Philip of France, still striving to increase his power at the expense of the Angevins, saw his chance, of course, and with a view to embarrassing his powerful rival, he supported Arthur's claim to some of the French fiefs.

**The Loss of Normandy.** John shortly played into the French King's hand by marrying a girl who was already betrothed to one of his own French vassals. Outraged, the prospective bridegroom appealed to Philip as his overlord to do him justice against the intermediate lord, John. When the English King refused to appear at the French court to answer the charges, his Continental holdings were declared forfeit under feudal law for disobedience to his suzerain. In the fighting that followed we get our last glimpse of the lion's brood in typical action. John's mother, Eleanor of Aquitaine, had been imprisoned by her husband after the 1173 revolt and was not released until Henry's death sixteen years later. Undaunted, at nearly eighty she took the field in John's behalf and was very nearly captured by her seventeen-year-old grandson from Brittany. John arrived only just in time to turn the tables, rescue her, and seize Arthur. The unfortunate nephew was thrown into prison at Rouen in Normandy, and there he disappears from history—probably murdered at the command of his uncle. John was now undisputed ruler of England, and he made some effort to improve on the work of his predecessors. For example, he tried to make the financial side of his government more efficient. His efforts, however, were seldom long sustained, and his cruelties, notorious even in a cruel age, alienated many of his supporters. By 1206 Normandy, Anjou, Maine, Touraine, and Brittany had been overrun by Philip, and this conquest was confirmed in 1214 by the result of a great battle at Bouvines, near Lille on the northern border of France. There Philip defeated John's last hope, an army of German and Flemish allies. Northwestern France thus passed out of English hands. Only Eleanor's heritage in the southwest—Poitou, Aquitaine (thereafter called Guienne), and Gascony—remained under John's control, largely because the lords in this area preferred the weakness of an absentee rule to the direct domination of a powerful French king uncomfortably near at hand.

**The Effect of the Loss of Normandy.** The loss of Normandy and the adjacent territories left a gap between England and John's possession in southwestern France and thus destroyed what semblance of geographical unity there had been in the so-called Angevin Empire. It also forced those lords who held lands on both sides of the Channel to give up their holdings in one place or the other, for Philip would no longer permit a divided allegiance. The result was a very marked development in England of the sentiment that we call nationalism. Instead of thinking of themselves as Norman-French regardless of their geographical location, those Normans who chose to retain their English holdings now began to think in terms of England alone and so to regard themselves as Englishmen. While there are earlier traces of national feeling among Englishmen—as, for example, in the story of the relations with Scotland and in the factional quarrels among the Crusaders—it is from this event that we may date the real amalgamation of Saxon and Norman into the later Englishman.

## HENRY III AND THE BARONIAL WARS

**The Succession of Henry III.** The story of John's quarrels with the Church and with his barons we must postpone for more detailed treatment in the next chapter (pages 113-5). Here it is sufficient to say that he sustained notable defeats in both controversies. In the course of a campaign growing out of the second, in 1216 he suffered from exposure, which, combined with a too hearty indulgence in peaches and new cider, brought him to his grave. The oldest child by his stolen bride was a boy of nine, who succeeded to the throne as Henry III. A regency was necessary, and the victorious barons and churchmen combined to supply this. William Marshal, Earl of Pembroke, who had begun as a poor squire and risen to prominence as a successful contestant in knightly tournaments, was the chief administrator of the kingdom, and managed it very well until his death in 1219. A papal legate, a prominent bishop, and a royal official trained under John then shared the control of the state for a time, and the last two continued to do so until Henry was declared of age in 1227, and indeed for several years afterward. Henry proved to be almost another Stephen or Edward the Confessor, personally attractive but no man for the crown. He was intelligent—part of his troubles sprang from a desire to substitute trained civil servants for unskilled feudal potentates in governmental offices—and he could be stubborn, but he was not capable of long-continued constructive action on his own initiative.

**The Reign of Henry III (1216-72).** The chief influences exerted upon Henry were those of foreign favorites and that of the papal curia, to which he never ceased to be grateful for protection in his minority. Henry's mother returned to France on her husband's death and married her first love in Poitou. Thereafter a steady stream of Henry's Poitevin kinsmen came to England to seek their fortunes. When the King married he chose a wife from Provence, on the southern border of France, and she was followed to England by hordes of poor relations. The easy-going Henry could not resist the demands of these ravenous place-hunters. After he obtained full control of the government he filled vacant positions either with his foreign connections or with men of low social station who would naturally be entirely under his domination. He thus alienated the bulk of the baronial class. The English churchmen, touched by the rising spirit of nationalism, were offended by the royal support given to papal efforts to tax them and also by the King's acquiescence in papal appointments of Italians to English ecclesiastical positions. The last straw, to barons and churchmen alike, was Henry's request for money to keep a bargain with the Pope by which Henry's second son was to be made king of Sicily.

**The Baronial Wars, 1258-65.** Seven years of upheaval, political experiment, and civil war followed—events to which we shall devote more attention in a subsequent chapter (page 127). Toward the end Simon de Montfort, Earl of Leicester, came into prominence as a leader with very advanced principles, notably a willingness to make room for the middle class in governmental activities. This proved too much for the more conservative of the barons, who, unstable at best, were now ready to go over to the royal side if adequate leadership could be secured. This was supplied by the King's oldest son, Edward, who defeated Simon at the battle of Evesham in 1265 and theoretically restored the control of the government to his father. Actually Edward himself dominated the situation to such an extent that by 1270 he felt safe in going off on a Crusade to Palestine, from which he was returning when his father died two years later.

## EDWARD I AND HIS FOREIGN POLICY

**The Character of Edward I (1272-1307).** Edward I, Longshanks, Hammer of the Scots, and the English Justinian—these three nicknames suggest some but not all of the features of the many-sided personality who dominated the English scene for the next thirty-five years. The tall, long-striding monarch schemed for many years to bring about a European peace so that he might resume his crusading activities. And he fought the Welsh and French besides the Scots. At home, where he had already demonstrated his military skill, his power was questioned but once, and then only in unusual circumstances. This political and military pre-eminence gave him the freedom of action that permitted the introduction of many new statutes. Edward in his role of Justinian (the imperial Roman lawgiver) belongs to later chapters. Here we must note briefly his dealings with neighboring powers.

**Relations with France.** Relations with France had been greatly improved by the Treaty of Paris negotiated in 1259. Previous to that time England had not formally acknowledged the loss of northwestern France, nor had the kings of France abandoned their claim to the Angevin lands in the southwest. In that year Henry III and Louis IX (St. Louis) agreed to recognize the status quo. Though some friction continued because the French did not restore certain territories belonging to Aquitaine, it was not until 1293 that serious trouble again broke out. Then a new French King, Philip IV—who with Philip II and Louis IX strengthened the power of the French central government, as William the Conqueror, Henry II, and Edward I did that of England—resolved to eject the English from his domains altogether. Taking advantage of his position as feudal overlord, he moved troops into part of Gascony because of certain depredations committed by her seamen, and then declared the entire area forfeited to him. After several years of fighting, in which England was aided by Flemish allies, Edward succeeded in making a treaty by which Gascony was restored to him in 1303. He gained no new territory by all this struggle, but it was something to have held his own in the country of as strong a rival as Philip IV.

**Wales.** The principality of North Wales, which Henry II had left semi-independent, had expanded since his day. Its princes, taking advantage of John's troubles and the weakness of Henry III, had become lords of virtually all the country outside the marches in the south and east. At the beginning of Edward's reign Llewellyn, who was then prince, failed to do homage to the returned Crusader. Edward's response was an invasion that forced on the principality a treaty divesting it of most of the territory acquired earlier in the century. Five years later the English King's efforts to replace tribal customs in this border area with the law of England produced a revolt in which Llewellyn rendered assistance to his fellow Celts. This time Longshanks determined to end the Welsh problem once for all. He marched west from Chester again, and thoroughly conquered the entire country. Llewellyn was killed, and the Welsh government completely reconstructed. By the Statute of Wales, enacted in 1284, counties were established and English courts set up to administer a law essentially English. There was a further revolt in 1294, and some more troubles in the later Middle Ages, but, generally speaking, after 1284 Wales ceased to be a separate political entity and was absorbed into the stream of English national life. True, the marcher lords still retained some special rights in their territories, and the Welsh remained distinct from the English in language and in some of their customs. But after the time of Edward I there was no Welsh problem to parallel the Irish and Scottish ones of the succeeding centuries. To cement the union thus achieved, the nominal government of Wales was committed to the King's oldest son, and these royal heirs have borne the title of Prince of Wales ever since.

**Scotland.** Edward prudently let Ireland alone. But he considered Scotland worthy of his attention. The death of the last representative of the Scottish royal line in direct descent gave him his opportunity, for, as we have noted in the case of John and Arthur, feudal theory was not yet clear on the rights of relatives in collateral lines. To avoid civil war the Scots consented

THE SCOTTISH SUCCESSION PROBLEM, 1290-92

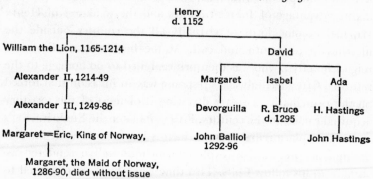

John Hastings had a poorer claim than that of Balliol, if the kingdom were to remain a unit, but since David's own estate had been divided equally among his three daughters (page 219), Hastings claimed a one-third interest in the kingdom also.

to allow Edward to act as arbitrator in the matter of the disputed succession. In 1291 he met the main claimants, John Balliol, Robert Bruce, and John Hastings, at Norham on the Scotch border. Before he would make a decision, however, he insisted that all the contestants acknowledge him as overlord, thus reviving Henry II's claim to suzerainty, which Richard I had allowed to lapse. The candidates for the throne were in no position to resist this claim, and made the required submission. In the next year, after consultation with English and Scottish commissioners who had studied the problem, Edward decided in favor of Balliol. This decision was based on the theory that the representative of the oldest surviving branch took precedence over any of the junior ones, even though these might be separated from the deceased by fewer generations, or joints in the family tree. This decision was of great importance to the law of inheritance of real property, as we shall see a little later (page 220).

**Outbreak of the Scottish War.** Balliol became king, but Edward claimed so many rights as suzerain—hearing appeals from Scottish courts and demanding Scottish troops for his Continental wars—that the nobility of the northern kingdom forced Balliol to resist, in much the same way that the English nobility had prevented Henry III from following papal directions. The English King's success in Wales, however, had probably led him to overestimate the effect of force rather than diplomacy in dealing with people of different traditions. It is possible that with patience and a reasonable number of concessions the Scots might have been won to a permanent alliance with England. This in turn might easily have resulted in a genuine amalgamation of the two kingdoms, for there had been a great deal of peaceful penetration by English influences, during the past century in particular (page 91). As it was, however, methods that were effective when applied to men of Edward's own country or its small Celtic neighbor to the west only stimulated the development of a separate nationalist feeling in the north. In 1295 Scotland concluded an alliance with France, thus beginning a policy that was to become traditional during the next three centuries. In 1296 Edward invaded the northern kingdom and carried all before him. Balliol was deposed, and English commissioners were appointed to rule the country in Edward's name.

**The Winning of Scottish Independence.** Scotland was not Wales, however, and guerrilla tactics made life miserable for the southern intruders. For eight years a knight named William Wallace led the opposition, and when he was captured and executed in 1305, Robert Bruce, a grandson of the original claimant by that name, took his place. Year after year Edward rode north to put down the "rebels." In 1307 he was so weak that he had to be lifted onto his horse at the beginning of each day's march. Still the indomitable old man pressed on, faint yet pursuing. Finally he could go no farther, but as he lay dying he gave orders that his body should be carried with the army until the enemy was subdued. His easy-going son and namesake—on the period of whose reign we trespass long enough to finish this topic—disobeyed his command, however, and had the corpse taken back to Westminster for burial. Thereafter Bruce continued to wear down the English power in Scotland until he destroyed it altogether at the battle of Bannockburn in 1314. From that time on the Scots were an independent nation. Hammering them had defeated its purpose.

## ECONOMIC LIFE

**Other Forces Operating in This Period.** During these two centuries and a half, while kings were scheming against their rivals men did not live by dynastic quarrels alone. Although humble subjects were greatly affected by these personal disputes, the other interests of these same subjects often played a great part in determining the outcome of the political struggles. Part of the reason why John and Edward could get aid from Flanders

against the French was that much of the prosperity of the Low
Countries depended on the supply of English wool, which was
there worked up into the finer grades of cloth. Some of the
troubles of John and even the mighty Henry II came because
they offended against the moral sense of the time. We must therefore turn to a brief mention of some of these powers behind the
throne.

**Agriculture.** Agricultural operations were little affected by the
Conquest. We shall note later that changes were made in the
legal arrangements governing landholding (page 209), but the
methods of tilling the soil changed slowly. The idea of having
three instead of two open fields around the typical village—which
had been introduced at the very close of the Anglo-Saxon period
—gained in popularity during this time, because it permitted the
cultivation of more land than did the two-field system. But the
grain produced—corn, the English call it—remained the same;
wheat, barley, oats, and rye, with the choice depending on the
demand and on the type of soil available. The chief development
in agriculture during these centuries was the increased emphasis
on wool production. The raw, damp climate of England forced
the sheep exposed to it to grow long thick wool. Very little cotton
was grown during the Middle Ages, and linen and silk were too
expensive for general use. England thus became the best source
of raw material for the clothing of medieval Europe. From the
amount of this commodity that she exported and from the generally agrarian nature of her economy she has aptly been called
the Australia of the time. One order of monks, the Cistercians,
made a specialty of settling in the "waste spaces" and developing
them. Sheep were ideal for areas otherwise unsuited to agriculture, and the Cistercians experimented with breeding until they
had greatly improved the strain.

**Mining.** Mining was of considerable importance in medieval
England. The value of the tin produced in Cornwall and Devon
was so great that the stannary workers (tin-miners) were allowed

to have their own courts (page 183). Lead was obtained in the
same area, and also in Derbyshire and Cumberland. There was
a well-developed iron industry on the Welsh border. This was
quite destructive of the surrounding forests, for the smelting was
all done with wood. Some coal was taken from surface or outcrop
workings during this period, but the art of using it in the smelting process had not yet been discovered. Good building stone
was quarried in many parts of the country and was generally
used near home because of the difficulty of transporting it.

**Manufacture and Trade: The Gild Merchant.** Though the
overwhelming majority of the population still lived in the country, the towns grew steadily, if undramatically. The boroughs
served as trading centers for the surrounding agricultural districts and provided markets where producers might bring their
goods for sale. There were also a good many small manufacturing
enterprises in the boroughs. In the early part of this period the
chief means of organizing and regulating this manufacturing and
trading activity was the gild merchant. This was an association
of all the merchants of the borough, somewhat like the modern
chamber of commerce in an American city. It commonly enjoyed
a monopoly of trading within the town walls and regulated the
conditions under which it could be carried on. By its code of
fair practice the principle of the just price was enforced. According to this medieval notion, as taught by the clergy and generally
accepted by the lay public, the selling price of a commodity was
not to be determined by the law of supply and demand but by
the theory that both buyer and seller should be benefited by the
transaction. In other words, the merchant should make a fair
profit and no more. Therefore no merchant was permitted to
"corner" the market, and if one of them made a particularly
successful bargain, he was required to share his good fortune
with the others, that is, to allow them to acquire part of his newly
bought goods at the same low rate. The gild was also an association for mutual help and protection. If a member was imprisoned

in another town, the gild endeavored to secure his release. If he left a "foreign" town owing money, any fellow gildsman who might come that way was obligated for the debts, though of course the home gild tried eventually to obtain a settlement from the original debtor. Members of the gild who undeservedly fell on evil days were helped back on their financial feet. Where necessary, assistance was also provided to gildsmen and their families in case of illness or death.

**The Craft Gilds.** By the thirteenth century the towns had grown so large that the merchant gilds began to be unwieldy. A new and smaller type of organization therefore developed. This was called the craft gild, and was composed of the practitioners of a single industry or craft only. Thus the weavers, the fishmongers, and many others formed their own associations. These took over the professional and benevolent activities of the gild merchant, subject to the overriding control of the borough government. The craft gilds naturally were able to regulate the conduct of a single industry very closely. They fixed wages, established standards of workmanship, and maintained inspectors to prevent the production and sale of defective goods. The gilds were also important as religious bodies, for in addition to their charitable activities they had their patron saints and their feast days, and also commonly supported special shrines. The ordinary member of the gild was known as a master workman. He usually made the goods in the back of his shop, sold them over a counter in the front, and lived with his family in quarters on the second floor. He was assisted by an apprentice or two who were bound to him for a long training period—usually seven years—and who commonly lived with him. He might also have one or more fully trained assistants who came in to work for him by the day. These were known as journeymen (from the French *journée*, by the day). It should be noticed that these craft gilds differed from the modern trade-union in that they were associations of owner-masters plus journeymen instead of wage-earners only. They also exercised much more supervision over their industry and had more official standing than the modern trade-union.

**Foreign Trade and Banking.** The English merchants were active in foreign trade and organized a kind of gild, called the Merchants of the Staple, to export the raw wool. The Staple itself was the Continental warehouse where English goods were deposited. What banking business there was, however, remained in the hands of foreigners, Jews—until their expulsion in 1290—and Italians. Though French visitors frequently considered the island country more prosperous than their own, England's economy was still primitive, much less well developed than that of northern Italy, the Rhineland, or the Low Countries.

**The Standards of Living.** Because of the comparatively undeveloped nature of England's economy her standard of living was relatively low. The poor still lived in huts, and even the stone castles of the nobles were not much more comfortable. Any well-dyed cloth had to be imported, and meat was considered something of a luxury. Starvation was common. The economy of abundance was a long way in the future.

## RELIGION AND CULTURE

**Religion.** During this period religion profited greatly by a succession of monastic revivals similar to the Cluniac revival of Saxon times. Though they began on the Continent, England commonly benefited from their effects. The Cistercians, whom we have already mentioned, came in the early part of the twelfth century, and another zealous order, the Carthusians, a generation later. In the thirteenth century the mendicant (begging) friars— the Franciscans and the Dominicans, followers of St. Francis and St. Dominic—performed even greater services. Instead of remaining in monasteries they moved among the people, preaching and teaching. The piety of all these genuinely religious men and their followers gave them great prestige. Hugh of Lincoln, a saintly

Carthusian, awed even John at times. Donations flowed in for the work of the monks.

**Culture.** Education and art profited by this flowering of religion. In the later twelfth and early thirteenth centuries universities grew up at Oxford and Cambridge, roughly fifty miles northwest and northeast of London, respectively. In them the system of theological learning called Scholasticism was soon brought to a high level of development. Throughout the country gray stone parish churches and impressive cathedrals continued to spring up. From about 1200 on, however, they were built in a new fashion, for the massive pillars, small windows, and imposing round arches of the Norman style began to give way to the clustered piers, larger windows, and pointed arches of the Gothic. But all was not learning and light in the cultural world of this period, even in the thirteenth century, the height of the Middle Ages and the so-called greatest of centuries. Far too much ignorance and superstition remained to plague future generations. "Every mixer of cough elixir was thought a vassal of Nick himself." A belief in witchcraft was taken for granted, and medical treatment was exceedingly primitive. Callous indifference to human suffering disgraced the age. Henry I once permitted the blinding of two of his own granddaughters whom he was holding as hostages during a quarrel with his son-in-law. Richard the Lion-Hearted and his rival Philip II of France also exchanged gruesome insults in the form of maimed prisoners. In the late thirteenth century the horrible punishment of quartering offenders was devised, and it was soon afterwards applied to the captured Wallace (page 100). Yet the atrocity stories seem to diminish somewhat toward the end of this period, and we may conclude that some progress was being made in the slow process of preparing the average Englishman to respect the rights of his weaker neighbor, to understand the problems of government, and to take an independent place in society instead of following the lead of a feudal lord.

# 5. THE DISTRIBUTION OF POWER

**The General Pattern.** The constitutional history of this central period of the Middle Ages naturally fits rather closely the general medieval theory of the division of power among the various political elements, to which we have already referred (page 31). King, Church, and nobles combined to control society. The high average level of ability among the Norman and Angevin kings, however, gave them a more important role than the Anglo-Saxon rulers had obtained. As explained in the preceding chapter (pages 81-82) William the Conqueror and his successors were much more influential than the Saxon Edwards and Ethelreds. Consequently we have devoted considerable space to describing their personal characteristics. But since the associates of the post-Conquest kings were Norman also, and therefore too vigorous to yield power without something more than a show of resistance, we have a series of what appear at first glance to be death struggles. Actually, closer observation shows that in practically all cases neither party really objected to the other's having some sphere of influence, but only to the extent of that influence. The fact that until about 1200 nearly everyone who could read and write was a clergyman and that accordingly most of the king's record-keeping officials were churchmen suggests not only the complicating factors in the rivalries of crown and Church, for example, but the underlying co-operation between them. We shall notice in this period, however, the beginnings of a middle-class movement that in time was to broaden the base of effective political factors on which the English social structure stood.

## RELATIONS BETWEEN CROWN AND CHURCH: THE CONQUEST SETTLEMENT

**The Conqueror and the Hildebrandine Program.** As we have seen (page 79), William had rallied his forces for the Conquest under a banner blessed by the Pope. He paid his political debt by allowing the Roman curia to institute in England many of the changes it was trying to put into effect in western Christendom as a whole. Under the influence of a great monk named Hildebrand, who later became pope himself under the title of Gregory VII, the Roman authorities were striving to convert the Church to the reforming ideals of Cluny (page 19). William had already accepted much of this program in Normandy, and he had no objection to bringing his new domain into line with the old. Norman clergymen who sympathized with the reformers were put in places of influence, including the all-important see of Canterbury. Clerical celibacy and the strict observance of monastic rules were enforced. More important for our purposes, though ecclesiastics continued for a few years to attend some secular tribunals,[1] the Church was permitted to have its own councils and its own courts.[2] Although there had been some such rudimentary tribunals before the Conquest, this was a sharp reversal of the general practice in late Anglo-Saxon times (page 38), and in line with Hildebrand's claim that the Church should have a right to control its own affairs without lay interference.

**William's Restrictions.** Farther than this William would not go. He laid down a set of rules to prevent the Church from securing Hildebrand's full objective in the field of government, predominance over the secular arm. These rules are sometimes called the Triple Concordat, or agreement between the Pope and

[1] See Walter Lichtenstein, "The Date of Separation of Ecclesiastical and Lay Jurisdiction in England," *Illinois Law Review*, Vol. III (1908-09), pp. 347-53.
[2] S-M, No. 17, pp. 35-36.

the secular ruler, though they are more properly four in number. (1) No pope was to be acknowledged without the royal consent, and (2) no papal legates or papal letters were to be admitted to the realm without the King's permission. (3) The King also reserved the right to veto the acts of English ecclesiastical councils, and (4) he prohibited the excommunication of any of the great men of the kingdom without his approval. This last step was designed to prevent the Church from putting political pressure on the royal councilors, for excommunication in those days theoretically amounted, as we have noticed (page 19), to social and legal ostracism besides constituting a threat of eternal damnation.

## LATER DIFFICULTIES: THE INVESTITURE STRUGGLE

**Remaining Sources of Friction.** These regulations perhaps provided as good a basis as any for solving the virtually insoluble medieval problem of having three co-operating authorities but no supreme head. The rules needed, however, firm and skillful administration, and they left many questions unanswered. Three of these questions were to be especially prominent in the Norman and Angevin periods. (1) Who should have the right to control elections to important ecclesiastical offices? (2) How extensive was to be the jurisdiction of the new church courts? (3) Did the secular government have the right to exercise control over ecclesiastical property? These problems presented themselves in that order during the two centuries after the Conquest.

**The Investiture Struggle.** We have seen that in Saxon times the king and the Witan chose men to fill the chief ecclesiastical vacancies (page 42). After his election the bishop promised to be the king's vassal—"did homage" was the feudal phrase. The king thereupon invested the bishop with his new office by giving him the symbols of his land, probably the figurative clod and twig (page 69), and also the symbols of his spiritual office, an episcopal ring and a shepherd's crook (pastoral staff). Hildebrand had objected to this practice and demanded that the Church should control its own elections and do its own investing. The royal answer was that since the bishops held great lands, the king had a right to see that none of his enemies secured such material power. The issue came to a head in the time of Henry I when Anselm, Archbishop of Canterbury, who had already gone into exile after quarreling with William Rufus over the recognition of a pope, refused to do homage to the new King. Henry exiled him again, and after prolonged negotiations Anselm was about to excommunicate the monarch when Henry's sister Adela arranged a compromise. Churchmen were to do homage; in exchange ecclesiastics were to have the right to invest with the spiritual symbols. It appeared at first to be a fair compromise, but actually Henry had won, for he continued to hold elections to clerical offices in his council, and by retaining the right of investing successful candidates with the temporalities (land) he kept an effective veto power over all choices. The right to exact homage gave the king a further hold over the important clergy.

## THE ECCLESIASTICAL COURT ISSUE

**The Growing Jurisdiction of the Church Courts.** Nevertheless, the Church gained ground in Stephen's troubled reign. In order to win support for his shaky throne that monarch made important concessions to the ecclesiastics by a charter issued in 1136. In it he promised them the right to control their own elections, and he defined very generously the jurisdiction of the ecclesiastical courts, a matter that had been left uncertain by William. Now the courts were granted full control over the clergy and their goods. The words of the charter, however, still left considerable room for interpretation, and with such a weak king the ecclesiastics were not slow to take advantage of the situation. According to the rules of the canon (ecclesiastical) law that was developing on the Continent the clergy were to have jurisdiction over ecclesiastical persons, things, and causes. Following this principle, English churchmen were soon claiming the right to settle all disputes that involved land held by ecclesiastical tenure, and the general public was scandalized because churchmen accused of crimes were getting off very lightly. This lenience in the matter of criminal offenses was in part a result of the regulation of the canon law that churchmen might not shed blood. The half-brother of William the Conqueror, Odo, Bishop of Bayeux, had evaded the spirit while observing the letter of this provision by fighting at Hastings with a smooth mace, but when it was to the churchmen's advantage to be more rigid in their interpretation of this rule they found it easy to be so. A light penance, such as a few prayers, might be the only sentence imposed upon a convicted cleric, even for very serious crimes. There was also a complaint from the laymen because in disputes over land the church courts nearly always ruled in favor of churchmen, and thus a means was provided for putting more and more wealth under clerical control. Furthermore, in case the ecclesiastics encountered difficulties in England they made use of a new device, an appeal to the papal court at Rome, where they almost always received support for their claims.

**Henry II's Attempt to Limit Ecclesiastical Jurisdiction.** With his strong instinct for restoring the royal power, Henry II naturally grappled with this problem of the Church and its courts. He concluded that the best way to handle it would be through a pliable archbishop, and on the death of the old incumbent of the see of Canterbury he secured the election of his friend and Chancellor Thomas Becket. Becket had shown little regard for spiritual matters in the past and was reluctant to take the post. He warned Henry in advance that if the King insisted on his doing so the worldly Chancellor would have to change his ways and do his duty by looking out for the interests of the Church. True to his word, Becket at once adopted the monastic way of life, and rejected Henry's suggestions for a limitation of clerical powers. In 1164 the King had his advisers draw up certain regulations called the Constitutions of Clarendon (from the name of the royal manor where they were first presented),[3] which were said by the King and his supporters to describe the usages of the realm in ecclesiastical matters as they had existed in the time of his grandfather, Henry I. There were prohibitions of such practices as excommunicating the king's chief men without his consent. Other articles dealt with the royal control over ecclesiastical elections, bans on appeals to the papal court without the royal permission, and regulations that seriously limited the jurisdiction of the ecclesiastical courts in civil cases having to do with lands (page 181) and debts (page 218). On the most dramatic of the issues, that of the criminous clerks, as the offending clergy were called, it was provided that while the trials might be held in ecclesiastical courts, defendants adjudged guilty should be turned over to the royal courts for punishment.

**The Struggle with Becket.** To a modern ear these arrangements sound reasonable enough, but it must be remembered that concepts of justice were different in those days. Just as each private individual in Saxon times had had his mund (area of jurisdiction, page 72), so special interests were supposedly entitled to special courts (page 102). If separate tribunals were to exist, the ecclesiastics felt it unreasonable that theirs should be restricted. "Touch not the Lord's anointed" was their cry. With a few possible exceptions, Henry and his supporters were correct in asserting that the Constitutions of Clarendon represented the practice of his grandfather's time. Becket did not try to deny it, but merely maintained that the antiquity of laws in conflict with spiritual principles could not give them validity. After some preliminary wavering he therefore refused to accept the Constitutions, and followed Anselm's example by fleeing to the Continent. For six years he remained in exile. During that time he negotiated occa-

[3] S-M, No. 30, pp. 73-76.

sionally with Henry, but neither would yield. In 1170, however, a reconciliation was arranged without a final settlement of the issues involved, and Becket returned to Canterbury. There he promptly disciplined some of the clergy who had taken the King's side in the great quarrel. Henry was on the Continent when he heard the news. In a fit of rage he cursed the men who took his bounty and let such insults go unavenged. Four of his knights at once crossed to Canterbury and killed the Archbishop in his own cathedral.

**The Settlement: Benefit of Clergy.** All western Christendom was shocked by the murder of Becket, and public opinion, which was a force long before the daily press was thought of, compelled Henry to change his course. The wily statesman found it convenient to make his Irish expedition (page 89) at this time. But when the worst of the storm had blown over he promised the Pope to allow appeals to Rome in the future and to end all encroachments on the liberties of the Church introduced in his own time. The Constitutions of Clarendon were not mentioned by name, however, and since Henry insisted that they were not innovations, he was able to retain some of their important provisions, notably the restrictions on the civil jurisdiction of the church courts. Benefit of clergy, the right of the criminous clerks to be punished by ecclesiastical courts, he had to concede. From this time on churchmen accused of crime were tried in the royal courts, but on conviction they claimed their clerical right. A Bible was produced, and if they could read the appropriate "noose verse"—usually "Have mercy upon me, O Lord" (Psalm 51:1)— they were turned over to their bishop for his sentence. Later, by several steps this privilege was taken away in the case of particular crimes (page 326), but it did not disappear entirely until the nineteenth century (page 586). Becket was generally recognized as a martyr to the cause of religion, and was soon canonized. To the great shrine of St. Thomas the Canterbury pilgrims made their way for centuries, and thus provided Chaucer with the set-

ting for his great tales. While the particular issue for which
Becket contended most bitterly is not such as to commend itself
to modern minds, it should be remembered that judicial authority was almost inseparable from political power in those days
and one could not be sacrificed without the other.

**Further Developments in This Field.** As long as the Church
retained its strength the secular authorities had to be on their
guard to prevent the ecclesiastical courts from exercising jurisdiction over cases involving such important secular interests
as real property and contracts. The judges of the royal courts
tried to meet this competition by issuing writs of prohibition
which forbade the church courts to proceed with cases over which
the secular courts claimed jurisdiction.[4] But a century later, in
1285, Edward I was forced to supplement this device by a special
writ or statute, called *Circumspecte agatis* (from the opening
words—"Act circumspectly"), which endeavored to define the
limits of ecclesiastical jurisdiction more narrowly.

## THE LANGTON CASE

**The Election Issue Again.** The reign of Henry's crusading son
Richard passed off without any notable conflict with the Church,
but in John's time another very important round was fought on
the election issue. The provision that the Constitutions of Clarendon had made for preserving the substance of royal control in
such matters was to allow the shadow of it to the protesting
clergy. They were allowed to elect, but they must do so in the
chapel at the royal court.[5] Since few churchmen were rash enough
to defy the king's will when surrounded by his henchmen, the
king's nominees were generally elected. By the end of the century, however, a pope named Innocent III raised the papal power
to a very high degree, and it seemed possible to challenge this
royal domination.

[4] S-M, No. 331, p. 85.                    [5] S-M, No. 30, Sec. 12, p. 76.

**The Langton Struggle.** Accordingly, when the Archbishop of Canterbury died in 1205, some of the monks who were the canons there immediately held a secret election on the spot and sent the man of their choice posthaste to Rome to claim the pallium. Unfortunately for their scheme, the successful candidate felt himself bursting with a sense of his new importance, and had not proceeded far on his journey before he had revealed the secret. Naturally, John was greatly angered and took steps to defeat the plan before it should be too late. He persuaded the frightened monks and the bishops of the province, who also claimed a share in the electoral rights, to name his candidate and lodge an appeal with the Pope. Innocent chose to show his authority by quashing both elections, and prevailed upon the delegation of Canterbury monks, who had gone to Rome to support their claim to independence, to elect his own nominee, an English cardinal named Stephen Langton. John was furious, and refused to invest Innocent's candidate with the archiepiscopal lands. For six years the Pope employed all his great powers to bring John to terms. Since he had reduced others, including the King of France, to submission with much less effort, the length of time that he required shows something of the continuing strength of the monarchy which Henry II had built up, a strength which had survived twenty years of neglect and misrule. England was put under an interdict, which meant the suspension of nearly all religious services except baptism and the rites for the dying. Innocent knew that John did not mind for himself, since the King had not attended mass since his coronation, but the move was designed to frighten the monarch's subjects into bringing pressure to bear upon him. In fact, however, they did not stir, and the King's response to the ecclesiastical challenge was to seize nearly all the property of the Church and to drive the higher clergy from the realm. Innocent then excommunicated him. This involved a threat of damnation to all who associated with the King (page 108), but by the royal order the first priest to leave court was caught and crushed to death with heavy stones. No one else abandoned his post thereafter, and the King's government went on. Finally, in 1213, the Pope acted on his claim to be the representative of the Heavenly King, the overlord of all earthly ones. He declared John deposed, released the obstinate ruler's subjects from their allegiance, and authorized Philip of France to carry out the sentence.

**The Settlement.** Since Philip was all too willing to help eliminate his English rival, John was at last forced to yield. He met the papal legate (page 37) at Dover, agreed to admit Langton as Archbishop of Canterbury, and to restore the property of the Church. Much more important, in theory, he acknowledged the Pope as his feudal lord, swore fealty to him, and agreed to pay tribute each year for England and Ireland. In 1214 John formally conceded freedom of election to the churchmen, and the next year this grant was repeated as the first article of the Great Charter,[6] of which we shall speak more fully later (page 124). Even so, by indirect means royal influence was still exercised over ecclesiastical elections, and it is believed that at least one-third of the successful candidates in the next generation owed their selection to their standing at court.

## THE PROPERTY ISSUE

**Mortmain.** The last of the issues that disturbed the relations between churchmen and the crown was the claim of the King to control ecclesiastical property. According to the Hildebrandine tradition the lands and goods of the Lord's anointed were as sacred as their persons, and therefore not to be touched by profane hands. Yet the Church was a wealthy institution, for it had a large fraction—probably at least a fifth—of the land of the country in its possession. And it was steadily growing richer. The churchmen were constantly persuading dying landlords, in fear

[6] S-M, Nos. 43-44, pp. 114-15.

of purgatory or hell fire, to better their chances in the hereafter by giving large amounts of their property to the Church. Furthermore, in theory at least, the Church never relaxed its grip on what it acquired. For it was a corporation that never lacked an heir and was never guilty of felony or treason. Its property therefore was never lost by escheat (page 121), nor was it ever forfeited to the crown. Because this never-relaxing grip reminded medieval observers of the clenched hand of the dead after rigor mortis had set in, frank almoin (ecclesiastical) tenure (page 120), was sometimes called mortmain (dead hand). To prevent his kingdom from getting out of balance by the unrestricted continuation of this process, in 1279 Edward I issued the Statute of Mortmain,[7] which forbade further alienation of land to the Church without a royal license. This permission was frequently given thereafter, but since it took a long time to secure it from Westminster, the abuse of deathbed transfers was considerably moderated, and, in general, bounds were set to the future accumulation of ecclesiastical wealth.

**The Taxation Question.** Another controversy about church property was decided in Edward's time. This was the question of its liability to secular taxation. Taxes of any sort were rare in Saxon times, as already noted (page 20), and so this had not been an issue before the Conquest. When the Danegeld was levied, usually in times of emergency, the churchmen paid with the rest. As the royal government came to depend more and more upon taxation for its support the question became a serious one, especially in view of the great wealth of the clergy. There were bickerings on this point in the reigns of Richard and John, but the real struggle took place under Edward.

**Edward's Victory over Boniface VIII.** During Edward's reign a pope named Boniface VIII interpreted the theory of papal supremacy in such sweeping terms as to prohibit the clergy of any country from paying taxes to the secular rulers without the

[7] S-M, No. 52B, pp. 169-70.

consent of the papacy. This formulation of ecclesiastical theory
was contained in a bull called *Clericis laicos,* from its opening
Latin words. Armed with it, the clergy refused to pay the assessments levied in 1296 for Edward's French war. The King met
this resistance by a device first employed by the ministers of
Richard I a century before. Since churchmen refused to support
his government, Edward deprived them of the use and protection
of his courts. This virtually outlawed the recalcitrants, and put
their goods at the mercy of anyone who cared to defy the ecclesiastical censures pronounced upon marauders. Since the French
King, Philip IV, adopted similar tactics, the Pope was soon
forced to modify his original statement so that the clergy might
make "gifts" to the secular rulers in lieu of taxes. Thereafter
whenever the laymen assembled to grant the king taxes the clergy
also assembled in their Convocations (page 153) and offered a
proportionate amount by way of a present to the king. As long
as the amount came up to the royal expectations the gift was
as sweet as though called by any other name, and thus the king
gained a decided advantage in the long controversy over the
taxation question.

## ENGLISH CHURCHMEN AND THE ROMAN CURIA

**The Struggle between Churchmen and the Roman Curia.**
Thus far we have been speaking as though churchmen were
always a unified class pursuing a single policy. Actually, however,
there were divisions among them, and the occasional clash of
papal and local interests must be particularly noted, for the
spirit of nationalism (page 94) was penetrating even the Church.
As the popes claimed and wielded more and more power the
English clergy frequently profited by their support, as we have
seen. But at times the Roman authorities showed their strength
in less acceptable fashion. Under the papal theory of the fullness
of power, which made the popes the dictators of all appoint-

ments if they chose to exercise their rights, the thirteenth-century pontiffs began to provide their friends and supporters with ecclesiastical positions throughout Christendom. These provisions, as the appointments were called, deprived the holders of advowsons of their previous rights, and were usually exercised in favor of foreign clergymen, especially Italians. The popes also tried to extract taxes for the benefit of the Roman curia from both laymen and churchmen, but particularly from the latter. Sometimes the popes demanded a percentage of the clergy's movable belongings—personal property, we should call it. Sometimes they asked for a fraction of their annual income. Finally, they came to demand annates—the full returns from the first year's occupancy of any ecclesiastical office.

**Lay Participation in the Controversy.** These papal claims adversely affected lay as well as clerical interests. By diminishing the incomes of the clergy they reduced the value of advowsons, which, as already noted (page 43), were in the hands of the laity. Consequently the English clergy who opposed these claims of the Roman curia had little trouble in securing co-operation from the nobility and other influential laymen. In a Parliament held at Carlisle in 1307 a protest was entered against provisions, and a rule was laid down prohibiting the papal agents from exacting any new payments. The King, however, revoked that part of the parliamentary decision which related to annates, since he and most of the other monarchs commonly found it very convenient to have a strong papal power with which to co-operate. Arrangements could often be made by which some of the papal revenues found their way into the royal coffers, or by which half the beneficiaries of papal provisions would be royal nominees. In spite of all the surface quarrels, co-operative sovereignty was the order of the day, as we have previously noted.

## RELATIONS BETWEEN THE KING AND THE BARONS: THE FEUDAL SYSTEM

**Feudalism.** The implementation of this co-operative attitude in the royal dealings with the lay nobles was the feudal contract. To this we have necessarily made occasional references in dealing with other post-Conquest topics. Now we must examine this contract more closely, for the story of the struggle over its interpretation is the story of how political power was shared by the crown with its associates, especially the lay lords. We have seen (page 49) that the Saxon arrangements of lordships did not constitute a fully developed feudal system according to Continental standards. This Continental organization of society was quickly established by William in England, and represents that speeding-up of tendencies already present in the evolution of Saxon England to which reference has already been made.

**The Feudal Contract.** Under the influence of developments across the Channel and also as a result of the Conquest, men came to believe that not only some but all land was to be considered as having been given out originally by the king as chief lord (overlord) in the country. There were no longer any free villages. All lands were to be held of the monarch under the terms of a contract called feudal because the individual tracts of land so held were called feuds or fiefs. Each of the royal vassals or tenants in capite (tenants in chief) might then parcel out some of his land to his dependents or subtenants by a contract of the same pattern, which the later English lawyers worked out with great care and which must here be described in some detail. The lord must give his vassal not only (1) the land, but also (2) protection, and (3) justice. He must guarantee the quiet occupation of the land by the vassal and do right by him in any quarrels that might arise.

**Services or Tenures.** In return the vassal owed to the lord a great number of things. (1) The most important of these was some kind of service. The different types of this were called tenures because they were the methods by which land was held. (a) The commonest was knight service, mounted military service to the extent of forty days a year, if requested. One or more knights must respond to the lord's summons and make part of his feudal army. (b) Ecclesiastical tenure was called frank almoin (free alms) because no tangible return was required. But the legal theory was kept intact by the assumption that the churchmen would pray for the souls of their feudal lords. (c) Nonmilitary service, such as filling a household office or carrying dispatches, was called tenure by sergeantry (sergeant = servant). One family held from the crown a manor near Dover on condition that the vassal accompany the monarch on his trips across the Channel and hold the royal head in case of seasickness. (d) A few men, probably the survivors of the Saxon class of free ceorls, made money payments for their land. This service was called socage tenure.

**Incidents.** The typical vassal also had many other obligations. These were called feudal incidents because they were incident (attached) to the tenant's status.[8] (2) He had to swear fealty or loyalty to his lord, and to do homage to him—that is, vow to be his man. Homage commonly involved an act of kneeling before the lord and putting the vassal's hands between the lord's hands. (3) He must do court service—that is, attend the lord's court, counsel him, and help to do justice to others, or submit to the court's decision in cases where he himself might be involved. (4) He had various financial obligations, called feudal aids. In general he was expected to help his lord in any time of need. Originally the lord had to request this assistance, and legally it

[8] The socage tenants and the less important of those who held by sergeantry (people who held by what was called petty sergeantry) were not called on to fulfill all the obligations, particularly those relating to wardship and marriage (to be described in this paragraph).

might be refused. When it was granted it was known as a gracious aid. But the king early formed the habit of levying a general aid in times of emergency and in three special cases both he and the lords slowly acquired a legal right to the help. These special aids —aids by right in contrast to gracious aids—were payable (a) when the lord was captured and needed a ransom, (b) when his oldest son was knighted, and (c) when his oldest daughter was married the first time. There were a number of other financial incidents. (5) A sum of money called relief was to be paid by the heir of a deceased vassal in order to succeed his father. This requirement grew out of the theory that the title to the land was in the lord's name and that the regranting of it was a matter not of right but of grace. That is, the tenant's son had no right to succeed to his father's land, and only did so by the lord's gracious kindness.[9] (6) If the heir was a minor, he could not render service, and the lord supposedly found it more difficult to protect him. Therefore the guardian-lord took all the returns from the land until the heir came of age. This right of the lord was called wardship, from the guardianship in which the minor heir was placed. (7) If an unmarried woman was the heiress, she could not marry without the consent of the lord, usually purchased by a fee. The theory back of this was the same as that involved in the royal claim to choose the bishops—that the lord could not be expected to have his lands held by enemies. This right was called maritage, or simply marriage. (8) By the right of escheat the holding reverted to the lord if the vassal died without heirs. (9) If the vassal was convicted of felony, the land was forfeited to the lord. (10) If the vassal broke the contract or disobeyed his suzerain in any important way, he also forfeited his holding to his lord. It was under this provision of the feudal contract that Philip could de-

[9] This theory and the resulting right of relief were further enforced in the case of tenants in chief by the practice of the king's taking possession of the land on the vassal's death, keeping it without obligation to account for the proceeds, and restoring it only on the doing of homage and payment of relief. The right to do this was called *primer seisin* (first possession).

clare John's French possessions forfeit, because John had not fulfilled the obligation of court service that he owed to the overlord
of his Continental domains.

**The Feudal Contract Vague.** It must not be thought that even
by the thirteenth century the lord and vassal drew up complete,
formal contracts setting forth these conditions and then kept
duplicate copies signed and witnessed. Had not convention fixed
upon the term "contract" for the purpose, it would doubtless be
better to call this arrangement a feudal understanding. For the
three paragraphs above are a rough summary of a great number
of vague, customary obligations, few of which were written out
and some of which were probably not quite fully developed or
clearly recognized at this time. It will be seen at a glance that
there was a great deal of uncertainty about some of these obligations. If land had been in wardship, was relief also due when the
heir came of age? What constituted a fair relief, or a fair aid, and
how often could general aids be demanded? Was a vassal's widow
subject to the lord's marriage right? What was a reasonable return for a guardian to take from a ward's land? Besides leaving
such great scope for differences of opinion, the contract provided
very inadequate means for settling them. In theory, had all the
oaths been properly kept the system would have worked fairly
well. With the help of those who owed him suit of court, the lord
was to settle quarrels between his vassals. But all the oaths were
not kept, and furthermore the lord could not be sued in his own
court. If the lord did not do his part under the contract, he also
was to forfeit his rights, but who was to determine when this
default had been made? Theoretically, the lord's lord was to
punish him for failure to deal fairly with his vassals, and sometimes he did so, as Philip disciplined John in the case of the
defrauded bridegroom (page 93). But who was to keep the
keeper? Who was to regulate the overlord? God was, said the
theory, and, as we have seen (page 114), the pope as his representative occasionally undertook to do so. More often the appeal

lay to the battlefield, where the judgment of the Almighty seemed to be obtained rather more directly. Just as the ordeal—slowly supplanting the blood feud pure and simple—was considered a fair method of trial in private cases, so it was in these semipublic matters. If the vassals felt that their lord had wronged them, let them prove it on the lord's body and those of his retainers. "Legalized anarchy," some have called this system, but that gives rather less than the true picture. If, as one historian phrased it, the Merovingian type of government, which preceded the system of Charlemagne in France, was monarchy tempered by assassination, then feudalism was a gentlemen's agreement tempered by licensed dueling. If worse than a centralized monarchy, it was better than leaving the problem of law and order to be dealt with by means of family feuds or a grossly inadequate system of public courts.

**Restrictions on Feudalism in England.** The great Conqueror had already begun to limit the powers of his feudal lords in Normandy, and by both accident and intent he was able to keep these troublesome subjects well in hand in England. The five-year delay in completing the Conquest naturally caused William to scatter out his grants so that no one lord held a large, solid block of territory. This complicated the problem of arranging a successful rising against the monarch in case the tenants in chief felt aggrieved. In 1086 at a great assembly on Salisbury Plain, in south-central England, he also established the principle that the rear vassals (vassals of these tenants in chief) should swear an oath of allegiance to the king superior to that sworn to their immediate lords. Thus they were theoretically bound to support the crown in case of a feudal revolt, or large-scale trial by battle (appeal to the God of Battles), as it should perhaps more properly be called. William also retained the institution of the fyrd (national militia), which gave him some armed forces independent of the feudal levy. Henry II, enlarging upon a practice instituted by Henry I, further weakened the baronial powers of resistance by permitting them to pay scutage (shield money), that is, to pay for the hire of substitutes to do military service in case of need. Those who took advantage of this opportunity tended to lose their skill in arms, and, like the Saxon farmers before them, were correspondingly weakened politically.

**Baronial Tactics: Warfare.** While these precautions did strengthen the hand of the monarch to some extent, they did not entirely eliminate the possibility of wars waged against the king by the barons, as the tenants in chief were called. When the royal title was in doubt, or in case of misrule, a rationalization for such strife could still be found. That it was, in fact, carried on we have already seen in our sketch of the general history of this period. But it was obviously an unsatisfactory method of dealing with the problem of delimiting the king's power, for however great were the victories that might be won by the baronial opposition, in time these victories lost their effect and the fighting had to be done all over again.

## THE GREAT CHARTER

**The Written Contract and Its Granting.** The next logical step was to cement the gains achieved in such conflicts by setting down the feudal contract in writing, with explicit interpretations of the points in dispute. This device was employed in John's reign, and resulted in the Great Charter (Magna Carta), so called originally because of its length rather than its importance. The barons were angered by John's heavy demands for money and feudal services, largely occasioned by the French wars that he conducted with such poor success. In a preliminary consultation held in 1213 someone mentioned the charter of Henry I (page 84), and the scholarly Archbishop Langton produced it at a meeting in London the next year. He was very anxious to substitute legal for violent means of settling these quarrels, and the barons accepted the idea of a new charter that John should sign, though they expected to employ force—or the threat of it—to secure this end. In May of 1215 they formally renounced their allegiance to the King, in keeping with the feudal theory which required this action before resorting to the trial by battle. John hastily made concessions to the Church and also to the citizens of London, in the hope of winning their support, but both of these elements sided with the barons instead. The King then saw that military resistance was hopeless. On June 15, 1215, he met the barons in a field called Runnymede (the meadow of Runny) near Windsor, along the Thames above London, and accepted their terms. Four days later the Great Charter was issued.[10]

**The Terms of the Charter: Feudal.** Magna Carta was primarily a clarification of the feudal contract, much of it in accordance with old Norman custom books. It regulated the size of reliefs and aids that the king might exact (Arts. 2 and 12). Widowed heiresses were not to be compelled to remarry against their will in order that the royal overlord might obtain the marriage fee (Art. 8). Land that had been in wardship was not to be subject to the payment of relief (Art. 3), and the profits of the wardship were restricted (Art. 4). The jurisdiction of the feudal courts was safeguarded (Art. 34; see below, page 177), and other baronial privileges similarly protected. The frequency with which scutage was to be levied and the rate of scutage per knight's fee were regulated by the provisions that no scutage should be levied, nor any general aid exacted, without the consent of the king's Great Council, which the barons and the churchmen controlled (Arts. 12 and 14).

**Terms for Other Interests.** Though the feudal clauses were the most important in the charter, sections were also included to reward those elements which had supported the baronial demands. Free elections were guaranteed to the Church (Art. 1), as already noted (page 115). London and other towns were protected in their claims to liberties and customs won at earlier dates

10 S-M, No. 44, pp. 115-26.

(Art. 13). Subtenants, merchants, and freemen in general also shared in some of the concessions (Arts. 20, 35, 39, 40, 41, 60).

**Governmental Terms in General.** Other provisions were inserted that applied to the working of the royal government in aspects which were neither feudal nor directed at any one class. The treatment of debtors (Art. 9), the means of exacting bridge service (Art. 23), and the method of conducting the royal courts (Arts. 18, 19, 20) were all prescribed. The King was made to promise that he would not sell, deny, or delay justice to anyone (Art. 40). No freeman was to suffer by imprisonment, loss of property, or otherwise "except by the lawful judgment of his peers and the law of the land" (Art. 39). These last-mentioned clauses did not guarantee the right of *habeas corpus* or trial by jury, as later lawyers maintained. The actual writ of *habeas corpus* was not devised until years later, and in 1215 trial by jury was only one of the testing methods to which a man's peers in court might subject him (page 197). But these clauses were virtually the equivalent of the original form of the "due process" clause in the American Constitution, and represented a triumph of Langton's principle of settling disputes by legal rather than violent means.

**The Significance of the Charter.** Subsequent reissues of the Great Charter eliminated some of these clauses, notably the provision for conciliar consent to the levying of scutages and general aids. But the charter established the principle, foreshadowed in the Charter of Henry I, of making the king definitely subject to a law set down in writing, a principle that was regularly honored by including an obligation to observe the charter in subsequent coronation oaths. Though the baronial element profited most from Magna Carta at first, by subsequent interpretations other classes later increased the small share they already had in the benefits of the great document.

**The Inability of the Barons to Enforce the Charter.** The weakest link in this chain of sixty-one articles which were to bind the

King was the last, which provided for sanctions. Twenty-five barons were to be appointed to see that the King kept his word. If he did not, these leaders, after giving due notice through a committee of four, were to lead "the community of the entire country" in waging war on the King and seizing his property, though sparing the lives of the monarch and the royal family. The defect in this arrangement lay not so much in the failure to provide a tribunal in which the issues could have been peacefully settled—that was too much to ask in that day—as in the number of barons who were expected to co-operate in this matter. For only on rare occasions, such as the one that has just been described, could these proud and touchy fighting men be persuaded to pull together, even for a short time. Dissension broke out, in fact, before the Runnymede conferences were concluded. Then the Pope, now John's acknowledged overlord, conveniently annulled the Great Charter, absolved the King from his oath to observe it, and threatened to excommunicate any baron who tried to enforce it. This completed the division in the opposition party, and enabled John to raise an army with which to conduct the civil war that occupied the last year of his reign. The barons needed more training in co-operation before they could hope to hold a predominant political position for long. This training was to be obtained much more easily by participation in the national government as such than by any further attempts to clarify and enforce the feudal contract. For the vantage point of a responsible position in a central government inevitably teaches the holder the necessity of compromise and co-operation, although he may not thoroughly learn the lesson all at once.

## ATTEMPTS TO CONTROL THE CENTRAL GOVERNMENT BY COMMITTEE

**The Provisions of Oxford.** The first halting steps in this new direction were taken late in the reign of Henry III when the

barons decided to resist the royal demands for money with which
to carry on the Sicilian venture (page 95). In 1258 the King was
compelled to accept their terms, embodied in a document called
the Provisions of Oxford.[11] According to this agreement a committee of fifteen was virtually entrusted with the royal power,
and given authority to reform and regulate the government as
the majority should choose. This committee was named by an
electoral board of four, selected by an ingenious arrangement
designed to ensure the choice of moderate men. A panel of twelve
barons and a similar group of twelve of the King's friends nominated two each from the other panel. Since each group of twelve
chose the two of the other group whom they considered the least
objectionable, this device produced a board of four who were
not extremists. The fifteen barons whom the four then chose
were to consult three times a year with a group of twelve selected
by the King's Council or with the Council itself, should it be
summoned. But since the fifteen were to remain in attendance
upon the King at all times they practically supplanted the Council, and were expected to dictate all royal appointments, with the
object of putting honest and capable officials in the important
administrative posts.

**Provisions of Westminster.** Unfortunately the committee of
fifteen could not agree on matters of policy. Some members were
genuinely in favor of reform, but others were chiefly motivated
by personal interests. The mesne tenants (rear vassals)—knights
and small landholders—were becoming sufficiently well-to-do to
make their political influence felt. Just as the barons a generation before had demanded a statement of the feudal contract that
would lessen their burden, so these subtenants were now asking
for modifications in their favor. Particularly they wished to limit
their lords' court rights, which bore heavily upon them. They
wanted to lighten the obligation of suit of court, and to secure
exemption from penalties for alleged false judgments. They de-

11 S-M, No. 47B, pp. 143-46.

sired the abolition of the practice of attaching their goods to
force them to appear before feudal courts in cases concerning
their freehold lands. They also protested against the custom of
compelling them to take oath without royal authorization, since
juries of freemen were originally available only in the royal
courts. These objectives were attained by them in 1259 when the
baronial government issued a document called the Provisions
of Westminster,[12] correcting these abuses in the feudal courts.

**The Mise of Lewes.** Those of the barons who wished to preserve their personal power through the feudal courts opposed
the agreement. The division caused by this issue, combined
with another convenient papal annulment of reforms restricting
the royal authority, gave the King his opportunity and led to
the outbreak of civil war in 1261. Simon de Montfort, Earl of
Leicester, whose party triumphed in 1264 at the battle of Lewes,
was willing to extend political power to the rising social classes.
Under the terms of yet another new constitutional document,
called the Mise (Agreement) of Lewes, he substituted a council
of nine men controlled by himself for the other oligarchic group
of fifteen, and proceeded to invite the lesser landlords and even
the townsmen to share in the control of the government. He included representatives of both these groups in a Parliament that
he called in 1265. This action alienated still more of his own
class, in addition to those offended by the Provisions of Westminster, and led to his defeat and death in battle the next year
at Evesham (near Worcester in the west of England).

**The Royal Settlement.** After that battle the successful royal
faction abolished the council of nine, put the King's appointees
back in their administrative posts, and annulled the reforms of
the oligarchic governments. Only the reforms of the Provisions
of Westminster survived—probably because they did not directly
affect the King's interests—and were incorporated in the Statute
of Marlborough in 1267. The baronial class had not yet learned

12 S-M, No. 47C, pp. 146-48.

to preserve effective unity of action or properly to appreciate the role of other political elements in society. During these last few years of civil commotion none of the barons in the opposition seems to have realized the contribution that the king could make, and which for the time, at least, was badly needed. Furthermore, too few of them were willing to admit to the councils of state men of lower birth and lesser substance, even though in the aggregate the influence of this upper middle class might be very important. The mention of a Parliament in connection with the troubles of 1265 suggests the mechanism that was to provide the necessary instruction and opportunities. But the story of its origins and development belongs to the next chapter.

## SIMPLIFICATION OF THE FEUDAL HIERARCHY

**"Quia Emptores."** Since the baronial class itself had ceased to rely primarily on the feudal contract as a means of securing its political ends, Edward I was able to secure the enactment of a statute that struck a deathblow at the pyramidical system of feudalism in which the important lords might have large bodies of mesne or rear vassals owing allegiance to them. By the Statute of Westminster III (1290) the English Justinian forbade further subinfeudation. He justified his action by alleging that people purchasing land subject to the condition that they be subtenants of the seller were depriving the original lord of his feudal rights. Accordingly one section of the statute [13]—called *Quia emptores* (Since purchasers) from its opening words—provided that in the future the seller in such cases lost all his feudal rights over the land and that the buyer should be feudally obligated to the lord of the seller in precisely the same way as the previous owner had been. In other words, no more subfeuds could be created, and as the intermediate lords ran out of heirs or were adjudged guilty of felony or treason the old subfeuds were gradually abolished

[13] S-M, No. 52F, p. 174.

and nearly every landlord came to hold his land directly from the king.

**The Small Share of the Middle and Lower Classes.** In general during this period, the height of the Middle Ages, practice conformed so closely to what we have called the typical medieval political theory (page 31) that the middle and lower classes had very little power indeed. In the baronial troubles under Henry III the upper middle class in the rural areas did assert itself to some extent, as already mentioned (page 128). In that and most other emergencies with financial implications, especially toward the end of this time, the voice of the mercantile elements as represented by the townsmen was also beginning to be heard. In periods of military stress at home doubtless some attention was paid to the sentiments of the villeins, who became temporarily important on such occasions. But generally the domination of both middle and lower classes by the elements higher in the social scale was very nearly complete. Furthermore, their means of manifesting what little power they had were intimately connected with agencies originally designed for those same higher elements. Consequently it will be best to describe the constitutional position of these less important classes in the following sections on the governmental machinery of the time (pages 147, 149, 161).

# 6. THE CENTRAL GOVERNMENT

## THE FEUDALIZATION OF THE CROWN

**Contemporary Statements about the Power of the Crown Vague.** Although the enhanced position of the English monarch following the Conquest was the major constitutional change effected by the invasion, it depended to such an extent upon the personalities of the individual rulers that formal documentary statements relating to it are hard to find. Dominating figures, and also people living in their immediate presence, commonly find it inexpedient to make explicit written pronouncements on the exact relationships prevailing. An accurate definition of the extent of monarchical power would not greatly aid a king who was pushing his authority beyond earlier limits, and might easily give representatives of interests adversely affected some tangible justification for opposition. Yet the situation may be clear enough to the observer looking back on the scene.

**The Change from Elective to Feudal Status.** The general effect of the increased power of the crown may be seen in the great mass of constitutional and judicial activity with which we shall have to deal in this period. Particularly the new status of the monarchs may be noticed in the increased importance of the hereditary, as opposed to the elective, factor in determining the succession to the throne. Whereas in Saxon times election played a very important part in determining which member of the royal family should succeed to the throne when a king died (page 32), the legal rules of heredity now became the chief consideration. From a position as semielective head of a people the kingship shifted to become the right of feudal lordship over a territory and its inhabitants, a right to which the succession should be determined according to the letter of the feudal law and not by a vote of the Council ratified by the Church. William the Conqueror practically willed his lands away (page 83). It will be recalled, however, that the bequest of England took the form of a letter to the Archbishop of Canterbury requesting him to make this arrangement if it could be done justly, so that while the monarch determined the succession, a gesture was made in the direction of the custom of the land. These old forms were definitely observed at the accessions of Henry I and Stephen, but the agreement between the latter and Henry of Anjou practically amounted to another disposal of the crown by royal will, and shows that now the wish of even a weak king was considered important in determining the transmission of the crown. From the time of Henry II on, the feudal theory began definitely to predominate, and if there was uncertainty about the succession after the death of Richard, it was because the feudal law on the subject itself was not yet clear. This strengthening of the feudal attitude appears in John's title, for he called himself King of England instead of King of the English, as his predecessors had done, and thus indicated a growing sense of proprietorship of the land itself. The new attitude is also evident in the assumption by both Richard and John that they might on their own responsibility acknowledge an overlord from whom they would hold their kingdom as a fief.[1] The award of Norham, which determined the succession to the Scottish throne in 1292 (page 99), was made on the basis of the feudal law of England and thereafter fixed the order of succession to all the real property in the land, including the kingdom itself.

**Abolition of the Legal Effect of Coronation.** Clearest of all indications of the decline of the elective factor, however, was the precedent set in 1272 at the accession of Edward I. It will

[1] Richard did homage to the German Emperor as one of the conditions of his release in 1194.

be recalled that heretofore the successful candidate had not
been considered actually in office until he had submitted himself to the church authorities by taking the oath and receiving
anointment in the coronation ceremony (page 33). Edward, however, was in Sicily when his father died, and he could not be
crowned for months. Meanwhile, according to the old theory,
there would be no king and the king's peace would lapse. This
was a highly unpleasant prospect, for a chronicler had recorded
how in similar circumstances after the death of Henry I "every
man that might soon robbed another." This emergency, combined with the development of the feudal theory already mentioned, induced the Council to proclaim Edward legally king
at once, without waiting for him to be crowned. After that time
the coronation ceremony had no legal significance, and the
Church therefore lost all its former veto power on the choice
of a successor when a ruler died.

**The Relation of King to the Law.** What few theoretical statements have come down to us from this period on the subject of
royal power have to do largely with the relation of the king to
the law. The tradition (page 36) was that the king, as well as
his Council, did no more than declare and enforce the customary
law. Therefore he was bound by the law of the land and must
rule in accordance with it. This doctrine was popular with all
those who wished to limit the royal powers—churchmen, barons,
and the upper middle class—and it finds more frequent expression than any other because, as already suggested, documentary
statements of principle are more useful in the hands of the
king's opponents than in those of his friends. A churchman
named John of Salisbury set forth this doctrine in the time of
Henry II, declaring that kings ruled by laws, while only tyrants
ignored them. To withdraw the king from the power of the law
is to make him an outlaw. The same attitude appears in the
movement that culminated in the Great Charter and in the
subsequent demands that rulers should swear to this and other

similar charters. The most striking instance of all was a Confirmation of the Charters exacted from Edward I in 1297,[2] in
which he was made to bind himself not to take any aids, tasks
(taxes), or prises (requisitions or custom charges) except "by
the common consent of all the realm." The same theory of royal
subjection to the law underlay the effort to bind Henry III by
the Provisions of Oxford and the Mise of Lewes. In practice,
however, the king broke these earlier bonds, as we have seen,
and Edward did not keep the promise given in 1297. Though
the powerful kings generally observed the forms of English law,
in effect they came close to acting on the rival theory of Roman
law. According to the imperial Roman tradition kings, far from
being bound by the law, made it, for the will of the prince
was law. This was quoted by one of Henry II's legal advisers
named Glanvil (page 202), and while he meant it to apply only
to part of the legal field, another writer of the time preached
all the essentials of the doctrine that was later to be known
as the divine right of kings. Rulers receive all their power from
God and are responsible to him alone, he said. They are not
bound by the common law of the realm, and subjects are not to
question their doings. We shall see that there was to be a long
struggle between the Roman and the common law theories on
this point before the matter was finally settled. At this time the
royal practice lay somewhere between the two extremes of theory,
but on the whole somewhat closer to the Continental notion
than to the traditionally English one.

## CHANGES IN THE HOUSEHOLD AND
## ADMINISTRATIVE OFFICES

**Growing Separation of Administrative Offices and Household.**
In the organization of the royal administrative offices a new
principle may be observed after the Conquest. The close con-

2 S-M, No. 51A, pp. 164-65.

nection between the royal household and the regular officials of the central government began to break down.[3] An important new post (the Justiciarship) was created which was not filled from the ranks of the household, and several of the most important officers, drawn originally from those ranks, no longer followed the king on his travels. Instead they "went out of court." This meant that they settled down in permanent stationary offices where they could do their work more efficiently and be more accessible to the general public than if they remained with the king.

**The Justiciar.** The Conquest, which put England along with great Continental territories under a single ruler, made it advisable to have some substitute—virtually a vice-king—who could wield the royal authority in England when the monarch was on the other side of the Channel. In the early Norman reigns the queen or some other member of the royal family frequently acted as regent in the king's absence. At the same time men called justiciars were frequently given the royal authority to determine a particular lawsuit or represent the crown otherwise, as for example in the case of the collection of the data for the Domesday Book (page 83). In the reign of Henry I the title came to be given to the king's chief legal and administrative assistant, an official who served as regent in his absence. For a few years in the time of Henry II there were two of these officials, but before the end of the reign the King reverted to the earlier practice. During the reigns of Richard and John the office was held by a succession of great administrators trained up in Henry's system, who were chiefly responsible for preserving the authority of the central government in those troubled times. After the loss of Normandy, however, the king no longer went abroad so frequently or for such long periods. Accordingly,

---

[3] For a fuller description of the royal household as it existed in the early part of the twelfth century and in the reign of Edward I, see S-M, Nos. 29 and 52C, pp. 65-70, 170-72. *Cf.* No. 42, pp. 113-14.

there was less need for this office, and after the first decades of Henry III it ceased to be of great importance. Under Edward I it was abolished altogether.

**The Chamberlain and the Treasurer.** The first administrative office to go out of court, as the process of settling in a permanent location was called, was an offshoot of the Chamberlain's organization. That dignitary himself continued to travel with the royal court and to have charge of the king's private quarters and all matters of ceremony. He also had custody of the small sums of money needed for the routine expenses of the court. But his chief financial duties had to be put in other hands. By the time of the Conquest it was no longer feasible to carry all the king's treasure wherever he went, and the bulk of it was deposited in the royal castle at Winchester with one of the Chamberlain's subordinates as treasurer. About 1130 this Treasurer became independent of the Chamberlain and thereafter was responsible directly to the king.

**The Exchequer.** Not only did the Treasurer keep the bulk of the royal funds, but with two helpers, at first called Assistant Chamberlains, he also kept accounts of the receipts and expenditures. A report, called the pipe roll—perhaps from the pipes (strips of parchment) that were stitched end to end to make it—was drawn up to show the state of the Treasury at the end of the fiscal year.[4] To assist in the computations use was made of a modified abacus, a table with ruled lines dividing it into columns for units of pennies, shillings, pounds, and scores of pounds, and crossbars to indicate the amount due, the amount paid, and possibly the balance.[5] By placing tokens in the various squares it was possible to make the reckonings clear to illiterate debtors. These tokens, the squares, and the rival parties

[4] S-M, No. 25, pp. 49-54.
[5] This is uncertain. If there was no such line, the computations must have been made by removing counters of equal value from both sides of the single line until one was empty.

on the two sides of the table gave the whole the appearance of
a chess game, and so this office came to be known as the Exchequer, from the Latin term *scaccarium* (chessboard). When

THE EXCHEQUER TABLE

| | £ 20 | £ 1 | Sheriffs Shillings | Pence |
|---|---|---|---|---|
| Amount due | | | | |
| Amount paid | | | | |
| Balance | | | | |

Royal Officials

(The royal officials usually occupied one end—or both ends—also.)

computations were completed, payments made, and accounts
settled, the sheriffs and other royal debtors were given receipts
in the form of tallies, notched wooden sticks about as big as
eight or ten inches of broom handle. These were cut in a subordinate office known as the Lower Exchequer, which also received the actual cash payments. The size and number of the
notches indicated the amount paid. The stick was then split,
the amount paid written on each piece, and half retained in
the Exchequer to guard against the possibility of a sheriff's
attempting to do profitable whittling in his spare time.

**Change in Location of Exchequer and Treasury.** As London
became more and more important it became increasingly inconvenient to make payments on the royal accounts at Winchester.
Probably by the time of Henry I the Exchequer for the enroll-
ing of receipts and expenditures was already transferred to
Westminster, a village near the city of London in which were
located a large royal palace and an abbey under the patronage
of the crown. In the reign of Henry II the Treasury itself was
moved from Winchester to the more convenient location of the
Temple, the buildings of the military crusading order called
the Knights Templar, located between Westminster and London. Later the Treasury was removed to the royal castle called

the Tower of London, on the other side of the city. In the reign of Henry III one of the clerks, previously loaned by the Chancellor's office to the Exchequer to act as auditor and keep a duplicate roll, was made an independent official, no longer responsible to the Chancellor, with the title of Chancellor of the Exchequer, and placed in virtual charge of that office.

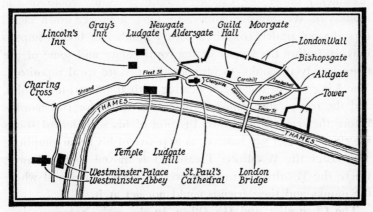

MEDIEVAL LONDON

**The Wardrobe.** Another branch of the Chamberlain's office that went out of court during this period was the Wardrobe. Originally the king had actually possessed a piece of furniture by that name (page 34) for the storing of all his clothing, and the Chamberlain and his clerks were responsible for its custody and transportation. Old accounts record payments to the man who furnished the cart to move it from one royal stopping-place to the next. Armor was, of course, included among the monarch's changes of costume, and so this side of the Chamberlain's office came in time to be charged with the custody of bows, arrows, spears, and munitions of war in general. As the government's store of these became too bulky to be moved from place to place, they were deposited in the Tower at London. This branch of the Wardrobe—called the Privy Wardrobe—therefore corresponded to the quartermaster's department of a modern military establishment. Surplus money, jewels, and plate belonging to the king's personal funds in the Chamber, as the Chamberlain's office was now called, were turned over to another group of Wardrobe clerks to guard in a separate treasury. In the thirteenth century this Wardrobe Treasury was located in the crypt (basement) under the Chapter House (assembly room of the monks) of Westminster Abbey. In 1303, a broken-down clerk, turned wool trader, conspired with a number of boon companions—including the keeper of the royal palace and some of the more convivial monks—to plunder this private royal repository. The King was in the north, dealing with the Scottish troubles, and the conspirators enjoyed their huge spoils for two months before the secret leaked out. In spite of his semiclerical status the chief offender was hanged, as were five of his lay accomplices. Thereafter the Wardrobe Treasury was moved to the Tower, where the Wardrobe's weapons were already stored and where the monks and their friends could not get at it.

**The Chancellor and His Office.** In the early Norman reigns the Chancellor acted as a kind of secretary of state for all departments. He and his clerks not only attended to all the royal correspondence, but kept records for the Justiciar, the Chamberlain, and the Treasurer. Always a churchman in this period, the Chancellor also had charge of the royal chapel, and was considered the keeper of the king's conscience. He advised the monarch on ecclesiastical matters, especially on the filling of vacancies where the king had the advowson right. Indeed, those of lesser value he filled himself, without consulting his royal master. With all these duties, plus his responsibility for the final form which all official documents should take, the Chancellor was already a person of considerable political influence in the reign of Henry I. By the end of the century he and his subordinates had developed many types of governmental records, of which the charter, patent, and close rolls were the most impor-

tant. These, given in the order of their importance, were duplicate copies of the royal communications. Charters were the most
solemn grants of lands or privileges. Letters patent were so called
because they were left open for all to see (Latin *patens,* showing)
and usually dealt with matters of some public interest. Letters
close were closed or sealed up, and concerned topics of a minor
or personal nature.

**The Chancery Goes out of Court.** The Chancellor remained
longer in court than the Treasurer, because of the desirability
of having the great seal (page 34) available for authenticating
the king's communications. Since, however, the Chancellor was
also charged with issuing the documents called writs, which permitted their purchasers to make use of the royal courts for civil
suits (page 186), it was extremely inconvenient for prospective
litigants to have him so often on the move. The baronial opponents of Henry III also wished to have the Chancellor stay at
Westminster, so that he might be less directly under the royal
influence. It was accordingly arranged between 1234 and 1238
that the Chancery, as the Chancellor's office was called, should
have a permanent office at the capital. Writs were thereafter
obtainable at Westminster, though the Chancellor followed the
king for some time afterward and the process of going out of
court was not complete until the time of Edward I. With the
rise of the Chancellor of the Exchequer in this same reign the
original Chancellor came to be known as the Lord Chancellor
to distinguish him from the less important financial official with
a similar title.

**Creation of the Privy Seal.** To take the Lord Chancellor's
place as the authenticating agent for the royal correspondence
the controller, or counterroller—keeper of the duplicate roll—
in the Wardrobe was given custody of what was called the privy
seal. Both the seal and the official in charge of it—who shortly
ceased to be connected with the Wardrobe—were referred to
thereafter by this title. Documents of minor importance were

issued under this seal. Those of greater consequence were sent through the Privy Seal office to the Lord Chancellor to be drawn up formally and stamped with the great seal.

**Other Administrative Officials.** The stewardship remained an office of dignity in this period, but never obtained great administrative importance. A Constable took the place of the Anglo-Saxon Staller. He was the highest military official and had under him one or more marshals as assistants.

## THE REVENUE SYSTEM

**Direct Taxes.** In medieval feudal theory the kings were supposed to live "of their own," from their estates and feudal dues. But the feudal principle that the vassal should aid his lord in time of need opened the way to supplementary taxation. We have seen (page 116) that in emergencies the Norman kings continued to levy the Danegeld, which usually amounted to two shillings for every hide of land. Stephen promised to abolish this levy, however, and it was not exacted after 1162. When Richard's captivity necessitated the raising of a large sum of money a tax called a carucage was devised.[6] This was really a revived form of Danegeld, which took the caruca (plowland of 100 acres) as its unit of assessment. In most forms of medieval taxation people obtained concessions or discovered means of evading them. In later centuries these tactics were met by a new assessment or an increase of rates, but at first a new form of tax was commonly invented in such circumstances. When the carucage thus wore out, it was replaced by a tax on movable (personal) property, the first tax of this sort in England. This was called the Saladin tithe, and was levied under Henry II for crusading purposes, to assist in the recovery of Jerusalem from the Mohammedan Saladin. By the middle of the thirteenth century, however, the royal government had taken over the idea

[6] S-M, No. 46C, pp. 134-35.

for secular use, first under the guise of an aid to assist in raising funds for Richard's ransom and later as a fractional levy of various proportions on personal property.[7] Finally it came to be known as the tenth and fifteenth, because people in towns and on the royal domain were required to pay the full tenth, while others were let off with the lesser fraction. Since movable property is relatively easy to secrete, the returns from this tax dropped off very sharply. In 1334 therefore the government began the practice of assigning a definite sum of money to each administrative unit (township, village, or borough) of taxation. After 1334 the amount of money raised in that year (roughly £38,000) became the standard unit for a tenth and fifteenth. Thereafter, when Parliament voted a tenth and fifteenth it meant that each administrative unit was responsible for raising its old quota regardless of how its wealth had increased or declined (though some exceptions were allowed). Eventually some of these charges came to be attached to certain parcels of land, and the tax became virtually a real property one.

**Indirect Taxes: Customs.** The control of trade and markets was a standard feudal right that the English kings had long been accustomed to exercise. Sometimes this control was used for military purposes, so as to regulate shipping during hostilities with France, for example. But most commonly it was used to impose tolls for revenue purposes. Before the reign of Edward I these tolls were of varying amounts and might differ from port to port, but that vigorous monarch undertook to put them on a regular basis and to deal with the merchants of England as a whole. In 1275 he succeeded in establishing a levy of six shillings and eightpence for each sack of wool (364 lbs.) exported, and thirteen shillings and fourpence on each last (144) of hides. This came eventually to be known as the Great and Old Custom in contrast to the New and Small Custom, which was an additional charge of 50 per cent imposed in 1303. At first

7 S-M, No. 46D and 46G, pp. 135-36, 138.

only foreign merchants were compelled to pay the latter, but in the next reign English shippers were brought to accept it also.

## THE COUNCIL, GREAT AND SMALL

**The Great Council: Its Composition.** Several factors combined during this period to bring about a marked change in the constitution and duties of the king's Council. The introduction of strict feudal principles, the enhanced power of the king, and the resulting increase in the amount of central government business to be transacted all helped to transform the Saxon witan into the Norman council. By the application of feudal theory to existing institutions the king's Council now became the king's court (Latin, *curia regis*) to which all his vassals owed suit. Accordingly, membership was now based not on vague considerations of personal importance, but on landholding. Every tenant in chief was obligated to attend when the king held court, usually three times a year—Easter at Winchester, Whitsuntide at Westminster, and Christmas at Gloucester in the west. These tenants in chief were all called barons, according to legal usage. Even the bishops and important abbots were absorbed into this class, and for feudal purposes seem to have been considered barons. There were over five hundred barons all told, however, and those of lesser importance found the obligation to attend these functions burdensome. Rarely, if ever, did all of them fulfill this requirement at the same time. The king, on his part, was not especially anxious to have them present at these sessions, and by the time of Henry I only the more important barons— who numbered some one hundred and seventy—were expected to attend council meetings. They received a special summons, and the lesser barons who were not included in the list did not come. In time the title of baron was confined to this select group. Even of them no more than seventy-five appear to have been present at any one meeting, the rest sending various excuses.

**Functions of the Council.** Since the Council was now the king's feudal court and not legally a national assembly, it lost some of its earlier functions. It was no longer necessary to secure conciliar assent to the alienation of royal lands or the appointment of important royal officials, such as earls or even churchmen. The imposition of the Danegeld or feudal aids was also in the king's province, though he sometimes found it convenient to associate the Council with his name in his financial decrees. The same is true of legislation, which might stand in the royal name alone, or be re-enforced by the endorsement of the Council. We have already noted how the importance of the Council as a body electing to the kingship declined in this period, though the forms were frequently observed, especially in the earlier part. The judicial functions of the Council, which we shall consider in greater detail in a succeeding chapter, increased in number and impor·tance, but they were strictly under the royal control. Only in a few special cases does the Council, in its advisory capacity, seem to have overridden the royal will.

**The Small Council.** The word "court," which was used interchangeably with "council" in the Middle Ages, originally meant not the body of men surrounding the king, but the place of his residence. Subsequently it came to be applied to the body of persons associated with that place. It was therefore not difficult to think of the king's friends, administrative officials, and members of the royal household, who remained in attendance on him when the feudal council broke up, as a royal court or council also. We have seen that the Saxon kings made use of household officials as assistants and doubtless took advice from them between meetings of the Witan. With a swelling flood of routine business pouring in upon the Norman kings they often found it convenient to call upon their available attendants for help with governmental affairs. Monarchs asked for advice, referred perplexing legal cases to these companions for their consideration, and had them witness grants of land and privileges. The resulting activities of these associates were also considered those of the king's court (Council). Since the king commonly dominated the Council, however large it was, and since at best many of the important barons did not attend the formal sessions, there seemed no reason to make any distinction on grounds of size. Legally the powers of both groups, or the same group at different numerical strengths, were identical. For the purpose of tracing subsequent developments we shall find it convenient to refer to them as the Great and the Small Council, but the contemporary legal mind only distinguished one Council (*curia regis*). In practice, the relations of the less formal to the more formal body were those of a modern executive committee to the large society which it represents. The more important matters were commonly reserved for general discussion, but in emergencies this custom was disregarded.

**The Development of the Organization of the Small Council.** Throughout the early Angevin period the Norman theory of the council was still followed in the main, but a distinction began to appear between the Great and Small councils. In the time of Henry II it was decided that a royal decree made with the consent of the Small Council was valid only during the lifetime of the king, while an enactment approved by the Great Council was considered binding for all time, unless repealed. A certain distinction based on the social classes represented is also noticeable, for the permanent council came to be composed more and more of what we should call civil servants, men without other means, trained as clerks in Chancery or as lay administrators in some such office as the Exchequer or Wardrobe. Some of these came eventually to rank with the greatest men of the realm. Hubert de Burgh, one of the regents during the minority of Henry III (page 95), is typical of this class. In fact, the minority of this king lent such additional importance to the permanent council that subsequently there was a clarification of its status and a definite effort by the barons to control its membership. A special oath was instituted in 1237, which all members of the Small Council were required to take, binding them to give the king good counsel—originally there was no distinction between "counsel" and "council," the advice and the body giving it—and not to disclose his secrets.[8] The permanent council was also given its own staff of clerks and was generally permitted to use the privy seal to authenticate its documents, though it did not always control the use of that instrument. The baronial reform of 1258, resulting in the Provisions of Oxford, and Simon de Montfort's alterations in the government a few years later, though they did not long survive, both involved the notion of a small permanent council of definite membership, which should not be dominated by the king.

## THE ORIGINS OF PARLIAMENT

**Early Special Instances.** At the same time there were occasional evidences of willingness to expand the Great Council. Henry II took the unusual step of summoning barons of the second rank during the quarrel with Becket in 1164, and deans of cathedral chapters frequently attended to re-enforce the clerical element. Important nobles commonly brought their own knights and other retainers along to add to the dignity of their appearance. Occasionally representatives of areas with special governmental problems were summoned. Under feudal theory the lesser tenants in chief had a right to demand justice of their lord, and so might attend the royal court without special summons, if they chose to go to the trouble of doing so. Furthermore, the Great Charter (in its short-lived Article 14) provided that general notice was to be given to these lesser tenants in chief in their respective county courts whenever a scutage or general aid was to be levied.

8 For later examples of this oath, see S-M, No. 53, pp. 176-77.

**The Use of Parliament for Taxation Purposes.** The tendency to enlarge the Great Council in special cases, particularly where finances were concerned, led in the thirteenth century to the development of the institution later known as Parliament. The steady opposition of the rank and file of taxpayers to financial levies (particularly to the direct taxes at first) led to a succession of efforts in the thirteenth century to include representatives of the upper middle class in the Great Council. It was not the taxpayers who desired this arrangement, but those who wished to impose the tax. Just as Henry II felt that the judgment of Becket would be more impressive and seem like that of the entire realm if the lesser barons were represented, so later rulers thought to secure compliance with their financial demands through having men of all the substantial classes combine to authorize the collection. In this movement the kings were supported by the lords, both spiritual and temporal, who had found difficulty in collecting levies from their subordinates and so were insisting that they had no power to bind others. After the inclusion of knights and burgesses in the sessions of the Great Council the upper middle class property-owners whom they represented could no longer feel justified in refusing to pay their assessments on the ground that they had not been consulted in making the original decision to levy the tax.

**The Representative Idea.** The representative idea was an ancient one, whose origins are buried in remote antiquity. The principle of representative government, which permits a large class to function in a governmental capacity through a few chosen men, was thoroughly understood and practiced in ancient Greece. The English had long made use of it in local government, where county and hundred courts acted for their communities, and groups of four and five men spoke for their villages. In many other ways, as local officials, as jurymen, as electors, in religious as well as secular activity, Englishmen had been trained by the strict discipline of king and churchmen (pages 114, 185) to act as authorized spokesmen for their fellows, who were usually considered bound by their actions.

**Rudimentary Parliaments.** As early as 1213 the king and his advisers began trying to force elected representatives of one or more supplementary classes to attend the meetings of his lay and ecclesiastical barons in the Great Council. Sometimes the lesser clergy were in demand, sometimes representatives of the Cinque Ports, the five Channel ports which supplied the bulk of the royal navy. More often the pressure was applied to county courts to delegate pairs of knights to speak for the lesser landlords of the county, or to towns to supply similar delegations of burgesses. In 1265 Simon de Montfort first summoned representatives of both the rural and the urban elements in the upper middle class to attend the same session of the Great Council.[9] Though Montfort was defeated shortly afterward, his shrewd opponent who later became Edward I appreciated the merits of his policy, and repeated the experiment many times in the succeeding reign. Representatives of the lower clergy were also present at some of these enlarged sessions of the Great Council.

## THE ROLE OF THE KNIGHTS AND BURGESSES IN THE EARLY PARLIAMENTS

**Their Weakness.** The business usually taken up at these gatherings was the demand for a financial grant to the royal government, though occasionally the authorities may have wished to obtain information about the state of the country or the reaction of these delegates to a proposed line of policy. Since the representatives of these less exalted orders were not considered fit to be seated or to speak at length in the king's presence, they must have played a rather indirect part in the affairs of the Council during the thirteenth century. Probably they answered questions and possibly by applause or murmurs showed

9 S-M, No. 48C, pp. 151-52.

approval or disapproval of speeches made by the lay barons and the important churchmen. At this time it was difficult for them alone, without baronial support, to do anything but accept the royal demands. It was therefore greatly to the advantage of the crown to have them present, since the fact that these representatives had once given consent considerably facilitated the subsequent collection of the taxes voted.

**Their Influence over Taxation.** In this period, however, the knights and burgesses did develop two rights that were to be of great importance later on. One was that of being consulted on all future proposals to grant financial assistance to the king beyond that provided by the monarch's "own." Since some such supplementary grants were originally supposed to be owed to the royal overlord under the terms of the feudal contract (page 120), the king had some grounds for exacting these revenues without consulting the commons, or even the magnates, when and if he chose to do so. Particularly was this true in the case of the customs, which were established in 1275 on the basis of an agreement between the king, the merchants, and certain of the nobles whose feudal interests were affected. In other words, they were set up as the result of a semiprivate bargain between the interested parties and not as a result of formal action by the national Parliament. Nevertheless, this bargain was announced as being made in Parliament and that body thus began to acquire a kind of shadowy claim to pass on such grants. Later royal exactions of excessive customs not confirmed in Parliament brought strong protests, culminating in the Confirmation of the Charters [10] which Edward was forced to accept in 1297. By it he bound himself in the matter of both direct and indirect taxes, promising that he would not again make any such assessments "but by the common assent of the whole kingdom." Since a similar phrase is used in another passage that dealt with the customs on wool, where the merchants were particularly

[10] S-M, No. 51A, pp. 164-65.

concerned, it is probable that the nonnoble representatives were included in the phrase "the whole kingdom." They are specifically mentioned along with the magnates in a document of the same year called *De tallagio non concedendo* (Concerning tallage which shall not have been granted), which provided that no tallage or aid was to be taken without their consent, though this document originally did not have official rank as a statute. This promise was not strictly kept, but it established an important precedent nevertheless.

**Their Influence over Legislation.** The second advance was the winning of the right to petition the king as a body for redress of grievances, a right from which later legislative powers sprang (page 256). Wherever the king went in the Middle Ages he was besieged by suitors requesting justice or favors of one kind or another. On ceremonial occasions, when the monarch, surrounded by churchmen, nobles, and representative subjects, was supposed to be in especially good humor and in a mood for business, the number of these petitions increased so greatly that in the thirteenth century it became necessary to appoint special committees of the Great Council to receive and try them. Some of the petitions were referred to the ordinary courts, while others were turned over to the king with a recommendation of some particular action. Conciliar meetings held to consider these petitions were thus very important, and the special name of Parliament was first given to those held for such purposes. Originally "colloquium," or "parliament" (talkfest, from the French *parler*, to speak), was considered merely another name for "council," and the technical significance of the term as applied to special sessions of this body developed but slowly. The knights and burgesses did not take part in the receiving and sifting of these petitions, but they did develop the practice of presenting joint petitions and requesting favorable royal action upon them at this time, commonly in conjunction with the magnates who made up the council itself. There thus developed the idea of a petition which was not that of a private individual, but one expressing the wishes of the members of Parliament as a whole. If the king wished to act favorably upon it, he and his advisers would draw up a decree or a statute embodying the substance of the request, which the Great Council thereupon approved. In this way representative knights and burgesses might make some small contribution to the process of legislation. In this period, however, they seem rarely to have initiated any petitions of their own, but rather to have supported those already drawn up by the nobles. Indeed, the presence of knights and burgesses was as yet not considered necessary, either at the session of Parliament that heard the complaints or in the meeting that approved the subsequent statutes. Parliament, as the term was then used, might and did often meet without either knights or burgesses when financial business was not to be taken up or when it had been disposed of and the representatives of the lesser orders dismissed.

## THE ECCLESIASTICAL SIDE OF THE CENTRAL GOVERNMENT

**The Roman Curia.** On the ecclesiastical side the central government was strengthened during this period by the increased power of the popes, to which we have already alluded (page 113), by the clarification of the relationship between the archbishops of Canterbury and York, and by the development of autonomy in the English Church. Here we can say little more about the first topic than to mention the strengthening of governmental machinery at the papal court, which dates from this period. Not only were the relationships of cardinals to popes made more definite,[11] but the arm of the pontiff was greatly

[11] Technically the cardinals were the cardinal (the most important) clergy of the diocese of Rome who elected the pope, as canons commonly elected the English bishops. Actually these men ordinarily held other offices in the Church besides the one that made them eligible to vote in these elections.

lengthened by the increased jurisdiction of his courts and by the invention of the practice of providing his friends with any livings that might fall vacant, if he so chose. Most striking was the development of a system of clerical taxation which paralleled that of the secular government. Besides their local tithes, laymen were obligated to pay Peter's pence, which was an assessment levied on every hearth in England. The clergy were taxed much more heavily, as has been explained (page 118), first by levies of fractional parts of their annual income, and later by means of annates.

**Canterbury and York.** At the same time the archiepiscopal administration of England underwent some centralization. With two rival archbishoprics friction was inevitable unless precedence was granted to one or the other. Canterbury, as the older, claimed this superiority, but the archbishops of York refused to concede it, in spite of royal pressure. After a great deal of unseemly quarreling, which even went so far at one time as to involve the forging of documents to support the claim of Canterbury, the southern archbishop obtained appointment as a papal legate. As such, he clearly outranked his rival, and when future archbishops of Canterbury were regularly given a similar honor the problem was solved.

**Clerical Autonomy: Convocations.** The restoration of separate ecclesiastical courts and councils at the time of the Conquest permitted the Church to regulate its own affairs, to legislate (subject to the royal veto and the overriding claims of the Roman canon law) on religious matters, and to make grants to the secular government. The assemblies exercising such powers for the northern and southern provinces were called Convocations, and reached their fully developed form in the reign of Edward I. They included not only the bishops and important abbots, but representatives of the lower clergy as well. The ecclesiastics thus kept pace with the secular rulers in their efforts to introduce efficiency into government and to broaden the base of consent upon which it rested.

# 7. LOCAL GOVERNMENT

**Local and Central Government Influenced by the Same Forces.** The same forces growing out of the Norman Conquest, whose effects we have been tracing in the development of the central governmental system, are also to be seen at work in the field of local government. The Roman heritage, the increased power of the king, the rigid framework of feudal law, and the new ecclesiastical autonomy are all reflected in the arrangements made for governing subdivisions of England also.

## THE COUNTY: THE SHERIFF

**The Elimination of the Earl.** After the Conquest county administration came much more directly under royal control. The system of earldoms, which had made unified administration almost impossible in the late Anglo-Saxon period, was quietly dropped. At first a few Normans were made earls with governmental duties, but William soon regretted this step. Consequently, as rebellion or death removed these officials from the scene their places were not filled, except in the marcher areas on the borders sometimes called palatine (palatial or royal) earldoms—those enjoying semiroyal rights of administration. Men who were given the title of earl in England proper thereafter held it as an honorary one with practically no official duties attached. It enabled them to outrank ordinary barons at ceremonial functions, but left them no official foothold in local government.

**The County Court.** As the bishop was now given his own governmental system to manage (page 107), the administration of the county was left to the sheriff and the county court. The court was summoned by the sheriff, and met every four or six weeks, depending on the county, with especially important sessions every six months. It was still made up of the important landholders in the shire, with at least occasional supplements in the form of representative groups of four men from each hundred and vill, plus the reeves and priests from the vills. Besides a great amount of legal business, which we shall discuss in the next chapter, considerable administrative work was carried on in the county court. Royal proclamations and grants were made public there. Military and financial matters were also attended to at these sessions. Many of the counties retained some peculiar customs, which preserved distinctions dating back to the days of the Danelaw and even the heptarchy. For the most part, however, they were dominated more and more by the royal sheriffs, as an enumeration of the duties of this official will show.

**Duties of the Sheriff.** The sheriff was the judicial head of the shire, and of the hundred as well. He often had charge of a royal castle, for which he exacted from the royal tenants in chief residing in the county a kind of military service called castle guard, and he regularly commanded the local fyrd (militia) in time of war. He was also the chief police officer of the area. He supervised tithings, arrested criminals, served the king's writs, and attached property to compel appearances at court. Furthermore, he looked after the monarch's financial interests. Each year he was responsible at the Exchequer for a sum called the farm of the shire, which represented the king's share of court fines, the return from the royal estates in the county during the early part of this period, feudal dues owed to the crown, and various other items. The sheriff also assisted the special commissions appointed to collect supplementary taxes, when they were levied, and he made disbursements for local needs at the king's order. As a mere incidental he was obligated to provide hospitality and transportation for royal guests traveling through the county, and for the king's messengers. To assist him in these activities he appointed an undersheriff, bailiffs, and usually several clerks, one of whom acted as treasurer, while another took charge of the writs.

**The Difficulty of Securing Honest Local Government.** For doing all this work the sheriff and his subordinates were given no stated salaries at all. It was generally understood that the assistants were to receive various fees and gratuities from those who had business with them, while the sheriff was granted the surplus, if any, remaining after the farm of the county was paid, plus a certain allowance for expenses after the time of Henry III. Yet, whether profitable or unprofitable, the office of sheriff could not be refused. Like military service, it was binding upon all whom the king chose to call. Naturally this system demanded careful supervision or substantial alteration if it was to work smoothly. The sheriff's assistants tended to use their official powers to supplement their uncertain fees by all manner of extortion and graft. One of many aggrieved petitioners to the king during this period declared that his horse, which had been attached in a lawsuit, was still in the sheriff's pound long after the suit was ended, and that the sheriff's man had been seen riding it to a fair in a neighboring county. The problem of securing an honest and efficient local government, of finding men willing to work faithfully in obscure corners for small compensation, has, of course, always been a difficult one, and we shall see that the English struggled long and hard before finding an approximately satisfactory solution.

**Status of the Sheriff.** With all his multifarious duties, the sheriff, as might be expected, became very important in the first two Norman reigns. Prominent barons held the place, and in many cases were succeeded by their sons or other relations. They acted almost as viceroys, and for a time it appeared that they might reproduce the evils of the old system of earldoms, though normally each sheriff now had only one county under his control. It was not easy to remove a strongly entrenched lord from the sheriff's office, especially when he had come to regard it as his by hereditary right. Many of these sheriffs therefore took advantage of their position to appropriate lands, commandeer animals, and wring excessive taxes from their districts. Complaints poured in against them as well as against their subordinates.

## REFORMING EFFORTS AND THE CORONER SYSTEM

**Reforming Efforts of Henry I.** The participation of some of these sheriffs in feudal warfare against the king forced Henry I to take the risk of removing some of them from their offices. As opportunities presented themselves he filled these posts with new men drawn from the ranks of the trained officials in the administrative offices connected with his court. This step, combined with the supervision supplied by the itinerant justices (page 170) sent out by the King, reduced the sheriffs to somewhat better order.

**And Henry II.** Yet the troubled reign of Stephen revealed a weakness in this arrangement. The men of no substance, who were put in office because this characteristic was supposed to render them easier to control and therefore more honest, seem to have reasoned that if they could easily be lowered to their former status they had best feather their nests while they had the opportunity. Henry II found that there were many complaints against the sheriffs of the new school. He therefore held a great investigation into the conduct of his sheriffs—the inquest of sheriffs, it was called—and, acting on its findings, removed all but seven from their posts. This discipline and the King's well-known attention to the details of administration brought about some improvement in county government.

**The Coroner System.** Even so, much power concentrated in the hands of one man called for some more effective check. Under Henry I and Stephen county justiciars were used for this purpose, but because they had become so powerful as to be dangerous the system was discontinued under Henry II. In 1194 Richard's regents devised a system of supplementary officers— usually four to a county—who were elected in the county court. Their chief duty was to keep a duplicate set of records of things that should be brought to the royal attention, especially criminal matters. Because they kept track of these pleas of the crown, as those items of special interest to the king were called, they were known as coroners (from the Latin term *corona,* crown). Gradually, however, they came to confine their attention to those preliminary investigations into mysterious deaths with which we still associate them.[1] But the survival in most American counties of the rule that only the coroner can arrest the sheriff shows that something of the original purpose of the office lingered on to later days.

**Baronial Reforming Attempts.** The baronial reformers of 1258 also grappled with the problem of county government. They proposed to have four knights appointed in each shire to report to the itinerant justices on the conduct of the sheriff. They demanded that sheriffs be elected in the county court, that they serve for a term of one year only, and that instead of men of little or no means being chosen, the office be restricted to men of substance, holding lands in the county whose affairs they administered. The object of this last demand was to obtain men who would possess easily accessible property from which damages could be recovered if they were proved guilty of maladministration. With the failure of the barons' general plan of reform (page 129) all of these suggestions in the field of local govern-

[1] S-M, No. 54D, pp. 181-83.

ment, except that relating to the property qualifications of the sheriff, naturally failed of permanent adoption, and the problem of securing honest and efficient county government was left to perplex later centuries.

## HUNDRED, MANOR, AND TOWN

**The Hundred.** Below the county came the hundred, in which the court continued to meet every three or four weeks, depending on local custom. There administrative as well as legal business was transacted, since the hundred served as a unit for military levies and the assessment of taxes. Twice a year the sheriff visited the court, supplanting the hundredman as the presiding officer. On these occasions he inspected the tithing system, which was now known as frankpledge, that is, free pledge as distinguished from the family one, which was supposedly compulsory in nature.[2] Frankpledge now included an obligation of general suretyship (guarantee of good conduct), as well as the police work of the Saxon period. On these visits the sheriff also looked into the condition of local roads, bridges, and fortifications, and took steps for their repair if necessary. The hundredman (headman of the hundred) was now called a bailiff, and like the sheriff he appointed assistants in the form of clerks and underbailiffs. After 1205 there was also a hundred constable who was charged with turning out the hundred posse to pursue criminals. He was also responsible for inspecting arms to see that they were kept in good repair and for supervising a system which provided bands of unpaid watchmen in each community. These constables lived by fees and various benefits and perquisites, of which per-

[2] In the northern and western border areas frankpledge was not established. Its work was rather done by sergeants of the peace working under the sheriff. They made arrests and presented for crimes. Quite possibly they are the survival of a primitive Anglo-Saxon law-enforcing officer working under the king's reeves, who perhaps even enforced process in the local courts. *Cf.* R. Stewart-Brown, *The Serjeants of the Peace in Medieval England and Wales*, Manchester, Eng., 1936.

haps the most interesting was the right in some places to take the profits accruing from the compulsory revelry of a hundred ale. This was a party on the order of a policeman's ball or a church supper (though with stronger refreshments), which citizens attended willy-nilly at a stiff price. The bailiff himself was chosen in various ways, depending on the local custom of the hundred. Some were elected; others were named by the sheriffs. When the hundred was in private hands—and by the time of Edward I 358 of the entire 628 were—either the lord himself acted as bailiff or he appointed one of his men to do the work. In those cases, of course, the sheriff did not visit the hundred on his tourn (tour) when he was holding "view of frankpledge."

**The Manor: Status of Villeins.** The figures just given on the number of private hundreds suggest something of the extent to which local government was feudalized at the hundred level and below. While we find references to village constables who were responsible to the hundred constables, there is practically no other trace left of the old free villages. They are now all manors, subject to the control of some lord. The men living in them are now bound not only to their lord, but also to the soil. No longer can they take their property and transfer to another master whenever they like. The link that binds them to the manor is a menial version of the feudal contract. Instead of doing military or some other form of "honorable" service, they work on the lord's domain two or three days a week, though in emergencies they are also herded out in their leather coats to do service as foot soldiers. They may not marry without their lord's consent, and they owe him an endless number of extra services, such as assistance with harvests and payments in kind or produce, at various seasons of the year. At the beginning of the Norman period the villein was still considered in law a freeman, and he often participated in the county courts as a full member. Eventually, however, the influence of Roman law, which maintained that all men must be either free or slave, made itself felt, and by the

thirteenth century the villein was considered unfree. One redeeming feature of this situation was that it merged the position
of the former slaves with that of villeins. Since the Church was
anxious to alleviate the lot of the lowest class, absolute slavery
disappeared, and the villein (or one of his fractional subdivisions
—bordar or cotar) now represented the lowest legal rank. By the
thirteenth century it came to be an accepted principle that the
villein, though bound to the soil, could not be sold away from it,
and he had certain rights in it. Since we find landless men buying
the status of a villein, we may be sure that the villein's lot was
not too hard. As a member of his lord's court, as reeve, constable,
possibly even as delegate to the county court, he participated in
the work of local government. Though the freeman (ceorl) of
Saxon times had thus fallen far in the legal scale, he had not put
himself quite beyond the reach of training in self-government.

**The Rising Status of the Towns: Burgage Tenure.** Some local
institutions even provided means of rising from villein status.
The towns, which originally had developed largely as military
centers (page 42), lost that importance when royal castles came
to replace fortified settlements as bases of royal influence. The
growth of trade now gave the towns greatly increased wealth and
a corresponding increase of political prestige. As the kings, or in
some cases the feudal lords, on whose lands they stood felt the
need of their financial support in times of crisis, these dignitaries
became more and more willing to bargain with the burghers. For
a lump sum, cash in hand, they could be persuaded to grant a
charter that made various concessions to the townsmen. The
capture of Richard I and his subsequent need of funds for his
ransom consequently made his reign a period of great advance
on the part of the towns. The most important of the concessions
commonly granted was that of burgage tenure—roughly corresponding to socage tenure in the rural areas—which entitled the
burghers to hold their homes and places of business in return for
an annual money payment only. This had the effect of making

the townsmen freemen. Usually the charters also provided that anyone who had lived in the town unmolested for a year and a day was to be considered a burgher. Accordingly, any villein who might escape from his manor and evade detection in some town for the required length of time could obtain his freedom in this way.

**Other Concessions.** A great many other concessions were made to the towns, of which some of the most common were grants of the rights to hold their own courts and markets, and to elect their own officials. These officials usually consisted of a mayor and aldermen, with sometimes a second council in addition to the aldermen. According to the charter of many towns the local sheriff was not permitted to enter them. All moneys due the king or the lord were collected by the chosen agents of the townsmen themselves, and turned over to the sheriff or the lord's reeve in a lump sum called the farm of the town (*firma burgi*).

## THE ECCLESIASTICAL SIDE OF LOCAL GOVERNMENT

**The Role of the Church.** The Church also provided an avenue of escape for the clever and ambitious villein. With the definite establishment of the principle of clerical celibacy as a result of the Cluniac reforms, the ranks of the clergy had to be recruited afresh in every generation. In other words, there were no hereditary ecclesiastical positions, and the necessity of finding men from other groups to fill the vacancies in church offices made for a very considerable fluidity of class lines. Many of the better places went to members of the upper classes, it is true, for the wealth of the Church naturally attracted the attention of prominent people looking for suitable positions for their relatives. An illegitimate son of Henry II, for example, became Archbishop of York. Furthermore, the kings made a regular practice of rewarding faithful administrative or clerical service in a government office with a lucrative ecclesiastical appointment. As in Dunstan's time, it helped one's chances of advancement in the Church to have a friend at court.

**Recruiting of Churchmen from the Villein Class.** Many an able and aspiring villein's son, however, attracted the attention of the local priest and was diverted from the fields to the study. With his lord's consent, which it was necessary to obtain, he could secure proper training, first from the parish priest himself, then at a monastic or cathedral school, and finally, it might be, even at one of the universities. Once he had his start in the educational system, the height to which he might rise was limited only by his abilities and the amount of political favoritism exercised in behalf of those better connected. The origins of many of the prominent clergymen of this period are lost in an obscurity which suggests little if any family background. Others among the greatest, however, such as Robert Grosseteste, Bishop of Lincoln, are known to have come of very humble parents.

**The Bishops.** Next to the archbishops, who had charge of the ecclesiastical side of the central government, came the bishops, now numbering nineteen, counting four for Wales. As a result of the reforms growing out of the Conquest the seats of many of the sees were moved from small country towns to the larger boroughs, which were then entitled to be called cities.[3] The purpose of this change was to put the bishop in a position where he could exercise greater influence than he could from a rural village. Many of the dioceses were very large, and those of London, Lincoln, Winchester, and Durham—the last-mentioned, being on the northern border, was also a palatine earldom—were almost as important as archbishoprics. The bishops now developed not only their own courts, but full staffs of administrative assistants—chancellors, registrars, and stewards. The ordinary canons—under their presiding officer, the dean—continued to be important, and with the help of Innocent III, as already indicated (page 115), won at least the nominal right to elect the bishop.

[3] In England the term "city" is applied only to towns with cathedrals.

**Archdeacons and Rural Deans.** Between the bishop and the parish priest there developed a set of officials called archdeacons, who roughly corresponded to hundred bailiffs in the secular government. Each of them had a subdivision of the diocese under his supervision. They were expected to visit each parish twice a year, hold court for ecclesiastical cases, and see that all was in good order. Below the archdeacons were other supervising clergy, the descendants of the minster clergy of Saxon times (page 43), who kept watch on smaller subdivisions of the archdeaconries while they did service as priests in their own towns or villages besides. These men were called rural deans.

**The Parish Clergy.** Aside from the enforcement of the requirement of celibacy, the chief alteration in the status of the ordinary parish clergy during this period came from changes in the ownership of advowsons. As the monastic movements grew in strength and popularity, many of the lay patrons were persuaded to turn over their appointment rights to a monastic body. That group usually bargained with a secular clergyman to serve the cure—as the post which involved the care (cure) of souls was called—and the monastery then put most of the parish income into its own funds. Bishops and colleges at the universities sometimes acquired these advowson rights in similar fashion. Where this substitute arrangement was made the incumbent was called a vicar—because he served vicariously for the monastic body or other holder of the legal position—or sometimes merely a curate (one having a cure). If the advowson remained in lay hands, however, and the clergyman received the full income of his position (his living), he was known as a rector, since he had the rule or direction of the parish legally committed to him.

# 8. THE ORGANIZATION AND JURISDICTION OF THE COURTS

## THE CONQUEST AND THE NEW CENTRAL COURTS OF COMMON LAW

**Effect of the Conquest on the Administration of Justice.** The introduction of Roman as well as fully developed feudal theories at the Conquest had a profound effect on the administration of justice in England. No longer was the chief court of the realm an assembly of magnates over which the king did little more than preside. The monarch, as prince and the highest feudal overlord, became the fountain of justice, which he dispensed with the aid of those vassals who happened to be present in the meetings of his Council, whether Great or Small (page 145). The theory that this justice remained that prescribed by the conscience of all good Englishmen was retained as a convenient form of expression, without too curious questioning as to how it could be harmonized with the royal practice.

**Extension of Royal Jurisdiction.** The imperious Norman rulers coolly appropriated huge areas of jurisdiction, and defied anyone to dispute their rights to them. The king's peace (page 33) was greatly broadened. It ran everywhere for eight days after the coronation, and for an equal time at Christmas, Easter, and Whitsuntide. It applied to the four great highways of the realm and for one hundred yards—a good bowshot—on each side. It covered navigable waters leading to cities and boroughs, and by the royal order it could be extended to markets and fairs, to whole classes of persons, or even to types of offenses. It was not far from becoming the peace of the whole land. These encroachments on other jurisdictions were not successfully made by force alone. The fact that the royal courts developed more speedy and efficient means of doing justice gave them a large measure of support from prospective suitors. It was therefore possible to poach on the preserves of both the baronial and the ecclesiastical courts, and to take over civil as well as criminal cases from them.

**Need of New Courts.** The mass of business thus acquired by the royal court demanded the development of an enlarged system of tribunals to cope with it. Not even a Henry II, with his capacity for combining perpetual motion and legal activity, could deal with the pressure of litigation. The classic illustration of this fact is the experience of the unfortunate Richard de Anesty, who won a case only after six years of following the King back and forth across the Channel, during which time he had twenty snatches of hearings, and spent a good share of the value of the lands in dispute.

**The Development of the Court of Common Pleas.** In 1178, responding to the need for simpler methods than these, Henry detached five members of the household part of the Small Council, three laymen and two clerks, and ordered them to remain in Westminster. There they were to "hear the complaints of the realm and do justice." Specially difficult cases were to be referred back to the king, but the five men were to settle ordinary disputes. For the rest of the century these judges appear to have merged with the remainder of the royal court whenever it was in the capital, and therefore to have had a kind of concurrent jurisdiction with the larger body. In the Great Charter, however, it was provided that common pleas were not to follow the king but to be held in a fixed place,[1] and this helped to produce a more distinct cleavage. During the minority of Henry III the courts merged again, but the division was completed in 1234 by the institution of a separate roll, called the *de banco* (bench) roll, for the new court. Thereafter common pleas business was recorded apart from the *coram rege* (in the presence of the king) roll of the parent court. In 1272 a Chief Justice was appointed

[1] Art. 17, S-M, No. 44, p. 118.

to this stationary body, and by the end of the century most of its judges were professional lawyers rather than administrative clerks. Since routine criminal cases eventually came to be taken care of in the local courts, the ordinary pleas heard in this separate court usually concerned what we call civil cases, and hence its jurisdiction was a civil one.[2]

**The Court of the Exchequer.** Another offshoot of the parent body which began even earlier than Common Pleas, but took longer to develop, is the Exchequer in its judicial capacity. As early as the reign of Henry I the Exchequer itself was taking on the double aspect we have already noted (page 138). As the Exchequer of Receipt it was a depository and tally-cutting body. When there were disputes about the royal tax claims, however, in the Upper Exchequer (Exchequer of Account), where the sheriff's records had to be audited, it was necessary to have full sessions of the Small Council to pass on them. These gatherings usually took place at Easter and Michaelmas (St. Michael's Mass, September 29), and were attended by the Justiciar, the Chancellor, the Chamberlain, the Constable, and one or more marshals, as well as by the Treasurer and the Chamberlains of the Exchequer. Other members of the Small Council were frequently present, but the official element predominated. This body took steps to enforce the royal demands, or to sanction compromise settlements. Only slowly, however, did its judicial functions become separated from its accounting ones, and from those of the king's council in general. As their other duties multiplied the Chancellor, Justiciar, and most of the household officials ceased to attend Exchequer meetings. By 1234 a group of Exchequer men called barons—from the general sense of this term to indicate a king's man—had assumed the duties of the Exchequer of Account. In 1235 a separate set of plea rolls begin, and by the end of the century mention is made of a Chief Baron, who,

2 For samples of cases at Common Pleas in the period when it still heard criminal charges, see S-M, No. 54A, pp. 177-79.

with some of his colleagues, came to be a professional lawyer rather than an accountant. But for a long time this court was so intimately connected with the administration of the accounting side of the Exchequer that it was considered inferior to Common Pleas. The jurisdiction of the Exchequer particularly applied to cases concerned with the royal revenue, as we have seen. Because it was also, in a sense, the Small Council, however, many of the early Exchequer sessions were concerned with routine cases of a general sort. Even after the separation from the Small Council the Barons of the Exchequer continued to hear a certain number of private debt cases. The court charged with collecting the royal revenue brooked no delay. It used speedy and effective methods of enforcing its judgments. Naturally, private creditors wished to enjoy similar advantages, and the king sometimes permitted them to use this court. Later this jurisdiction over private cases was to become very important.[3]

**Beginnings of the Court of King's Bench.** The parent body of Common Pleas and Exchequer, the king's court, began to show signs of one more fissure before 1307. The court held *coram rege* (in the king's presence) exercised a general residual jurisdiction. It heard specially difficult cases to which established law did not seem to apply, corrected errors made by lesser courts, and heard cases not assigned to other courts—those concerning important individuals and, in particular, civil cases in which force had been used.[4] In the exercise of these last types of jurisdiction it necessarily became more and more technically legal. Both criminal and civil cases demanded definite rules, and so did the supervision of the work of the lesser courts, especially Common Pleas. The result was the appointment to the king's court of professional lawyers and in 1268 a Chief Justice, whose particular duty it was to hear such pleas *coram rege*. It was no longer

---

[3] For samples of cases tried in the Exchequer in this period, see S-M, No. 54C, pp. 180-81.

[4] For samples of *coram rege* cases in this period, see S-M, No. 54F, pp. 184-85.

considered necessary that the king should attend sessions of his court held for these purposes, and the tribunal did not always follow him on his travels. By the time of Edward I we therefore have the beginnings of the court that was later to be called the King's Bench. Not for another century, at least, is its separation from the council and the presence of the king complete, but it has progressed far enough to enable us to see the direction in which the cleavage is developing.

**Supervisory Jurisdiction of the King's Bench.** The supervisory jurisdiction of the King's Bench needs further explanation. The early medieval mind, as we have seen (page 56), recognized no such thing as a retrial of a case once heard. Theoretically, a decision once reached could not be upset. If the disappointed suitor wished to proceed further, he must start a new action by alleging some delinquency in the conduct of the earlier suit. This might take the form of an accusation of fraud against the judges or jury—after the development of this body (page 195). More often it meant the assertion of an error in the record made of the case. By examining these allegations of "error" the higher court could, in effect, hear an appeal from the lower one, in spite of the theory. Much ingenuity in the employment of technicalities was necessary to make this device fit the needs of suitors, but where the fees were sufficient lawyers were generally able to devise the means. Besides hearing these cases in error, the King's Bench set the bounds to the jurisdiction of rival courts by means of writs of prohibition. These forbade other courts, such as the ecclesiastical ones, to proceed with a particular matter that in the opinion of the royal judges should be dealt with elsewhere (pages 113, 401).

**The Common Law.** The three central courts whose origins we have been describing remained until the nineteenth century the backbone of the English legal system. All were royal courts and, as such, administered a single set of legal principles. Because these principles were common to the whole country and also

because they were not artificially dependent, as it were, on particular statutes, this set of principles came to be called the common law, as contrasted with the diverse and variegated codes
enforced in the local and feudal courts on the one hand, and on
the other, with the special varieties of law introduced afresh at
later times.

## THE ITINERANT JUSTICES

**The General Eyre.** The story of how this royal common law
was extended until it virtually choked out its lesser rivals is
largely the story of the itinerant justices. In early Norman times
the rulers, overwhelmed by the pressure of business, frequently
delegated to subordinates their power to hear a particular case
or type of case in some distant area (page 136). These subordinates might be members of the royal court or prominent men
of the locality concerned, or a mixture of both sorts. Henry II
extended and regularized this practice. The most general commission given was that to hear all pleas. The justices who held
it were known specifically as justices in eyre (Latin *iter*, journey),
and their sessions were called a general eyre. They took over and
superseded the ordinary meetings of the county court, and their
coming involved not only the hearing of civil and criminal cases
but a general overhauling of the whole machinery of county
government. In other words, these visits did for the county what
the sheriff's tourn did for the hundred. The records of the sheriffs
and the coroners were produced, and strict inquiry was made
into the matters there mentioned. The justices also brought rolls
of their own with numerous written queries to which answers
must be given, questions about police administration, misconduct of officials, the usurpation or misuse of franchises, and encroachments upon the rights of the crown such as escheats, ward-
ships, and other sources of revenue. Panels of jurymen were
sworn in to answer these queries, and if the answers of the jury

did not correspond with the records of the sheriff and the coroner, those who had failed to report properly were fined. Then the various suspects were tried. It can be seen that the justices in eyre constituted not only a legal tribunal of some consequence, but also a very important link between the central and the local governments, and a major factor in preserving law and order in the country. So searching were their inquiries and so severe the penalties they exacted that in 1233 the inhabitants of Cornwall took to the woods rather than face the justices. It came to be an established rule that a general eyre should not be held more often than once every seven years. After the development of Parliament as a body with local representatives from whom the central government could obtain information if it chose, this form of visitation was discontinued.

**Other Commissions.** Other more strictly judicial commissions, however, continued to be issued to itinerant justices. Those of gaol (jail) delivery were designed to relieve the pressure on the inadequate prison system of the country (page 62). They empowered their recipients to try all the prisoners in a certain jail, and thus deliver it. Usually they were directed to important men of the community. The commission of oyer and terminer was a broader one, and usually given to royal judges. It authorized them to hear (French *oyer,* hence the modern court attendants' cry of *Oyez,* Hear ye) and settle criminal cases, whether those of men in prison or those out on bail. It might be a general commission or one confined to a particular type of crime, a special place, or even a single offense. The most important commission, short of a general eyre, was that to hear assizes. Originally "assize" meant simply a sitting of a court or assembly (French *assis,* seated). From that it came to apply to the things done, the enactments passed, in such a place. Some of these assizes in the reign of Henry II—to be described in detail later (page 189)— provided arrangements for hearing important real property cases. It was for these that the original commissions of assize were issued, at first only for a single case at a time, then for all of this class in a given area. Later, other powers, such as those included in the criminal commissions mentioned above, were added to these, and as technical legal knowledge became more and more necessary to follow such cases professional lawyers were regularly appointed to exercise them. The Great Charter provided that these assizes be held four times a year in each shire at sessions of the county court.[5]

**The "Nisi Prius" System.** The way was therefore prepared for Edward I, the English Justinian, to integrate the system of itinerant justices with his central courts of common law. Before his return from Sicily, in the first year of his reign four definite circuits had been laid out, to which two judges were to be sent regularly.[6] In 1285, by the great Statute of Westminster II, the final connection with the royal courts was made by means of what was called the *nisi prius* (if not before) system. It was provided that anyone beginning a case in the royal courts, which usually met in the great hall of the royal palace at Westminster,[7] was to be assigned a day in court there, on which the matter was to be heard *if* the assize justices did *not* come into his county *before* that time. If they did, the case was to be heard by them and the decision reported back to Westminster for recording on the roll of the appropriate court there, just as though it had been fully heard and settled in the central tribunal. Since the itinerant justices were expected to come to each county at least once a year, and since the day assigned at Westminster was commonly more than a year in advance, it can be seen that the effect of this statute was to make royal justice easily obtainable in every locality. Specially important cases continued to be heard at Westminster, but ordinarily it was no longer necessary to go to the expense of sending a local jury all the way to the capital.

[5] Art. 18, S-M, No. 44, p. 118.
[6] For a later arrangement of circuits in his reign, see S-M, No. 52G, p. 175.
[7] Exchequer had a special chamber elsewhere in the palace, in which its sessions were held.

At Westminster the courts kept four terms a year, named after the ecclesiastical holidays that immediately preceded them—a long one called Michaelmas, lasting eight weeks in the autumn, and short ones of three to six weeks after Christmas (Hilary, St. Hilary's Day, January 13), in the spring (Easter), and in early summer (Trinity). In the intervening vacations the provincial assizes were held under the *nisi prius* system. Thus it was possible for royal justice to compete most effectively with that of rival lesser courts in the different localities, and it was possible also to give people living at a distance from London a periodic touch of the royal dignity. For the assize justices carried on some of the less objectionable traditions of the justices in eyre. They opened their sessions with a general address to those present, in which they frequently expounded the current royal policy—foreign as well as domestic—and they also reported back to Westminster on the conduct of local governmental officials and popular sentiment on public affairs in the areas which they visited.

## THE COUNTY AND HUNDRED COURTS

**Decline of the County Court.** In the face of such keen competition the jurisdiction of the county court declined markedly in this period. At first the sheriff had often been commissioned as a royal justice, and had turned the county court into a royal one, after the manner of the justices in eyre. The constant complaints against the sheriffs, however, caused their judicial powers to be limited. The Assize of Clarendon (1166) reserved to the royal justices itinerant all jurisdiction over robbery, murder, and theft.[8] Ten years later the Assize of Northampton added forgery, treason, and arson to the special list.[9] The Great Charter virtually finished off the criminal jurisdiction of the county courts by forbidding the sheriff to hold any plea of the crown (page

[8] Art. 1, S-M, No. 31, p. 77.    [9] Art. 1, S-M, p. 80.

158).[10] On the civil side, Henry II reserved all land cases for the royal and feudal courts. The Statute of Marlborough (1267) ordered all pleas of false judgment heard in the king's courts and thus destroyed the quasi-appellate jurisdiction which the county court was in effect exercising over the hundred courts. Finally the Statute of Gloucester (1278), in order to prevent the overcrowding of the royal dockets with minor cases, provided that no case should be heard in the king's courts where the amount at stake was less than forty shillings. By a breath-taking display of royal power and legal imagination the king's judges interpreted this regulation to mean that no case involving more than forty shillings should be heard in the county courts. As the value of money shrank with the years this left the county courts with very little legal work to do.

**And the Hundred Court.** The courts of the free hundreds suffered a fate similar to that of the county tribunals. Their civil jurisdiction was destroyed by the competition of the assize justices. The sheriff's tourn, which was a royal court of record—that is, one which kept a roll of its proceedings that could be referred to later in case of dispute—took over the criminal functions of the ordinary hundred court. As the king's agent, the sheriff came twice a year, and turned the session of the hundred court into a royal court, as the justices in eyre did the county sessions. Besides taking view of frankpledge (page 159), he empaneled a jury from the hundred, which questioned the chief pledges of the tithings and the reeve and four men from each vill as to offenses committed in the hundred since the last tourn. Men accused of the more serious crimes were sent to the itinerant justices. Lesser offenders over whom the court had final jurisdiction were tried and punished (usually by fines) on the spot. In other words, the sheriff's tourn did the work of a modern police court. Drunkards and brawlers might expect justice there. So also those persist-

10 Art. 24, S-M, No. 44, p. 119.

ently pestiferous individuals who sold lightweight bread or over-
charged their customers for flat beer.

## THE FEUDAL AND OTHER PRIVATE COURTS

**Honor Courts.** The feudal courts, though also hard pressed by
royal competition, fared somewhat better in this period than the
county and free hundred courts. This was largely due to the fact
that they represented the interests of the landed class, who naturally used their not inconsiderable political power to protect
them. The establishment of legally complete feudalism on English soil by the Conquest meant not only the reconstruction of
the king's Council on a feudal basis, but also that the vague and
informal relationships existing between the royal vassals (tenants in chief) and their subordinates would also be regulated
according to feudal theory. Those powerful vassals who were
important enough to have many mesne (rear) vassals holding of
them in honorable tenure set up honor courts in which they
administered justice to these freemen. Whenever the lords chose
to hold these courts, the mesne vassals were bound to attend, by
their obligation to suit of court, and a few of these honor courts
became of some importance. Each had its own set of rules, which
might vary greatly from those of its neighbor, but in general
they were empowered to enforce all the terms of the feudal contract and to settle disputes between mesne vassal and mesne
vassal.

**Leet and Manorial Courts.** Below the honor court in the feudal
scale came the court of the individual manor. As the manorial
system had absorbed the remaining free villages of Anglo-Saxon
days, it may be said that every village was under some manorial
court, though there was not a manor for each village, for often
two or three villages would be included in the same manor. The
manorial court, in other words, was the ordinary court for the
medieval villein and the few small freemen, such as socage

tenants, who might live on the manor. But because frequently the lord of the manor also held the franchise for the local hundred court (page 48), the sessions of the tribunals for the manor and the private hundred were often held jointly, and it is not always easy to distinguish between them. The records were frequently kept on a single roll, which recorded the administration of justice for the hundred as a whole and for the manor simultaneously. Where a distinction is possible, the lord's court for the hundred, or at least that part of it which did the work of the sheriff's tourn, is called the court leet, and the session for the manor is again divided in two. That for the free men, where they existed, is entitled the court baron, and that for the villeins is known as the customary court. These courts met every three or four weeks, except the court leet, which like the sheriff's tourn came twice a year. The lord's bailiff usually presided. Where hundred business was included in the work of the court these private courts dealt with cases already mentioned as belonging to the hundred or the sheriff's tourn. In the manorial court the most petty kind of grievances arising from medieval village life were handled. A quarrel between two women over an odd loaf of bread in a joint baking in the lord's big oven might occupy the court. Boys stealing fruit from the lord's orchard were also disciplined there. Even in these court records, which might be expected to show only the seamy side of life on the manor, signs of paternalism appear to remind us that feudal lords, as well as kings and churchmen, did not always insist on the full measure of their legal rights. When a man accused of poaching fish from the lord's pond pleads that his wife was ill and needed this food, the bailiff waives the defense with the reminder that under the circumstances the defendant might have secured this tidbit in a more honorable way.[11]

[11] For a sample of cases heard in the manorial court, see S-M, No. 54H, pp. 187-89.

**Decline of the Honor Courts.** The manorial courts continued to exercise this petty jurisdiction for centuries, and in fact many of them still exist. It was on the jurisdiction of the honor and franchise courts that royal competition bore most heavily. The chief bone of contention between the royal and the honor courts was the right to hear land cases. As long as the lord could retain this jurisdiction over his mesne vassals his court possessed genuine significance, since land was the chief form of wealth. Henry II and his judges attacked this jurisdiction in two ways, which will be explained in greater detail in the next chapter (pages 188, 195), but which must be mentioned here. They invented the very popular system of trial by jury, and forbade the use of juries of freemen in any but royal courts. They also issued writs of *praecipe* that arbitrarily ordered the defendants to hand over the land in dispute to the plaintiff or else to appear before the royal court regardless of feudal obligations. The feudal lords were not strong enough to do anything about the jury matter. They could compel their villeins to take oath and do jury service, but with royal support freemen resisted all efforts to force them to do so outside the king's courts (page 129). In the baronial program incorporated in Magna Carta, however, it was provided (Article 34) that in the future the writ *praecipe* should not be "issued for any one concerning any tenement whereby a freeman may lose his court"—that is, the writ was not to be used to deprive feudal proprietors of their court jurisdiction.[12] This resulted in a temporary setback to the growth of royal jurisdiction, but the feudal methods, lacking the jury of freemen, proved so inadequate and unpopular that within a few years another royal writ (page 191) was devised which evaded the restriction in the Great Charter and restored to the royal court the monopoly on land cases originally claimed. This was a body blow to the honor courts. A second blow, lesser but yet important, was delivered by the Provisions of Westminster (1259), later

12 S-M, No. 44, p. 120.

confirmed by the Statute of Marlborough (1267), which sharply limited the obligation of suit of court resting on mesne tenants (page 129). It provided that this duty could only be enforced if it had been performed within the preceding thirty-nine years, and that subsequent divisions of the property should rather diminish than increase the responsibility. The clauses in the Statutes of Marlborough and Gloucester which confined cases in error and matters of more than forty shillings in value to the royal courts (page 174) further crippled the honor courts.

**And of the Franchise Courts Also.** The franchise courts (pages 48, 176) were effectively dealt with by Edward I. In 1274, as soon as he was well on the throne, he held a sweeping investigation—along the lines of the Domesday inquest—into the question of private jurisdictions. This resulted in the compilation of what were called Hundred Rolls, which give minute information concerning the local government of the period. At a convenient time a few years later the king sent out commissioners armed with writs of *quo warranto,* which empowered them to demand by what warrant, or right, the holders of franchises claimed them. Those who could not show a legally correct written warrant from the crown were to be deprived of their jurisdictions. The commissioners interpreted this rule very strictly in the king's favor, and many who had written authority, of a sort, for their holdings were threatened with deprivation. This resulted in a great protest in which others joined, especially those whose families had exercised these rights for generations without any original documentary proof, or after discarding it as no longer necessary. When asked to produce his warrant one earl brought out an old rusty sword by which, as he said, his ancestors had secured their courts when they aided William the Conqueror, and by which he proposed to retain his. Edward was wise enough to compromise on this issue. By two statutes of 1290 he conceded a liberal interpretation of the written grants, and also confirmed the holdings of those who could prove that their families had had un-

interrupted possession of their franchises from the first year of
the reign of Richard I. By this provision 1189-90 was fixed as the
limit of English legal memory, the time "whereof the memory
of man runneth not to the contrary." To the present day, whatever can be established as having existed in that first year of
the Lion-Hearted's reign is considered for legal purposes to have
existed always. Nevertheless the *quo warranto* procedure brought
about a sharp drop in the number of franchise courts, and the
subsequent strict administration of the royal rules—which evaded
the spirit of the promises of 1290—resulted in a slow but steady
decline thereafter.

## THE ECCLESIASTICAL COURTS

**The Bishop's.** Thanks to Becket and his papal supporters, the
ecclesiastical courts set up after the Conquest fared best of all in
their struggle with the crown, and remained important down
to modern times. We begin with the episcopal courts, which in
their organization and jurisdiction were the most typical of the
church tribunals. Normally the bishop's jurisdiction was exercised by his chancellor in what was called a consistory court.
The bishop might, however, hear cases himself, or he might delegate his judicial authority in certain parts of his diocese to a
special official called a commissary, whose court was therefore
known as a commissary court.

**Their Jurisdiction.** The jurisdiction of these episcopal courts
was a very wide one. On the criminal side, as we have seen, it
included all the offenses of the clergy that would otherwise be
punishable at common law—though after 1170 the criminous
clerks were often tried in the secular courts and only punished in
the church ones—and a large number of other offenses, whether
committed by clerks or by laymen. Some of these offenses were
specifically religious, such as heresy, witchcraft, and blasphemy.
Others had to do with sexual misconduct, drunkenness, slander,

and usury. Men were even prosecuted for plowing up the church path that ran through their fields. On the civil side the ecclesiastics naturally had jurisdiction over specifically religious matters, such as the proper forms of excommunication and the legality of ordination rites. They heard disputes about church goods and finances that did not involve real property. They also had jurisdiction over cases having to do with two very important social institutions, marriages and bequests. Since marriage was considered a sacrament by the medieval Church, it is not difficult to see the origin of this jurisdiction. It included all questions of annulments and legitimacy. The origin of ecclesiastical control over testamentary cases is lost in obscurity, but it was never challenged, even by Henry II. Probably it goes back to the custom of late Saxon times when churchmen were urging laymen to make wills and often drawing them up for their illiterate parishioners. In any case, the jurisdiction extended to the probating of wills,[13] the distribution of the movable goods of intestates, and the conduct of executors and administrators, when these officials developed. This, naturally, put a great deal of power in the hands of churchmen.

**Other Ecclesiastical Courts and Their Relationships.** This sweeping jurisdiction, which in the original theory belonged to the bishop, was in time actually divided with lower and higher courts. The archdeacon in his subdivision of the diocese exercised control over the smaller criminal cases and those having to do with ecclesiastical rites. An appeal lay from his court to the bishop's. This frank recognition of the right of appeal distinguishes the church courts from the secular ones, and did much to slow down their procedure. From the bishop's courts one might appeal to the archbishop, and from him to the papal curia. Even there it was difficult to settle a case permanently, as

---

[13] These covered only personal property in this period (page 221) and should more properly be called testaments, since, strictly speaking, the term "will" is reserved for a document dealing with real property.

the popes were reluctant to commit themselves finally and were regularly willing to grant rehearings, and incidentally to collect new fees. The chief court of the archbishop of Canterbury—presided over by an official Principal—was that of the Arches, so called because it met in the Church of St. Mary le Bow (St. Mary of the Arches), London, which had a steeple supported by arches. This court heard the appeals from the episcopal courts, and also built up a sizable original jurisdiction for itself by poaching on the episcopal preserves in various ways. There was also a Court of Audience for cases that the archbishop wished to hear himself, and for probate cases a Prerogative Court, so called because it drew its authority from a special assertion of the archbishop's power (prerogative). By claiming jurisdiction over all cases in which a man left movable property in two dioceses it acquired most of the important testamentary jurisdiction in the country. The archbishop of York had similar courts for his province.

**Restrictions on Ecclesiastical Jurisdiction.** Two major restrictions on ecclesiastical jurisdiction must be pointed out before leaving this subject. After 1066, when feudal practices and theories were fully developed (page 119), land could not be willed, and if not sold before death had to pass to the heir according to the rules of feudal law. Otherwise, where the land was held by knight service or grand sergeantry, the lords could have been defrauded of their rights of wardship over minor heirs by the willing of the land to an adult relative. This new rule meant that the probate powers of the church courts, when these were established, did not extend to lands, and explains why the rules of succession for real and personal property developed along different lines (page 585). Secondly, the insistence of Henry II and his successors on bringing all land cases into the royal courts took away from the churchmen all power of deciding such important questions as disputed claims to clerical offices. For since the church livings were invariably endowed with lands or tithe rights, they were regarded as real property and treated as such. The Constitutions

of Clarendon provided (pages 111-2) that if there was a dispute
as to whether land was held by lay or clerical (frank almoin)
tenure, the issue was to be settled in the royal court under a
writ called *utrum* (whether).[14] Though it was specifically stated
at the time that if the decision under this procedure was that
the land was held by frank almoin, the case should be finally
settled in the church courts, this rule was subsequently reversed.
The exact process by which this was accomplished remains uncertain, but by the thirteenth century all land cases had been
taken away from the church courts.

## COURTS OF SPECIAL JURISDICTION

**The Boroughs.** There remain to be mentioned several courts
of minor importance, which also remind us that the arm of royal
justice in this period, though long and strong, was nevertheless
far from all-embracing. The feudal lords were not the only ones
who enjoyed franchises. Boroughs also commonly secured the
right to have their court leet for petty criminal cases, as well as
a civil court with jurisdiction roughly corresponding to that of
the court baron, or the civil court for freemen in the feudal system. In addition, these civil courts were by charter frequently
given powers that normally were exercised in the royal courts,
so that most of them had jurisdiction over disputes involving
more than forty shillings, and many even heard cases involving
real property.

**Other Courts of Special Jurisdiction.** Other special interests
also acquired the right to their own courts. Some of these privileged interests, like the towns, were predominantly commercial.
Towns frequented by foreign merchants often set up courts that
decided cases according to the customs of those engaged in foreign trade. Courts merchant, these were sometimes called. In the
port towns these courts paid special attention to the problems of

14 Art. 9, S-M, No. 30, p. 75.

sailors and shippers and decided questions according to the custom of seafaring men. Individuals or boroughs controlling fairs were frequently given the right to administer the mercantile type of justice to those in attendance. Since these were often peddlers, who came with dusty feet (French, *pied poudré*), these courts came to be known, from the Anglicized form of the phrase, as piepowder courts. The tin-miners of Devon and Cornwall had their special courts, called stannaries from the Latin term for "tin." Professional as well as commercial and industrial people pressed their special claims. The ordinary ecclesiastical courts we have already mentioned. Besides them the churchmen making up the universities at Oxford and Cambridge were given extensive jurisdiction in both criminal and civil matters. A student might commit any offense short of mayhem against a townsman in the happy assurance that, as one who enjoyed clerical status, he would answer for it only in his benevolent court. The king himself made use of this system of special jurisdictions and had separate courts of his own for particular purposes. Of these the most important were those for his hunting-preserves, the forest courts in which special coroners duly conducted solemn inquests on the bodies of deer found slain. For when not out killing them himself, the Conqueror "loved the tall stags as if he were their father," and his successors also guarded them zealously. In addition, the king had a special tribunal for the army, the Court of the Constable and Marshal (page 142), which administered martial law, that is to say, the rules of military discipline. These royal tribunals enforced almost savage penalties on their victims. Hanging was the usual punishment for poaching the royal game. This may serve to remind us that in spite of numerous and striking examples of special privilege in this period, the royal courts were the agencies of justice chiefly feared. That fact in itself marks the great advance of the Norman and Angevin system of justice over the Saxon one.

# 9. PROCEDURE AND THE LEGAL PROFESSION

**General Changes Produced by the Conquest.** In the field of legal procedure the period following the Conquest is marked, as might be supposed, by a sharp decline in the amount of self-help required and a great extension of the areas in which royal assistance was available for the conduct of a case at law. It is also noteworthy for the increase in the complexity and technicality of the law, which made necessary the development of a professional class of lawyers to cope with the new system. Any hasty conclusions as to the advisability of this change should be postponed until it is also possible to see the greater flexibility, subtlety, and comprehensiveness which this development brought to the substantive law of the time.

## THE INITIATING STEP IN CRIMINAL CASES

**Appeal.** In discussing the whole topic of procedure, we naturally consider first and in greatest detail that employed in the royal courts. At the beginning of this period it was still the custom for the victim of what we now call crimes to initiate his own case. He did this, however, not by serving notice on his adversary, but by accusing him in open court. This act was called an appeal, and is not to be confused with a request for a rehearing of a case. But if the charge was a serious one, it was considered a plea of the crown, and the king and his agencies co-operated in pressing it. The sheriff was required to make any necessary arrest, and the royal courts took jurisdiction of the offense.

**Jury Indictment.** Often, however, no one dared to make such an appeal when the offender was a prominent or powerful man. Henry II undertook to remedy this difficulty by bringing the great engine of the jury to bear on the problem. This institution was one which the English owed to the Roman-Carolingian heritage (that of Charlemagne's empire) which the Normans brought with them. The term "jury" comes from the Latin *jurati,* meaning a body of sworn men, and was originally applied to such a body put on oath to tell the truth in answer to some particular question. The Romans had used juries to extract the information necessary to make proper tax assessments. The Carolingian kings of the Franks used it for obtaining the facts on all manner of topics of governmental interest. There is one slight trace of such an institution's being used for accusing suspected criminals in Anglo-Saxon England, which perhaps represents a preliminary borrowing from the Continent. For certainly the great popularity of the jury on the island dates from Norman and early Angevin times, and the English jury is therefore Norman rather than Saxon in origin. William the Conqueror employed it in compiling the Domesday Book. He and his successors used it occasionally for judicial purposes, such as settling disputes over rights to property. Accordingly it was not difficult for the energetic Henry II to develop it to meet the need of restoring law and order after he became king. In the Constitutions of Clarendon (1164) Henry offered this royal support to the ecclesiastical courts in their efforts to punish lay offenses that belonged in their jurisdiction—an offer conditional, of course, on the churchmen's doing the royal bidding in the matter of real property actions and criminous clerks:

> If the guilty persons are such that no one wishes or dares to accuse them, the sheriff, on being asked by the bishop, shall have twelve lawful men from the neighborhood, or the vill, placed on oath before the bishop to set forth the truth in the matter according to their own knowledge.[1]

1 Art. 6, S-M, No. 30, p. 74.

Two years later, by the Assize of Clarendon, the same practice was adapted to the secular courts.[2] The itinerant justices and sheriffs were charged with holding such inquests (as the inquiries were called) into robbery, murder, and theft (page 173). In the Assize of Northampton (1176) arson and counterfeiting were added to the list, and the practice of employing the indicting jury in the royal courts became general thereafter.[3] We have already noticed (page 174) the sheriff's employing it on his tourn, and holding the accused for the sessions in eyre or the later assizes.

**The Survival of Appeal.** Procedure by appeal was not immediately displaced by the use of the jury to obtain indictments or presentments, as they were called. It lingered on through the Middle Ages, partly as a device by which a criminal might turn king's (state's) evidence and accuse his accomplices. It was also used occasionally by those who were not satisfied by the results of a criminal trial under the jury system. For it permitted such a case in which the defendant had been acquitted to be reopened by the different type of accusation, which in the eyes of the law made it an altogether new case.

## THE INITIATION OF CIVIL CASES

**The Writ System.** Civil cases, as we call them, were begun in the royal courts by means of the writ system. Because the suitor wished to make use of the king's court rather than his own hundred or shire court, he had to pay for the privilege, and he did so by purchasing from the Lord Chancellor's office (Chancery) a document giving him permission to begin his action in the royal court. These written documents were called writs, and because they were used to begin a case they were called original writs. This was in contrast with mesne (intermediary) writs, such as a writ of prohibition (page 169), which might be employed

[2] Art. 1, S-M, No. 31, p. 77.          [3] Art. 1, S-M, No. 32, p. 80.

after a suit was once begun to direct, hinder, or aid its further progress. The particular original writ secured gave explicit directions to the sheriff as to the steps to be taken, and in that way largely determined the subsequent procedure to be followed in the case, in other words, the form of the action. The original writs and the forms of action which they began came therefore to be known by the same name. As already indicated (page 55), English practice allowed adjective law to have a very great effect on substantive law. The legal doctrines employed in a given case thus came to be greatly influenced by the form of the action. Consequently, though the forms themselves have now been abolished in most jurisdictions, they rule us from their graves, in the phrase of the great legal historian Maitland. So it is necessary to explain this system in some detail.

**Its Growth.** The royal justices, as we have seen (page 168), became very technical and sometimes rigid in their interpretation of the law, perhaps partially from a desire to make more business for their courts and more money for the king. Accordingly they often refused to recognize the validity of a writ already purchased, on the ground that it did not properly cover the case in hand. "It is not for us," said the justices to a disappointed suitor who asked on such an occasion what writ would be satisfactory, "to tell you what writ is needed. But you must find that out for yourself." Although the Chancery clerks were required to obtain the authorization of the king and the Council for all new writs, they seem in practice to have secured this rather easily, and to have been able to devise new writs almost at will. Since they probably received extra fees for inventing new writs, they were glad to co-operate in multiplying their number. Thus eventually there came to be several hundred in all, with which the medieval lawyer had to be familiar. For our purposes it is sufficient to describe some of the leading ones. We begin with those for real actions.

## THE WRITS FOR REAL ACTIONS

**Right.** The oldest of these was the writ of right, which empowered the purchaser to begin an action concerning the ownership of land.[4] This action normally was heard in the feudal court of the suitor's lord, but as the royal claim to supervise all land actions made itself felt, this type of case, although feudal, could not be begun without this writ. When the royal prerogative became even stronger in the thirteenth century, the feudal courts were prohibited from proceeding with such actions at all. This writ was called the writ of right because it commanded the feudal lord to give the claimant who secured the writ full right (justice) in the matter at issue.

**"Praecipe."** Closely related to the writ of right was the writ *praecipe* (command), which instructed the sheriff to command the defendant to restore the land in dispute or answer for his refusal in the royal court.[5] This writ was at first used only by the king's tenants in chief, but mesne tenants who wished to avail themselves of royal justice were later permitted to purchase it also. The resulting encroachment on the feudal courts was temporarily stopped by Article 34 of Magna Carta (page 177), which barred the use of this writ in such cases. Because the writ *praecipe*, like the writ of right, was used to settle disputes about the ownership of land it came in time to be known as a writ of right also.

**Weakness of Writs of Right.** This was because it finally settled —as between the contending parties—the question of right, or ownership, in contrast to mere possession, with which another set of writs was concerned. Since land was the chief form of wealth in medieval England, the courts gave elaborate protection to rights in it. They were extremely reluctant to deprive a man of his title, and did not do so without giving him every oppor-

---

[4] S-M, No. 33E, p. 84.          [5] S-M, No. 33F, p. 84.

tunity to protect his interests. One of the safeguards observed
was the provision that no man might lose his right to land unless he was present in court when the case was heard. A defendant who realized that he had no right to certain property could
hold it for years by resisting process. The law permitted an
essoin (delay) of a year and a day for illness. By giving an accom-
plice a half-interest in the property and having him conveniently
taken ill as the first year's delay drew to a close, what was called
a fourched (forked) essoin (of which the two parts fitted together like the tines of two forks) was set up which might delay
proceedings almost indefinitely, though the courts were empowered to investigate and punish fraudulent essoins. Another weakness of the writ of right was that under it the defendant always
had the option of choosing trial by battle, in which some plain-
tiffs were reluctant to engage.

**The Possessory Assizes: "Novel Disseisin."** To provide substantial justice in such cases Henry II's advisers, true to the already
traditional practice of not abolishing an old rule that had proved
unsatisfactory but devising a way of getting around it, worked
out a new kind of writ. Because the provision for this writ happened to be incorporated in the Assize of Northampton (1176)
it, and others like it, were called assizes, but in effect they were
original writs. This invention was *novel disseisin* [6] (French, recent dispossession), an assize, or writ, that empowered its purchaser to have a jury empaneled to answer the question "Did
A dispossess B of his land since the king last crossed the sea [or
some other recent date]?" If the answer was in the affirmative,
B was to be restored to his possession (seisin) at once. No final
settlement had been made, however, because only possession and
not right had been determined, and if A still felt that he had
the better *right* to the property he might purchase a writ of
*praecipe* (right) and begin the longer action. Because this possessory writ theoretically gave only a temporary decision, the

6 S-M, No. 33B, p. 83.

action could be conducted in the absence of the defendant, who might stay in bed as much as he liked without delaying the case. Accordingly this form of action became very popular. So many requests were made for it that the commission to take the assizes became, as already noted (page 171), one of the chief ones held by the itinerant justices.

**Others.** Soon there were demands for other possessory writs for cases which *novel disseisin* did not cover. The most important of these was *mort d'ancestor* (death of the ancestor).[7] This was used by heirs who had been prevented from obtaining possession of their father's, uncle's, or brother's (or the corresponding female relative's) lands after the death of the ancestor. Because the heirs had never been in possession themselves, they could not say that they had been disseised, and therefore *novel disseisin* would not help them. *Mort d'ancestor* allowed them to have a jury asked whether their immediate relative died possessed of the property. If an affirmative answer was given, they were to be put in possession, while the other claimant was allowed to sue further under the writ of right if he chose. Such were the technicalities of the time that the original limits of this writ were interpreted very strictly, and other writs had to be worked out where the relationship involved was more complicated than those covered by the first writ. In the thirteenth century three new writs, *aiel, besaiel,* and *cosinage,* were devised to cover the cases in which the heir was trying to secure seisin of lands left by his grandparent, great-grandparent, or cousin respectively. For no other good reason except that they were newer, these three original writs carried with them a more efficient process and procedure at later stages of the case than did the older forms of possessory actions. Another important possessory writ dating from the time of Henry II was that of *darrein presentment* (last presentment) for temporarily settling disputes over advowson rights.[8] It gave the temporary privilege

[7] S-M, No. 33A, pp. 82-83.        [8] S-M, No. 33D, pp. 83-84.

of appointing to a church living in dispute to the one who had last presented a candidate to the living, and left his rival to have recourse to a writ of right of advowson if he was so inclined.

**Entry.** The last of the important real property writs to be developed in this period is that of entry. This gave the purchaser the privilege of obtaining an answer to the question "Did A, who is the present tenant, enter upon the disputed land by means of a particular faulty title as alleged by the plaintiff?" This was originally useful in cases where a disseisin had been committed but the guilty party had died before the case could come to trial, and the land had passed into other hands. After Magna Carta outlawed the writ *praecipe* it was possible to expand the uses of this writ to cover virtually all forms of actions in right. This development began soon after 1215 and was completed by 1267. Because the procedure used under entry was simpler than under either right or *novel disseisin*, this writ by the end of the period came to be used for practically all types of actions concerning the ownership of land, though in theory it only supplemented the older forms of action, and the assizes were still used in many individual cases.

## THE PERSONAL WRITS

**Covenant, Debt, Detinue, and Replevin.** The important original writs for what we call personal, as opposed to real, actions do not require so much explanation. Covenant was a writ which covered cases of promises made in writing and formally sealed, usually those having to do with leases of land, which were not considered fit subjects for real actions because they gave only a temporary control of the property. A writ of debt permitted the purchaser to sue in the royal courts for money owed. Detinue granted a similar privilege in case the thing loaned was a chattel (originally identical with "cattle," but later used as the equivalent of any movable goods) instead of money. If the plaintiff was successful, the defendant could restore either the chattel or its money equivalent, and thus we see the beginning of the historical distinction between real and personal actions. Replevin covered goods taken by distress and illegally held thereafter. The law would not yet enforce contracts, or promises not made in the form of covenants under seal, and consequently no writs were available for such a purpose during this period.

**Trespass.** The most important of all the personal writs was that of trespass *vi et armis* (by force and arms). This permitted the initiation of cases for damages caused by trespass on one's person, goods, or land. Since the offense involved violence, it was considered a semicriminal one, and if the defendant lost, he might be punished as a criminal besides having to pay damages to the plaintiff. The law therefore allowed arrest as the process in this form of action. Consequently it was much speedier and more effective than the others, in which process depended, for the most part, on distress (page 57). As a result, there was a strong tendency to enlarge the action of trespass so as to make it fit the cases covered by the other forms of action. A section of the Statute of Westminster II (1285) contributed to that end. Because of a protest by the barons in the Provisions of Oxford (1258) against the multiplication of new writs the Chancellor's clerks had been somewhat restricted in the freedom with which they issued new ones. Since this proved to be too drastic a check on the development of the law, the new statute provided that instead of turning men away empty-handed when no writ could be found which exactly fitted the need, the Chancery clerks should give them one if there was a legal writ that applied in a similar case (*in consimili casu*). By alleging some sort of trespass in connection with the injuries that gave rise to the other personal actions, we shall see (page 291) that later lawyers were able greatly to expand the scope of this form of action.

## PROCESS AND PLEADING

**Process.** In criminal cases, as already suggested, the normal process was by arrest, in which the inhabitants of the locality where the offense occurred were expected to co-operate with the constables and the sheriff. If a fugitive evaded arrest, he was exacted, that is, asked for or demanded, in five successive county courts. If at the end of that time he did not appear, he was outlawed. Thereupon all the outlaw's property was legally forfeited, and he himself might be slain by anyone on sight. In real property cases one theoretically compelled appearance by the sheriff's summons, the taking of pledges, the attachment of chattels, or eventually the seizure of the land and the award of it to the plaintiff subject to a subsequent suit in right if the defendant chose. Actually, endless essoins were permitted in right cases, as we have seen (page 189), and in the others an obstinate defendant with a clever lawyer could bring about almost as many delays. Process in personal actions was carried out in much the same way as that for real actions, except that usually it was impossible to seize the actual thing in dispute. Here also a little stubbornness mixed with ingenuity could easily hold up a final decision for several years.

**Civil Pleading.** If and when the defendant appeared in court, the pleading followed. First the defendant repeated the flat denial of Saxon times, but exceptions or supplementary answers were now allowed, and these permitted greater flexibility in determining the exact nature and the amount of the disagreement. To the plaintiff's original declaration (count) the defendant could, of course, answer with an admission of fault and confess judgment. Otherwise he might answer it in one of several ways. He could enter a demurrer or a plea. The defendant who demurred admitted the facts alleged in the plaintiff's count, but denied that they involved any legal cause of action.

That raised an issue of law. Otherwise he entered one of several pleas. There were a variety of these possible. The defendant might plead to the jurisdiction of the court—denying its control over the case; he might allege some matter, such as infancy,[9] that would suspend the action; he might plead in abatement, asserting a defect in the writ or declaration; or in bar—that is, give an answer on the merits of the count. This last might take the form of the flat denial, now called a traverse, or of confession and avoidance. The latter was an admission of the facts alleged but with the production of other facts to avoid the conclusion originally drawn. If this last course were taken, the plaintiff replied with either demurrer, traverse, or confession and avoidance, and so on until an issue of law or fact was reached. A great deal of legal learning was expended on the permutations and combinations possible under this system, for the most important objective in many cases was to get an issue favorably stated.

**Criminal Pleading.** Criminal pleading followed much the same pattern, though on simpler lines. Because suspects were not allowed legal advice until the nineteenth century, the judges compensated them for this handicap by permitting a great deal of latitude in the number of technical pleas permitted them. For this and other reasons a man might have an indictment thrown out because it alleged the commission of a crime on the Feast of St. Peter without specifying which of the two annual feasts of that saint was intended. This is the background from which many of the hair-splitting devices of modern criminal lawyers have been developed.

[9] That is, that he was a minor and therefore not obligated to defend the suit until he became of age.

## METHODS OF TRIAL

**Battle.** As methods of trial the Normans continued the use of the Saxon compurgation and ordeal, but introduced two very important supplementary devices. Compurgation was employed in the routine civil cases, and the pre-Conquest types of ordeal often served to test accusations of a criminal nature. A new kind of ordeal was brought in, however, for civil actions in which land was concerned and as an alternative method in criminal cases. This was ordeal (trial) by battle, of which the new rulers were very fond. As late as the time of John we find inserted in the arrangements for a suit the notation "Let this duel be held before the lord king, for he wishes to see it." As the name implies, this device was a combat between the plaintiff or complaining witness and the defendant, which involved a simple appeal to the God of Battles to give victory to the cause of right. Men were armed with long staffs, or sometimes swords, and required to fight until one was vanquished, or even slain if he refused to admit defeat. If no decision was reached by the time the first star appeared, the defendant won if still on his feet. Women were allowed to be represented by a male champion.

**The Jury.** By the time of Henry II people began to doubt whether God always did what was expected of Him in these ordeals. There was more than a little suspicion that the wounded hand of many a sturdy culprit healed so rapidly that its owner escaped the punishment due him, and that in trial by battle it was more important to be strong and skilled at arms than to have a just quarrel. Accordingly men began looking for an alternative method of trial. The Saxon tradition of trial by witnesses, combined with the Norman experience of the jury as a fact-finding body, provided a natural solution for the difficulty. As already noted (page 185), the jury was used sporadically by the Norman kings as a method of settling judicial disputes. Henry II and his legal advisers considered the problem of disorder during many night watches (*multis vigilliis*), as Bracton, the legal writer of the next century tells us, and then decided to regularize this jury procedure.

**Civil Uses.** We have already noted the use of the jury for trial purposes in the possessory assizes (page 189). Many other uses for it in civil actions soon developed. As a supplement to the writ of right or *praecipe* it was provided that the defendant to the suit might purchase the privilege of having the matter at issue decided not by battle but by a jury. This type of jury was called the grand assize to distinguish it from the possessory juries, whose proceedings were not considered so important because they did not determine ultimate ownership. The grand assize procedure protected the peaceful landholders from the legal robbery practiced by their more warlike neighbors. No longer did they have to lose land and honor, or life, in judicial battles. The contemporary legal writer Glanvil said:

This assize is a kind of royal benefit, granted to the people through the kindness of the prince on the advice of great men, by means of which men's lives and the integrity of their status are so helpfully taken into consideration that in maintaining the right which they possess in free tenement of land, men are able to avoid the doubtful issue of trial by battle. And thus it happens that one can escape the extreme sacrifice of an unexpected and premature death, or, if not that, the stain of eternal disgrace resulting from that hateful and untrue word ["*Craven*": I am a coward and yield] which sounds so shamefully in the mouth of the conquered.

As pleading grew more complicated, it was readily realized that the right to use the jury as a method of trial would have to be extended beyond the bounds of the original assizes. For example, if an heir secured his estates and then sold them, he could, at first, defraud the purchaser by bringing an action of *mort d'ancestor* and recovering possession of them while still retaining the proceeds of the sale, for his relative had certainly died seised of the land in question. Naturally, the defendants in such cases began putting in exceptions in their pleas, avoiding the force of the original allegation by asserting the facts that put the matter in its true light. Though no provisions for a jury trial of such supplementary allegations were made by the original assizes, it was soon recognized as only proper and fair that the person who submitted his quarrel to an assize procedure must allow the jury to pass on all its aspects. In this and similar ways trial by jury was extended to cover the great bulk of civil cases, though compurgation was for many years still permissible under some of the older forms of action, such as debt.

**Criminal Uses: Distrust of the Ordeal.** On the criminal side the matter was more complicated, because the proving of a serious charge commonly meant mutilation or death. Men in such jeopardy were thought to be entitled to the most sacred of all trials, the ordeal. It was commonly considered unjust to punish men severely after a verdict obtained by human means when a divine tribunal was available. Yet the suspicion of the validity of the ordeal had reached such a state by 1166 that in the Assize of Clarendon it was provided that if a suspect "made his law" and was cleared by it, he should nevertheless be banished if he was "of very bad reputation, being publicly and shamefully denounced by the testimony of many lawful men." [10] In other words, the opinion of the indicting jury constituted, in effect, a reserve means of trial, as a result of which some punishment was meted out even when the ordeal failed to bring about a conviction. A similar provision was repeated in the Assize of Northampton ten years later.[11]

**The Writ "De Odio et Atia."** Another factor contributing to the growth of trial by jury in criminal cases was the use by blackmailing ruffians of an appeal method of initiating a suit. An unscrupulous bully, knowing that he could easily beat a

---

[10] Art. 14, S-M, No. 31, p. 78.     [11] Art. 1, S-M, No. 32, p. 80.

prosperous but peaceful man in a trial by battle, would threaten to appeal him of a crime unless a good-sized payment were forthcoming. To counter these tactics, the king and his judges permitted the accused to purchase the right to have a jury determine whether he had been accused in good faith or merely out of hate and spite (*de odio et atia*). If the jury answered that the charge had been brought from such motives, this virtually, though not necessarily, ended the case. In effect, therefore, the offering of this writ constituted permission for many suspects to have a jury trial if they wished, and by the end of the twelfth century those who were presented by indicting juries were given a similar option. These trial juries were known as small or petty (French *petit*, small) juries to distinguish them from the indicting or grand jury. The grand jury was so called, probably, because as the initiating body it was considered more important, but perhaps also because it was commonly a larger body of from twelve to twenty-four men.

**The Decline of the Ordeal as a Means of Trial.** There remained, however, the class of obviously guilty persons who refused to be tried by their country, as this representative method —the jury acting as representatives of the district concerned— was called. The problem they presented was made very much more acute in 1215 by the action of the great ecclesiastical council—called the Fourth Lateran Council, from the Roman church where it met—in prohibiting priests from taking any further part in ordeals. The motive for this rule was to protect the priests from the temptations of secular interests in general, and particularly from that of accepting bribes in their capacity of judges of the condition of wounds. Its effect was to terminate the use of the old Saxon ordeals by iron and hot water. Trial by cold water had come to be used only in special cases. Trial by battle, in which priests were not needed, could still be used when a criminal case was begun by an appeal, but where the accusation had been made by a jury there was no one to fight the suspect if he demanded that the charges be proved on his body. Neither the king nor any champion of his fought in cases in which he was concerned, and jurymen could not be expected to do so.

**"Peine Forte et Dure."** Nevertheless the conscience of the time could not bring itself to require that the accused accept human means of trial. The result was the development of a curiously indirect means of attaining the desired end—a procedural device quite typical of the English law, as we have already seen (page 177). When the castles and mills were filled to bursting and notorious sheep-stealers went on placidly declining to accept the logic of the situation and be tried by their fellow mortals, harassed officials decided to use stronger arguments than reason. They loaded the recalcitrants with heavy chains, and sometimes neglected to feed them. This kind of treatment induced some of the victims to take the long chance of escape that a jury trial afforded. Others remained obstinate, however, because they had property, which throughout this period was automatically forfeited on conviction of serious crime (page 121). They preferred to suffer any misery rather than leave their families destitute. In such cases it soon became the practice to do away with the prisoners by an elaboration of the original technique of persuasion. Stones were piled on these unfortunate prisoners until they were crushed to death. This practice was known as *peine forte et dure* (pressure hard and severe). Those who died in this way did so without having been legally convicted of any crime, and thus their families succeeded to their property.

**Character of the Early Jury.** By these methods, trial by jury was extended to nearly all cases, both civil and criminal. It should be noted, however, that the jury in this period was not identical in character and function with the modern body which carries its name. Its numbers remained uncertain, though twelve was coming to be a favorite size. In criminal cases the distinction between grand and petty jury was not yet clear, and the trial jury was often merely the indicting jury consulted a second time, or the indicting jury afforced (strengthened) by the addition of supplementary members. Certainly to the end of this period individual members of the grand juries frequently served on the trial body. Most important of all the primitive features of these early juries is the fact that they were still considered as sources of information rather than judges of fact. They were chosen from the immediate neighborhood concerned because they were supposed to be able to tell the truth of matters in dispute if they could only be forced to divulge it. They were themselves sworn bodies of witnesses, so to speak, and not impartial judges of fact listening to other witnesses. One by-product of this status as witnesses was that until after the end of this period unanimity was not required of juries, since it was supposed that their statement reflected merely the preponderance of the evidence and not an absolute judgment of the truth or falsity of a fact. No other witnesses were known to the law of this time, and the absence of any provision for them led to great looseness and complication in the pleading stage of trials. For the parties concerned naturally endeavored to bring in facts of supposed evidential value by putting them in the pleading.

## THE REMAINING STEPS

**Judgment.** The judgment continued to follow the result of the trial, though some leeway was left to the judges, especially in criminal cases where the amount of the penalty was not definitely fixed.

**Appeals in Error.** Appeals as such were not permitted in the secular courts during this period, but, as already explained (page 169), by the device of alleging an error in the record of the case something of the same end was attained. Common Pleas had jurisdiction in error over the county and hundred courts, and the King's Bench over Common Pleas. Charges of errors in Exchequer were heard by a special commission, which commonly included the original judges (barons) with afforcements from other royal officials.

**Attainting the Jury.** Another method of securing justice after failure in the first attempt was to purchase a writ of attaint and sue the jury that had rendered the faulty decision. This was a semicriminal action which the courts allowed on the ground that the jurymen knew the truth and were sworn to tell it. Therefore they were liable if they did not do so. By the end of this period attaint procedure was allowed in all actions concerning land, and later it was extended to personal ones.

**Execution.** The execution of the judgments of the royal courts was uniformly committed to the sheriff and his assistants. For as the state grew stronger self-help at this stage of the case became virtually unknown. If necessary the sheriff seized the defendant's goods to collect the judgment in civil cases, but the loser's lands were considered exempt for the reasons suggested above (page 188). After the Statute of Acton Burnel (1285) the defaulting debtor might be imprisoned. In the serious criminal cases, where death was the usual penalty (page 225), and appeals were not permitted, execution followed the judgment very summarily. "Let him see a priest" is the ominous ending of many records of criminal cases.

**Procedure in Other Courts.** Space does not permit of detailed explanations of the procedure in those other medieval courts which, though very important at the time, have not had material effect on the later development of Anglo-American legal procedure. All that can be said is to remind the reader that the right to employ juries of freemen was a royal prerogative that set the king's courts apart from, as well as ahead of, their rivals. The Church and the nobles were driven to depend on "inquisitorial" methods in which judges took the lead in extracting evidence from reluctant witnesses and in deciding the cases. These methods in time came to be regarded as "un-English," and so help to account for the unpopularity of the tribunals which used them.

## THE LEGAL PROFESSION AND ITS LITERATURE

**Growth of the Legal Profession.** All the niceties of legal procedure that we have been describing did not grow of themselves. They were carefully worked out by men who made it their chief business, men who could sit up nights thinking them out because they were royal officials and could devote their full time to this activity. Some of these were merely Chancery clerks who devised new writs. Others were the royal judges and Justiciars who might technically be churchmen, paid only indirectly by the crown through ecclesiastical preferments, but who were in reality full-time civil servants. An Italian named Vacarius taught Roman civil and canon law at Oxford in the middle of the twelfth century, and the legal advisers of the crown ordinarily combined a background of Roman theory with a day-by-day experience of English realities. The result was the production of a legal literature not unaffected by Continental principles, but yet adapted to the established customs of the land with which the authors were dealing.

**Glanvil and Bracton.** The first of these expositions—*Treatise on the Laws and Customs of England*—goes by the name of Ranulf de Glanvil, Justiciar under Henry II, though it was more probably written by someone else, possibly his nephew Hubert Walter, later Justiciar himself under Richard I. The work gives, at any rate, our clearest information as to the theory and procedure in the great formative period of English law. In the middle of the next century a similar work—*Concerning the Laws and Customs of England*—was compiled by a judge who is known as Bracton, though his name actually was Bratton or Bretton. He had a very good background of Roman law, and since his large work proved a mine of information for later students, he did a great deal to import and naturalize the more highly developed law of the Continent. Yet he accepted the traditional English attitude on the relation of the king to the law (page 134). In a celebrated passage he maintained that while superior to all other men, the ruler should be under God and the law, because the law makes the king. Britton and Fleta, who wrote in the reign of Edward I, borrowed largely from Bracton, though they contributed some additional information on the state of the law in their time.

**The "Year Books."** Besides the official records such as the court rolls and the statutes, which were put upon a separate unofficial Chancery roll in 1299, the other important type of legal literature to develop in this period was the *Year Book*. This was an annual collection of outstanding cases, made unofficially and as a commercial enterprise, to sell to lawyers. As the law came to depend more and more on precedent (page 208), such collections became very popular among the legal profession. Bracton, for example, had copied down some two thousand important cases for his own use. The series of annual volumes began in the reign of Edward I.

**Pleaders, or Barristers.** The legal profession, in the sense of a body whose services were available to the ordinary layman as distinct from the king, dates from the thirteenth century, though traces of amateur activity in this field may be seen in Norman times. From its earliest appearance the profession was divided into two categories, the pleader and the attorney. As early as the time of Henry I a man was allowed to have a pleader speak for him, so as to escape the rigor of the Anglo-Saxon rule that a slip of the tongue meant the loss of the case. The party to the action listened to his pleader and had the right to disavow any of his statements. The increasing complication of the law in general, and pleading in particular, further stimulated the demand for skilled pleaders. Churchmen often did this work, but after 1180, as suggested above (page 198), the ecclesiastical authorities frowned on such secular interests of the monks and priests. Though the regulations were occasionally evaded, they led to the development of lay practitioners of the pleading art. By 1253 these lay pleaders had a definite organization and were taking apprentices. The apprentices were taught partly by lectures, but largely by having them attend court and observe the conduct of suits. In 1305 a Chief Justice was puzzled by a knotty case that he suspected had been devised by students who purchased a writ to have it tried to see what the decision would be.

**The Attorneys.** In England the pleader (or barrister, as he is now called from the fact that he appears at the bar of courts) has always outranked the other lawyers, from whom he has held himself apart. Perhaps part of the reason for this is that because pleading was originally such an important part of the law, it demanded much more learned practitioners than did the attorney's work, much of which could be done by rule of thumb. For the business of the attorney at first was largely to lighten his client's burden of suit of court in the feudal system. Since a man was obligated to attend his lord's court, and since he might hold land from several different lords, this requirement, as the Provisions of Westminster (page 128) showed, was a real source of annoyance to tenants. If someone could be retained to make the necessary appearances, the tenants would be glad to pay for this service. The law, which could admit the right of a man to secure assistance in conducting his business in court, was, however, slow to grant the individual the right to be absent from court altogether when he was legally concerned in its deliberations. For such a concession royal permission was commonly considered necessary, but conditions resulting from the Crusades finally compelled a certain generosity in this respect. Obviously a Crusader could not fulfill his obligations of suit of court in person, and substitutes had to be allowed. Once such permission was secured by some people, it was difficult to refuse it to others, even though they were not Crusaders, and the practice of having attorneys therefore became more general. Those who had many appearances to make found it worth while to have a full-time attorney. Some of these professional attorneys did little more than attend feudal courts, but others were used by their masters to draw up legal papers and do other routine work of this sort. Since the right to have an attorney was considered a great privilege, the courts supervised the system carefully, and the royal ones required that all litigants should appoint their attorneys in court. As the custom of employing attorneys developed, the courts continued to regulate the practice and keep control of the profession. This is the origin of the modern rule that an attorney is an officer of the court and not merely an employee of his client.

# 10. SUBSTANTIVE LAW

## NORMAN IDEAS OF LAW AND AUTHORITY

**The Relation of Norman Law to Roman and Saxon.** The transition at the Conquest from a weak to a strong monarchy had very important effects in the field of substantive law. In Saxon times the law was hesitantly and timidly asserting its claims over the most obvious sources of social friction. After 1066 it marched forward like William himself, occupying domain after domain and defying any rival to offer resistance. Yet, like the Conquest also, this advance was all made under the claim of being the rightful heir of Edward the Confessor and his England. The laws of Edward were not repudiated; rather they were appropriated for the new regime, and much of the ensuing progress was accomplished ostensibly in the effort to compel William's subjects to respect and observe the old Saxon laws. True, the Conqueror had a vast reserve arsenal of semi-Roman legal weapons upon which he might draw when the English equipment seemed inadequate to meet the need for law and order. A very great resource this was, too, built up during centuries of commercial prosperity and world rule in the time of the Roman Empire. Later it had been adapted to the rough-and-tumble conditions that followed the breakup of Charlemagne's empire, but it remained a resource capable of furnishing with suitable legal theories a highly developed society in as great a state as even a Norman might hope to construct. Yet William and his successors were too practically and politically minded to wish to substitute such a foreign system as a whole for the one they found. They knew that such a drastic change was not necessary, and even had the cult of the Roman civil law been as strong in the eleventh century as it was in those following, it is doubtful whether the English rulers would have yielded to its claims much more than they did. They were no pedants, but men of affairs, keeping order in their kingdoms first and worrying later, if at all, about a justification for their methods. The natural thing was to appease the conquered as far as possible by allowing them to retain their old codes, while whatever chinks and gaps appeared in the earlier structure were filled in with Continental ideas and devices borrowed from the developed feudalism of that area, or ultimately from the Roman civil code.

**Survival of the Saxon Theory of Law.** So it happened that the cornerstone of the Anglo-Saxon legal structure survived to do similar service in the greater edifice the Normans erected, just as many a bit of humble Saxon masonry was actually incorporated in the stout round-arched walls with which the large-minded conquerors dignified the old building sites. The conscience of the collective Englishman was still considered to be the source of law. The royal councils and courts were only declaring the law, not making it. Now and then this principle seemed to be obscured by the sweeping generalization of a clerical theorist or by a highhanded royal action, and no doubt it was frequently forgotten in practice. Roman legal principles were widely quoted in the twelfth and thirteenth centuries, and the royal ordinances and statutes of the period look suspiciously like the product of modern legislative action. But underneath was the old feeling, which reasserted itself sufficiently often to remain fundamental to any understanding of the law of the time. "We do not wish the laws of England to be changed," said one baronial assemblage, and in their basic theory these laws were not changed.

**Growth of the Principle of "Stare Decisis."** Along with this traditional attitude went the steady development of the corollary principle of *stare decisis* (pages 66, 510), that the courts should be bound by the decisions of their predecessors in similar cases. We have seen the effect of this idea in Bracton's collection and the *Year Books*. A similar attitude may also be seen in the provision of Westminster II (1285) permitting the Chancery clerks to issue writs for a new type of case provided a similar writ could be found (page 192). By the fifteenth century lawyers were beginning to argue that for convenience' sake precedents must be followed by the judges, since otherwise students and practitioners could never be certain of the law. Nevertheless the courts were not fully bound by this principle. Until modern times it was theoretically possible—as it still is in practice—for the courts to chart a new course that might appeal to the current English conscience, even though the weight of precedent was against such a procedure. A few specious legal arguments, however weak in precedents or even logic, sufficed when coupled with social demand. As we look at the growth of legal doctrine in its more important fields we shall see several illustrations of this fact.

**Significance of the Order to Be Followed.** It is typical of the contrast between Norman and Saxon law that we may now discuss the law of real property first and relegate criminal law to a minor position later on. No longer is society so hard pressed to deal with the most glaring injustices that it cannot cope with most of the subtler disorders. On the contrary, the law of real property has been elaborated and refined almost out of all recognition. Between the land law of the Saxon period and that of the centuries following the Conquest there is a marked contrast. Distinctions that either did not occur to the Saxon or were beyond the power of his shaky legal system to cope with are now both noticed and provided for.

## REAL PROPERTY: ENTAIL AND ESTATES

**Relation to Feudalism.** The basis of Norman and Angevin land law was the developed feudal system (pages 119-24). Whatever may have been the original difference between bookland and folkland was no longer of any consequence, for after the Conquest all land was held directly or indirectly of the crown by some kind of feudal "contract." The type of service prescribed in that contract determined the tenure by which the land was held. The other provisions of the understanding, or set of undertakings, which we call the feudal contract largely fixed the lines of the further development of the English law of real property. The right of *primer seisin* connected with relief in the case of land held directly from the king (page 121 n.) doubtless made it possible for the law to distinguish between ownership and seisin, as we have noted in the case of the possessory assizes. But the complicated system of vassals, lords, and overlords also made it possible to see a multiplicity of rights (and even seisins) in the same land. If a lord and an overlord might have certain rights in a vassal's manor—rights that they could protect and enforce in their own courts—why should not the vassal himself divide up his own rights in any way that happened to suit him? This led to the development of what were called estates—which were really the collective right of the vassal, or some division of that right. They may be divided into estates in possession and estates in expectancy (future estates). Of both kinds of estates there is a further subclassification into freehold and nonfreehold estates. The reason for these distinctions should appear from the description of these estates.

**Estates in Possession: Freehold, the Fee Simple.** The basic one of these estates was the fee simple, that is, the vassal's collective or undivided interest in his property. It was called a fee because it was a fief (feudal holding), and called simple to distinguish it from the subdivisions of it that are to be described later. On payment of a routine fee to the feudal lord, it could be freely bought or sold at the vassal's will. In the early Norman period there was some uncertainty as to whether it could or could not be willed, but the logic of feudal law eventually determined that it could not be. For testamentary disposition of the land would break down the principle of primogeniture, on which feudalism depended, and also might deprive the lord of his wardship rights (page 181).

**Pressure for Restrictions: The Conditional Fee.** The second of the estates is the fee simple conditional. This introduces us to one of the longest chapters in the history of the law of real property, and also to one that is intimately connected with political and social history. It is an outgrowth of the effort of landed proprietors to determine the way in which their lands should be held after their death. Prominent families early wished to devise some means by which their line would remain wealthy and powerful for an indefinite period in spite of the appearance of an occasional weakling or black sheep. The holder of a fee simple therefore endeavored to pass his land on to his heir with strings attached, that is, under certain conditions. In the first two centuries after the Conquest this took the form of selling it to a living son—let us say—on condition that it descend to his heir, and so on. This was called a fee simple conditional.

**The Opposition of the Royal Courts Destroys Its Effect.** The crown, however, as we have seen (page 157), was generally not in favor of allowing families to become too strongly entrenched, and therefore the royal courts usually championed the cause of free alienation, the right to sell one's land freely no matter what conditions original donors might have imposed. This policy also found some support in the general feeling that people of a generation long past should not be allowed too much control of affairs in later periods, whose conditions they could not have foreseen. By the latter part of the thirteenth century, therefore, the royal courts were interpreting the terms of the original grant to a man "and his heirs" as words of limitation and not of purchase, the germ of what was later to be known as the rule in Shelley's case. This meant that the sole beneficiary of the transfer was the ancestor, and that the words "and his heirs" were merely to define the estate (interest) which had been transferred to him. The heir, on the other hand, had not purchased any right in the property, but was merely mentioned to limit (describe) the person to whom the sale was made. Therefore as soon as an heir was born to the purchaser, the description (limitation) was complete and the purchaser might convey his estate in fee simple to a third party.

**"De Donis Conditionalibus": The Estate Tail.** In 1285 the baronial faction, apparently alarmed not only by this line of interpretation but by a further threat against the magnates' property contained in concessions made to creditors by the Statute of Acton Burnel in the same year (page 201), succeeded in obtaining a reversal of this trend. Why Edward I consented to this cannot be determined with certainty, but since the important clause in this Statute of Westminster II, called *De donis conditionalibus* (Concerning conditional gifts), is followed by a great many others that stiffen up the royal control of the country in other ways, it is possible that it was granted as part of a compromise settlement of outstanding grievances. In any case, *De donis* provided that in the future land should descend according to the order (*formam*) expressed in the charter, so that those to whom the holding was thus given on condition should have no power to alienate and thus defeat the original purpose of the donor. By this statute estates tail were created. These were so called because they were limited, or cut down (French, *taillé*) to the line of descent named in the original charter setting them up.

**Other Freehold Estates in Possession.** Besides the fee simple, the fee simple conditional, and the fee tail, the law recognized other types of freehold estates in possession. One of these was the life estate, in which the life period for which the land was to be held might be either the life of the holder or that of someone else. Dower, the right of a woman to receive one-third of her husband's estates of inheritance (inheritable interests) on his death, and curtesy, the right by which a surviving husband enjoyed all his wife's estates of inheritance until his death if he had had a child by her, were both recognized as types of life estate. Still another type of estate in possession was that of one to whom land had been mortgaged for a debt. In this case the land in question had originally been conveyed to the creditor (the mortgagee) for the term of the mortgage only, with the proviso that it be returned when and if the money was paid, but otherwise to belong to the mortgagee. Under this arrangement, however, the mortgagor lost seisin, and the mortgagee, though entitled to use other writs, was not protected by the assizes. As a result the conveyance was changed to one in fee simple, with a proviso that if the debt was paid by a fixed date, the land should be reconveyed. This set up an estate defeasible (terminable) upon condition subsequent, that is, a condition yet to be fulfilled (in this case the repayment of the money loaned). This type of estate was considered a freehold estate in possession.

**Nonfreehold Estates.** There were other types of estates that were not considered freehold because they could not be protected by the real actions, for a reason to be explained in this paragraph. When one's interest in property was for a definite period less than life or a period that might be terminated within that limit, the seisin of the land was considered to remain in the hands of the one who created and transferred the limited or limitable interest. Since seisin was an essential of a freehold, these estates could not be considered freehold estates. Among these limited or limitable estates were those of the tenant for a term of years, and the tenant at will, whose tenure might be terminated at any time. Because these estates did not involve seisin, they were not protected by the real assizes, such as *novel dissei-sin*, but were considered chattels and protected by personal rather than real actions.

**Estates in Expectancy.** It is obvious that in the case of estates less than fee simple not all the rights in the land in question were assigned to the holder of the immediate estate, since that estate was less than fee simple and therefore there must be further rights. These further rights were those of the persons who if living at the expiration of the interest of the current estate-holder were either certain to succeed to the property, or had some possibility of doing so. Thus in the case of a fee tail, for example, the heir of the estate-holder (the issue in tail) had an interest (called a remainder) in the property that was to remain (abide) for him when the current holder of the estate should die. There was also the line of the original owner to which the

ESTATES IN EXPECTANCY

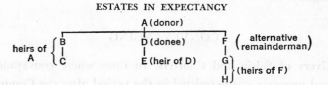

land would revert in default of anyone eligible to receive it under the terms of the original entail, and there might also be another remainderman, who with his heirs might have been originally named as an alternative recipient of the land in case the line of the first donee ran out. Consequently in the case of land entailed by A "to D and the heirs of his body and then to F and the heirs of his body," in addition to the fee tail that D received there would be an estate in expectancy for E, his heir under the entail, perhaps one for F and his heirs as alternative remaindermen—those for whom the entailed land was to remain (abide) in default of heirs in the original line—and one for A and his heirs B and C as reversioners. These estates in expectancy were considered real property, and the law provided means of protecting the rights of their holders as against the holder of the fee tail—when he might be cutting down trees or allowing an uncontrolled stream to wash away the soil, for example. The estates in expectancy so far described were all freehold estates, but just as in the case of estates in possession (page 212), where the period involved was for less than life the estate in expectancy was also considered nonfreehold.

**Lesser Interests.** There were incorporeal (intangible) interests in land that could be protected by real actions, though they were considered less than freehold. These included advowsons, privileges to share in common fields, rent charges (income guaranteed by the proceeds of certain rents, somewhat on the order of a modern debenture bond), and easements (such ancillary rights as that of access or of not having one's land damaged by a neighbor's excavation).

## CONVEYANCING

**Livery of Seisin and Charters.** In cases where conveyancing of real property was permitted in the period after the Conquest, it could still be done by the Saxon method of livery of seisin combined with certain symbolic actions, such as the handing over of a lump of earth, a twig, or a knife. Though this was a perfectly legal method of transfer, it was not always easy to establish the exact interest for which seisin was delivered, whether for life or in perpetuity. It therefore became customary to draw up a charter in which the terms of the transaction were described in minute detail, and this served as evidence of the original intent. It did not convey the land, however. Livery of seisin was still necessary for that, though the handing over of the charter came to fill the role of the symbolic act with the twig or the knife.

**The Fine.** Charters were commonly guarded very carefully, but still they might be lost. Therefore a demand naturally developed for some better system of recording important land transfers, and one that would quiet (guarantee) the title conveyed. The result was the development of the method of conveyancing by fine. We have already noticed that the royal court was frequently used as a place in which grants were witnessed (page 36). Possession acquired as a result of a positive court order was considered an even stronger guarantee of title. Glanvil's nephew Hubert Walter met the demand by allowing collusive suits in the royal court. A wished to sell land to B. B paid him the money and then entered suit for the land. A, having already received payment, did not defend the case, and the land was awarded to B under the fine, or final agreement (Latin *finis*, conclusion). A record of the transaction was then made in triplicate on parchment, which was then cut with irregular lines as

THE METHOD OF RECORDING FINES

indicated in the diagram. Each party to the transaction received one of the top pieces, while the foot was placed in the roll of the court. Should any question arise at a later date, the official record could be consulted at the court. There is a continuous series of these Feet of Fines, as they were called, still in existence, ranging from July 15, 1195, to 1836. The cutting in jagged or indented (hence the term "indenture") lines was an additional precaution, since forged documents could be detected by producing one of the other parts of the original and fitting them together, as in the tally system at the Exchequer. Sometimes a figured design was drawn on the inner margins before the parchment was cut, as yet more insurance.

**Villeins' Holdings.** All that has been said about the law of real property applies only to free tenures. The villein on the manor was considered legally unfree, and whatever rights he had in his thirty acres held by menial service were not at this time protected by the courts of common law. What recourse he had was in his lord's court. He could sell his holding with his lord's consent—purchased by a fee. But in this and all the other aspects of real property law, as far as it concerned the villein—or anyone else—holding by menial service, the custom of the manor ruled. Thus it must not be forgotten that in this period, while actions concerning the larger and more valuable holdings were heard in the royal courts, the great majority of Englishmen had their extremely variable real property law administered elsewhere.

## PERSONAL PROPERTY AND CONTRACTS

**Personal Property.** As already suggested (page 192), it is in this period that we see the beginning of the concept of personal property, that is, property for which only the equivalent money value and not the thing itself can be recovered in legal actions. Originally the law made no such distinction, and it was possible to sue for the recovery of a particular cow, or even a particular coin, just as for a particular pasture. The reason why this practice was dropped seems to be partly that cattle were often used as money—in Latin the term *pecunia* (money) originally meant cattle—and partly because of the remedies provided by Norman and Angevin law. There was no great point in demanding the identical coins back in payment of a debt, and so frequently any other cattle could be substituted for those claimed. Because cattle were the most common kind of movable property, the rules that applied to them came to be applied to all movables, as may be seen from the fact that the legal term for such property, "chattels," is merely a variant of "cattle" (page 191). Furthermore, in the case of movable property the ordinary means of recovery allowed by the Normans was an action for theft, as a result of which the thief might be hanged and the property restored. But as the royal power grew stronger the king's courts confiscated the criminal's goods, and with their greedy ways they often included the stolen property. If the complainant recovered anything, therefore, it was more likely to be money, which was not so intimately connected with the original action. With the development of trespass as a form of action a branch of it, called *de bonis asportatis* (trespass of goods taken away) did the work of the old action of theft. Since, however, trespass actions retained some of the criminal flavor of the parent form, as we have seen (page 192), and since damages in such cases were always assessed in money, even under this procedure only a monetary compensation was secured.

**Roots of the Later Doctrine of Contract: Ecclesiastical.** In an age to which the concept of credit was not so familiar as it is today, and whose little banking business was in the hands of foreigners, the law of contract as we understand it was almost undeveloped. The enforcement of mutual agreements on sufficient consideration to do or forbear in the future was perhaps not too difficult a problem for the Angevin lawyers to solve, but it was one that they were not frequently asked to attempt. There were, however, in this period some roots of later ideas that must be noted here. We have observed (page 214) that symbolic acts ac-

companied livery of seisin in land. From this custom there developed the practice of binding a bargain with a handclasp, or
later by a pledge of Christian faith—pawning one's religion, as
Maitland described it. If the agreement were not kept, the
church courts might be called on to punish this misuse of religion. The quarrel between Becket and Henry II, however, resulted in the royal courts' using writs of prohibition to stop
this ecclesiastical effort to acquire jurisdiction over commercial
transactions, for the Constitutions of Clarendon declared that all
pleas of debt "belonged to the king's justice." [1]

**Debt and Covenant.** The procedure in debt (page 189) available at common law provided another foreshadowing of con-
tractual ideas, for in a way it permitted a man to enforce an
agreement. The theory back of it, however, was rather that of
a man recovering his own property that was being wrongfully
kept from him. Lastly, the action of covenant under seal afforded
a way to secure compliance with the terms of leases. If these had
been put in the form of a written agreement sealed "by the party
to be charged therewith," the law would enforce them. By the
end of this period these actions were allowed to cover movables
of all sorts, but the agreements were required to be in writing
and sealed by the person bound.


## INHERITANCE

**Inheritance of Real Property: Primogeniture.** We have already
noted that the Norman Conquest introduced primogeniture into
England (page 133). Strictly speaking, the initial step was only
to insist that the feudal holdings be impartible (indivisible). If
a man had a fief in Normandy and one in England, each held
by a separate service, he might give one to one son and one to
another, so long as the service obligations were not subdivided.
Not until the time of Henry II was this desire for simplicity

[1] Art. 15, S-M, No. 30, p. 76.

of control allowed to go the full length of requiring that all real property left by the father be held by the eldest son. Some minor exceptions must, however, be noted. Some socage tenures that were created before the time of Henry II were divisible among the heirs, since no military service was involved. In Kent all sons of well-to-do peasants still shared equally in the inheritance, by the custom of gavelkind (page 73). On some manors and in some towns, by a custom known as borough English the youngest rather than the eldest son inherited the entire estate. This custom of borough English prevailed in cases where no military service was owed, and probably became the accepted procedure because the younger children were thought to be more likely than the older to need help at the death of the father. Getting back to the normal rules of inheritance, if there were no sons, daughters might inherit, but in this case the eldest was given little preference over her sisters. Since she was as incapable of performing military service as her juniors, there was no point in giving her the entire inheritance. She was commonly permitted to hold the castle, if there were one, and was sometimes allowed to do the only homage for the family. Toward the end of this period, however, lords were exacting homage of all the daughters equally. For in this way the lords acquired marriage rights over all the heiresses. Furthermore, the other arrangement, which gave the eldest sister control over her fellow heiresses, was considered to put too much power over their destinies in her hands, since, for reasons of self-interest, she might wish them to die childless. Whatever arrangements were made as to these details, however, the bulk of the property was divided equally among the daughters, as in the case of David's heirs in Scotland (page 98 n.). The coheiresses of this sort were called coparceners (equal sharers).

**Collateral Heirs: The Parentelic System.** When a property-holder died without direct issue, the law found itself in considerable uncertainty as to what was to be done with his lands and goods. Under the developed feudal system the lands could not be willed, but at first there were no clear notions as to which of the collateral relatives was to succeed. In the case of John and Arthur we have seen (page 92) that a younger surviving brother of the deceased took precedence over his nephew who represented the claim of an older brother, also deceased. The theory of inheritance right which was used to justify John's succession in that case is called the gradual theory, because it awarded the inheritance to the person who was separated from the deceased proprietor by the fewest *gradui* (steps or joints), in the family tree. The results of John's reign, however, were not such as to encourage the English to follow this precedent. For a few more years, it is true, until the death in 1241 of Arthur's sister Eleanor—carefully imprisoned by Henry III so that she could have no heir—the royal courts could not very well reverse themselves and follow the rule that supported the claims of nephews and nieces in such cases. But after that convenient demise it was possible to do so, and the parentelic system became the standard one. This provided that a man's children could represent his claim in case of the parent's death, and that therefore the entire oldest surviving branch (*parentela*) of a family must be exhausted in the search for an heir before going on to the next branch. It was under this principle that the crown of Scotland was awarded to Balliol in 1292 (page 99), and it thereafter remained the law in such cases. Where it was necessary to go farther afield in search of an heir, the rule was that he must be related by blood to the original purchaser, that is, the one who last acquired the estate by means other than inheritance. Thus one's father's sister could not inherit from the nephew land that had descended to him through his mother. Beyond that there was a great deal of uncertainty. It was decided that the limit of relationship for purposes of inheritance should be sixth cousins, but no clear method was known for determining whether a mother's brother had a better claim on land purchased by a childless deceased person than had a cousin on the father's side.

**Inheritance of Personal Property: Testaments.** As we have seen (page 73), the Church encouraged the making of testaments (or wills). Lands were excluded from them after the twelfth century, not only for feudal reasons but to protect the interest of the heir against the deathbed begging of the churchmen (page 115). Personal property was conveyed by testament, however, subject to certain rights of the family known as the *légitime*. If a widow survived, but no children, she received half the estate. Similarly if children were left, but no widow, they were entitled to half of their father's personal property. If, however, both widow and children survived, they were given one-third each. The ecclesiastical theory was, of course, that the free fraction would be given to the dead, that is, to the Church to pray for the souls of the departed. Executors were named, and the testament was probated in the church courts, as already noted (page 180). Intestacy was regarded with horror, as showing a niggardly spirit, and in such cases the church courts took charge of the goods and distributed them as the churchmen saw fit, presumably according to the rule for the *légitime* just mentioned.

## FAMILY LAW

**Decline of the Status of Married Women.** In the field of family law the husband during this period increased his powers at the expense of the wife. This was a result not only of the feudal theory, which preferred male heirs to female ones, but also of the increased influence of the Church. After 1066 the English Church, now closely tied to the papal curia, observed the principles of the canon (ecclesiastical) law as it had developed on the Continent, in this and practically all other matters. Though strenuous efforts have been made to show that the Church in England was legally separate from the Continental one during the Middle Ages,[2] we have clear evidence for the adoption of the Continental canon law in England soon after the Conquest. The theological ideas that made of husband and wife one flesh and prescribed subordination to the woman as a result of the Fall seriously undermined the favorable legal position women had occupied in Saxon times. By marriage the husband now acquired an estate in all lands held by his wife as tenant in fee. This estate endured for the duration of the marriage, and could be alienated without the consent of the wife. If a child were born, the estate was extended by the rule of "curtesy" for the life of the husband (page 212), and this additional interest could be similarly alienated. Without her husband's consent the wife could not dispose of her lands during the marriage, but if the husband wished to convey a fee simple in her property, her permission was necessary. A widow was entitled to receive as dower one-third of all lands of which her husband was seised (possessed) during the marriage, if she had not consented to a less advantageous arrangement. The married woman thus retained some rights as far as land was concerned, but immediately on marriage all the wife's movables became the absolute property of the husband, and could be disposed of as he pleased. The wife was not permitted to make a testament (will) without the husband's consent, though this concession was frequently made. In general the relation between husband and wife did not quite amount to a community of goods, but was rather a guardianship that worked very largely to the advantage of the guardian, the husband.

**Marriage.** The actual marriage itself did not need to be blessed by a priest, nor was it even necessary that it be a public ceremony. The mere statement of mutual taking each other as husband and wife, delivered in terms of the present tense (*sponsalia per verba de praesenti*) was all that was legally essential.

[2] See the comments on patriotic motives in the interpretation of history on page 81 n.

The Church strongly urged the employment of a priest in this sacrament, but rather than encourage informal unions dissoluble at will this simple ceremony was permitted. Children of seven were allowed to contract legal marriage, though until consummated it was voidable if the young parties later chose to renounce the tie.

**Annulments and Separations.** The church courts took jurisdiction over matrimonial cases, as we have mentioned (page 180). Because of the sacramental character of the marriage ceremony, divorce with the privilege of remarrying was theoretically not permitted, except to one of an infidel pair who became converted to Christianity without the other.[3] This served further to lower the status of women in this period, since, once married, they had no straightforward way of regaining their complete freedom of action, no matter what abuses they might be subjected to. Some provision for separation and remarriage was, however, made through the canonical doctrine of annulments. If it could be established—and by hard swearing it commonly was—that a husband or a wife had been previously espoused in terms of the present tense, even though that marriage was not consummated, the second was thereby annulled. Consanguinity or affinity were also grounds for annulment. In 1215 the Lateran Council prohibited all marriages within the fourth degree counting from a common ancestor—that is among all descendants of the same great-great-grandparent. Since marriage made husband and wife one flesh, these same degrees—now called of affinity in the in-law relationship—also applied to relatives by marriage. Even people who stood as godparents at baptism were considered spiritual relatives for the purposes of annulling bur-

---

[3] The Church used the term "divorce" as the legal term "separation" is used today, and thus under certain circumstances granted "divorces" from bed and board (*a mensa et thoro*), but these were not from the marriage tie (*a vinculo*) and thus did not permit of remarriage. This loose use of the term "divorce" in medieval times in part accounts for the confusion in the terminology applied to the first "divorce" of Henry VIII (page 323), though in that case it was actually an annulment that was sought.

densome marriage ties. Legal separations—which stopped short of divorce with permission to remarry—were permitted in cases where one of the parties had committed adultery.

**Children.** Children were of course subject to parental discipline, but they were also capable of being enfeoffed (put in possession of fiefs), suing, and being sued. They might, however, allege their infancy and so postpone troublesome actions. The lord's right of wardship in the case of lands held by knight service or grand sergeantry furnished a guardian for infant heirs in case of the death of the father. The other surviving children were doubtless supported by the mother on her dower privileges, but when the elder brother came of age, it was generally expected that he would make some provision for them. Illegitimate children could not inherit from anyone, and therefore, strangely enough, were all considered freeborn—since they could not inherit villein status, even though one or both parents were villeins.

## CRIMINAL LAW AND THEORIES OF LIABILITY

**The Development of Criminal Law.** Between these fields of what we now know as civil law and the sphere of serious social offenses there was slowly developing the distinction that was to put criminal cases in a separate category. It was not yet complete by 1307, but we can see many signs of its growth. We have already spoken of the concepts of the king's peace and the pleas of the crown that asserted the ruler's special interest in offenses of certain types, or those committed in special places or circumstances (pages 158, 165). The classification of punishable acts as misdemeanors, felonies, and treasons was a product of this royal interest. Misdemeanors, though the word used in its technical sense belongs to a later period, were the minor offenses, such as "blind blows" that did not draw blood or break bones. Some of these might be punished in the royal courts, but often they were left to the local and feudal courts. The felonies were the serious crimes, such as homicide, robbery, mayhem, and arson, over which the king claimed jurisdiction. They were so called from the term "felon," meaning wicked or cruel. They involved punishment by the loss of life or member, and the forfeiture of property to the feudal lord. Treasons were the worst of all crimes, those involving some kind of betrayal of the king or an attack upon his office. They were not covered by benefit of clergy, and the property of the convicted man was forfeited to the king rather than to the immediate feudal superior of the guilty man.

**Criminal Liability.** A new principle of criminal liability was also introduced during this period, largely as a result of the influence of the Church. Not motion but the guilty mind was the important thing, said the moralists. In theory, the agent (the one acting or moving) in accidental homicides was still punishable and had to obtain a royal pardon, but he owed nothing to the family of the deceased. For conviction of a crime it was necessary to establish some degree of criminal intention or mental guilt.

**The Early Idea of Tort as a Civil Action.** It will be seen that the wer and the bot were thus abolished in some cases. The law, however, still permitted the injured parties in many circumstances to collect damages for wrongs to their person or property, and the action for this purpose gradually separated itself from the criminal charge. This special provision originally grew out of actions of *novel disseisin,* in which the sheriff was empowered to see that not only possession of the land was restored, but also the original chattels or their value. Afterward the special action of trespass was developed for this and similar cases. From it descended most of what we now know as the law of torts. This whole development of the idea of a civil action for damages in addition to the criminal charge of course left the guilty man in a much worse position than before, since he might have to pay the equivalent of bot or wergeld and still have to answer the criminal charge.

**Civil Liability.** In these civil actions the theory of liability was less generous than the criminal one to those in any way concerned with the infliction of injuries. For the law was still anxious to placate the injured, even though a criminal punishment was not in order. The master was held liable for wrongs his servants had committed if they were acting directly under his orders. If they were uncommanded wrongs, the servant was required to pay if he could. Otherwise, especially if the injuries had been committed in the course of the servant's ordinary duties, *respondeat superior*—let the superior (the master) answer for the damages. Still, trespass as yet applied only to injuries inflicted by violence, not to such incidents as the laming of a horse by a clumsy smith. Before 1307 the royal courts provided no proper remedy against fraud, defamation, or even perjury and forgery. Over some of these the local and ecclesiastical courts had a partial jurisdiction, but they did not exercise it satisfactorily. The law had begun a bold advance in difficult and unexplored territory, but there were yet many important areas to be occupied.

# The Late Middle Ages

# 11. GENERAL HISTORY
## 1307-1485

**Character of the Period as a Whole.** The fourteenth and fifteenth centuries are generally known as the last of the Middle Ages, and with good reason. They still show all the fundamental traits that we have come to associate with medievalism—the alliance between king, Church, and nobles, the low standard of living, the otherworldly faith, learning and art dominated by religious considerations, and the rest. Yet in spite of some notable individual exceptions, such as Chaucer, it was a tired age, listlessly going through its prescribed routine. The zest had gone out of life with the passing of the era of Innocent III, St. Louis, and St. Francis. Neither by the invasions of new peoples, by the acceptance of new religious ideals, nor by intellectual discoveries was western European society awakened or the tempo of its daily round quickened. This period seems at first glance to be a long pause in the story of human progress. Yet on closer inspection it will appear that much useful work was being done in preparing the ground for future advances. Those who despair of the prospects for modern civilization would do well to acquaint themselves with the era of the waning of medievalism.

## THE WEAKNESS OF THE MONARCHY

**Fundamental Causes.** The fortunes of the English monarchy in this period reflect this general failure of nerve, to borrow a phrase originally applied to the situation at the end of classical times. For nearly two hundred years after the death of Edward I there was no king of England who was able to enjoy undisputed possession of the royal powers his predecessors had established. In part this circumstance, as suggested, is to be attributed to the spirit of the age, which seemed to put a premium on conformity and dead tradition rather than on vigor and initiative, or even loyalty to the real spirit of the past. In part it is to be explained by the peculiar development of the machinery of the central government, which, as we shall find in a later chapter, although originally designed to serve the monarch's purposes, was even better suited to the work of advancing the interests of his rivals.

**Personal Causes: Edward II (1307-27).** Another major contributing factor, however, was the series of biological and psychological accidents that determined the succession to the throne, and the personalities of those who held it—or tried to hold it. Edward II was a failure. It is hard to follow in office one who has been an outstanding success. Furthermore, few great men—witness William the Conqueror and Henry II—can bring up their sons without somehow malforming their characters. In this respect Edward I was no exception, and as a great man's son Edward II ran true to type. He lost Scotland, as we have already seen. At home, for twenty troubled years he enjoyed himself, played favorites, and alternately blew hot and cold on matters of state. He was a hard drinker, a gambler, and a spendthrift, more fond of practical jokes and his pet lion than of attending to official business. Under pressure from his barons he would accept terms, and discard the objectionable upstarts whom he normally chose as his bosom friends to the great scandal of the older nobility. But when the old baronial failing of lack of cohesiveness appeared, he regularly fell into his old ways and started the cycle over again. At last he sided with one of his favorites against his own wife, Queen Isabella. She thereupon went into the opposition camp, and then the game was up. Forming an alliance with Roger Mortimer, Earl of March, she took the field, captured her husband, and seized control of the government in the name of her son. Parliament was summoned, and soon succeeded in extorting a semblance of abdication from the royal prisoner.[1] A few months later he died in captivity—reputedly stabbed to death with red-hot pokers.

## EDWARD III AND THE HUNDRED YEARS' WAR

**Edward III (1327-77).** The nominal successor, Edward III, was fourteen at this time, and consequently the management of the government was left to his mother and her more than friendly ally, Mortimer. In three years of scandal and greed they wore out their welcome. The opposition to them was then strong enough to permit the young King to declare himself of age, have Mortimer executed, and take the control of the government away from the Queen Mother. Edward was a kind of early Miniver Cheevy who appreciated "the medieval grace of iron clothing." He

> loved the days of old
> When swords were bright and steeds were prancing;
> The vision of a warrior bold
> Would set him dancing.

As a boy he had read of King Arthur and his knights, and, like Peter Pan and some college alumni, he never grew up. He doted on titles, ranks, orders, glory, and more glory. He wanted to be able to confer a higher title than earl, and so in his early manhood he created the rank of duke to honor his seven-year-old son. He thus began that complication of hierarchical titles which still characterizes the English nobility.[2] He also gathered those

---

[1] S-M, No. 59, p. 205.

[2] In 1386 Richard II inserted the rank of marquis between those of duke and earl. The regents of Henry VI in 1440 devised the title of viscount—vice-count (count = earl)—to rank between baron and earl. This was the last of the strata of lords. Two hundred years later James I introduced the title of baronet, which conferred the hereditary title of knighthood (Sir), but baronets did not rank as nobles, and, like knights, they are not members of the House of Lords.

whom he especially wished to honor—mostly nobles—into an order of knighthood modeled on the Knights of the Round Table. This was known as the Order of the Garter, probably because of an incident in which the chivalrous King came to the rescue of a lady in distress. It is said that when the Countess of Salisbury had the misfortune to lose one of her garters at a court function she was greatly embarrassed by the reactions of certain rude spectators. Thereupon the King picked up the ribbon and tied it around his own leg as a decoration, remarking as he did so, *"Honi soit qui mal y pense"* ("Evil to him who evil thinks"). This sentence afterwards became the motto of the order, which took the blue band of the garter for its badge.

**Edward's Foreign Wars.** Such a king would inevitably look for glory on the battlefield. He regretted a treaty made during his minority, by which the independence of Scotland was recognized. He attacked his northern neighbor and gained some successes, but when France came to the aid of her ally his attention was turned to the Continental adversary. Thus began the so-called Hundred Years' War. Besides the Scottish complications there were many other pretexts for this extended series of conflicts. The French were still whittling away at the English holdings in southwestern France. They were trying to dominate Flanders, which was the chief outlet for English wool and therefore a very important part of the English economic system. There was intense rivalry between French and English sailors. The best excuse of all, from Edward's point of view, was a claim that he had on the French throne. His mother, Isabella, had been a sister of Charles IV of France, who had died without issue. The French barons, anxious to avoid a foreigner's rule, had awarded the crown to Philip of Valois, a cousin of the late king. Edward had acknowledged the legality of this settlement and had done homage to Philip for his French lands. Yet when he decided to fight he was enabled to revive his claim by the fact that in ordinary feudal law a nephew had a better right than a cousin to inherit from a deceased tenant in fee. Naturally this fact also made good propaganda for his side. The real cause of the war, however, was obviously the growing national spirit in the two countries and the rivalry between them. Both had come through a period in which powerful monarchs had built up strong, efficient central governments. Now the ruler of one of these countries was the feudal lord of part of the other and wanted to extend his power even further. Like quarrelsome twelve-year-olds feeling their strength, the two countries decided to fight it out. So they did, and for a time at Edward's court there was glory enough to go round. But at long last in the next century the English were left with nothing to show for their trouble except the French Channel port of Calais.

**The First Phase of the Hundred Years' War.** The war began in 1337. There was an English naval victory at Sluys off the Flemish coast in 1340. In 1346 at Crécy, on the river Somme in northern France, a small English army of dismounted knights and longbowmen, fighting side by side, withstood the charge of the disorderly feudal assemblage of French knights and then calmly shot them down. Afterward Calais was besieged and taken. Ten years later at Poitiers in west-central France Edward's oldest son and namesake, known as the Black Prince, repeated the tactics used at Crécy. He won another great victory, and this time captured the French King John II, who had succeeded Philip in 1350. During the period between these two great battles western Europe had been ravaged by a plague known as the Black Death (possibly the bubonic plague), which killed something like a third, or possibly even a half, of the population. France was now apparently exhausted, and in 1360 accepted the Treaty of Brétigny, so called from the place where it was drawn up—a town south of Paris. This gave the English outright possession of Calais, an area around Crécy called Ponthieu, and a very much enlarged Aquitaine. Appearances, however, are deceiving where such intangibles as national spirit are concerned.

A new French King, Charles V, quietly built up his resources and in 1369 renewed the war on a different plan. Departing from the old feudal tradition, he chose for his commander one Bertrand du Guesclin, reputedly the ugliest man in Brittany, who relied on professional soldiers. Avoiding pitched battles, the new commander gradually wore the English down by those guerrilla tactics which have so often proved the undoing of invaders far removed from their base of supply. The Black Prince was ill and unable to lead the English forces, so the blame for the losses was fixed on his successor in command, a younger brother, John of Gaunt, Duke of Lancaster, whose first title came from his Flemish birthplace, Ghent (Gand). By 1375 Calais and two other coast towns, Bordeaux and Bayonne, were practically all that the English had left of their Continental holdings, and they were glad to arrange a truce, which lasted until the death of Edward in 1377.

**Its Cost.** The war had temporarily brought the English monarch the military glory he wanted, but otherwise it had cost him dear. Bankrupt in the 1340's, he defaulted on loans secured from Italian and other Continental bankers. "We grieve, nay, we blush," said the King in response to one dun, "that we are unable to meet our obligations." In this emergency he was forced to seek the help of Parliament and accept terms that made great inroads on his control of the governmental machinery (page 256). While fortune smiled on his arms during the war he enjoyed considerable popularity with his subjects, but he retained it, as just suggested, only by making substantial concessions to the upper and middle classes at the expense of his royal prerogative. The last years of his reign were marred not only by the military reverses in France but by the King's dotage, during which the government became the plaything of his mistress and of aristocratic factions.

## RICHARD II AND THE LANCASTRIAN DYNASTY

**Richard II (1377-99).** Edward the Black Prince died shortly before his father, and so the crown passed to his son, the ten-year-old Richard II. During the years of regency the war with France dragged on until the mounting financial levies, combined with other factors arising from the breakdown of the manorial system (page 265), produced the Peasants' Revolt in 1381. This uprising resulted in the capture of London and the mob murder of those whom the peasants considered their chief oppressors, ministers of the crown, taxgatherers, and lawyers. It was, however, put down by a combination of bravery and bare-faced lying (page 266)—otherwise known as diplomatic presence of mind—in which the young King played a leading part. In 1385 he began to assert his own will in governmental policy, but in the following year he was forced to accept an arrangement by which a reform council was commissioned to manage the government. Its members are known as the Lords Appellant because two years later they used the appeal procedure to make criminal charges in Parliament against some of the King's friends. In 1389, however, Richard, following the precedent of Edward II, succeeded in gaining control of the government himself. After eight years of reasonably good rule he suddenly began to show a tyrannical streak, probably because of the death of his wife, Anne of Bohemia, who had been a restraining influence. Supported by some of the younger lords, he dealt severely with certain Lords Appellant. He packed Parliament with his friends and had them delegate their power to a small committee under his control. He declared roundly that the laws were "in the king's breast." Then he made a double misstep, and the precedent of Edward II returned to plague him. After banishing his cousin Henry Bolingbroke—son of John of Gaunt, Duke of Lancaster—for his part in a private duel, the King broke his promise not to touch

Henry's ancestral lands and took them when the father died a few months later. With one falsehood he had come into political prominence, and with this one he was to go. When he followed up this blunder by incautiously going to Ireland to inspect the situation in that land of perpetual trouble, his cousin seized the opportunity and returned from the Continent. Henry claimed his estates and was given such rousing support that he added the realm of England to the original demand. Richard hurried back from Ireland, but was forced to come to terms. A Parliament was called and the King was compelled to sign a formal abdication. He was imprisoned, and four months later it was announced that he was dead—"of starvation," people whispered.

**Henry IV (1399-1413): The Weakness of His Title.** Henry of Lancaster, then thirty-two, claimed the crown in Parliament, and it was granted to him under the title of Henry IV. Richard died without issue, but because there were living daughters of an older brother of John of Gaunt Henry did not have the best hereditary claim on the crown of England according to the parentelic system. This had important consequences, the least of which was that the following kings were considered to form a new dynasty, called the Lancastrian, instead of the Angevin (Plantagenet), which had begun with Henry II and ended with Richard. The crown had not passed to the new line through a woman, but it had not followed the normal feudal course. Hence the change of name. This irregular succession was later to bring on a bitter dynastic war. For the time being, however, the most important effect was to weaken the legal position of Henry and his successors to such an extent that they had to be very deferential to Parliament, the only legal source of their title. This gave Parliament increased importance in affairs of state.

**Henry's Struggle.** Henry had to supplement the parliamentary endorsement of his claim with active military campaigning before he could make it good. Richard's second wife had been a daughter of the King of France, and that ruler seized the oppor-

tunity to reopen the Hundred Years' War. Scotland joined in
the fray and there were revolts in Wales and in the north of
England. Not until 1405 did Henry definitely begin to get the
upper hand over this combination of enemies. In 1406 the heir
to the King of Scotland was accidentally captured by English
pirates, and the next year factional feuds which broke out in
France led to a truce with that country. In 1409 Henry was
finally secure in his position, such as it was. The ten years of
fighting had been too much for him, however, and by 1413 he
was dead.

**Henry V (1413-22).** Brought up amid alarms and excursions,
the new King, Henry V—the Prince Hal of Shakespeare's plays—
was a man of action. He had helped his father put down the
Welsh and northern risings, and already had an established reputation as a soldier. Succeeding to the throne, he promptly resumed the old quarrel with France. Another Edward III, he obtained much glory and little permanent profit. In 1415 he won a
great victory at Agincourt, between Crécy and Calais, whose chief
importance today is that it furnished Shakespeare with the background for some of his best lines on courage. Five years later
circumstances induced one of the French factions, the Burgundians, to make a treaty with the English King, recognizing Henry
as regent of France and successor to the then insane French King
Charles VI. With a fine disregard for the biological principles of
heredity, it was required that the English King bind the bargain
by marrying Charles's daughter. He did so, and when his military exertions brought him to an early end in 1422 he left a
nine-months-old son and namesake of royal blood and weak
mind to make what he could of his inheritance.

**Henry VI (1422-61): End of the Hundred Years' War.** The
chief Protector appointed was Henry V's brother, John, Duke of
Bedford. He loyally tried to enforce his nephew's claims to
France, but of course the Burgundians' rivals, the Armagnacs,
did not accept the Burgundian bargain. When Charles VI died,

also in 1422, the Armagnacs put his son on the throne as Charles VII, and the war went on. It was hopeless for the English to attempt to conquer and absorb permanently such a huge block of alien territory. Sooner or later the French national spirit was certain to rise above factionalism and reassert itself. The appearance in 1429 of the religiously militant peasant girl Joan of Arc provided the needed impetus. Though she was captured and executed as a witch in 1431, by 1435 the French schism was mended and the doom of the English sealed. Bedford died that year, and one disaster followed another until Charles VII triumphantly entered Bordeaux in 1453. This marked the end of the Hundred Years' War. The gist of it all was that the English had marched into France and then out again. Only Calais was left in their possession.

## THE YORKISTS AND THE WARS OF THE ROSES

**Factionalism and Disorder at Home.** The closing of the long run of the military drama in France permitted many of the English actors to play roles in a tragedy that was soon staged at home, and here again factionalism and bloodshed made up most of the plot. A brother of Bedford, Humphrey, Duke of Gloucester, had developed a semipopular party that was contending for power with one composed mostly of nobles and their dependents led by Cardinal Beaufort, a son of John of Gaunt by his mistress and third wife, Catherine Swynford. When Gloucester and Beaufort both died in 1447, their roles were taken respectively by Richard, Duke of York, and Beaufort's nephew, Edmund, Earl (later Duke) of Somerset. Richard was supported by the ambitious Earl of Warwick, while Somerset was actively assisted by Margaret of Anjou, a French noblewoman who had become Henry VI's queen.

**Outbreak of the Wars of the Roses.** The struggle was carried on with a technique made possible by the political and military

developments of the preceding century. During the early part
of the Hundred Years' War easy-going, glory-loving Edward III
had hit upon the idea of getting the professional soldiers he
needed for his type of military tactics by reverting to something
like the practice of prescutage feudal days and encouraging his
nobles to raise and equip their own private bands of fighting
men. With a weak monarchy and ample opportunity for using
these forces at home as well as abroad, the English magnates
took full advantage of this opportunity. During the fifteenth
century, and particularly after the end of hostilities in France,
the land was overrun with these bands of armed retainers wearing the private uniform (livery) of their patron. The Earl of
Warwick had a thousand such men bearing his insignia of the
bear holding a ragged staff (roughly lopped tree trunk). The
example of the greater nobles was imitated by the lesser. Public
and private quarrels were inextricably mixed. Heiresses were
kidnapped with impunity and married off by force. If such cases
were taken to court, the liveried retainers appeared to support,
or maintain, their fellows' cause by overawing juries and intimi-
dating judges. Should a major political crisis develop, the minor
frays were stopped while the liveried men hurried to join the
army of their lord's choice. The man who should have suppressed these disorders was, of course, Henry VI. But the King,
who was declared of age in 1437, was quite incapable of dealing
with the situation. He meant well but meant it feebly, to borrow
one of Theodore Roosevelt's phrases. Helplessly he looked on
while the great partisans contended for the power that should
have been his. Then in early middle age he began to have recurrent spells of his grandfather's insanity. These, coupled with the
fact that the King had no child until 1453, gave the Yorkist
party the opportunity to turn the factional quarrel into a dynastic one. It is now time to look at the genealogical table, without
which it is impossible to understand the events of the so-called
Wars of the Roses during the next thirty years. There is an old

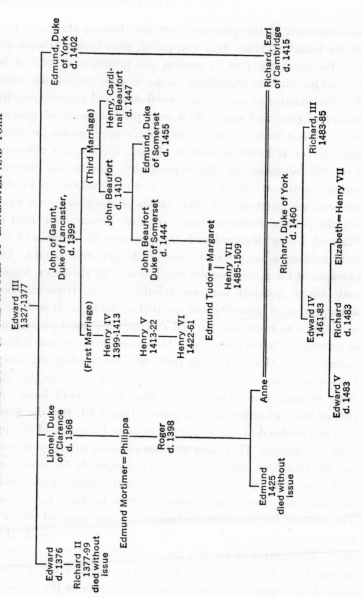

ABBREVIATED GENEALOGY OF THE HOUSES OF LANCASTER AND YORK

Edward III
1327-1377

Edward
d. 1376

Richard II
1377-99
died without
issue

Lionel, Duke
of Clarence
d. 1368

Edmund Mortimer = Philippa

Roger
d. 1398

Edmund
1425
died without
issue

Anne

John of Gaunt,
Duke of Lancaster,
d. 1399

(First Marriage)

Henry IV
1399-1413

Henry V
1413-22

Henry VI
1422-61

(Third Marriage)

Henry, Cardi-
nal Beaufort
d. 1447

John Beaufort
d. 1410

John Beaufort
Duke of Somerset
d. 1444

Edmund, Duke
of Somerset
d. 1455

Edmund Tudor = Margaret

Henry VII
1485-1509

Edmund, Duke
of York
d. 1402

Richard, Earl
of Cambridge
d. 1415

Richard, Duke of York
d. 1460

Edward IV
1461-83

Richard
d. 1483

Edward V
d. 1483

Richard, III
1483-85

Elizabeth = Henry VII

saying that "The Wars of the Roses, so I have heard, were caused by too many children of Edward the Third." It will be seen that by the marriage of Richard, Earl of Cambridge, and Anne Mortimer, the Yorkists, though descended on their father's side from Edmund, had inherited the Mortimer claim, which came through Lionel and was therefore superior, according to the parentelic theory, to that of the Lancastrians, which came through the younger John of Gaunt. The Mortimer claim had not been pressed in 1399, however, because of the peculiar circumstances of Henry's return and because Roger's children, who represented it, were under age at that time. It had been held in abeyance for obvious reasons during the reign of the militaristic Henry V. Nor was it urged during the early years of Henry VI, because as long as that monarch remained childless the Duke of York was the logical heir and so saw no need to hurry his fortune. When, however, a son was born to the royal couple in 1453 and the King presently went mad, Richard demanded appointment as Protector. With Warwick's help he obtained this temporarily, but when the King unfortunately recovered his few wits, Richard took to the field. The symbol employed by the Yorkists was a white rose, and years later the Tudors, who drew their chief claim from the Lancastrian line, used a red rose. Historians accordingly have called the ensuing tumults by the strikingly inappropriate title of the Wars of the Roses.

**The Course of the Wars: Edward IV (1461-83).** Richard was successful in 1455 and became virtual regent for a short time. Margaret of Anjou refused to accept this arrangement, however, and in 1460 Richard was defeated and slain in a battle with her followers at Wakefield, in Yorkshire. But the next year his son Edward was victorious at the battle of Towton in the same county and took over the government as Edward IV, the first of the Yorkist line. Still more troubles followed. It was several years before Henry could be captured and imprisoned. And then Warwick became disgruntled. Having done so much for the House of York, he naturally expected to be the chief man in the king-dom, and when Edward disregarded his advice in the matter of marriage, and otherwise showed his independence, the powerful Earl went over to the other side. By turning out Edward and restoring Henry in 1470 he earned the title of "King-Maker." But the next year the Yorkist returned from the Continent, where he had taken refuge. He regained his throne at the battles of Barnet, near London, and Tewkesbury, near Gloucester in the west, killing Warwick in the process. The son of Henry VI was also slain in this fighting, and Edward saw to it that the father did not long survive. It was given out that he had died in prison "of pure displeasure and melancholy," but when the body was displayed men noticed evidence of more physical causes. For the next twelve years the country was comparatively peace-ful. The chief troublemaker during the period, the King's brother the Duke of Clarence, was eliminated in 1478, being drowned, according to an unofficial report, in a vat of his favor-ite drink, Malmsey wine.

**Edward V (1483): Richard III (1483-85).** Whatever the exact manner of Clarence's going, Edward would have been well ad-vised to serve another brother, Richard, Duke of Gloucester, in the same way. This ambitious hunchback unfortunately survived, however, and became Protector when Edward suddenly died in 1483. For while Edward left five daughters and two sons, the older boy, the dead King's namesake, was only twelve. Richard at first professed allegiance to his nephew, the boy ruler Edward V, but soon contrived to get him into the Tower, which was commonly used for prisoners of state as well as for storing muni-tions. The frightened mother took sanctuary in Westminster Abbey with the other children. On the thin pretext that young Edward was lonesome and needed a playmate, the helpless dow-ager was forced to surrender the younger brother, who was also named Richard. With the two boys in his power Richard the uncle brought trumped-up charges against the validity of their

parents' marriage and usurped the crown as Richard III. Soon
the two princes disappeared. In all probability they were smoth-
ered to death and their bodies buried under a stairway in the
Tower where two small skeletons were subsequently found.

**Bosworth and the End of the Wars.** Outraged representatives
of both Yorkist and Lancastrian factions now devised a method
of getting rid of the usurper and healing the long-standing
breach between the two parties. Elizabeth, the oldest daughter
of Edward IV, who was with her mother in sanctuary, now had
the best Yorkist claim to the throne. The direct Lancastrian line
had run out with the death of Henry VI's son in 1471. A grand-
nephew of Somerset, Henry Tudor, Earl of Richmond, had something of a claim through John of Gaunt, however. His great-
grandfather—Cardinal Beaufort's brother John—had been born
to Catherine Swynford before she was more than the mistress of
John of Gaunt. Though Parliament had later legitimated the
children, Henry IV had ruled that this action did not cover
claims to the crown. Nevertheless, a clouded title is better than
none, and when politics so require technicalities can be overlooked. It was arranged that the claim of Henry Tudor—who
was prudently biding his time in France—should be supported
by both Lancastrians and Yorkists if he would agree to marry
Elizabeth. He promised, and in 1485 returned to England, where
he met Richard in battle at Bosworth, near Leicester in the midlands. Richard did not play the coward and offer his kingdom
for a horse, as Shakespeare and the propagandists of a later age
would have us think. According to the contemporary account,
"If he lost his life, he died a king," with the crown on his head,
trying to hack his way through Henry's bodyguard. The battered
headgear, picked out a thornbush after the battle, was placed
on the brow of the Earl of Richmond, now proclaimed King of
England as Henry VII. With this event the Wars of the Roses
ended. Historians have also found it a convenient stopping-point
for their descriptions of the Middle Ages in England, though of

course no definite date can really be assigned for the shading of one era into another.

## RELIGIOUS MOVEMENTS

**The State of the Church.** If the kings thus gave to the fourteenth and fifteenth centuries the appearance of decadence and the nobles seem to have been relapsing into—or giving free expression to their natural—barbarism, we may rightly expect that the Church was not in the best of condition at this time either. Throughout the height of the Middle Ages that great institution had been kept abreast of the moral consciousness of its day, as already indicated (pages 19, 104), by a succession of revivals of religious interest. The strength of the Church lay in its flexibility—in its being able to accept and absorb these new moral and religious ideas. The orthodox theory of authority, which ranked tradition and ecclesiastical interpretations of the Bible along with the Scriptures themselves, was admirably suited to preserving this ability. Unfortunately, however, the concentration of authority at Rome tended to make the Church bureaucratic. No longer was it willing to accept reforming innovations, but rather turned the wonderful instrument of its doctrine of authority to protecting the special interests of the bureaucrats and ecclesiastical politicians. Instead of welcoming the reformers as the essential white corpuscles in the clerical blood stream, the church authorities now treated these necessary nuisances as troublemakers and heretics.

**Wyclif.** Chief among the movements so persecuted in England was Lollardry, based on the teachings of John Wyclif, an Oxford priest and professor. Shocked by the idleness of the clergy—particularly the monks—and the abuse of their wealth, he applied feudal theory to the situation. About 1374 he began to suggest that financial power, like any other dominion, belonged only to those who use it rightly, and was forfeited when not employed according to the terms of the original contract. Let the secular authorities, therefore, take back the ecclesiastical holdings, he argued. According to his theory the churchmen, poor again like the original Apostles, would then recover some of the original apostolic zeal.

**Wyclif's Followers.** Such teaching naturally attracted much unworthy support. Many selfish noblemen, such as John of Gaunt, were willing to help out in the godly work of divesting the Church of its fine trappings. There were, however, many humble people who gladly heard the call to reform and accepted it sincerely. The wandering exhorters who spread this doctrine, the natural successors of the Friars of the preceding century, were called Lollards, from an old English word for wandering minstrels.

**Wyclif's Doctrinal Innovations.** When in 1378 the western Church was rent by the so-called Great Schism, a cleavage growing out of a disputed succession to the papacy, Wyclif was driven to even more searching criticisms of the established ecclesiastical order. He began to substitute the authority of the Bible for that of priests or the organized Church. He attacked the doctrine of transubstantiation, which declared that the substance of the communion bread and wine were miraculously changed to Christ's body and blood when the priest consecrated them. He put the responsibility on the individual for making his peace with God and obtaining salvation. In short, he championed virtually all the important principles of what we call Protestantism.

**The Suppression of the Movement.** Like Simon de Montfort's efforts in the preceding century, however, Wyclif's were generations in advance of their time. The ecclesiastical authorities set themselves to stamp out Lollardry. Wyclif they could not destroy, for when summoned to a church court he appeared leaning on the arm of John of Gaunt. But they did force him out of Oxford, and when in 1384 he suffered a fatal stroke as he was administering communion, the conservatives accepted the incident as both an appropriate fate and a sign of divine disapproval of his doctrines. They then took steps to suppress his teaching. For some years Parliament refused to sanction persecuting legislation, but when Henry IV came to the throne he tried to secure the support of the orthodox Catholic clergy by using his influence in their behalf. In 1401 a statute was passed providing for the burning of heretics.[3] After a revolt led by a Lollard named Sir John Oldcastle in 1414, this statute was vigorously enforced and the movement was driven underground. Only the humbler citizens continued to read the English version of the Bible that Wyclif's followers had prepared, and only these obscure men and women were brave enough to furnish an occasional martyr to the cause during the remainder of the century.

**Pecock's Proposed Solution Rejected.** Other efforts to revive the Church and its thought were similarly repressed. A bishop named Reginald Pecock who tried to win Lollards back to the fold by advocating the claims of reason as the ultimate religious authority was speedily imprisoned, though the conclusion he drew from his premise was that any reasonable man would accept the authority of the Church. So the moral vigor of the age declined. Monks feasted and amused themselves in the ways that Chaucer and Boccaccio have made famous. Here and there a few protesting voices were heard crying in the wilderness, but they went unheeded.

## ECONOMIC LIFE

**Government Control on a National Basis.** Only in the towns and among the agricultural laborers were there real signs of constructive activity. Manufacture and trade increased throughout the period, though not steadily. These economic activities were now organized and controlled on a national rather than a local basis, just as the governmental organization of the country was

[3] S-M, No. 69B, pp. 274-75.

taking on a more and more nationalistic (instead of feudal) aspect (page 268). Edward III, anxious to develop more financial resources for his wars, encouraged the English to do their own spinning and weaving instead of sending the raw wool abroad. The spiny plant whose cultivation he encouraged because its burs were useful for dressing cloth is still known as Edward III's cocklebur. His policy of levying high taxes on exports of raw materials gave an added inducement to home manufacture. Similarly, to ensure the protection of the royal interests and to counteract the effects of the Black Death the national government now undertook to control and regulate trade. For example, royal inspectors enforced fair standards in the manufacture of all exported woolens. In the reign of Richard II the first of a long series of navigation acts was passed, giving preference to the use of English ships by Englishmen engaged in foreign trade. This effort to devise and operate a nation-wide economic policy which would build up the wealth of England as against that of other countries marks the beginning of what was later to be known as the policy of mercantilism (page 314).

**The Rise of Capitalism: The Domestic System.** The growing prosperity of the very complex cloth trade led to the development of a new form of industrial organization. There were many processes in the making of cloth, from the carding (combing) of the original wool to the fulling (dressing) of the finished product. It therefore occurred to some of the cleverer masters of single processes, such as fulling, that instead of buying the woven cloth to dress, they might make more money by buying the raw wool and paying wages to carders and weavers for putting it through the other processes under their supervision. These entrepreneurs (French, undertakers) accordingly soon blossomed out as clothiers on a large scale, men who supplied the capital and management for the cloth trade while the rank and file worked for wages only. Since much of the piecework on the raw materials thus supplied was done in the workers' homes, this method of production in this period is known as the domestic system. Today, because of the low wages commonly paid where this system is employed, it is known as the sweatshop system.

**Changes in the Gilds.** The craft gilds, which had originally been associations of small masters (page 103), naturally opposed the development of this new type of economy. For example, the gilds commonly adopted rules prohibiting any master from having more than a small number of apprentices. Nevertheless the gilds themselves were largely responsible for the development of the new system, since they had come more and more under the control of the wealthier members and had therefore shaped their policies to fit the interests of this class. The rule limiting the number of apprentices was in part dictated by the desire to keep down competition and strengthen the personal monopoly of the few privileged members. For the same reason membership fees and general gild expenses were greatly increased, so that the ordinary journeyman found it very difficult to maintain full membership in the gild. The result was that the livery—a few members who could afford the costly festival dress (livery)—came to control the organization, while the poorer masters and journeymen occupied a subordinate rank and were known as yeomen. In other words, the organization of the gilds reflected the general oligarchic trend in the towns as a whole (page 262). The rising capitalistic entrepreneurs commonly evaded the gild restrictions, however, by moving their establishments to the country, beyond the reach of gild regulations. Because this made for freer trade, it was doubtless a step forward, economically speaking.

**Foreign Trade and Banking.** Since England was now manufacturing her own cloth, it was natural that merchants trading overseas should organize for marketing this product just as the Staplers had for the export of the raw wool (page 104). These new traders were known as merchant adventurers, but since they traded in various parts of Germany, Scandinavia, and the Low

Countries, several different companies were established to regulate the trade in the different areas. The Staplers protested against this development and claimed the right to handle manufactured cloth themselves, but the English government steadily overruled their objections. In these foreign trading companies each merchant traded on his own responsibility; the company was only a kind of trade association that established and enforced codes of fair practice. These companies were therefore called regulated companies, because the trade which their members carried on was a regulated one. It is significant of the growing prosperity of the merchant class that after defaulting on the Continental debts in 1345 it was possible for the government to finance the French campaigns by loans raised in the home market. The infant banking industry thus passed into native hands.

**General Prosperity of the Trading Classes.** The disorders of the fifteenth century did not have such a disastrous effect on the economic life of the country as might be supposed. Throughout the Lancastrian and Yorkist periods the towns generally held aloof from the dynastic quarrels and continued to grow and even flourish, while the brunt of the Wars of the Roses was born by the aristocratic classes and their dependents. The large perpendicular Gothic churches put up by the wool towns of the eastern counties in this century bear eloquent witness to the prosperity of those communities and their different gilds.

**The Agricultural Situation: The Enclosure Movement.** During the early part of this period economic life in the country went on much as before. The open fields of the manor were subjected to their annual rounds of cultivation and biennial or triennial cycles of crop rotation much as they had been in the earlier Middle Ages. In the fifteenth century, however, the prosperity of the wool industry combined with other factors, to be explained later (page 264), brought about a great change. This was a marked increase in the practice, not unknown in earlier centuries, of the landlords' enclosing the open fields and using

them for sheep pastures. Since this activity required fewer workers than did the raising of grain, the tendency was for the peasants to be evicted from their holdings in places where eviction
proved to be possible. These enclosures produced bitter complaints and led the peasants to claim legal rights to certain privileges that they had been gradually securing from their lords
during the preceding century. But as the effort to establish these
rights involved constitutional points yet to be explained, it is, in
Kipling's phrase, another story, and must be postponed to the
next chapter.

# 12. THE DISTRIBUTION OF POWER

**General Characteristics.** In looking more closely at the constitutional side of society in the late Middle Ages, we see governmental power still being distributed roughly according to the medieval pattern, which should now be familiar. King, Church, and nobles continue to share the rule. But there are some noteworthy variations in the general pattern. The kings are no longer such strong rulers, and on the whole, the Church is losing its grip. The nobles are employing a new device, Parliament, to make their influence felt. Social groups lower in the scale than king, Church, and nobles are clamoring for political attention. The towns are growing into powers of major consequence. Even the small rural landholders, twanging faithfully with their yew bows at Sunday afternoon shooting practice, are learning a symphony whose theme will become more and more insistent.

## THE CROWN AND THE CHURCH

**The Monarchy: Personal Factors.** Personal factors continued to be very important in determining the distribution of power in late medieval English society. The fondness of Edward II for his gambling companions put him at the mercy of his jealous nobles. But when a countess insulted his wife by refusing her admission to a castle where she sought shelter, he showed that he could rouse himself temporarily from his indolence and reassert his authority. Had Richard II not so soon lost the wife of whom he was so fond, the whole constitutional history of the fifteenth century might have been different. The desire of Edward III for glory and the mental weakness of Henry VI were also important elements affecting the balance of power during this time. The fact that there were so many weak kings and so few stark and wrathful ones distinguishes this period constitutionally from its predecessor.

**The Church: Its Difficulties.** During the fourteenth and fifteenth centuries the Church continued to claim all its earlier powers. The theory of Boniface VIII (page 116) remained unchanged, though the political realities of the time caused it to be greatly modified in practice. The declining moral prestige of the Church, combined with the effects of the Great Schism (page 245), made for a further separation between the ideal and the actual situation. The Church was therefore not able to take advantage of the opportunity presented to it by the weakness of the kings.

**Nationalism.** The rise of the national spirit was one of the political realities that weakened the power of the international clerical organization. Even within the ranks of the clergy themselves nationalism tended to diminish cohesiveness and discipline. At the great church council held at Constance in Switzerland in 1414 the churchmen present demanded and obtained the privilege of voting by nations rather than as common members of the mother body, and the English were recognized for the first time as a separate nationality. In England we have seen this spirit of nationalism manifesting itself in opposition to the claims of the papacy as early as the time of Henry III (page 95) and appearing again during the next century in the last year of Edward I when Parliament insisted on passing the Statute of Carlisle (page 118). This internal quarrel among the churchmen weakened their hold over the laity. Not only did the clergy tend to lose the prestige conferred by their earlier united front, but at the same time the protesting clergy welcomed the support of large sections of the laity that made their voice heard in their own interests with a petition against the papal claims. It was a dangerous precedent, since if laymen were encouraged to protest against the authority of one part of the Church, they might become impatient of any clerical restraint.

**Lay Feeling: Provisors and "Praemunire."** Yet the clergy continued to solicit lay support in their struggle with Rome, and when the kings found it to their interests not to enforce the Statute of Carlisle, the agitation in Parliament was renewed. The English laity were particularly hostile to the papacy after the outbreak of the Hundred Years' War, because at that time and for forty years afterward the popes were residing at Avignon on the southern border of France and were very much under the French influence. The English suspected that moneys paid to the pope eventually found their way into the enemy's war chests. So strongly did the English feel on this point, in fact, that after the battle of Poitiers they boasted that if the Pope was French, Jesus was English. For they had appealed—successfully, as it seemed—to the God of Battles against His alleged agent on earth. The culmination of this feeling was reached in the Parliaments of 1351 and 1353, where two important statutes were passed. The first, called the Statute of Provisors,[1] decreed that anyone who accepted a papal appointment to an English benefice should be imprisoned until he paid a fine and surrendered all such claims to office. Two years later the Statute of *Praemunire* was passed to strengthen the hand of the royal courts in their jurisdictional struggle with the papal ones.[2] It re-enforced an already established principle by providing means whereby litigants appealing to the court of "another" in matters "whereof the cognizance

[1] S-M, No. 62E, p. 226.
[2] S-M, No. 62G, pp. 227-28. The commonly accepted interpretation of this statute as providing for drastic penalties is a mistake, since the original *Praemunire* act was concerned mostly with process in such cases, and the severe punishments were laid down in later statutes. See E. B. Graves, "The Legal Significance of the Statute of Praemunire in 1353," *Anniversary Essays in Medieval History by Students of Charles Homer Haskins*, Houghton Mifflin, 1929, pp. 56-80.

pertaineth to the king's court" could be forced to appear in the royal courts for trial and punishment. Later statutes dealing with this problem provided that people guilty of such actions should be imprisoned for life and forfeit all their goods. This new type of legislation did not affect established areas of ecclesiastical jurisdiction, such as those of marriage and probate work, but it did provide a means of enforcing the Statute of Provisors by punishing those benefice-hunters who tried to summon the pope to their aid. During this period also the English suspended the payments of the tribute promised by John when he acknowledged the Pope as his overlord. When the Pope pressed for payment in 1366 Parliament renounced the obligation entirely, on the ground that John had no right to bind the realm without consulting the lords and commons.

**Underlying Co-operation of King and Pope.** Thus on the old controversial points of control of personnel, court jurisdiction, and finance there were renewed troubles in the relation of temporal and spiritual arms during this period, with attacks made on the papal powers in each case. Since so much of the power of the Church in England depended on its international character and the support it received from abroad, it is clear that these onslaughts tended to diminish the share of political power which the clergy exercised. Yet the fact that the kings generally did not choose to enforce the Statutes of Provisors and *Praemunire* shows that the Church continued to be an integral part of society and to enjoy the co-operation of the secular authorities in the great majority of its efforts. Although supplementary legislation designed to enforce the Provisors and *Praemunire* principles was passed by Parliament from time to time, the monarchs still found it convenient to make bargains with the pope (page 118). By allowing violations of the Statute of Provisors, particularly, the rights of private patrons could be taken from them and divided between the two august conspirators. In this way the king continued to exercise a considerable voice in the filling of important vacancies in the ecclesiastical establishment.

## THE NOBLES AND PARLIAMENT

**The Power of the Nobles.** In general, however, the king and the Church declined in political influence, as we have seen, and as they declined, the nobles and their allies gained in relative strength. This they sometimes showed by the method of the time of Henry III, seizing control of the Council and either working through it or appointing a particular reforming body to carry out their will. The latter device was attempted in 1310, when a body of twenty-one lay and ecclesiastical magnates was appointed to reform the government. These were known as the Lords Ordainers, and their decrees, issued the following year, were known as the Ordinances of 1311.[3] As we have noticed, however (page 230), this experiment soon failed because of divisions in the baronial party. Similarly the efforts of the Lords Appellant (page 235) under Richard II to control the government by means of the Council also failed.

**Parliament as a Tool of the Nobles.** The strength of the nobility was much more effectively shown in Parliament. This body, being so much larger than the Council, was far more difficult for the king to control, and the story of the development of its powers in this period is largely the story of the increasing importance of the nobility in late medieval England. During this period Parliament made good its claim to control all nonfeudal taxation. In the early years of the century, it is true, Edward I secured papal absolution from his Confirmation of the Charters (page 150), and subsequently he and Edward II made agreements with merchants by which, without parliamentary consent, they increased the indirect taxes (customs duties) on the export of wool. But Parliament was jealous of the principle, and several

[3] S-M, No. 56, pp. 193-98.

times passed legislation authorizing these past collections in order to keep alive the principle that there was no such right of taxation without its approval. In his financial difficulties of the 1340's (page 234) Edward III was driven to consent to a restatement of the old rule.[4] All levies of aid or charge of any kind without parliamentary consent were now forbidden. Edward ignored this restriction on one or two later occasions when he again raised the customs rates by making bargains with the merchants or his Council. Parliament continued its protests, however, and by statutes of 1362 and 1371 prohibited these private bargains and ensured its own control of the very important power of the purse. The King still had his "own" income—his feudal revenues and the return from his lands—which was independent of parliamentary control. But this was insufficient to support his government in full, and the necessity of securing parliamentary permission for the raising of the supplementary income seriously weakened the royal power. By threatening to withhold its consent to essential taxes Parliament was able to secure concessions in several other important fields also.

**Legislation.** In the sphere of legislation Parliament made particularly notable gains. While in the time of Edward I nearly all the acts of Parliament originated with the King or his Council, now the procedure by petition (page 151) became much more common. In the weak reign of Edward II, when during much of the time the barons had control of the government, the royal officials did little more than draft the statutes or ordinances to fit the parliamentary pleasure. In the first year of Edward III the knights and burgesses asked that their petitions might be made into statutes. By the end of the reign the majority of the legislation passed by Parliament came from that body itself rather than from the King or his Council. To the end of the Middle Ages the monarchs in approving statutes or ordinances occasionally made modifications in the original petition, either

[4] S-M, No. 62B, pp. 223-24.

as to its substance or as to the time during which the statute should have effect. But they did not presume to give it a contrary meaning. Furthermore, the Commons in 1414 claimed the right—and to a large extent secured it in succeeding reigns—of acting on these amendments. After an act had passed both houses of Parliament, however, the king might veto it altogether. This he did with the euphemistic expression, *"Le roi s'avisera"*—"The King will think it over." When the power of the crown revived under the Yorkists, the influence of Parliament on the shaping of legislation naturally declined. In the last years of this period most of the acts passed seem to have originated in the royal Council.

**Administration.** Over the actual administration of the government Parliament was able to gain some measure of control, though not a very extensive one. In 1340-41 it claimed and exercised the right to audit the royal accounts—that is, to see that the money voted had been spent as originally promised—and thereafter this right was never directly denied. Another area of administrative power on which Parliament made inroads was the control of the king's ministers. The Ordinances of 1311 provided that royal officials were to hold office only with the consent of Parliament, and though the Ordinances were later repealed, in 1341 Edward III was forced to accept a similar arrangement.[5] He shortly repudiated it, on the ground that his consent to it had been given under duress,[6] but as previously mentioned (page 235), Richard II was subjected to similar restraints for a brief period. In 1406 Henry IV was also compelled to accept for a short time a Council nominated by Parliament and virtually responsible to it after the manner of a modern English Cabinet (page 496). Another effort in the same direction was the claim of Parliament, being the largest and most important of the royal courts, to the right of impeachment, that is, to accuse the royal

5 S-M, No. 61E, pp. 213-17, particularly p. 215.
6 S-M, No. 62C, pp. 224-25.

officials of misconduct and to try them on such charges. In 1376, during the dotage of Edward III, this claim was asserted and exercised in the case of two royal officials whom a baronial faction controlling Parliament undertook to punish. Impeachment proceedings were also carried through at various other times when the crown was virtually powerless. Occasionally Parliament also undertook to control the administration of the government by presuming to force advice upon the king under the threat of withholding funds. But the success of this method of dominating governmental policy rarely outlasted the session of the body itself.

## PARLIAMENTARY CLAIMS OF PRIVILEGE

**Freedom from Arrest.** Even more shadowy were the claims of privilege by which members of Parliament strove to strengthen their position. They asserted that as members of a royal court engaged in official business they must be free from arrest during the meetings of Parliament and for a reasonable time before and afterwards. This claim did not apply to suspected felons, and was designed mainly to free debt-ridden parliamentarians from the most unpleasant importunities of their creditors. It did, however, have some constitutional significance, since if this privilege were recognized, it would serve to prevent intimidation of members of Parliament or their forcible detention from the sessions of their body when an important vote was to be taken. But the fact that some members of Parliament did suffer arrest in this period shows that the claim was not yet fully established.

**Freedom of Speech.** The same consideration applies to the much more important claim of freedom of speech in Parliament. If the members of the royal court, so ran this claim, were to give the king sound advice, they must be permitted to speak their minds freely and even voice sentiments which might be offensive to the royal ears. A corollary to this privilege was that, also claimed, of having free access to the king, through their Speaker, to take up with the monarch any matter which the Commons wished to have considered. These claims seem reasonable enough to an age brought up in a democratic tradition, but in 1376 one Peter de la Mare, Speaker of the House of Commons, was imprisoned for his part in the so-called Good Parliament, which had impeached the royal ministers in that year. Again in 1451 a member named Yonge proposed that the crown be given to the Duke of York, and was speedily thrown in prison for his rashness. In both cases the victims were released when the wheel of political fortune took a turn, and high-sounding claims of this privilege were then freely made. But throughout the fifteenth century Parliament commonly confined its attentions to the matters set before it by the Council, and did not presume to speak on forbidden topics, such as those relating to the king personally.

**The Usefulness of Parliament.** However imperfectly developed the powers of Parliament may have been at this time, the institution yet served a very useful purpose as a mechanism for bringing the influence of the nobility to bear on the problems of government. Though troublesome baronial factions continued to be all too plentiful in this period, the experience of co-operating in parliamentary activities doubtless served somewhat to reduce their number, and was excellent training in the art of class government that was later to be so important in England.

## THE KNIGHTS AND BURGESSES IN PARLIAMENT

**Powers of the Knights and Burgesses.** We have spoken thus far as though Parliament were a vehicle for the expression of the power of the nobility only. But the knights (who were not nobles, page 231) and burgesses played an increasingly important part in its deliberations during this period. We have noticed (page 150) that by the terms of the Confirmation of the Charters in 1297 their consent to the imposition of any nonfeudal tax appears to have been considered necessary. These social elements were not included, however, in the Parliaments envisaged by the Ordinances of 1311 as hearing complaints and disciplining royal officials. But they were present at times of important crises, such as the adoption of the Ordinances, and their repeal in 1322. On the latter occasion it was enacted in the Statute of York[7]— so called from the place where Parliament was meeting—that "the matters which are to be established for the estate of our lord the King and of his heirs and for the estate of the realm and of the people shall be treated, accorded, and established in Parliament by our lord the King and by the assent of the prelates, earls, and barons, and commonalty of the realm." In other words, the commons, as the knights and burgesses were called, were to be consulted on all matters with a serious bearing on the national welfare. The statute itself was primarily concerned with the repeal of the Ordinances, and this phraseology was inserted casually, as though merely describing a reasonably well-established practice. Nor was the promise always strictly observed in the years immediately following. Nevertheless, it reflects a growing sentiment as to the importance of the commons, and thereafter the representative knights and burgesses were more and more regularly summoned to the sessions of Parliament along with the nobles. In the reign of Edward II they also developed the practice of initiating their own petitions instead of merely following the lead of the nobles and endorsing the requests of their social superiors. By the middle of the fourteenth century the House of Commons was definitely established—with a formal organization (page 277)—as an important element of Parliament, and after that time Parliament did not act on matters of major consequence without the consent of the knights and burgesses.

[7] S-M, No. 58, pp. 204-05.

**Continued Subordination to the Nobles.** This is not to say, however, that by 1350 the so-called commons enjoyed an equal voice with the nobles in political affairs. In the majority of cases where governmental initiative appears to come from the House of Commons closer investigation seems to reveal that the knights and burgesses who did the unpleasant work were acting on the advice and suggestion of nobles who did not wish to appear too prominently on the scene. Since the king might easily take vengeance on a few lords, the magnates found it expedient to seek shelter behind the comparative anonymity of a sizable House of Commons, many of whose members were their relatives or dependents in one way or another. For example, Peter de la Mare, whose troubles we have recounted above (page 259), was the steward of the Earl of March. Furthermore, before the end of this period the original idea that a parliamentary burgess must be a citizen of the community he represented was abandoned, and neighboring magnates were sometimes allowed to name one or more of their younger sons or other dependents as burgesses (page 276). Because of this alliance between the opposition nobles and the House of Commons, it is exceedingly difficult to say just how much the power of the small landlords and wealthy merchants had actually grown.

**But Some Advance Made.** This development cannot have been wholly illusory, however. The fact that battles were now fought more by archers and mercenaries than by armored men on horseback diminished the importance of the nobles and increased that of the classes which could supply the new sinews of war. Though to the end of the period the influence of the knights and burgesses remained much below that of the lords spiritual and temporal, it steadily increased as the countryside became more peaceful before the Wars of the Roses and as the towns grew in prosperity.

**Classes Affected.** However much power they held, these new classes, it should be carefully noted, were not common in the

ordinary sense, or even middle class as Americans would use the
term. They were only common in the sense that they did not
have titles of nobility. They were actually upper middle class
or better, in the sense that they had enough to live on without
working any regular hours. In 1429, when membership in Parliament had come to be considered a privilege, the right to vote in
the county courts which elected the knights of the shire was
restricted to forty-shilling freeholders—that is, to people who
held land in honorable tenure to a rental value of forty shillings
a year or over.[8] This restricted the county franchise, in practice,
to the landed gentry, since if yeomen held lands of that value,
they were commonly copyhold (page 266) rather than freehold.
In the same century an oligarchic movement in the towns
reached its climax. As a result most of the town corporations,
which elected the burgesses, fell into the hands of a small inner
circle of wealthy merchants who controlled matters to suit themselves. What we in America would call the middle and lower
classes, therefore, still remained virtually disfranchised and without appreciable voice in the government. What had happened
was that political power was being acquired by more and more
elements at the top of the social scale.

## CLASS LINES AND THE MERCHANTS

**Fluidity of Class Lines in the Upper Levels.** This upper-class
monopoly of power may be seen more clearly when we observe
that the English system of titles and primogeniture made for
easy passage from one branch of the upper class to another. In
England the younger sons of nobles were not considered nobles,
as they were in France. The oldest son alone inherited the title,
and the others were technically commoners. They might receive
a manor or two by some special settlement and become ordinary
knights or country gentry. They might even be apprenticed to

[8] S-M, No. 69E, pp. 276-77.

merchants in a neighboring town. On the other hand, the married woman took her husband's rank, and then as now a wealthy merchant's daughter was considered a good catch by scions of the less prosperous nobility. A merchant's grandchildren might therefore be titled nobility in their own right. Some successful traders themselves were raised to the nobility, the first being Michael de la Pole, the son of a Hull merchant, who was created Earl of Suffolk in 1385. The English upper class therefore regularly tended to broaden out. The frequent comings and goings between town and country made for considerable fluidity of class lines as between landed gentry and prosperous merchants.

**Similar Fluidity in the Towns: The Resulting Peacefulness of Town Life.** In the towns this fluidity of class lines was to be seen not only at the top, but all the way down the ladder. The ambitious apprentice, however poor, might hope to rise in a single generation to a position of prominence in his gild and community. This open door of opportunity in the towns relieved most of the pressure from the disfranchised burghers—the smaller merchants—since the able among them, their potential leaders, could rise above their original station in life, and did not feel the necessity of agitating for an increase of political privileges for their class. In most English towns of this period, therefore, we do not find those stern struggles between the larger and smaller gilds which at this time mark the history of the older Continental towns, where class lines within the community had hardened. There are a few exceptions, as at Bristol, where there was practically a civil war for two years in the time of Edward II, but for the most part town life was peaceful during the later Middle Ages.

## THE DECLINE OF FEUDALISM

**The Longbow and the Black Death.** In the country, however, there was a definite legal barrier to be attacked. That was
villeinage, which sharply marked off the free from the unfree,
the honorable tenant from the menial. We have noticed that
the methods of husbandry continued almost unchanged during
the fourteenth century (page 249). It was natural, therefore, that
the legal framework of this system should not readily yield to
demands for change. Yet powerful forces were working to this
end. (1) The innovations in military tactics and organization we
have already noted. When longbowmen learned to bring down
armored knights, it was more difficult for the latter to dominate the neighborhood and intimidate the peasantry than it had
been before. (2) The Black Death (page 233), by reducing the
available labor supply at least a third, put the surviving villeins in a very strong bargaining position. It was obviously to
the landlord's interest to cling to his old rights of work service
as tightly as possible, and had the landed proprietors been able
to stand together, the plague might have resulted in a perpetua-
tion of feudal practices. In 1351 they did put through Parliament a Statute of Laborers,[9] which prohibited any alteration in
the rate of wages customary before the pestilence. But in spite of
the appointment of special justices to enforce it—justices who
enjoyed some success at first—employers attempting to steal a
march on their fellows in the search for laborers gradually broke
down the restrictions and enticed men from their former loca-
tions by paying more than the statute permitted. The workmen also paid fines rather than comply with the terms of the
law. The result was that to hold any villeins on a manor at all
it was necessary to grant them more generous terms than they
had previously been able to obtain.

[9] S-M, No. 62D, pp. 225-26.

**Commutation.** (3) This led to the speeding-up of a process called commutation, which had already been going on since the thirteenth century. As England became more prosperous, there was more money in circulation, and under an enhanced money economy it was easier for the ambitious villein to secure the means of bargaining with his lord when the opportunity presented itself. Just as the towns had purchased charters from royalty and nobles in distress, so the villeins offered cash down in exchange for the right to pay only sums of money in the future instead of fulfilling all the various service obligations under the original "contract." Because a great number of different obligations were covered by the one annual payment, this process was called commutation, just as the monthly ticket that covers the cost of many different daily rides on the suburban trains today is called a commutation ticket. All through the Middle Ages the landlords had been commuting labor services or reimposing them, as their interests seemed to dictate, and the developments of the fourteenth century were merely a continuation of this process, though the advantage now happened to be in the hands of the villein tenants.

**The Peasants' Revolt.** This improvement in the peasants' status naturally whetted their appetite for further progress in the same direction, even at the cost of violence. For revolutions are more frequently attempted by impatient classes already rising than by a people in absolute destitution. The peasants began to protest against the conditions of service, where any remained, about the amount of rent demanded, and against the legal status of villeinage itself.

> When Adam delved and Eve span,
> Who was then the gentleman?

they inquired passionately. A priest named John Ball preached such doctrines around London. Wyclif, by his contemporary agitation against the wealth of the Church, unintentionally added fuel to the flame. Eventually, in 1381, the imposition of a poll tax, which bore heavily on the lower classes, furnished an issue on which the peasantry—in combination with dissatisfied elements in the towns—made a determined effort to throw off their legal bonds and obtain political rights. Led by one Wat Tyler, they succeeded in capturing London and securing the promise of their legal freedom and a reduction in rent. After the revolt was suppressed by the gentlemanly means already alluded to (page 235), these promises were all broken, and the radical movement came to nothing.

**Copyholders.** Nevertheless the process of commutation went steadily on, and by the end of the Middle Ages there were very few villeins left who were obligated to do personal service for their holdings. The vast majority now rendered only the annual payments, and were called copyholders because they held their land by virtue of a copy of the manorial record of their customary rents taken from the original record in the roll of the lord's court. In practice they were now considered freemen. Whether or not this copy constituted a legal title that could be maintained in case the lord wished to evict them from their holdings and enclose his manor for some such purpose as a sheeprun, or pasture, was a matter of great dispute. The king's courts of common law, hungry for jurisdiction and anxious to carry out the royal policies of keeping down the overmighty subject and treating the common man paternally, protected the copyholders wherever they could find a reasonable excuse for doing so. In theory they were bound by the custom of the particular manor, which originally had nearly always been in the lord's favor (page 121). But in perhaps half the cases brought before the royal courts the king's justices found what they considered sufficient grounds for interpreting this custom in favor of the copyholder and thus allowing him to sue the lord for ejecting him from his holding.

**The Growing Strength of the Lower Orders.** The lower class and the lower middle class were thus improving their economic and legal status during this period. Politically they failed to obtain any definite foothold, but indirectly they were exercising some influence. The triumph of the Yorkists under Edward IV over the Lancastrians was in part a victory for the party that commanded the greatest amount of popular support. With changing military and economic conditions the power that in late Saxon and early Norman times had been absorbed by the upper strata of society was beginning to seep back to the ordinary people, who once more, as in the early Saxon period, supplied a considerable share of the important social needs. That is to say, the people who now bore the brunt of the fighting and were increasingly important in the processes of producing goods and creating wealth were also on the way to securing political influence. For political power is normally a function (product) of service to society.

# 13. THE MACHINERY OF GOVERNMENT

**The General Change from Personal to National and Official Outlook.** Although the nobles, the gentry, and their burgher allies obtained a larger share of political power in this period than they had enjoyed in the preceding one, it has been noted that they exercised it not through the medium of the old feudal "contract" but through the machinery of the central government, which the monarchs had originally created. Instead of trying to set up or maintain little semiautonomous units of government of the sort envisaged by the barons as late as the time of the Great Charter, they now attempted to control the Council and to use its enlarged form, that is to say, Parliament, to make their influence felt. They were not now attempting so much to limit the central government as to determine its course of action. In other words, royal machinery now became national machinery, and its personal aspects tended to become lost in its official ones. That is a difficult distinction to catch, but one that is essential to the understanding of the period. The actions of a president of a modern college fraternity or class may appear much the same whether they are taken at his own pleasure or at the instance of an executive committee of the whole group. But we all know that there is a vast difference between the one type, which is predominantly personal, and the other, which is largely official.

## THE MONARCHY

**Establishment of the Parentelic System of Succession.** Just as some student presidencies may be tightly controlled by restrictive forces, so it was with the institution of monarchy in this period. For appearances' sake the old rules built up by the strong monarchs of the preceding period were observed wherever possible. But there was growing up the notion of monarchy as an exalted office that might be bigger than the person who happened to fill it, and in case of necessity this concept took precedence over the other. After the disappointing experience with John—whose legal claim to the throne, as we have seen (page 92; *cf.* page 220), depended on the gradual theory—the parentelic system of succession was accepted as normal, even though it subjected the nation to the difficulties of minority rule in the cases of Edward III, Richard II, Henry VI, and Edward V. Actually this feudal practice was not so well adapted to the monarchy as to vassals, for after the disavowal of the papal overlordship there was no one legally bound to supply the necessary protection to minor heirs. As already indicated (page 237), the wardship in such cases had to be furnished by committees of those who were properly vassals. Yet the feudal principle of parentelic succession had a strong hold, and except for a minor departure from it at the accession of Henry VII—when his mother, who transmitted the hereditary claim to him and who was still living, was quietly passed over—the only time when it was disregarded was in the special circumstances surrounding the deposition of Richard II and the accession of Henry IV. And the woes which followed on this departure from the letter of feudal law were sufficient to discourage further inclinations to deviate from the rule.

**Growth of the Official Theory of Monarchy.** Yet the very succession of minor heirs which this system involved hastened the development of the official theory of kingship. When a commit-

tee of regents was acting for Edward II or those of his successors who reigned as minors, it was inevitable that the office
should be regarded as something apart from the person who
technically held it. For example, the governess appointed for
the infant Henry VI was given authority by the conciliar ordinance issued in the royal name "to chastise us reasonably from
time to time as the case may require." The kingship was also
removed from the category of a mere feudal overlordship by
the passage in 1352 of the Statute of Treasons, which formally
put disloyalty to the crown in a class by itself among crimes.[1]
Besides punishing offenses against the royal person and family,
this statute also ranked as treason the offenses of counterfeiting
the king's seals or money, and killing the royal judges while engaged on official business. In other words, the office was protected as well as the individual who held it.

**"Constitutional" Monarchy.** This attitude, as already suggested, made possible the deposition of Edward II and Richard II, on the theory that the office was bigger than the man
and that they were incapable of filling it properly. It is noteworthy, however, that for the sake of legal appearances in each
case an effort was made to secure a formal abdication, and that
the successor, while confirmed by Parliament, was not chosen
from among the citizenry at large but was of the blood royal.
These depositions show that the monarchy was by no means absolute. Whoever filled the office did so with the possibility of
enforced abdication never entirely absent from his consciousness. As Bracton had suggested (page 203), he was under the
law, and whoever controlled Parliament decided what the law
was. It is not improper to refer to this period, particularly the
Lancastrian part of it, as an experiment in constitutionalism,
using that term in the restricted sense which the historian Hal-
lam popularized, as referring to a limited monarchy.

[1] S-M, No. 62F, p. 227.

# THE MACHINERY OF GOVERNMENT

**Functions of the Monarchy.** Whether a person or a group controlled the office, however, it was responsible for most of the
work of the central government. It represented the state in foreign affairs, headed the army, nominated the incumbents of most
of the offices, awarded titles, participated in all Council meetings, and supervised the administration of justice. It was easily
and unquestionably the main cog in the machinery of central
government.

## CHANGES IN ADMINISTRATIVE OFFICES AND THE COUNCIL

**General Trend in Administrative and Household Offices.** In
the administrative and household offices the trend from personal to official attitudes may also be seen.[2] In the struggles between the king and the nobles which distinguished the fourteenth century, especially under Edward II, the tendency was
for the older of these offices to fall into the hands of the baronial
opposition. The monarch might then try to develop new agencies to do his will, but in the end they too were limited or taken
over altogether. In the heat of the strife both sides were driven
to institute, or at least to support, administrative reforms, so that
the outlines of the later system of central government administration were quite largely developed at this time.

**Chancery and Exchequer.** Both the Chancery and the Exchequer remained out of court, and were therefore captured relatively easily whenever the opposition rose. By carefully prescrib-
ing rules for the conduct of these agencies, in such documents
as the Ordinances of 1311 (page 255), the nobles' party was able
to make its voice heard in administrative matters, and also to
do its share of reform work.

[2] For a detailed description of the household offices of Edward II, including
many of the more personal ones, see S-M, No. 57, pp. 199-204.

**The Wardrobe.** Over the Wardrobe there was a keener struggle, because as yet it was more closely connected with the court. Though the so-called Privy Wardrobe and Great Wardrobe—for military and general stores respectively—had been localized in the Tower, the parent Wardrobe body had continued to travel with the king and have charge of his personal finances. As these tended to get out of hand and absorb more and more of the national revenue for the festivities and favorites of Edward II —not forgetting his lion, whose expense account is carefully itemized in the records—the barons naturally tried to secure control of this agency also. It was dealt with by the Ordinances of 1311, but not until 1318, when the Wardrobe was definitely subordinated to the Exchequer, was anything approaching effective control established.

**The Chamber.** The royal answer to this move was to revive the Chamber, the body from which the Wardrobe had originally sprung. By attaching manors and other sources of revenue to it and having the proceeds paid in directly to the Chamber the king was still able to retain some privately controlled financial machinery. Not until 1355-56 did the opposition succeed in enforcing its demand that this body should also be responsible to the Exchequer, receiving its funds through the major treasury and accounting to it.

**The Privy Seal.** At the same time the growing complexity of governmental problems, combined with the political rivalry between king and nobles, led to further developments on the record-keeping side of the government. In order to prevent the king from employing the Privy Seal to interrupt lawsuits and otherwise secure obedience to his will, the barons seized control of that agency in the 1311 reforms. The Controller, or Keeper, as he was now called, was separated from the Wardrobe, given a distinct office, and temporarily made subject to Parliament. While this latter restriction soon broke down, the Keepership of the Privy Seal remained a separate office, which was frequently, but not always, out of court. Although still employed by the king for some purposes, the seal was also used by other branches of the government, notably the Council, in such a way as to confirm its semi-independent position.

**The Secretary.** It was therefore necessary for the king to develop yet another agency for his own correspondence. After experimenting during the middle of the century with various minor seals, the monarchy at the beginning of the reign of Richard II hit upon the device of having an official Secretary charged with the custody of the king's signet (finger ring), of which the setting could be used to stamp sealing wax with the royal insignia. Probably this was because the king was a minor at the time, and he was considered incapable of keeping and properly employing his own means of authenticating documents. From this time on it became customary for the king when he wished the Chancery to issue a letter patent, for example, to write a note with his own signature—the sign manual, it was called—to the Secretary, who drew up the desired document and sent it on under the signet to the Privy Seal, who repeated the process, so that eventually the Chancellor, authorized by the Privy Seal, issued the formal letter. This was a long and cumbersome procedure which indicates the degree to which the monarchy and its agents had become officialized. Yet it should also be pointed out that in the fifteenth century, as the nobility found in Parliament a more and more convenient means of making its power felt, the household and administrative offices came back into closer relationship with the crown. Whatever control over them Parliament was to exercise for some centuries thereafter was largely through the monarchy itself and was not applied directly. It is from the office of Secretary, incidentally, that most of the important administrative agencies were to develop in modern times (page 562), and from it we in America have borrowed the pattern for most of our cabinet posts.

**The Council.** The Council, like the household and administrative offices, developed considerably in this period and for much the same reasons. At times the opposition relied on it as a weapon against the king. More frequently all parties joined in leaving to it the great mass of routine work that the growing complexity of the government necessitated. The Small Council, now called merely the Council and later the Privy Council, became in this period definitely separated from the Great Council, which became virtually the House of Lords, the upper house of Parliament. While the Council still commonly followed the king in his travels, it was given a definite home in Westminster, where it endeavored to meet regularly at certain times a year for legal business. Besides employing the Privy Seal for its most important documents it had a definite staff of clerks to keep its records. The Council usually consisted of ten to twenty important personages, both ecclesiastics and laymen, including the Chancellor, the Treasurer, and one or two other royal officials. All were sworn to secrecy and to give honest counsel. The Council met several times a week and sometimes daily, but by no means all its members were present at its sessions. Four was generally considered a quorum, and the average attendance was not far from that figure. The king himself was now rarely present at the meetings. The Council lived up to its name by giving the king advice from time to time—advice that he did not always accept. It also issued ordinances that are difficult to distinguish from statutes, but which did not possess quite the same authority, since they were concerned rather with administrative regulations than with statements of fundamental law. It heard special legal cases of a type that will be described more in detail in the next chapter (page 287). It did a vast amount of routine government business, hearing complaints, considering the problems of overseas possessions, struggling with the royal debts, arranging for the supply of munitions of war, feeding garrisons, and even providing for the animals in the inevitable royal zoo.[3]

## PARLIAMENT AND THE REVENUE SYSTEM

**The House of Lords.** The machinery of Parliament was also becoming more definite in this period. The king was still considered an integral part of his High Court of Parliament, and the actions of this body were said to be those of the king in Parliament. He might attend and preside over the House of Lords in person, but commonly this prerogative was exercised by his representative, the Lord Chancellor. Because of the importance of the wool trade in the English economy (pages 101, 247) that official when presiding usually sat upon a conveniently shaped sack of wool, so that he would be reminded at all times to do nothing harmful to this great industry. The woolsack thus became the symbol of the office of Lord Chancellor. During the fourteenth century the Council as such ceased to sit in the sessions of Parliament. In part, this is to be explained by the fact that the Council now had its own quarters and tended to withdraw to them. But to some extent it must also have been the result of the nobles' objection to having royal officials sit with them as equals. After the middle of this century, unless the members of the Council were otherwise qualified, they did not attend. Accordingly, we find a clearer notion of peerage developing. Membership in the House of Lords now came to be considered rather an honor than a duty, and the royal advisers exercised a more careful scrutiny over those summoned than they had formerly done. Those barons who were selected came to be called regularly, and their sons after them, so that a hereditary peerage was established. The higher nobles were also summoned, as a matter of course. In addition, from the last part

[3] For samples of the records of council business, see S-M, No. 70, pp. 279-85.

of the fourteenth century new nobles were created from time to time by letters patent. All the bishops were invited to sessions of the House of Lords, but the number of abbots and priors was reduced. Whether the bishops were summoned as barons or as separate spiritual peers has never been quite determined, but by the end of this period we have a definite House of Lords, consisting of two archbishops, nineteen bishops, thirty or forty abbots, including three grand masters of important crusading orders, and some forty secular lords.

**The Commons: Membership.** At the same time the House of Commons was taking on a definite form, as has already been suggested (page 259). Besides the two knights from each shire, in the reign of Edward III there were some ninety-nine boroughs that sent two representatives—four from London after 1376. More parliamentary boroughs were created in 1445 and later. These boroughs with parliamentary rights were not evenly distributed according either to wealth or population, since approximately one-third came from the relatively minor counties of Cornwall, Devon, Somerset, Dorset, and Wiltshire in the west. No clear explanation of this situation has ever been offered, though the fact that these counties were so organized that it was less easy for them to evade the royal summons in the early days of parliamentary organization may have had something to do with it.[4] The elections were held with the restricted franchise already mentioned (page 262). At first the method of election appears to have been merely the suggestion by some prominent individual present of a name that would be greeted by general assent. Later it became customary to vote by a show of preference, with the will of the majority prevailing, though some deference was still paid to rank. The precedent permitting the election of nonresidents (page 261) dates from 1462. Repre-

[4] Mary McKisack's demonstration (*Parliamentary Representation of the English Boroughs during the Middle Ages*, Oxford Press, 1932, especially pp. 18-22) that the towns were not so anxious to evade this responsibility as has been commonly supposed casts doubt on this suggestion of L. Reiss.

sentatives of the lower clergy were required to attend the earlier Parliaments, but they objected to fulfilling this burdensome obligation. Since they made their grants, or "presents," to the king in their own Convocations (assemblies; page 117), the crown was not very insistent on their presence, and after the fourteenth century they were no longer represented in Parliament. With the cessation of the practice of summoning other special categories, such as merchants and lawyers, representation in Parliament for those below the rank of lords was left to the knights and burgesses.

**Organization.** Once assembled at Westminster, the knights and burgesses found themselves forced by contemporary etiquette to do no more than answer questions while in the presence of the king. It was this restriction on their deliberative activities which made it relatively easy for the thirteenth-century authorities to extract consent to grants from them. By the early part of the next century, however, the Commons were beginning to refuse to give an affirmative answer to questions on such matters until they had withdrawn to talk things over by themselves. This led to the practice of the knights and burgesses listening to the royal wishes in full Parliament and then adjourning from Westminster Hall to the Chapter House (assembly room) of Westminster Abbey across the road. This custom, incidentally, hastened the fusion of these two classes of representatives—already bound together by social ties and a similar status as elected representatives—into the one House of Commons, as already mentioned (page 276). The bicameral (two-house) legislature was therefore not originally and deliberately designed with the intention of introducing checks and balances into the legislative process, but was produced merely by the rigidities of contemporary social customs. In their separate session in the Chapter House the Commons decided upon the course they were to take, and this was reported back to the parent body by their presiding officer, who was therefore called the Speaker. This official was elected by the house, though often on the royal nomination. There was a clerk of Parliament as a whole, originally borrowed from Chancery, who at the conclusion of each session prepared a roll containing what he considered the important bills and other records of noteworthy transactions of the body. These Rolls of Parliament date from the reign of Edward I. By the middle of the thirteenth century some royal officials began to compile collections of statutes, the ordinances of Parliament that were considered of most permanent importance. After 1299 such rolls were kept in the Chancery, and it became the practice for the clerk of the Parliament to refer all bills passed to the royal judges for editing before they were publicly proclaimed in the county court of each shire and included in the statute rolls. By the fifteenth century Parliament had repealed so many of its statutes that permanence was no longer considered the chief test for inclusion. Thereafter, whatever was considered of general concern for the population at large, or at least for a sizable class or group of men, was enrolled as a statute. Ordinances that were administrative regulations "touching governance to be exercised by the lords of the council and of the realm" were not enrolled as statutes.

**Finance.** By the time of Edward III the king's own—the revenue from his estates and feudal dues—had shrunk to a mere third of the royal income. Out of an annual average of £140,000 some £50,000 came from this source. The rest was about evenly divided between direct and indirect taxes. Clerical tenths and parliamentary tenths and fifteenths supplied the bulk of the former. These were assessed by county committees, but collected and afterward paid into the Exchequer by the hundred constable, with occasional assistance from the local sheriffs. Customs revenue made up the indirect tax account. Export customs were levied on wool, leather, and other products, at rates supposedly fixed by Parliament, though this restriction was not always observed. Import customs were called tunnage and poundage because there was a flat rate of two shillings per tun (barrel) of wine and threepence per pound sterling ad valorem (roughly a 1.25 per cent levy) duty on all other entering goods. These rates were confirmed by Parliament, and after the time of Henry VI were regularly voted to each monarch for life. When the budget got too far out of balance, the authorities resorted to various expedients. The poll tax we have already mentioned (page 266). It was an assessment of so much per poll (human head). The rich were supposed to pay a larger sum than the poor, but it was not always possible to enforce this regulation, and hence the distress in some areas where quotas had to be met at the expense of the lower classes. Borrowings that the king did not mean to repay, called forced loans, and outright grants, called benevolences, were sometimes extorted from the citizenry by threats of the royal displeasure, though Parliament outlawed this practice in 1483.[5] If nothing else availed, debts might be repudiated, as we have noted (page 234), or the currency be inflated after the age-old manner of governments. The late medieval method of doing this was to increase the number of coins minted from a pound of silver or gold and to force their acceptance at face value in payment of government debts contracted in terms of coins with a higher content of precious metal. By pocketing the additional number of coins thus manufactured, the government was able to show a profit on the transaction.

## LOCAL GOVERNMENT

**Little New Machinery.** With the breakdown of feudalism it might be expected that in this period we should see a great development in the machinery of local government, but such was not the case. The need was largely met—so far as it was met—by the increased efficiency of the central government and its itinerant justices. The hundred with its court and hundred

[5] S-M, No. 69H, p. 278.

bailiff no longer played an important part in local government. Even the county court—now organized on a clearer membership basis (page 262)—ceased to be of much consequence except as an electoral body for parliamentary knights of the shire. The sheriffs and the coroners, however, continued to operate as before, with the periodic visits of the assize justices to keep them in order, though the general eyre itself was discontinued after the time of Edward III.

**The Justices of the Peace.** The one considerable addition to the old machinery of local government is the addition of the justice of the peace. Keepers of the peace were known as early as the time of Richard I, but the institution had its chief development in this period. We have already seen (pages 158, 170) that the central government was constantly trying to devise some system of keeping tab on the sheriffs, and was also inclined to call on prominent local figures for assistance in its judicial business. At the beginning of the fourteenth century conservators of the peace were being used to receive indictments of suspected criminals, but the actual trials were conducted by the itinerant justices. In 1329 the central government began to experiment with using these conservators as trial judges. The efforts to enforce the Statute of Laborers led to the development of a special corps of justices for that purpose, as already indicated (page 264), and this possibly suggested a thoroughgoing application of the same theory to the problem of local law and order. Statutes of 1360 and the following year authorized the appointment of a group of these justices of the peace in each county.[6] It was also provided that, like the sheriffs, they should be men of substance who could answer to the king and the people for any maladministration of their office, but in practice many permanent officials of the royal court were appointed on such commissions during this period. At first the duties of the justices were mainly in the sphere of criminal law, and these will

[6] S-M, No. 62I, pp. 230-31.

be discussed later. But in time a good deal of administrative work was given them also. They met at least four times a year (once a quarter) in what were called quarter sessions, and there they not only tried cases having to do with the disturbance of the peace, but also heard complaints against mayors, bailiffs, and even sheriffs in their areas. After the abolition of the special justices of laborers these men regulated wages and prices, weights and measures. Though almost, if not entirely, unpaid, they became the chief burden-bearers in the sphere of local government. In the days of weak central governments the system was very popular with the commoners, who felt the need of the protection it sometimes afforded against plundering nobles. But though capable of doing excellent work when controlled from Westminster by a strong hand, the system cannot be said to have operated very well in the fifteenth century, when it lacked effective royal support.[7]

**General Disorder: The Church.** For the rest, the story of local government in the late medieval period is not an inspiring one. It is to be feared that the liveried bands of retainers played a much greater role than the itinerant justices, and that corruption among bailiffs and sheriffs' clerks went almost unchecked. Nor were the churchmen always above suspicion, by any means. Bishops, canons, and abbots lined their pockets by making fraudulent leases, and even sales, of church property, and their subordinates, in their narrower spheres of influence, too often followed their superiors' example. Occasionally a conscientious bishop or archdeacon attempted to conduct a careful visitation of his area and to enforce the ecclesiastical law whose high standards in theory still obtained. But in practice these efforts came to little, and the machinery—and, still more important, the spirit—needed to make possible good local government remained undeveloped.

7 See *Proceedings before the Justices of the Peace in the Fourteenth and Fifteenth Centuries, Edward III to Richard III*, ed., by Bertha H. Putnam, London, 1938.

# 14. THE LEGAL SYSTEM

**General Characteristics.** In the legal world the period 1307-1485 is not notable for major conflicts, or for the introduction of important new principles. The new baronial policy of seeking to control the central government rather than to rival it removed the question of the jurisdiction of the royal courts from the immediate area of political conflict. When we find feudal lords suing in the king's courts to enforce their feudal rights against those who held of them, we may be sure that the feudal courts are no longer capable of seriously threatening the pre-eminence of the king's tribunals. Since the challenge of the Roman law had been successfully repelled in the thirteenth century, it was no longer likely that the accepted doctrines of the law would undergo anything approaching cataclysmic changes. Rather this was a period of steady growth in the legal system, with the professional lawyers gaining more and more control and introducing more and more refinements of the original doctrines. Indeed it is probable that there was not enough external pressure on the system for its own good; for technicalities and legal fictions bulked larger and larger, often to the extent of obscuring the true aims of justice.

## KING'S BENCH, COMMON PLEAS, EXCHEQUER, AND THEIR RIVALRIES

**The Relation of the King's Bench to the Council and the House of Lords.** In this period the separation of King's Bench

from the person of the king himself and from the Council became final and definite (page 169). By the time of Henry IV,
the monarch ceased to attend sessions of the Court of the King's
Bench, and as the Council became distinct from Parliament the
King's Bench began to reject the Council's authority in matters
of common law. Since Parliament was the body that made, or
declared, the statutes which the King's Bench enforced, the
judges recognized it alone as the place where their errors might
be corrected. This principle was definitely stated in 1377. Parliament thus acquired a jurisdiction in error over the King's
Bench, a jurisdiction which in practice was exercised by the
House of Lords because that body represented the survival of
the old Great Council. The House of Lords also came to have
certain original jurisdictions, as in the case of impeachment,
and in criminal cases where the defendants were lords, who, like
all other Englishmen after the acceptance of the Great Charter,
were entitled to be tried by their peers (equals).

**Rivalries Among the Common Law Courts.** By the beginning
of this period the three central courts of common law (page
169) were separate and distinct, with a definitely recognized system of jurisdiction in error above them. But their jurisdictions
were beginning to overlap to a remarkable extent. In part, this
was due to the pressure from suitors who wished to have their
cases tried in the court where they could get the speediest and
most effective justice. But besides this, each court was often
anxious to increase the area of its own jurisdiction. This was
largely because the judges' incomes were greatly affected by the
number of cases they heard. In the normal course of events the
judges were paid poorly and irregularly. But like the holders
of other royal grants, such as lands, they were allowed to make
what they could from their position. Just as a tenant in chief
originally might subinfeudate his holding, so the judges were
allowed to appoint their own clerks. These clerks usually made
a good living from the fees they collected from the suitors. The

more business the court had, the more clerks there would be, and the more they would be willing to pay the judges for their appointments. There developed accordingly a rivalry between the courts of common law, and a number of ingenious legal fictions were invented to further the interests of the contending parties. These were directed chiefly against the Court of Common Pleas, since civil cases, then as now, were the most profitable.

**Extension of Exchequer Jurisdiction: "Quo Minus."** The simplest of these devices was the one employed by individual creditors and the Barons of the Exchequer to give that court jurisdiction over the lucrative field of the collection of private debts. Many statutes and ordinances, notably those of 1311,[1] forbade the Exchequer to hear common pleas, but the desire of creditors for the speedy process that this court employed in the collection of royal debts enabled the judges to overcome these obstacles. The creditor alleged himself to be one of the crown's debtors who was having difficulty meeting his obligation to the king because of an uncollected private debt owed to him, by reason of which he was the less (*quo minus*) able to pay the royal bill. The hearts of the Barons of the Exchequer were touched by this lamentable prospect of the king suffering financial loss, and so they kindly offered to put the machinery of their court at the private creditor's disposal, purely in the interests of the crown, of course. By this *quo minus* fiction, as it was called, which can be found as early as the first half of the fourteenth century (1345-46), the Exchequer took jurisdiction over the many debt cases that creditors wished to bring before them.[2]

[1] Art. 25, S-M, No. 56, p. 197.
[2] Harold Wurzel, in "The Origin and Development of Quo Minus," *Yale Law Journal*, Vol. XLIX (1939), pp. 39-64, argues that this fiction was not fully developed before the middle of the seventeenth century, since prior to that time it was necessary to prove an actual debt to the king. But he grants that no proof was required of inability to pay the crown in case the private debt was not collected.

**Extension of the King's Bench Jurisdiction: The Bill of Middlesex and "Latitat."** From the other side, the Court of Common Pleas suffered a more general assault by a rather more complicated device of the judges of the King's Bench. Since courts were considered more or less as the feudal domain of their judges, it was general medieval practice to allow them to mete out justice of any sort to their subordinates. To summon a clerk from King's Bench, which was already in the legal business, to answer a plaintiff in the Court of Common Pleas would have been considered an insult to the sister court. It was not difficult to extend the concept of subordination to cover prisoners in the power of the King's Bench court. Thereafter if a defendant could be brought, even on a trumped-up charge, into the Marshalsea prison, which was the one used by the King's Bench, any civil action could proceed against him before the King's Bench. This desired imprisonment was achieved by what was called a bill of Middlesex, an order to the sheriff of Middlesex to arrest the defendant on a criminal or semicriminal charge, such as trespass (page 192), and lodge him in the Marshalsea. If the defendant did not reside in Middlesex, this bill was supplemented by a writ called *latitat* addressed to the proper sheriff informing him that the suspect was lurking (Latin, *latitat*, he lurks) and running about in his country, and ordering him to apprehend the accused and put him in the power of the court. Once that was done, the civil action was begun and the more serious charge was forgotten. The Common Pleas judges protested against such encroachments, but were powerless against the suitors and the rival court combined. By these devices original civil jurisdiction, which had formerly belonged only to Common Pleas, was distributed among the three central courts of common law.

**Justices of the Peace.** The itinerant (assize) justices continued to make Westminster justice available in the provinces under the *nisi prius* system, but the heavy load put upon them led to the development of the system of justices of the peace already mentioned (page 280). At first, in the time of Edward III, the jurisdiction of these local amateur justices was restricted to specific crimes mentioned in their commissions, such as riots. But by the end of our period they were charged with hearing cases involving all criminal offenses short of treason, that is, all felonies and lesser crimes. The former were handled with the assistance of indicting and trial juries at the regular quarter sessions. Minor offenses might be dealt with between sessions informally by one or two of the commission without a jury. Most of the criminal justice of the country was thus administered by these J.P.'s, as they are commonly called, though specially difficult cases were sent to the assizes. The justices of the peace had no civil jurisdiction, however; cases of that sort were left to the itinerant justices.

## THE DEVELOPMENT OF CHANCERY

**Its Organization.** The greatest change, however, in the court system during this period was the development of the Court of Chancery. We have already seen (pages 151, 168) that provision was made before 1307 for special cases in which the courts of common law for one reason or another did not give justice. Before the cessation of general eyres in the time of Edward III itinerant justices armed with such commissions heard cases of this type and provided remedies, though most of this residual jurisdiction was exercised by the Council. With the separation of Council, the House of Lords, and King's Bench, some clarification of their legal relationships was needed. As already noted (page 283), jurisdiction in error went to the House of Lords. But this did not supply all the existing needs. Not only was an agency necessary for correcting mistakes of the lower courts that could be demonstrated according to the letter of the common law, but one for making good the weaknesses in the judicial structure which sprang from too narrow a reliance on tech-

nicalities, written documents, and precedents. The sense of justice in the breast of the proverbial average Englishman—what
the Romans called the natural law—had to find a means of
expression. It continued to do so at first through the Council,
which originally advised the common law judges in special cases,
and even overruled them at times. But as this body became more
and more occupied with the executive routine of the government it tended to delegate this authority to the Lord Chancellor.
This was natural, not only because he was an important member of the Council, with a permanent office in Westminster, but
for two more specific reasons. (1) Since the Chancellor issued the
original writs and was authorized to make use of some leeway
in expanding the scope of their applicability, he was presumed
to be familiar with the remedies obtainable at common law
and thus able to deal with complaints that justice had not been
done there. (2) He was usually an ecclesiastic—originally his office was connected with the royal chaplaincy, it will be recalled
—and therefore he could be presumed to know what should
be done on moral, as opposed to strictly legal, grounds. Because
of his ecclesiastical character he was often called the keeper of
the king's conscience. During the fifteenth century, therefore,
the Chancery developed a court jurisdiction separate from that
of the Council. Twelve assistants called Masters in Chancery,
headed by a Master of the Rolls (originally a custodian of records) aided the Chancellor in this legal work—examining witnesses and serving as referees to hear the cases themselves and
make recommendations to the Chancellor for his final decision. The Court of Chancery held its sessions in one corner of
the great hall of Westminster Palace, where Common Pleas and
King's Bench also met, though in the corners on the other side
of the aisle. With the three knots of wrangling suitors surrounding the judges in the one big room, the scene presented must
have resembled that of an old-fashioned country Sunday school,
with each group trying to make itself heard above the noise

of the other. A slight difference of atmosphere is suggested, however, by the numerous complaints about pickpockets circulating among the crowd.

**And Jurisdiction.** In the early years of Chancery as a court it often heard cases having to do with aliens who were not under the English common law, and certain civil and criminal ones involving powerful subjects who were defying the ordinary courts. The type of jurisdiction, however, that had the most lasting consequences was that which we have been describing, in civil cases of the type that the common law did not cover. The theory was that the common law had "no fault nor flaw." When its powers and remedies had been exhausted, justice had been done. All that could be expected when one "crossed the aisle" at Westminster was not justice but mercy. Therefore this jurisdiction of the Chancery was called jurisdiction in equity (fairness, or natural justice) as opposed to law (common law justice).

**Uses.** This equitable jurisdiction was of many different sorts, all of which involved some weakness in the common law. Two of the types most frequently encountered, dealing with uses and frauds, will do for purposes of illustration. A use was what we should call a trust. It is a very old institution, found in early Germanic law and in England at least as early as the time of the Crusades. Men going on such expeditions often put their property in the hands of a friend or relative to hold to the use (originally *opus*), or on behalf, of their children who were not old enough to look after it themselves. By the thirteenth century the device had become quite common, and was frequently employed to evade the feudal prohibition of the willing of land (page 181). Under this arrangement A conveyed land to B to hold for the use of A. B was obligated to administer the legal estate he received according to the wishes of A, and this obligation was not confined to the lifetime of A. A might therefore

indicate that he wished the income from the property after his
death to go to a younger son or a daughter, who could not be
provided for by will under the feudal law.[3] After the issuance of
the Statute of Mortmain (page 116) this device was also employed
to defeat the intent of that statute and to make gifts to the
Church which could not legally be made in outright fashion
without a license. B, the trustee, would be a layman and so
capable of taking title, but the income from the property would
go to the Church as desired by A.[4] Before the development of
the Court of Chancery the chief objection to such arrangements
had been that the common law would not enforce the trust,
that is, would not compel B to carry out the wishes of A, since
B held the legal title and therefore presumably might use the
property as he chose, or even sell it and pocket the proceeds. As
the keeper of the king's conscience, however, the Chancellor
might be expected to punish misappropriations of this sort,
and as a churchman he was naturally anxious to do so.

**And Frauds.** Frauds based on the rigidity of the common law
also brought the Chancellor many cases. The common law had
already established the principle of evidence that a written document takes precedence over oral testimony. Therefore if A
paid B a debt of £1,000 but failed to secure the return of his
bond, he could be compelled at law to pay the sum a second
time, no matter how many witnesses he might have to the first
payment. He must go to the Chancellor for relief in such a case.
If a mistake that increased the debtor's obligation had been
made in the original bond, or if an accident had prevented
him from making payment by a certain penalty date, he could
also appeal to equity.

[3] For a case of this sort, see S-M, No. 71C, pp. 286-87.
[4] Soon after the passage of the original statute a supplementary act was,
in fact, adopted prohibiting the simple uses to ecclesiastical purposes of the
type here described. But more complicated uses involving the holding of
land in trust for the endowment or purchase of church services were devised
to evade this act.

## ADMIRALTY, MERCHANT, AND CHURCH COURTS

**Admiralty.** Another important court that administered a type of justice not based on the common law rose to prominence in this period. This was the Court of Admiralty. As the name indicates, it was a court of special jurisdiction, confining its attention to maritime cases. Its background we have already traced in the preceding period (page 182). As English overseas trade increased in quantity and value the old separate courts in the port towns became inadequate to their task. Speed of decision had to be sacrificed to the superior technical skill and defense against encroaching common law jurisdictions which could only be provided by a central court. Naturally these could be furnished by the Lord Admiral, who was already exercising a disciplinary jurisdiction over the fleet under his command, one similar to the martial law of the army. In the 1340's and 1350's this broader jurisdiction was slowly developing, and in 1357 we find a clear reference to a Court of Admiralty. From that time on the court has a continuous history. Its jurisdiction, though at first largely criminal, in time came to include civil cases as well. It extended to shippers' contracts, prize claims, wrecks, and quarrels arising on the high seas and on vessels in the main stream of rivers near the sea. The legal doctrines followed were those of the code of Oleron, a French port that had pioneered in the development of these principles and whose code was already generally accepted among seamen.

**The Ordinary Merchant Courts.** Admiralty law was really no more than a special branch of the law merchant, which was followed in the courts merchant and piepowder courts already mentioned. These other merchant courts, however, lacked any central agency to protect them from the competition of the established royal courts of common law. They therefore gradually gave way before their powerful rivals.

**The Church Courts.** The church courts underwent no notable development in this period. Their matrimonial and probate jurisdiction was still important and extensive, but it was not greatly altered during the fourteenth and fifteenth centuries. In the criminal field benefit of clergy was extended to all who could read, whether ordained or not, but various statutes provided that it should not apply to individuals suspected of treason, highway robbery, and one or two other serious offenses. In this period, also, it became established practice that the benefit should be claimed only after the trial in the king's court. This gave the crown the goods of the accused if he was convicted.

## COMMON LAW AND CHANCERY PROCEDURE

**Original Writs.** Turning to the subject of legal procedure, we find only minor variations from the pattern already described as existing in 1307. The chief changes have to do with the greater technicality of the law and the desire to make the courts more efficient. The main development in the field of the original writs is the extension of the scope of the action of trespass to cover all the ordinary torts, and some contracts as well. As early as the middle of the thirteenth century complainants were able to secure from the Chancery a special writ to fit the special circumstances of a particular case. This practice was strengthened by the Statute of Westminster II (1285), which permitted the Chancellor to issue an old writ for a slightly different type of action *in consimili casu* (in a similar case; page 192). Thereafter it was possible to allege that any kind of personal injury amounted to trespass, and this type of writ, called trespass on the case, or sometimes merely case, not only permitted the recovery of civil damages in what had formerly been criminal actions, but made possible process by arrest in this type of civil action. Another form of trespass on the case, called *assumpsit* (to be explained later, page 302), was developed for the purpose of enforcing contracts. In later centuries trespass was also to be extended to other important civil fields, such as those of debt and real actions (pages 403-5).

**Process.** Process was still carried on by the same means as before (page 193), but the use of the procedure by the bill of Middlesex in the King's Bench meant that arrest was much more commonly employed in civil cases than it had been in earlier times. The development of the action of trespass, just mentioned, also pointed in the same direction, since that was originally a semicriminal action and in its first forms involved a grant of process by arrest. The pains of outlawry were now moderated so that only the sheriff could execute the suspect, and then he was required to have a proper warrant. When used to compel appearances in civil cases, outlawry came to involve only the forfeiture of the outlaw's goods, and was therefore known as minor outlawry to distinguish it from the more serious variety.

**Pleading and Trial.** At the pleading stage in common law procedure we see the beginning of a trend toward written pleadings, stimulated by the custom of leaving a note of the plea with the clerk who drew up the record of the case. During this period the pleadings themselves became very complicated, in part because of the importance of having the issue favorably stated, but also because they afforded opportunities for suitors with weak cases to delay the trial. By having recourse to confession and avoidance (page 194)—also known as a special traverse or special plea—it was possible to avoid joining issue at once, and consequently this field of special pleading was explored quite thoroughly by members of the legal profession. For the trial the jury was by far the predominant method employed. In criminal cases the grand jury by this time has become quite distinct from the trial one. That is to say, no one who served on the grand jury might later serve on the trial body, as was frequently the case in the earlier period. Witnesses were being slowly distinguished from the jurors. Witnesses to a disputed deed might be summoned to court along with the jurymen. Documents might also be introduced in evidence. But the pleading stage was still used to introduce facts of which the jury might otherwise have been ignorant.

**Chancery Procedure.** Procedure in Chancery as distinct from common law procedure was exceedingly informal. No jury was employed there, and consequently it was unnecessary to resort to the elaborate pleading devices by which the issue was supposed to be made crystal-clear for the trial body at common law. It was sufficient to present the Lord Chancellor with a written document, called a bill, in which the grounds of complaint were set forth. That official then ordered the defendant under penalty (*sub poena*, hence the name of the writ employed) of royal displeasure to make his answer, similarly in writing. If further evidence was desired, it could be obtained by submitting written questions to either party or to third parties. This evidence was taken in secret, commonly by a specially appointed commission, and was not revealed to the other parties concerned until the matter was finally before the court. Oral arguments might be heard, but these were not necessary. The decision was supposedly based on all the available evidence, however gathered.

## THE PROFESSION: ITS LEADERS AND LITERATURE

**Markham and Fortescue.** During this period the legal profession tended to become more and more highly organized and class-conscious. With a few exceptions the royal judges eschewed politics and tried to do their work without regard to the political interests involved. Sir John Markham, Chief Justice of the King's Bench, deserves to be remembered as a judge who lost his post rather than strain a point to secure a conviction in a treason case for Edward IV in 1469. Though charges of bribery and political corruption of the sort that Markham resisted were

all too common and frequently all too well grounded, the tradition that the law was to be honored above the will of the
king and that of any private individual was still strong. The
greatest exponent of this doctrine was Sir John Fortescue, Chief
Justice of the King's Bench in the reign of Henry VI. He differed from most of his fellow judges in becoming so involved
in politics (on the Lancastrian side) that he was forced to go
into exile after 1461. On the Continent he wrote a work in
praise of the English law (*De laudibus legum Angliae*) in which
he elaborated on the supremacy of the law over the king. Though
in exile himself, he contrasted the government of his native
land, with its limited monarchy, very favorably with that of
France, with its absolute one. He also included a description for
laymen of the common law as it then existed. He later made
peace with the Yorkists and returned to England. About that
time he composed a treatise called *De monarchia* or *The Governance of England,* in which he described the Lancastrian government and analyzed its weaknesses. Consequently, this work is
one of political science rather than one of law.

**Littleton.** A more strictly legal writer was Sir Thomas Littleton. He was a judge of the Court of Common Pleas under Edward IV who composed a treatise on the real property law of
his time. This work, *Tenures,* deserves to rank with those of
Glanvil and Bracton for interpretative ability and the summing-
up of the contemporary status of the law. For though it was confined to one field, real property, that one, as we have seen, was
by far the most important and complicated division of the law
at that time. Littleton composed the treatise in the form of a
set of letters for his son, then a student at Cambridge. The first
two books treat of the estates and tenures at real property; the
third and last deals with the inheritance and alienation of land.
Littleton relied on the *Year Books* for his material, but he tried
to get behind the separate decisions to the principles and doc-

SIR THOMAS LITTLETON, 1422-1481

Notice the expression of orthodoxy and loyalty (*Ung Dieu et Ung Roy*—One God and One King) which Littleton is represented as uttering. *Ung Dieu et Ung Roy* is the fifteenth-century form of the modern French *Un Dieu et un Roi*. Once the student acquainted with modern French becomes familiar with such variations in spelling, he should not have too much trouble in reading the French of earlier centuries. There is a grammar of medieval Norman-English (law) French in the introduction to *The Year Books of Edward II, 1307-1309*, ed. by F. W. Maitland, Publications of the Seldon Society, Vol. XVII, London, 1903, pp. xxiii-lxxxi.

trines that they illustrated, the "arguments and reasons of the law."

**Law French.** Littleton's book is also notable because it was not written in Latin, as Glanvil's and Bracton's had been, but in law French. This suggests not only the declining influence of Roman law in this period but also the conservatism and upper-class character of the legal profession. Norman French had, of course, been the language of the invaders in 1066, and until the fourteenth century it remained the speech of the ruling classes of society. Then, however, the effects of the loss of Normandy and the rise of English nationalism began to be felt, and Middle English, as popularized by Chaucer, came into general use. In 1362 a statute required its employment in the courts when suitors did their own pleading, since otherwise the laymen could not understand what was going on. The professional lawyers, however, continued to plead in the current variety of French, which eventually became peculiar to them. It was still in common use in the profession as late as the eighteenth century.

## THE INNS OF COURT

**The Chief Inns.** A much more important aspect of the growth of the legal profession was the development among the pleaders of the system of the inns of court and the organized body of sergeants, which dates from this period. The inns began as law schools, but soon became fraternities of practicing lawyers as well. They seem to have grown up in imitation of the universities, which had developed in the twelfth and thirteenth centuries virtually as gilds of scholars with masters, bachelors (corresponding to journeymen in an ordinary gild), and undergraduates (apprentices). At first the law students hired masters to lecture to them in some inn or tavern where they found it convenient to lodge. As the legal profession prospered, these training schools became better and better established, and the control passed into the hands of the older lawyers, just as at the universities the original halls were mostly transformed into, or absorbed by, colleges controlled by masters. The most logical place for the legal inns was between the city of London and Westminster, in other words, halfway between the clients and the lawcourts. In that area (page 139) there developed four chief inns, Lincoln's Inn, Gray's Inn, and the Middle and Inner Temple. The first two were named from the original owners of the property, which the lawyers at first rented, Thomas de Lincoln and Lord Gray of Wilton. The other two used some of the buildings that had formerly belonged to the Knights Templar, the military crusading order founded to protect the route to the site of Solomon's Temple. Under Edward II the order was dissolved as a result of charges brought against it by those who perhaps cared more for its wealth than its morals. After some vicissitudes most of the buildings were occupied by the lawyers, who in time divided into the Inner and Middle group, so named from the relation of their buildings to the city boundary. That part of the Temple buildings which lay outside the area under the control of the London corporation never came into the hands of the lawyers, and thus there was never an Outer Temple. The two groups of lawyers in the Temple buildings continued to use the same chapel, and for a long time the exact location of the dividing line between their holdings was uncertain. It is not difficult to imagine the zest and ingenuity with which these rival groups through the centuries exhausted the law of real property and the resources of their profession in suing each other.

**Their Organization.** Each inn was governed by a committee of benchers, who co-opted new members in case of vacancies. With the assistance of readers the benchers controlled the inn and directed its educational program. The benchers were so called because at mealtimes they sat on the bench behind the elevated (high) table at one end of the hall. In most of the vaca-

MIDDLE TEMPLE HALL

The benchers and members are represented "taking commons" (eating a dinner in common, or at the common expense) during the early part of the nineteenth century. Those seated at the table in the foreground are the benchers. Since at the date of the picture there was little legal instruction at the inns (page 508), the diners are all mature lawyers and no students are in evidence.

tions, when the courts were not in session, the readers lectured
for, and held discussions with, the students. In termtime the
students attended sessions of the courts at Westminster. In the
evening during termtime or in learning vacations—that is, in all
but the summer-holiday recess—there were discussions in the
inns of difficult cases, and practice (moot) courts were also held.
Since the judges had prevented the students from practicing on
the real courts (page 204), these evening sessions were a very
important part of the curriculum. A good deal of humor might
be introduced into them. It seems to have been common practice for a member to sue the inn's cook, possibly alleging the
commission of some kind of a tort in the preparation of the
dinner, of which the remnants, useful as evidence, would be
still before the company. But for all this levity these were occasions for genuine legal training. On the forms (low benches)
that were placed before the high bench to make the bar (dividing barrier) of the court, the counsel on both sides took their
places. One or more experienced lawyers sat on the outside ends
of these forms; the junior students sat on the inner sections.
For this reason the full members of the inns, who had been
admitted thus to act as pleaders at its bar, though originally
known as apprentices, came eventually to be called utter or
outer barristers (later merely barristers), and the learners inner
barristers. The older men took the lead in conducting the case,
while the inner barristers rehearsed some of the pleadings and
tried to handle occasional minor parts. In this way the students received close supervision in their work and the benchers
and readers were able to tell when the students were ready to
become utter barristers, that is, be called to the bar. No other
call was necessary for practicing in most of the real courts at
Westminster, for the judges recognized full membership in an
inn as a satisfactory qualification, and the only one. If a lawyer
was ejected from his inn, he lost his professional standing. Dis-
barment powers were thus placed in the hands of the four rival

inns, each jealous of its reputation and familiar with the conduct of its members. This accounts to some extent for the high standard of professional conduct the pleaders have generally maintained in England. It should also be pointed out that the expense of this residential system of legal instruction was such as to put it beyond the reach of students without some means. Eventually the inns claimed to accept none but sons of the gentry, though actually many of their members were from the families of burghers and even yeomen.

**The Chancery Inns.** To each of the four main inns were attached others which served as preparatory schools for the larger inns. These were known as Chancery inns, not because they were in any way concerned with instruction in equity or were in any other fashion connected with the Court of Chancery, but because in them the beginner was expected to master the complexities of the system of writs, which, of course, issued out of Chancery in the sense of the Chancellor's office, not the court. When this work was completed, the student moved on to the mother inn.

## SERGEANTS, ATTORNEYS, AND SOLICITORS

**The Sergeants.** The sergeants were an inner circle of barristers, the ablest and most experienced members of the profession. Theoretically they were chosen by the Common Pleas judges—though probably the judges merely accepted the nomination of those who were already sergeants. In the court of these judges the sergeants early obtained a monopoly of the practice. From the ranks of the sergeants the judges were normally chosen. The sergeants had special inns called sergeants' inns, and were distinguished by wearing a white silk skullcap, called a coif. Some of the most distinguished sergeants were appointed king's sergeants. They represented the crown in the courts, and supplemented the legal advice given the monarch by the judges.

**Attorneys and Solicitors.** Besides the pleaders (barristers), the attorneys (page 204) continued to flourish, and at this time were even admitted as members of the inns of court, though considered only on a level with the inner barristers. As the Court of Chancery developed, another branch of the legal profession appeared. This was a body known as the solicitors, originally clerks in Chancery who solicited extra business by aiding litigants before that court with the task of drawing up the necessary papers. In time the demand for their services became so great that some of them gave up their clerkships and became full-time lawyers, practicing this specialty.

## SUBSTANTIVE LAW: CRIMINAL

**General Characteristics.** In the sphere of substantive law, as we have already seen, the Roman influence was on the decline, and the period was one of steady development in the field of common law. Parliament and the English conscience still declared the law, and the judges enforced it, with a careful eye to the precedents, though these were not yet considered absolutely binding. It is impossible from this time on even to suggest the general lines of development in all the different aspects of law that can now be recognized. That work must be left to the separate courses the law student will take in particular fields. All that can be done is to point out a few of the most striking alterations in the basic pattern of the common law, already described.

**Criminal Law.** In the field of criminal law we have already noted (page 270) the creation by statute of treason as a special crime ranking above felonies and considered deserving of special pains and penalties. Mere hanging was thought too good for men guilty of this crime, and to this punishment various additions were made, which began with the indignity of being dragged to the place of execution through the streets. Later this was modified to the drawing of the guilty man on a wooden frame (hurdle). After the hanging the victim's body was beheaded and quartered and the portions were impaled in various prominent places, such as on London Bridge and at Temple Bar —the boundary of the City of London on the road to Westminster—as a warning to others treasonably inclined. Furthermore, the real property of a subtenant convicted of this crime went directly to the crown by forfeiture instead of to the feudal lord, as in the case of ordinary felonies. The rebellion of a wife against her husband, resulting in his death, or of a servant against his master, with similarly fatal results, was considered petty treason and was punished by some such special means as burning at the stake. Below felonies the royal courts left lesser offenses, which would later be called misdemeanors, to be dealt with by the action of trespass or else before the justices of the peace or in other local courts.

## REAL PROPERTY AND CONTRACTS

**Common Recovery.** Of all the details that might be culled from Littleton's great work on real property we must content ourselves with explaining the very important device of common recovery, which was developed in the fifteenth century as a means of evading *De donis*. We have seen that the crown was opposed to the creation of perpetuities, estates that must legally remain in the hands of one family indefinitely. It could also be argued that perpetuities were contrary to public policy, since by means of them an age long dead might control the destinies of future generations, of whose circumstances the original donors were completely ignorant. Consequently, the royal judges undertook to defeat the intent of the statute. This was done by a device known as common recovery. There were several forms of this device, of which we shall describe only the simplest. After the middle of the fifteenth century the royal judges permitted B, holding an estate tail, who wished to alienate his land in fee simple to F,

COMMON RECOVERY

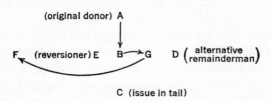

C (issue in tail)

to do so by means of a collusive suit, somewhat after the manner of the old method of fine (page 215). Having paid for the land, F entered suit against B, who thereupon alleged that he obtained his title to the land from a third party G, and vouched him to warranty—after the old Saxon practice in sales cases involving personal property (page 71). G thereupon acknowledged the grant, but defaulted (failed to answer the charge). He thus allowed the land to be awarded in fee simple to F by court order. The entail was thus destroyed (barred). Obviously C, the issue in tail, D, the alternative remainderman, and E, the reversioner, were deprived of their estates by this process. When they complained to the courts, however, they were gravely told that they had not been unjustly treated, since they had a right to recover lands of equal value from G. G, however, was the court bailiff, or some such straw man, carefully chosen because he did not have enough property to make him worth suing, and so the intent of *De donis* was effectively defeated. After the so-called Taltarum's (more properly Talcarn's or Tolcarn's) case in 1472, when the judges indirectly approved its use, this method of recovering land from under an entail was employed so frequently that it came to be called the common recovery. It was a method obviously unfair to the issue in tail, the alternative

remainderman, and the reversioner, but like many other governmental actions is to be justified, if at all, on the larger grounds
of public policy. It is not to be thought, however, that this marks
the end of the struggle to create perpetuities. We shall see
further rounds of the battle in subsequent chapters (pages 413,
510).

**Contracts.** The most notable development in the field of legal
doctrine during this period, however, is the development of the
common law to cover contracts not under seal. We have already
noticed (page 217) that the earlier medieval law had practically
no such provisions. But when the church courts and the Chancery
began to cater to this lucrative business, the common lawyers
began devising their own remedy, which in time supplanted the
others. This was an extension of trespass on the case to cover
broken contracts, on the ground that when one assumed (*assumpsit*) an obligation to do a thing he trespassed against the
peace of mind of the second party if he did not keep his promise,
and so was liable for damages. At first this variety of the writ
of trespass, *assumpsit,* was permitted only in cases where the
plaintiff had been injured by the defendant's misfeasance (careless performing of his duty), which shows how closely related this
writ was to the idea of tort. For example, if a man undertook
to ferry cattle across a river or to treat a sick horse and did the
work badly, so that the cattle drowned or the horse died, the
writ was allowed to lie. But if he did nothing at all, one could
not at first sue him under trespass. By the reign of Henry VI,
however, the judges were permitting the writ in some cases of
nonfeasance, that is, where the defendant had done nothing to
carry out his agreement. They did not feel it wise, however, to
try to enforce all such promises, but were inclined to limit their
services to cases in which the plaintiff had paid something to
bind the bargain. This was the beginning of the doctrine that
bare agreements (*nuda pacta*) would not be enforced, but only
those in which some consideration was involved. This consider-

ation was known as a *quid pro quo* (something for something), which the promisor had accepted and by which he incurred a liability because the position of the promisee had been altered in the process.

**Common Law "versus" Equity.** From these few illustrations it will be seen that the common law was becoming not only wider in its scope but more technically exact in its rulings. After learning of the device of common recovery and also of the rise of Chancery one may be inclined to contrast the rigidity and technicality of the common law with the greater flexibility of the rules of equity as applied in Chancery, and not always to the advantage of the former. While it is probably true that the sharp distinction between law and equity, and their administration in separate courts, were great misfortunes for the cause of English justice, it must also be remembered that chaos would have resulted from any move to scrap the common law and throw all cases into the Chancellor's jurisdiction. Definiteness in the law is important as well as fairness. Equity varies with the length of the Chancellor's foot, said one shrewd observer. If business could have looked to no more certain rules of conduct than those of equity, its activities would have been paralyzed. The greater exactness of the common law, with its statutes and precedents, gave the landowner and the trader definite rules to go by. This in itself was of great value, even if it did involve an occasional injustice and a certain time lag in the matter of keeping pace with the changing needs of society.

# The Tudor-Stuart
# Absolutism

# 15. THE SETTING UP OF THE TUDOR-STUART ABSOLUTISM
## 1485-1547

**A Transitional or Revolutionary Period.** In the three preceding sections of this work we have seen three different aspects of medievalism, early, middle, and late. Although they differed in many ways, as we have noticed, still they were variations on a single theme. The transitions from one phase to another in 1066 and 1307 did not therefore call for detailed explanation. After 1485, however, and again after 1637, the whole theory of English government underwent a profound transformation. These changes were so fundamental and important that they were neither quickly accomplished nor are they easy to describe. It will therefore be necessary to preface the last two sections of this work with preliminary chapters on the transitional periods in each case. The years covered by them saw such great alterations in the structure of English government that they are sometimes called revolutionary periods.

## THE TUDOR ABSOLUTISM

**Absolutism.** The change in the period after 1485 is from medievalism to a system known as absolutism, or the absolute monarchy. It is so called because the crown instead of sharing its control of English society with the nobles and the Church now became almost the sole legal authority in the land. Its power was no longer limited or restricted by that of its associates in the medieval system, but was practically unrestricted, or absolute. This alteration was largely the work of two rulers, Henry VII

and Henry VIII, and the process of accomplishing it extended
over the period of their two reigns, down to 1547. The first monarch destroyed the power of the nobility and the second that of
the Church, thus leaving the crown virtually alone as a controlling factor in English government.

**A Popular Despotism.** The reader should be reminded at the
very beginning of this section, however, of the general principles
stated in the opening pages of the volume (page 26)—that while
one or another political element assumes a dominant political
position from time to time, the others are never completely
eliminated, but merely subordinated. When we speak loosely,
for convenience' sake, of the destruction of the power of the
nobles or the Church, all that we actually mean is that this
power was very greatly diminished. Obviously, if no Saxon ruler
could handle all governmental problems himself, the Tudors
could not hope to do so in their very much more complicated
system. They had to have assistants, and to that extent they
shared their power. Furthermore, the Tudors had no standing
army and therefore were always at the mercy of their subjects
if the militarily significant majority of them chose to rebel. They
consequently relied, as even dictators with a standing army must
to some extent, on the arts of popularity and on providing their
subjects with a type of government that prevented all but a
politically negligible minority from attempting an insurrection.
For this reason the Tudors kept a close eye on the interests of
the rising elements in the upper and upper-middle classes—the
country gentry and the merchants—and drew many of their administrative assistants from that source. They also revived and
strengthened the medieval attitude of paternalism toward the
working class and the poor (pages 50, 176). For these reasons
the Tudor system is sometimes called a popular despotism.
Legally the kings were almost absolute; practically they were
considerably less than that. The Tudor prayer book spoke of
God as One in whose service there was perfect freedom. The

unrestricted absolutism of the Tudor monarchs was something of the same sort. In the service of their subjects they had perfect freedom. Once more power was a function of service.

## HENRY VII AND HIS TITLE TO THE THRONE

**Henry VII Dominates the Nobles: Mercantile Support.** In part, Henry VII was able to limit the political power of the nobles because England was tired of the uncertainty and confusion of the Wars of the Roses. It is true that England as a whole had not been really devastated by the troubles of the past thirty years, but there had been quite enough turmoil to produce a growing sentiment in favor of law and order. The mercantile class in particular was strongly of this mind. Not only did the merchants desire peace at home, but they felt that in a period of increasing international competition a powerful national government would assist their growing overseas trade.

**Henry's Personality.** It was Henry's personality, however, which focused this vague public opinion and made it effective. The new King was the direct antithesis of Edward III. He cared nothing for sentimental, medieval notions of kingship, and everything for the hard, cold facts of the current political situation. He saw clearly enough that to waste his time, strength, and money—above all, his money—in the quest for military glory was to give hostages to the nobility, who controlled Parliament, the body he would have to ask to pay the bills. He therefore deliberately embarked on a policy of increasing his own power, regardless of medieval tradition. This new royal outlook is one of the chief reasons for dating the beginning of modern English history in 1485, the year of Henry's accession. It also justifies us in considering him one of the great men in human history, one of those who by their character and efforts have contributed greatly to shaping the course of future events.

**His Care to Ensure His Title to the Throne.** First, the twenty-eight-year-old King took pains to ensure his title to the throne. Immediately after his victory at Bosworth he called a Parliament, and while it was still under the spell of his recent victory had it confirm him in the royal office, without regard either to his ancestry or to his promise to marry Elizabeth of York (page 243).[1] He was thus able to base his claim primarily on the consent of the politically vocal elements in the country, and only in a secondary way on the medieval rules of heredity. But he nevertheless proceeded to guard against that weakness of hereditary claim which had been a source of so much difficulty for the Lancastrian monarchy. Having made sure that his prospective wife could not tell him that he owed the crown chiefly to her, he carried out his marriage bargain. In this way he provided that any son of the pair should have an even stronger hereditary claim than either parent, and when one was duly born in 1486 and another in 1491, the future of his house seemed definitely assured.

**The Pretenders.** It was still necessary, however, to deal with some sections of the Yorkist party that did not accept the Tudor settlement. These disgruntled schemers managed to find various claimants to the throne whom they could use as tools in their opposition program. The most important of these were Lambert Simnel and Perkin Warbeck, two impostors who were persuaded to impersonate respectively the son of the deceased Duke of Clarence (page 242) and Richard, the younger brother of Edward V. In 1487, however, Henry defeated Simnel and his supporters in battle, and captured Simnel in the process. To show the royal contempt for the masquerading captive, the impostor was made a scullion in Henry's kitchen. Warbeck proved more of a problem, for he secured considerable support at different times from Ireland, Scotland, France, and Burgundy. Not until 1497 did Henry manage to capture and execute him. At the same time an excuse was found for sending to the block also the genuine

[1] S-M, No. 73A, pp. 298-99.

son of the Duke of Clarence, whom Henry had been holding captive ever since his accession. There was very little of what private people call justice about this latter procedure, but it was very effective in strengthening Henry's title to the throne. In 1506 another Yorkist claimant, the Earl of Suffolk, was seized on the Continent by Henry's obliging allies and soon lodged in the Tower. People began to conclude that it was unwise to question the Tudor right to the throne.

## FINANCIAL POLICY AND FOREIGN RELATIONS

**Henry's Financial Policy.** The second great string to Henry's bow was his policy of husbanding his resources. It was all very well for medieval kings to make princely gifts and distribute favors with such lavish hands that harassed Councils groaned under the necessity of raising taxes and the populace was driven to periodic revolts. Henry had been a destitute exile and knew what poverty meant. In fact, he had been so hard pressed for funds that he had been forced to leave two of his friends in Paris as a pledge—in pawn, so to speak—for the repayment of the French funds advanced to finance his expedition in 1485. He proposed never to be in such a humiliating position again, and he never was. If he ever blushed in his long reign, it was not because of inability to satisfy his creditors (page 234).

**In Its Relation to War.** He avoided wars like the plague they are, for he well knew their cost. This is not to say that he was a pacifist. "He knew the way to peace was not to seem to be desirous to avoid wars. Therefore would he make offers and fames of wars till he had mended the conditions of peace," said Francis Bacon in describing the policy of this king. No one could accuse of cowardice the man who had stood foot to foot with his rival at Bosworth and won his crown on the battlefield. He knew the rules of the military game, and he was good at making feints. In 1491 he obtained a large grant for the popular purpose of renewing the perennial war with France. Once the army was across the Channel, however, he readily listened to the offer of the French King to make it worth his while to withdraw. From the resulting payment—virtually a bribe—and the unexpended balance of the parliamentary appropriation Henry pocketed a neat profit.

**And Matrimonial Diplomacy: Spain and the Hapsburgs.** Marriage alliances were more to his liking than military activity. He lived in an age when Europe was being greatly impressed by the growing fortunes of the house of the Austrian Hapsburgs, who owed their success mostly to a series of successful matrimonial adventures. "Happy are you, Austria," ran the proverb. "Other nations fight. You only marry." Taking a leaf from the Hapsburg book, Henry, who by the end of the century had four children—two boys and two girls—proceeded to use them in his diplomatic business. In 1501 he married his oldest son, Arthur, to Catherine of Aragon, a daughter of the Ferdinand and Isabella of Spain who sent Columbus on his western voyages. As the Spanish house was also allied by marriage to the Hapsburgs, this match cemented a friendship of England with Austria and Spain that was to endure, in general, until almost the end of the century. In the next year, however, the sickly Arthur fell ill and died. Henry, anxious to retain the Spanish-Austrian alliance—and incidentally Catherine's dowry—made arrangements for the young widow to marry his surviving son and heir, Henry. Since Catherine and her new fiancé were within the prohibited degrees of affinity (page 223), this projected marriage involved various ecclesiastical complications that necessitated a papal dispensation and which were later to be of very great importance (page 323). But at the time they aroused little concern.

**Scotland and France.** In 1503 Henry's oldest daughter, Margaret, was married off to James IV of Scotland. In this fashion the Tudor ruler began a policy of friendly relations with his northern neighbor that eventually was to result in a union of the crowns of the two countries. He even paved the way for matching his six-year-old Mary with Louis XII of France, though the marriage did not take place until after his death. Henry's own wife, Elizabeth, died in 1503, and if his children had not proved to be enough pawns for his diplomatic game, the middle-aged widower would have been willing to marry anyone whom political advantage might dictate. There is still extant a kind of questionnaire that he gave to some of his ambassadors during some tentative negotiations of this sort in 1505, when it seemed that he might be forced to marry himself off in order to preserve his influence at the Spanish court. He wanted to know not only about the looks of his prospective bride, but also about her estate and "whether she be a great feeder." He found means to keep the Spaniards in uncertainty, however, by having his son threaten to renounce the marriage with Catherine, and the other project was not pushed.

**Other Financial Devices.** Besides substituting marriage alliances for costly wars Henry worked out many other devices for improving his financial position. Since the value of money was steadily declining and rents were rising, he persuaded Parliament to annul all the long-term leases of the lands in the royal domain, so that new ones could be made at higher figures. This constituted, of course, a repudiation of governmental obligations in the manner of modern currency devaluations, but it was very profitable to the crown. He also made trade treaties with the Hapsburg-Burgundian family that controlled the Low Countries, so that English merchants obtained great concessions in those areas. By heavily taxing the export of raw wool and putting only a light impost on the manufactured cloth, he further built up the weaving industry at home (page 247) and enabled the merchant adventurers—who controlled the cloth trade (page 248)—to compete successfully with Continental rivals. The more goods that came and went, the greater was Henry's customs revenue, even though the rate per piece was low. He also tried to build up a balance of exports over imports, so that England would sell more than she bought and thus accumulate a large store of gold and silver. This policy of stimulating and protecting native industries so as to obtain a "favorable balance of trade" and build up the nation's stock of hard money is called mercantilism, and is similar to the modern doctrine of protection.

**The Chamber: Forced Loans.** Henry also reorganized the financial machinery of his government. The Chamber (page 272) was revived, and special agents put in charge of its financial work. Archbishop Morton, Empson, and Dudley—we shall hear more of the Dudley family—were three of the chief ones. They not only kept all the ordinary revenue apparatus tuned up, but also resorted to benevolences and forced loans as well. The statute forbidding this kind of extortion (page 279) was waved aside as the work of a usurper. If a prospect lived on an extravagant scale, he was told that he could certainly afford to contribute something to the King. If he lived simply, he was told that he must be saving enough to be in a position to do the same thing. This two-horned dilemma was known as Morton's fork, though the Archbishop was not really to blame for the policy he carried out. Criminal prosecutions of wealthy citizens under obsolete laws were instituted in order to secure large fines for the royal treasury. Among the British Museum manuscripts there is a copy of one of Dudley's account books initialed by the King on every page in such a way as to show that he inspected the book carefully and regularly. When Catherine of Aragon came to England as Arthur's bride, Henry complained that the silver service she had brought along as part of her dowry was not good enough. He hoped that the Spanish ambassador would supply a better one and leave both in England. He obtained the new and superior set, but Ferdinand's representative disappointed him by carefully collecting the other and sending it home.

## EFFECTS OF THESE POLICIES

**The Financial Strength of the Government.** It should not be imagined, however, that Henry was the complete miser. He recognized the political value of display in a monarchical system of government, and he spent a decent amount for this purpose. But otherwise he was extremely cautious. The result was that by the middle of his reign his finances were in excellent condition and he was beginning to pile up savings. Some of these he put in jewels, but other funds were loaned to merchants engaged in foreign trade, usually on the explicit understanding that they should import or export a certain amount of goods and thus swell the royal customs revenue. When Henry died in 1509, it was reported that he had left to his son and heir a balance of some £1,300,000, more than nine times the average annual income of the government.

**Effect on the Nobles: Few Advancements and Strict Discipline.** Henry's strong claim to the throne and the financial strength of the monarchy put him in a position to deal effectively with the political power of the nobles. He did not give them many official positions, and chose the ministers of his Council mostly from the ranks of the more easily controlled "new men," the merchants and lesser gentry. He also fixed the pattern for the Tudor monarchy by coolly resisting most claims for advancement in rank and title. Dukes became very rare, and lesser peerages almost equally hard to secure, while simple knighthoods were made to do duty as rewards of merit in most cases. This stand weakened the nobles by reducing their numerical strength. Surprisingly enough, their numbers had not declined appreciably as a result of the slaughter of the Wars of the Roses. The long-continued Tudor policy of refusing to create many new peerages when the titles to the old ones ran out, or were forfeited for treason, proved a much more effective check on the development of this class. Among those who felt aggrieved by this attitude was Sir William Stanley, who with his brother, Henry's stepfather, had decided the battle of Bosworth in the young Tudor's favor by coming to his assistance at the crucial moment. Disappointed at not obtaining his expected peerage, he joined a Yorkist rebellion. When he was captured, Henry had him condemned and executed in spite of his relationship and past services. This served to warn others of the dissatisfied who might have been considering revolt of what they might expect—and incidentally swelled the King's coffers from the proceeds of the confiscated Stanley estates.

**Parliament.** The newly developed financial strength of the King also made it possible for him to be virtually independent of Parliament, which had served the nobles' purposes so well in the late Middle Ages. No longer did the monarch have to beg for money and grant concessions to the baronial group in order to get it. In the last twelve years of Henry's reign Parliament met only once, and then did little more than the royal bidding.

**Livery and Maintenance.** As we have seen, the last resort of the medieval nobles, as of all dissatisfied political groups in any era, was force. Henry therefore took pains to clip the military wings of his magnates. From his first Parliament, called together in the political honeymoon following the Bosworth victory, he extracted an oath to observe existing Statutes of Livery and Maintenance—laws prohibiting the practice of having private, liveried armies and of their maintaining causes before the common law courts (page 239). The nobles demurred, grumbled, but finally obeyed. Henry did not expect to bind these overmighty subjects with words, however. He was merely making sure that when they violated the law they would be without excuse. It remained to be seen whether the law could be enforced. By breathing new life into the activities of his council, the grim Tudor, the spiritual as well as legal heir of the Conqueror, Henry II, and Edward I, showed that enforcement was possible.

## THE PREROGATIVE COURTS AND THE WEAKENING
## OF THE POWER OF THE NOBLES

**Their Organization.** We have already noticed (pages 168, 287) that the Council had a residual jurisdiction which it either exercised itself or delegated to the Chancellor. We have also seen that this included offenses of subjects too powerful to be restrained by the net of the common law courts. In 1487 Henry took back this criminal jurisdiction from the Chancellor and put it definitely in the hands of the Council.[2] This body was ordered to have regular meetings for court purposes in a particular room in Westminster Palace. Probably because the ceiling of the room was decorated with stars on a blue background, in imitation of the sky on a clear night, it was called the Starred or Star Chamber, and the Council meeting as a court came to be called by that name. The Star Chamber did not use the common law system of justice, but tended to employ the methods of the Roman law, which were very much more favorable to the executive. There was no jury; the suspect was not allowed to cross-examine or, in some cases, even to see the witnesses against him. He might be tortured to extract evidence against accomplices if the case was a very serious one and the Council thought this procedure necessary. Finally, he could be sentenced to any kind of punishment short of death, but including mutilation. Branch councils, the Council of Wales and the Council of the North,[3] were also set up in the troubled areas of the west and along the Scottish border. In their capacity as courts they exercised all the powers of the parent body, and were commonly headed by one or more people who were also members of the central Council. Because these courts relied not on the common law but on the royal power (prerogative) for their authority and

2 S-M, No. 73B, p. 299.            3 S-M, No. 75, pp. 321-23.

the method of their procedure, they were called prerogative courts.

**And Operation.** The prerogative courts could be used for nearly any purpose to which the crown wished to turn these very efficient engines. This might be to punish some offense against the Statute of Maintenance. For example, the Star Chamber once imprisoned an individual for surreptitiously "feeding two men on a jury that they might starve out their fellows" in those days when juries were kept without food, drink, or fire until a unanimous verdict was reached. On the other hand, the prerogative courts could be used to strike at the most powerful lords in the land. After the passage of a supplemental Statute of Liveries,[4] in 1504 Henry went on one of his progresses, and was entertained in the midlands by John de Vere, the thirteenth Earl of Oxford. That representative of a very old and proud family, in cynical defiance of the new statute, paraded his six hundred liveried retainers for the royal entertainment. Henry was not amused, however, and disregarding his position as a guest, coolly informed his host that he should see the royal attorney. That official served the astonished Earl with a summons to appear before the Star Chamber. There he was fined the enormous sum of £10,000 for violating the statute.

**Effect on the Power of the Nobles.** This lesson was not lost on the other nobles, who began to realize that Henry meant business. "What he minded, he compassed," said the King's biographer. The importance of the nobles, so great in the fourteenth and fifteenth centuries, sank in a single generation to comparative insignificance before the rising mercantile civilization of the towns, the demand of the small landholders for peace in the country, and the determination of one man to gratify the needs of these newly important elements of his kingdom. When Warbeck invaded England from the north, "not a man" would rally to his cause. Soon afterward, according to a picturesque account,

[4] 3-M, No. 74F, pp. 302-03.

a Leicestershire copyholder, of the class of virtually free farmers now coming to be called yeomen, had his young son buckle him into his leather jacket so that he might go out to fight for the Tudor King. Hundreds of others like him did the same, and the menace was averted. The influence of the nobility was on the decline.

## HENRY VIII AND THE MOVEMENT FOR CHURCH REFORM

**The Succession of Henry VIII (1509-47) and the Continuation of His Father's Policy.** If there were any hopes that this diminution of the strength of the aristocracy was merely a temporary thing, the work of one extraordinary genius that would end with his death, they were dispelled by the actions of his successor, Henry VIII, who came to the throne in 1509. In 1513 the King had the imprisoned Earl of Suffolk (page 311) executed without any further legal steps beyond an old attaint (condemnation without trial) in Parliament. Shortly after this Henry took as his chief adviser an ambitious churchman, Thomas Wolsey, who soon became Archbishop of York, cardinal, and Lord Chancellor. In the last capacity he presided over the Court of Star Chamber. Under his vigorous administration, which lasted nearly fifteen years, this body extended its already growing jurisdiction and more and more put the fear of the law into the turbulent nobles. With the Star Chamber punishing contempts and perjuries committed in the common law courts, the older tribunals also became increasingly effective against powerful offenders, and the King was able to secure convictions almost at will. In 1521 Edward Stafford, Duke of Buckingham, who had a semblance of a hereditary claim to the throne through descent from Edward III, dared to comment on the apparent ill-health of the King, who lacked a male heir, and to say what he would do to Wolsey when he came to the throne. When word of this reached the ears of

Henry, he acted with all his father's ruthlessness. The Duke was arrested, tried, convicted, and executed, all within the space of six weeks. Other nobles were afterwards dealt with as summarily, but in reality these early examples were all that were needed. The powers of the English nobility did not revive appreciably until the eighteenth century.

**The Restriction of the Political Power of the Church: Nationalism.** The great contribution, however, of the second Tudor Henry to the constitutional history of his country was, as already suggested, the virtual elimination of the political power of the Church. Like his father, he successfully accomplished his great destructive work because he was able to bring to bear on his opposition certain hostile forces that needed only leadership to make them effective. Nationalism, the movement for religious reform, and anticlericalism were notable forces in the late medieval period (pages 244, 253). They had continued to grow throughout the fifteenth century, and there were signs of them in the early Tudor period. Nationalism was stimulated by that competition in the field of foreign trade to which we have already referred (page 309). Its effect on the English religious world can be seen in the willingness of Henry VII to take sides against the popes in his diplomatic negotiations whenever it suited his convenience.

**The Reform Movement.** The movement for religious reform was a complex but growing one. Lollardry had not completely died out, and there was a marked recrudescence of it in London at the turn of the century. Its demands for changes in the old religious regime were re-enforced by the rise of two new movements. One was the Renaissance, the revival of learning, which in northern Europe under the leadership of the Dutch scholar Erasmus began to direct attention to existing evils in the Church. This reforming activity is sometimes called humanist, or humanistic, because Erasmus and his followers were interested in humane scholarship, or the humanities. It grew naturally out of an interest in classical studies, since a knowledge of Greek stimulated scholars to read the New Testament in the original and to contrast the system there pictured with the one they saw around them. At Cambridge and Oxford in the early 1520's English students were beginning to imitate Erasmus, and one of the most prominent of them was Hugh Latimer, the yeoman's son who has told us of buckling on his father's "harness" when he went to fight for his Tudor king in 1497. The other, and more powerful, re-enforcement of the Lollard movement came from the Continental Reformation initiated by the German monk Martin Luther and soon taken up by Huldreich Zwingli and other Swiss leaders. These men had humanistic backgrounds, but they were more religious-minded than Erasmus. They developed theological doctrines—such as justification by faith alone, without the need of consulting priests—and they consequently put more fire into their movement than Erasmus the intellectual did into his. By the middle 1520's they had followers in the English universities and in London who were taking the lead in the reforming movement away from the Lollards and Erasmians. Their most prominent representative was William Tyndale, who once more (page 246) began the translation of the Bible into English, and in 1526, after fleeing to the Continent, put out the first printed New Testament in the vernacular.

**Anticlericalism.** All the reforming movements just mentioned contributed to the growth of anticlericalism. Erasmus stressed morality as opposed to sacerdotalism (the dependence on priests), and Lollard, Lutheran, and Zwinglian alike emphasized the duty of the individual to make his own peace with God, to the neglect of priestly ceremonies. The anticlerical movement, however, received much support from laymen as well. As the zeal and morality of the priests declined in the fifteenth century the common man saw less and less reason why they should be supported in idleness and comparative luxury when they did so little to justify this relatively high standard of living. In town and country, but particularly in the towns, men objected to the efforts of the clergy to enforce their old tithe rights and many other similar ones. Some joined in the hue and cry against the churchmen from even more questionable motives. Many objected to the policy of the clergy in restricting economic activities by such means as trying to hold laymen to the medieval doctrine of the just price (page 102). These aggrieved individuals wished to buy and sell freely, charging what the traffic would bear and openly collecting interest on their loans, a practice forbidden by the teaching of the Church. So strong was the feeling against the clergy in London by 1514 that when a churchman was accused of murdering a Lollard prisoner in that year, his bishop had to appeal to the King to stop the proceedings. A fair trial could not be obtained, said the prelate, since the people of the capital were so malicious that any twelve men in the city would condemn any clerk, even though he was as innocent as Abel.

**Importance of the Royal Attitude.** Eventually all these forces making for change might by themselves have brought about an English Reformation. But it would have required a long time, for the Church was still strongly entrenched, protected by its wealth and political position. The English kings were accustomed to co-operate with the popes and lesser churchmen. Lollards had been burned, and other reformers forced to work in secret. In 1514 the young Henry VIII, responding to the episcopal request in the traditional fashion, protected the clergy from the wrath of the laity, and later went so far as to write a book against Luther. So long as he retained that attitude the progress of the Reformation on English soil was slow. It was his change of front in the 1530's that brought the Church down so rapidly.

# THE ROYAL "DIVORCE" AND THE REFORMATION STATUTES

**The King's "Divorce" Project.** This shift in the royal attitude was caused by personal and political rather than by religious motives. Catherine of Aragon was six years older than Henry, and the only surviving child of the union was a daughter, Mary. There was no precedent for a woman ruler in England, with the possible exception of the unpromising one of Matilda's stormy career in the twelfth century. Many feared a renewal of the dynastic wars after the King's death. About 1527 Henry fell in love with one of the Queen's attendants, Anne Boleyn (pronounced Bōŏl'ĭn). He decided to secure a divorce [5] and to marry Anne. For this it was of course necessary to apply to the ecclesiastical authorities. There were some technical difficulties in the way; for, as we have seen (page 312), a papal dispensation had been issued to authorize the marriage in the first place and it was difficult for one pope to reverse the decision of another so explicitly stated. Still the Roman curia had surmounted as great obstacles in other royal cases—including some that involved Henry's own sisters. Catherine, however, was the aunt of Charles V, who as the result of the fortunate Hapsburg marriages had inherited Spain, Austria, and the Low Countries and had subsequently been elected Holy Roman (German) Emperor. What was worse, his army had captured Rome in 1527 and was virtually holding prisoner the Pope, Clement VII, who had supported Charles's great rival, Francis I of France, in the diplomatic maneuverings of the time. Under the circumstances, therefore, it was hard to expect the Pope to annul the marriage of his captor's

[5] More properly an annulment, for the Church, as we have seen, did not recognize what we call divorce, with the privilege of remarrying (page 223). But "divorce" was the term used at the time for such annulments, and the one historians have employed in describing this case.

aunt and thus to declare Charles's cousin Mary illegitimate and her claim to the English throne void.

**Henry's Devices to Sway the Pope.** Still, Henry was a deter-mined man, and he directed all his energies to securing his objective. For two years he besieged the already besieged Pope with embassy after embassy demanding a decision in his favor. Various legal arguments were offered, of which the one most fre-quently employed was that a pope (in this case Julius II, Pope in 1503) had no right to issue a dispensation allowing a mar-riage specifically prohibted in the Bible, as Henry now read it. But the question was, in fact, a political rather than a legal or theological one, and the Pope took refuge in delay, hoping that something would turn up to rescue him from his difficulty. When, in 1529, Henry decided that the means already used were not strong enough, he dismissed his chief minister, Wolsey, who had hitherto managed the negotiations. He took a more active charge of state affairs himself, and summoned Parliament. At first he used this body as an auxiliary in his negotiations with the Pope. He had it pass minor bills of a sort hostile to the powers of the clergy, such as an act reviving the old royal right to veto all ecclesiastical legislation. He hoped that the threat of more severe anticlerical acts on such matters, after the manner of the medieval Statutes of Provisors and *Praemunire,* would bring the Pope to terms. If an invading French army could have made a little more progress in Italy, this might have been pos-sible, but the military hope failed, and in 1533 Henry decided to take even more drastic action.

**The Reformation Statutes.** In the next twelve months a series of statutes passed by the Reformation Parliament, as it was called, virtually destroyed the political power of the Church, and incidentally gave the King his annulment. The Act of Appeals (1533) [6] supplemented the Act of *Praemunire* by forbid-ding ecclesiastical appeals of any sort to go out of the realm

[6] S-M, No. 74B, pp. 304-05.

thereafter. Accordingly it was immediately possible for Henry's new and pliable Archbishop of Canterbury, Thomas Cranmer, to hear the great case of the "King's matter," and give the desired decision without fear of being reversed on appeal. It was thereupon announced that Henry had already married Anne Boleyn, and in September a child was born, a girl—to Henry's intense disappointment—who was named Elizabeth. Since the Church of Rome would, of course, not recognize the legitimacy of Elizabeth or any subsequent issue of the new marriage, the King and Parliament proceeded to sever all ties with the Continental Church and to set up one distinctively English. The Act of Supremacy (1534) made the King Supreme Head of the Church in England, and conferred upon him practically all the rights belonging to the pope before that time.[7] The Act of Annates [8] of the same year made final a similar measure, tentative and threatening, of two years previous, forbidding the payment of annates, which constituted the chief source of papal revenue from England (page 118). It also provided that future elections to bishoprics should proceed according to a system known as the congé d'élire (privilege of election). According to this arrangement chapters of canons could not elect until they had the royal permission and then must choose the man named in the written congé, in other words, the royal nominee. After the passage of this act the king named the bishops as he named sheriffs, though once in office the bishop was theoretically irremovable. An Act of Succession, settling the crown on the issue of the marriage with Anne, completed the so-called Reformation statutes.[9]

**Their Constitutional Effect: Severance of the International Tie.** No doctrinal changes were made by these acts, unless the alteration in the earthly headship of the English Church be so considered. But it will be seen that constitutionally they were of the greatest significance. They struck at one of the chief

[7] S-M, No. 74G, pp. 311-12.  [9] S-M, No. 74F, pp. 310-11.
[8] S-M, No. 74D, pp. 307-08.

sources of ecclesiastical strength, and they settled in favor of the crown every major controversy that we have seen disturbing medieval relations between the spiritual and temporal arms. The severance of the ties with Rome that was brought about by the Acts of Appeals, Supremacy, and Annates deprived the English churchmen of that international support which had proved so valuable in all their earlier struggles with the secular authorities. No longer could they appeal to Rome for assistance, to English laymen to do their duty as members of an international body, or even to the established practice in other Christian countries. For England was now a law unto herself, and consequently English churchmen had to stand on their own feet thereafter.

**Powers of the Ecclesiastical Courts.** Specifically, the acts dealt with the old questions of court jurisdiction, control over the personnel of the clergy, and ecclesiastical finance, which had agitated church and crown relationships in earlier days (pages 108-117). The Act of Appeals took the starch out of the ecclesiastical courts. While those in England still retained most of their old jurisdiction, their independence disappeared with the loss of their connection with Rome. Henceforth ways could be found to see that they did nothing contrary to the royal will. A symptom of their new position was the increasing number of minor acts, which began as early as the thirteenth century (page 112) and were now much enlarged in scope, taking away from one type of case after another the clerical privilege of claiming benefit of clergy.

**Elections and Finance.** The Act of Annates, as we have said, definitely settled the question of the control of ecclesiastical elections—the thorny topic that had troubled William Rufus, Henry I, and John. In combination with the Act of Supremacy, it also went a long way to end the age-old problem of the wealth of the semi-independent Church with which Edward I and so many other medieval kings had struggled. By substituting the crown for the pope as head of the English Church, ecclesiastical as well as secular taxation was put in the royal hands.

## THE DISSOLUTION OF THE MONASTERIES AND ITS RESULTS

**Dissolution of the Monasteries.** Yet the bulk of the Church's wealth was not directly affected by these measures, since theoretically no more taxes were required after their passage than before, only a different recipient for some of them. Indirectly, however, these acts served to put all the Church's wealth at the mercy of the crown and eventually to reduce the clergy to comparative poverty. As Supreme Head of the Church, Henry was entitled to supervise and discipline the churchmen, both regular and secular. He was not as economical as his father, and some futile French wars had emptied his coffers well before the "divorce." He and his advisers were not slow to see the financial possibilities inherent in his new powers. Through an agent named Thomas Cromwell, he conducted an investigation into monastic morals. The results so roused the solicitude of this "pious" monarch for the spiritual welfare of the monks and nuns that he decided to abolish their institutions and confiscate their property. This he did, with the consent of Parliament, between 1536 and 1540. The regular clergy, as such, thus ceased to exist in England.

**Far-reaching Effects of the Dissolution.** The elimination of the regular clergy, however, was only one of the effects of the dissolution. The property that thus passed into the royal hands was soon given or sold at a very low rate to the King's friends and their friends. This created a powerful class of landlords whose position depended on preventing any restoration of lands to the Church. Consequently, when the anti-Roman movement later took on a definite religious complexion (page 331), they tended to support the Protestant movement and to oppose any

revival of Catholicism. The dissolution of the monasteries therefore helped to speed up the Reformation and to strengthen the
chances that the alterations which it effected in England's ecclesiastical structure would become permanent. The dissolution also
had very important economic effects. Most of the people who
received monastic lands belonged to the rising class of enterprising landlords who had been affected by the trend toward the
capitalistic organization of economic activity (page 247). Not
content with a mere living from their property, they wished to
derive from it the maximum income possible. Consequently they
did not content themselves with the old customary rents, but
sought to exact from their tenants all that the market would
bear. This new type of rent was called rack rent, because it
seemed to contemporary observers to operate as did the torturing device of that name. Furthermore, these new landlords much
more frequently tried to enclose their lands (page 249) than had
the old ecclesiastical proprietors (cf. page 392). With the profits
they obtained in these ways the new-style landlords might buy
more lands and repeat the process, or they might invest in some
of the new manufacturing and trading schemes that were springing up. Partly because of the amount of wealth that the dissolution of the monasteries thus made available for such investments,
England developed very rapidly as a capitalistic nation during
the next century. These religious and economic changes also
had a great effect on the problem of poor relief, which we shall
consider later (page 391).

## OTHER EFFECTS OF THE CHANGES IN THIS REIGN

**Impoverishment of the Secular Clergy.** The secular clergy
were almost as harshly treated as the regular, though the pressure was applied to them more slowly. Those employed as
chantry priests—clergy supported by endowments to say masses
for the souls of the departed, and commonly to teach school

also—had their endowments finally confiscated just after the close of Henry's reign. The ordinary parish clergy, most of whom had always been poor enough, were not greatly affected in a financial way by the Reformation, though they were left at the mercy of neighboring laymen if their parishes happened to have any property worth taking. But in the course of time the bishops and other high clergy whose appointments could be dictated by the crown were easily shorn of most of their lands by the simple process of the sovereign's refusing to nominate anyone who would not accept the royal terms. These terms commonly included the surrender to the crown of this or that manor or lease, so that after a few such appointments to a see most of its endowments would be in the monarch's hands.

**Tudor Absolutism Established.** Wyclif's dream of secular control of ecclesiastical funds was thus realized. But economic and political power go hand in hand, and with the property of the clergy went their political strength. A few brave souls, such as Sir Thomas More, Lord Chancellor and author of *Utopia,* John Fisher, Bishop of Rochester, and a handful of monks, dared to resist these changes—or at least to refuse to co-operate in making them—but they paid for their boldness with their lives. The leaders and many of the participants in a general rising of religious conservatives in the north of England, called the Pilgrimage of Grace, met the same fate in 1536. The power of the Church was thus broken by Henry VIII and his supporters, just as the power of the nobles had been by Henry VII and his. From 1535, or 1540 at the latest, we may date the establishment of Tudor absolutism. In the latter year Parliament was induced to pass an act which gave statutory force to royal proclamations, provided they did not involve the death penalty or the fundamental law of the land. Thus the English came very close to accepting that Roman theory which had been used as a rationalization for earlier Continental absolutisms—that the will of the prince is law.

# 16. GENERAL HISTORY
## 1547-1637

## EDWARD VI AND THE PROTESTANT MOVEMENT

**Edward VI (1547-53).** Henry died in 1547 and was succeeded by Edward VI, the son he had so greatly desired. But Anne Boleyn was not the mother of the child. She had been executed on a charge of infidelity in 1536 and her place was taken by a young lady of the court named Jane Seymour, who bore Edward in 1538. She died a few days later, and was succeeded by three more queens, whose comings and goings are not important for our purposes.

**Edward's Short Reign.** As a nine-year-old boy, Edward had to rule through regents. They assigned the young King tutors who were so conscientious about giving their equally conscientious royal charge a thorough classical education that they quite possibly worked him to death.[1] At any rate, he died in 1553 at the age of sixteen. The boy King's short reign is therefore memorable more for his advisers' doings than his own.

**The Religious Question.** The religious problem was the chief concern of these ministers. As already noted, the legislation of Henry VIII had had little doctrinal significance. The reformers of the Tyndale and Latimer school—now called Protestants because their German allies had protested against a degree of a German Diet (parliament) at Spires in 1529 forbidding further religious changes and refusing toleration to Lutherans in Catho-

---

[1] The writer is indebted for this suggestion to Professor T. W. Baldwin of the University of Illinois, who has made a special study of the subject.

lic states—were therefore clamoring for advances along this line.[2] Edward's uncle, Edward Seymour, Duke of Somerset, who acted as Protector during the early part of his reign, and John Dudley, Duke of Northumberland—the son of the financial agent of Henry VII—who virtually succeeded him, though without the title, were both inclined to Protestantism, and so furthered the movement. In 1549 Parliament passed an act permitting the clergy to marry. In the same year by another statute, called the Act of Uniformity,[3] a new prayer book was introduced that all clergymen were compelled to use in conducting the services of the Church. It was confused and vague on doctrinal points, but it translated the services into English from the medieval Latin formerly used, and otherwise suggested a tentative Protestantism in some places. Although there was a revolt in the west, public opinion in most of England seemed to accept these changes and in 1552 a more thoroughly Protestant prayer book was substituted [4] for the one of 1549. In it the communion was treated as a memorial meal, after the Zwinglian practice, instead of a sacrifice, as the Catholics considered it. The next year the Council issued a creed of Forty-Two Articles in which the doctrine of

GENEALOGY OF THE TUDORS

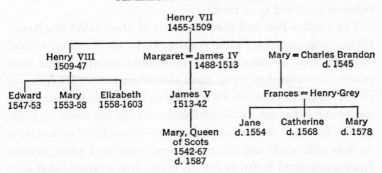

2 Tyndale himself had been seized on the Continent and executed for heresy in 1536.

3 S-M, No. 77A, pp. 325-26.          4 S-M, No. 77B, pp. 326-27.

transubstantiation was flatly denied and five of the seven Catholic sacraments were dropped. Plans for even more sweeping reforms were under way when Edward died in July, 1553, leaving
a problem about the succession.

## THE SUCCESSION OF MARY: HER POLICIES

**The Succession Question.** Henry VIII had secured parliamentary authorization to will the crown as he chose. With a fine
disregard of the niceties of both law and theology, he fixed the
order of succession as (1) Edward, (2) Mary, (3) Elizabeth, and
then (4) the Grey sisters, who were descended from his sister
Mary by her second marriage, with Charles Brandon, later Duke
of Suffolk.[5] He thus disregarded the facts (1) that both Mary and
Elizabeth had been declared illegitimate by act of Parliament,
(2) that the child Mary—Queen of Scots, as she was called—was
descended from an older sister and had a better hereditary claim
than the Grey girls, and (3) that his daughter Mary Tudor had
been brought up a Catholic and might therefore be expected to
reverse the policies of both Edward and himself. In spite of all
these difficulties, however, his settlement commanded great respect, and since it had the endorsement of Parliament, most Englishmen regarded it as final.

**The Dudley Plot and the Succession of Mary (1553-58).** Nevertheless, the ambitious John Dudley, Duke of Northumberland,
realizing that a Catholic sovereign would mean his fall from
power, determined to try to upset this arrangement. He reasoned
that if he could persuade an acceptable Protestant woman claimant to marry his son, Guilford Dudley, and if she could be made
queen, he might retain his position as virtual ruler of England.
As Edward's declining health became more and more evident
Northumberland began to lay his plans. It is probable that Elizabeth, who had already had her fingers burned in one abortive

[5] S-M, No. 76, pp. 323-24.

plot, refused to have anything to do with the scheme. In any case, she was passed over on the grounds of her legal illegitimacy, and the parents of Lady Jane Grey were induced to participate in the scheme. They duly ordered the necessary marriage, which thereupon took place, according to the custom of the time by which children were expected to obey the parental dictates in such matters. The dying Edward was persuaded to recognize his cousin Jane as his successor, and on his death she was proclaimed queen. Public opinion would have none of this scheme, however, and when Mary evaded arrest and sent out a call for assistance, the response was overwhelming. She then had little difficulty in taking possession of London and imprisoning her rival. Thereafter few disputed her right to the throne. The extent to which the Protestants were involved in this Dudley plot, which Mary could only regard as treasonable, must not be forgotten in considering the events of her short reign.

**Mary's Foreign and Religious Policies.** As the offspring of Henry's marriage with Catherine of Aragon, Mary was virtually committed to a Spanish-Hapsburg policy and also to a Catholic one. That they both failed disastrously must not be considered a reflection on the personal qualities of the Queen, who was, with the possible exception of her young half-brother, personally the most honorable and conscientious of all the Tudors, and perhaps therefore the least responsive to public opinion. She regularly did what she thought right, regardless of the consequences. She secured from Parliament the restoration of the Catholic creed and worship,[6] though she could not obtain the restitution of the monastic lands nor—at first—the repeal of the Act of Supremacy. Then she arranged a marriage with her cousin Philip, son of Charles V and his heir in Spain and the Low Countries. This deeply offended the nationalistic spirit in England, which feared the domination of the Spaniard. Several revolts occurred, of which the last, led by Sir Thomas Wyatt, son

[6] S-M, No. 78A, p. 328.

of the sonnet-writer, was very serious and only suppressed after the Queen had been in great danger. In the executions that followed, Lady Jane Grey—called the Nine Days' Queen because of her short "reign"—and others of her party were sent to the block. The marriage with Philip thereupon took place, and the prospect of a Catholic heir put Mary in a somewhat stronger position politically. By the usual process of exerting pressure on the lord lieutenants (page 389) and sheriffs who managed the elections she obtained a compliant Parliament. It restored the Roman supremacy over the Church [7] and also revived the fifteenth-century legislation against heresy (page 246), which had been repealed in Edward's reign.

**The Persecution of Protestants.** For the next four years, from 1555 through 1558, the Queen and her advisers endeavored to stamp out Protestantism, according to the traditional theory of persecution. This held that it was the duty of the authorities to inflict a few earthly pains in order to spare heretics—if they could be terrorized into repentance—and their potential followers infinitely greater torments in the next world. Nearly three hundred men and women were burned at the stake. One of these was Cranmer, who had granted Henry the "divorce" from Mary's mother. Latimer and several other bishops were also executed in this way. Instead, however, of destroying the rival religion, this persecution served only to strengthen it, for the blood of the martyrs is proverbially the seed of the Church. At the stake Latimer remarked to a fellow bishop who was to die with him, "Be of good comfort, Master Ridley, and play the man. We shall this day light such a candle by God's grace, in England, as I trust shall never be put out." A zealous Protestant propagandist named John Foxe saw to it that his hopes were realized. By gathering up all the stories of these sufferings he could find, and publishing them—with woodcut illustrations— early in the next reign, he formed an association in the English

[7] S-M, No. 78C, pp. 329-30.

mind between Catholicism and religious persecution that has never been completely dispelled. This near-Ku Klux Klan spirit, which in the popular mind fixed upon the Catholic Queen the title of Bloody Mary, became part of the English national consciousness. It must be kept in mind in order to understand later political and constitutional developments in England, particularly those in the next century and a half.

**The Failure of Mary's Foreign Policy.** The opposition to the royal program which grew out of these executions was confirmed and strengthened by the Queen's eventual childlessness and the failure of her foreign policy. Soon after the marriage Philip retired to the Continent, never to return, but he managed to persuade his deserted spouse to aid him in a war with France. As the Pope chose to support the French cause, the devoted Catholic Queen thus found herself under the displeasure of the one for whose interests she had made such great exertions in the past. The crowning blow came in 1558 with the French capture of Calais, that trophy of the Hundred Years' War on which English national vanity had so long fed. This was more than her subjects could forgive. The disheartened Queen told her courtiers that when she died "Calais" would be found written on her heart. In a few months she took to her deathbed, and amid bonfires and other sixteenth-century signs of general rejoicing her sister Elizabeth succeeded to the throne.

## ELIZABETH AND HER CAUTION

**The Character of Elizabeth (1558-1603).** The keynote in Elizabeth's policy was caution. Twenty-two years' experience of imminent danger in the midst of plot and counterplot had given her character as definite a set as the years of exile had that of her grandfather Henry VII, whom she resembled in many ways. Once when imprisoned by her sister on suspicion of complicity in the Wyatt plot she is said to have written these lines with a diamond on the window pane of her room in the Tower:

> Much suspected by [of] me;
> Nothing proved can be.

The authorities of that day could indeed prove nothing against her, and she spent the next half-century in equally successful efforts to prevent anybody else from maneuvering her into a disadvantageous position.

**Her Religious Policy.** The religious problem she solved for her lifetime by adopting a middle-of-the-road policy and refusing to be pushed to either side. She could not very well be a Roman Catholic in view of the circumstances of her birth. But that did not mean that she had to be very much of a Protestant either. She could retain a certain number of Catholic ceremonies and keep the doctrine of her Church so vague that men of widely differing opinions could be accommodated in her establishment. The prayer book that she had the 1559 Parliament approve [8] was a changeable-silk masterpiece of ambiguity. Catholic and Protestant phraseology were so woven together that when using the communion service the Anglican (Church of England) priest was almost enabled to say the Catholic mass and administer the Protestant supper at the same time. By variations of emphasis the moderates of either party might be satisfied with the same words. From this strategically vague position she never allowed herself to be moved very far, though in 1571 she felt it politic to consent to the adoption of a moderately Protestant statement of faith called the Thirty-Nine Articles. Extremists of both sides she frowned upon, but she avoided shedding blood for religious convictions alone. Only in cases of a semipolitical nature was corporal punishment inflicted. Everyone was required by law to attend services in the Established Church, but the dutiful subject did not have to agree with what

[8] S-M, No. 81B, pp. 346-48.

he heard and might hold to his own religious opinions as long as he did not try to spread them or disturb the peace.

**Foreign Relations and the Succession.** With a similarly judicious caution Elizabeth dealt with her other major political problems: foreign relations and the succession question. These were inextricably intertwined, because Elizabeth was unmarried, and it was assumed that she would accept one of the foreign princes who were being proposed as possible consorts. The history of England in the preceding century seemed to show that when sovereigns married their own subjects, troubles followed inevitably, and this kind of a move was considered out of the question, especially in the case of a woman ruler. Since a foreign marriage in those days meant a diplomatic alliance, the succession question was an integral part of the problem of foreign relations.

## ELIZABETH AND MARY QUEEN OF SCOTS

**Mary Queen of Scots.** The situation was further complicated by the fact that the chief powers with whom an alliance would be worth while were France and the Spanish-Hapsburg combination,[9] and both of them were Catholic. Since the adherents of the old religion did not recognize Elizabeth's claim to the throne, nor Henry's right to will the crown, they supported the claims of Elizabeth's cousin, Mary Queen of Scots (see the table, page 331). If Elizabeth married a Protestant prince, both Catholic houses might unite to depose her and put Mary on the English throne. If she consented to marry a representative of one of the Catholic states, she ran the double risk of being dominated by one of the strong Continental powers and having the disappointed rival actively championing Mary's cause.

[9] The German possessions of the house were now under the control of Philip's uncle, Ferdinand I, but the two rulers were naturally in close agreement.

**Elizabeth's Courtships.** In these difficult circumstances Elizabeth's supreme caution led her to adopt an admirably successful policy. By alternately or even simultaneously holding out matrimonial hopes to both the great Catholic rivals she paralyzed their military arms. Why should they risk a costly war when they might soon attain their ends by the happy means so successfully employed by the Hapsburgs at the beginning of the century? Never a Penelope played her suitors more adroitly than did Elizabeth. Now she was sending an embassy to get a picture of an Austrian archduke and verify a report that his head was as large as the Earl of Bedford's—apparently the biggest one at the English court. Now she was dallying with the French King's brother, a pock-marked and undersized specimen whom she affectionately dubbed her "little toad." As she thus spun out the years, France became involved in a long series of civil wars fought on the issue of religion, while a prolonged revolt of the Protestants in the Low Countries, which led to the rise of the Dutch Republic, similarly exhausted Spain. All those years England husbanded her strength and slowly caught up with the declining Continental powers. The island kingdom, it has been remarked, remained in the dry while outside the rain of internecine war was falling on the fools.

**The Downfall of Mary Queen of Scots.** While this policy effectively preserved England for a generation from overseas attack, it did not contribute anything to the settlement of the succession question, or the claim of Mary Queen of Scots to immediate possession of the southern kingdom. But Mary herself did a good deal to simplify this problem. Being a very emotional and impetuous woman, the very antithesis of Elizabeth, she soon quarreled with her own subjects on the question of religion; for she was half French and had been brought up a Catholic, while Scotland, under the influence of a reformer named John Knox, had turned Protestant. When she fell out with her second husband, Lord Darnley, and married the Earl of Bothwell, who was generally believed to have conspired with Mary to murder Darnley, her scandalized subjects rose in revolt. Mary, after being imprisoned, escaping, and twice suffering defeat in battle, decided that the least of the evil choices which confronted her was to flee to England and throw herself on Elizabeth's mercy, which she did in 1568. Her son by Darnley she was forced to leave in Scotland, where he was brought up a Protestant and allowed to reign nominally as James VI.

**Her Imprisonment in England.** Elizabeth's mercies on Mary were not too tender, but at first they were not as bad as they might have been. After some hesitation Elizabeth put her rival in semihonorable detention, justifying the action on the ground of Mary's alleged complicity in Darnley's murder. There the English Queen kept her "guest" for nearly twenty years. She spared Mary's life, however, although Elizabeth's agents discovered several plots to assassinate the Protestant ruler so as to pave the way for the succession of her Catholic rival.[10] The English Parliament regularly petitioned Elizabeth to permit the trial and execution of her dangerous cousin, but the Tudor sovereign was reluctant to establish a new precedent for the beheading of queens.

## ENGLISH ECONOMIC DEVELOPMENT

**The Question of Colonial Trade.** Eventually, however, time and changing circumstances combined to end Mary's life and demonstrate the strength that England had been steadily building up in the long years of evasion and delay. In spite of opposition from the older gilds, the trend toward the capitalistic organization of industry and trade (pages 247, 328) had continued. By the greater specialization of labor and the superior

[10] The two surviving Grey sisters, Catherine and Mary, had contracted unfortunate marriages that were generally supposed to render their candidacies out of the question.

planning for large-scale production made possible by this system a greater quantity of goods could be made for a fixed sum of money than had been possible under the gild system. With an increasing quantity of manufactured goods to dispose of, the English naturally began to look for overseas markets. From the middle of the century English merchants and seamen had not only been trading industriously along the coasts of Europe but had been endeavoring to get a foothold in those new worlds which Columbus and other contemporary explorers had discovered. According to the current theory of colonization, however, the dominant political power in an overseas territory reserved to its own nationals the exclusive right to trade in its colonial possessions. Between them Spain and Portugal had been given all the new lands by Pope Alexander VI in 1493. If the Dutch or English wished to trade in these areas, therefore, they could only do so by force of arms.

**The Joint-Stock Companies.** Nevertheless the potential profits from such trade were so great that many ventured into it. Overseas enterprise was further encouraged by the development of joint-stock companies. The first of these—the Muscovy Company —grew out of an expedition led by Willoughby and Chancellor in 1553. On this hazardous voyage the North Cape route to Archangel was discovered after a brave struggle against icy dangers, in which Willoughby and two of the three ships were lost. Since, however, the investors had owned all the ships jointly, all shared in the profits arising from Chancellor's safe return. By the application of this principle of joint investment, with which we are so familiar today, merchants thus eliminated the most serious of the risks in foreign trade.[11] Prior to this time a man was commonly made for life if his ship came in, but ruined with equal thoroughness if it did not, since all his eggs were in the one bottom.

[11] For the charter of a very important joint-stock company, the East India Company, see S-M, No. 88B, pp. 401-02.

## THE WAR WITH SPAIN

**The Sea Dogs.** During the 1560's and 1570's, therefore, a swarm
of English adventurers, known as sea dogs, half-trader and half-
pirate, were attacking Spanish overseas possessions. With these
exploits of Hawkins, Drake, Raleigh, and their colleagues the
reader is doubtless already familiar from his study of American
history. Spain protested, but tolerated these minor nuisances
rather than risk losing the great matrimonial prize in London.

**The Armada.** By the 1580's however, it was evident that Elizabeth did not intend to marry. And in any case she was past
the age of childbearing. Other reasons induced the Spanish to
try conclusions at this time. In 1587 Elizabeth felt strong enough
to give a "reluctant" consent to the execution of the imprisoned
Mary. Her cousin's French blood had formerly made the Spanish lukewarm in their support of the Catholic claimant, but
now they were free to invade England without fear that the
French would profit as a result of a Catholic victory. The Spanish were also angered by English support given to the Dutch in
their revolt. So in 1588 a great navy, or Armada, as it is called
in Spanish, was organized and dispatched to end the English
nuisance. It was to sweep the defending fleet aside and then ferry
Spanish troops across from the Low Countries to complete the
conquest. Drake, Hawkins, Howard, and other English sea dogs,
assisted by a convenient storm, defeated these plans, however.
The wreckage of the Armada was strewn along the Channel
coasts, out into the North Sea and up around the tip of Scotland, whither the survivors fled on their way home. Men rubbed
their eyes, and suddenly realized that England had become a
great power. Although much smaller in area and population
than either of her great Continental rivals, she was now able
to hold her own with them as she had with disorganized France
at the beginning of the Hundred Years' War. All the ground

lost during the fifteenth century had been more than made up under the Tudors. Like the story of Bannockburn in the annals of Scotland, this Armada episode, in which a small country vindicated its claim to equal status in the family of nations by successfully defending itself against an apparently overwhelming invading force, makes one of the proudest chapters in the national history. In the succeeding three and a half centuries as Englishmen went out to conquer and defend a great world empire they were inspired by the example of such leaders as Drake, and came to feel that his spirit was still with them, guiding, counseling, and even ready to lend more tangible aid in emergencies.

Call him on the deep sea, call him up the Sound,
　Call him when ye sail to meet the foe;
Where the old trade's plyin' and the old flag flyin'
　They shall find him ware an' wakin', as they found him long ago!

**The Age of Shakespeare.** Elizabeth thus ended her reign in triumph. For the last fifteen years her warships harried the Spanish coasts or lurked behind tropical islands to intercept her enemy's returning treasure fleets. At home, like the jubilant victors in all wars, people strutted about, boasting of their power and claiming the lion's share of the credit for their own particular group. This spirit—combined, of course, with many other influences—helped to produce the great works of literature and music that were the artistic glory of the Elizabethan age. The cheerful exuberance that is reflected in many of Shakespeare's works carried over into the next reign, and is to be seen even in the account of the destruction of his Southwark theater, the Globe:

Nothing did perish but wood and straw and a few forsaken cloaks; only one man had his breeches set on fire, that would perhaps have broiled him if he had not by the benefit of a provident wit put it out with bottle ale.

## JAMES I AND HIS PROBLEMS

**The Succession of James (1603-25).** A strong and merry age it was, but the change of rulers brought in a monarch who was not likely to do so well as Elizabeth in keeping England at high pitch. This was James, the son of Mary Queen of Scots, who now became James I of England though he was the sixth James of the northern kingdom. Elizabeth had strenuously refused to recognize anyone as her successor, since, as she put it, people naturally turn to the rising rather than the setting sun. But with the discrediting of the Grey line (page 339 n.) and the execution of James's Catholic mother the English generally came to look upon the Scottish King as the logical heir to the throne, and he succeeded without difficulty in 1603. Since his claim had come through a woman—in fact through two, his mother and his great-grandmother, Margaret, daughter of Henry VII—he began a new English dynasty called the Stuart, from Darnley's surname.[12]

**His Problems.** James's difficulties as a ruler of England were many though not insuperable. Being a mere man, he could not hope to command the affectionate respect that had marked Elizabeth's declining years. As a Scotchman he was considered a foreigner, and his dialect and his friends highly offensive. He had no stomach for a fight, wished desperately to avoid war, and took elaborate precautions against assassination. He had a shambling gait and did not make a regal appearance. Furthermore, he was passionately fond of airing the pedantic learning that had been imparted to him by his conscientious Scottish tutors. None of these traits, of course, endeared him to the swashbuckling veterans of the Armada struggle.

12 This happened to be the same as Mary's maiden name, for he was her cousin. The Stuarts were so called because they were descended from the family that held the hereditary Lord High Stewardship of Scotland.

**His Character.** James's chief weakness, however, was that he took the attitude of a retired businessman. He had been a successful ruler in Scotland, one who upon reaching maturity had in twenty years or less of active reign thrown off the restraints imposed by both nobles and churchmen and got the upper hand over both sets of rivals. In other words, he alone had done in the northern kingdom, before he was quite middle-aged, what Henry VII and Henry VIII had needed practically two whole lives to accomplish. He therefore possessed the ability to do great things in England had he so chosen. But for years he had been dreaming of the day when his second cousin should die and he would come into his great inheritance. Scotland was poor, weak, and barren compared to England. In the eyes of contemporaries the Scots were lean and starved cattle about to be turned loose in the lush green pastures of the south. So poor, in fact, was the Scottish monarchy that when James brought Anne of Denmark back from the Continent as his bride in 1590 he had to ask his nobles to bring their own food to the welcoming banquet at the royal palace. James had therefore developed a kind of complex during the years of waiting, a fixed conviction that when he became King of England all his troubles would be over and he could relax. Sure enough, when the great day came he proceeded to enjoy himself, spend freely, and run up debts. Visiting the chief English minister, Sir Robert Cecil, whom he soon created Earl of Salisbury, James decided that he would like the Cecil country house as a base for hunting, of which the pacifist King was passionately fond. So he persuaded his host, who could not well refuse, to accept one of the royal manors, Hatfield, in exchange for the Cecil estate—Theobald's Court, some fifteen miles north of London. There he proceeded to dawdle away a good part of his time watching his favorite hawks tear other birds to pieces while Salisbury did what he could with the government at Westminster. This put a great advantage in the hands of the parliamentary opposition, of which we shall speak in the next chapter.

## THE FOREIGN POLICY OF JAMES I

**Scotland.** Yet when James did care to concern himself with affairs of state, most of his policies in the field of international relations were sound, judged by later standards. He tried hard to secure a political and economic merger of England and Scotland in addition to the mere union of the crowns. A single kingdom of Great Britain was his aim. But the English were loath to share their green pastures. They feared to open their commercial world to the free competition of the northern peddlers, who would tramp through Poland with packs on their backs, as one horrified Englishman put it. Parliament rejected nearly all bills with such aims, and genuine union was postponed for a century.

**Ireland.** Ireland, as often, is an exception to the rule, for James's policy there has not commended itself to later critics. James may be defended to some extent, however, by pointing out that his policy in dealing with the neighboring island was really an extension of a Tudor one. We left Ireland still in a state of semichaos at the time of the visit of Richard the Second. Henry VII tried to bring some order out of this confusion by sending over a governor, Sir Edward Poynings, who succeeded in establishing the English authority throughout the island. He introduced an arrangement by which all the acts of the Irish Parliament had to be approved in advance by the English council, a restriction known as Poynings' law.[13] Government by such English lord lieutenants or deputies as Poynings, with an army at their backs, cost money, however, and when the Tudor sovereigns desired to economize they often entrusted the rule to a representative of one of the two leading and rival

---

13 S-M, No. 73D, p. 301.

Irish families, the Butlers (Earls of Ormonde) or the Fitzgeralds (Earls of Kildare and Desmond). These local potentates commonly abused their trust by using their official position to settle old scores with their rivals. By Elizabeth's time, when religious differences had developed to complicate matters—for the Irish naturally rejected the new faith of their conquerors and remained Roman Catholic—adventurers of the Drake and Hawkins type persuaded the English authorities that the best policy was to confiscate the lands of some of the most troublesome Irish and settle (plant) these areas with Englishmen. A new English migration to these plantations therefore took place, much after the manner of Strongbow's emigration four hundred years earlier (page 89). When James came to the throne of England he inherited, along with the great prize, a good-sized revolt in northern Ireland—in Ulster. When it was finally suppressed, a plantation of that whole area was undertaken and carried out more thoroughly than any of its predecessors. It was difficult, however, to attract the ordinary nonadventurous Englishmen, who, according to the original plans, were to till the soil. So the lean and hungry Scots, barred from England, were diverted there, and the result was the development of that Scotch-Irish Protestant Ulster which after three hundred years of strife still blocks the way to a united Ireland.

**Continental Relations.** In his dealings with Continental powers James consistently strove for peace, as already suggested. He promptly ended the war with Spain and proceeded to enjoy fifteen years of European quiet. During that period he married his daughter Elizabeth to the Elector Frederick of the Palatinate, a leading German Protestant prince. Unfortunately this royal son-in-law became involved in the disastrous Thirty Years' War that devastated Germany and disturbed the peace of Europe from 1618 to 1648. In 1619 Frederick accepted election as King of Bohemia, roughly the modern Czechoslovakia. In November, 1620, however, the Catholic party drove the Winter King—

as he was called from the brevity of his stay—out of his new territories and soon overran the Palatinate as well. In England the men of 1588 cried out for a return to the old methods of dealing with Catholic invaders, but James, who in 1618 had ordered the execution of the belligerent Sir Walter Raleigh on an old charge of treason, would have none of them. Instead he set himself to obtain the restoration of his son-in-law's original domains by peaceful means. To this end he proposed to marry Charles, his only surviving son, to a Spanish princess, whose parents, of course, were on the Catholic side in the Continental struggle. The Palatinate was to be returned to Frederick as part of the Spanish marriage settlement.

**The Spanish and French Matches.** The prospect of a Catholic queen waked memories of the days of Bloody Mary in English minds and roused a storm of opposition. In the face of it Charles romantically took the risk of a visit to Madrid to court his prospective bride in person. But the Spanish terms proved to be too stiff. Charles managed to return in safety and a bachelor, to the intense relief of his father's subjects. James, however, proceeded to impale himself on the other horn of the Catholic dilemma by arranging a match between Charles and a French princess, Henrietta Maria. The wedding had scarcely taken place when the King died and left Charles to deal with the situation as best he could.

## CHARLES I AND HIS FOREIGN POLICY

**The Character of Charles I (1625-49).** Charles was much more attractive personally than James. Though shorter than his father, he made a good appearance, had been brought up in England, and had no Scottish accent. But in his early years he had not had his father's hard training in the art of ruling, and especially in the art of ruling Scots. In time this inexperience was to cost him dear. Yet for a dozen years he held his position firmly enough, and had he been ruling England alone he might have continued to do so indefinitely.

**His Foreign Policy.** The breaking-off of the Spanish match meant a short war with the old adversary. Then an early quarrel with Charles's French father-in-law brought on hostilities with the power that was supposed to be his ally. But the new King's difficulties with Parliament (pages 372-5) would not permit of much indulgence in such expensive luxuries as foreign wars, and after 1628 he religiously kept the peace. Under an able Lord Deputy, Thomas Wentworth, Earl of Strafford, Ireland was given the best government it had ever known or was to know for many a long year. For once, the accounts of the troublesome island actually showed a profit to the English government. However much Englishmen grumbled about the pacific policy of Charles and his father, it was actually a great benefit to them. Once more the Continental fools were being exhausted by war while England was safe in her island shelter, manufacturing quantities of goods by the new capitalist domestic system, filching trade from her rivals otherwise engaged, colonizing, building up her strength, and preparing for the day of world empire, which was to come when the question of the control of her own government had been settled.

# 17. THE DISTRIBUTION OF POWER
## 1547-1637

**The Predominance of the Crown.** We have already seen that the power of the English crown was overwhelmingly predominant in the century following the Reformation. Detailed examination of its relations with the other political elements in the state will show something of the method by which this predominance was maintained. It will also serve to show, however, the way in which the ground was prepared for the overthrow of this absolutist system in the middle of the seventeenth century.

**Divisions among the Religious Forces.** The effect of the Reformation on the power of the Church was shattering. Not only was it legally subordinated to the secular arm, in the fashion previously described (pages 324-9), but it was so divided as to make recovery of its old position exceedingly difficult. Besides being deprived of its foreign support, it lost the strength that came from unity at home, and it never quite managed to regain this unity. From the time of Henry VIII on there were Roman Catholic, Anglican, and Puritan parties among the churchmen, each opposing the claim of the other to dominate the Established Church.[1] Though the Anglicans, with the help of the crown, managed to keep the upper hand—except for the short period under Mary—the effect of this fratricidal quarrel among the religious forces of the country was greatly to weaken their political influence.

[1] The Puritans were so called because these advanced Protestants wished to go further than the Anglicans in "purifying" the Church of Catholic practices.

## THE DECLINE OF CATHOLIC INFLUENCE

**The Roman Catholics under Elizabeth.** After the disastrous reign of Mary Tudor the hold of the Roman Catholic Church on the English people was pretty well broken, as we have noted (page 335), and it seems questionable whether it could ever again have regained its former position without outside help. But its foreign support and the fact that for many years it numbered among its adherents the most logical successor to the throne in the person of Mary Queen of Scots made it politically dangerous. Elizabeth was keenly aware of the Catholic menace, especially up to the time of the Armada. After the Pope excommunicated her in 1570 and absolved her subjects from their allegiance in order to aid a Catholic plot in that year, the Queen was driven reluctantly to take strong measures against the Catholics. This persecution was not for their religious beliefs, but because of the political effects of those beliefs. Religious and political ideas, however, were so interwoven that most of those executed in this repressive campaign must be considered martyrs for their religion. When the representatives of the old religion sent missionaries to England in the 1570's and 1580's, Elizabeth had Parliament pass more and more severe legislation against them, until in 1581 it became an offense punishable by death to convert a person to the Roman Catholic religion, while even the saying or hearing of mass was forbidden under heavy penalties. Elizabeth and her chief advisers—Sir William Cecil, afterward Lord Burghley,[2] and Sir Francis Walsingham, who was an adept at ferreting out Catholic plots—did not exact the extreme penalties under these laws any oftener than they thought necessary to keep the Catholic danger down to reasonable proportions. Of the many arrested in the Queen's long reign less than one hundred and thirty were executed. Others were kept

[2] Father of James's minister the Earl of Salisbury.

in prison, and after the Armada victory more subtle means were found for curbing the political menace of the Catholic faction. Some of the missionaries were secular clergymen, and others—including some of the most outstanding martyrs—belonged to the newly founded order of the Society of Jesus. By carefully fostering the jealousy of the seculars for the Jesuit regulars, even to the extent of arranging for the publication of books written by the prisoners, Elizabeth's government managed to divide and rule, and so weakened still further the Catholic influence. It is estimated that the proportion of English Catholics to the total population never rose above 3 per cent after the early years of Elizabeth's reign.

**And under the Early Stuarts.** In the succeeding reigns the Catholics made little progress, though the Stuart policy of favoring peace and Catholic marriages involved a relaxation in the enforcement of the penal laws. Public opinion would not tolerate further concessions, especially after the discovery in 1605 of the Gunpowder Plot. This was a project of some Catholic extremists, led by one Guy Fawkes, to blow up King, Lords, and Commons at the opening of Parliament on November 5. The exposure of this insane scheme, which even if successful could only have aroused general opposition and so defeated the ultimate ends of its inventors, served to confirm the half-century-old popular impression of Catholicism as a thing of violence and horror. As the years went on and generation after generation of Englishmen was brought up in the Protestant religion, Roman Catholicism became stamped as an alien faith, and its power shrank to negligible proportions. Only when some bogeyman was needed by politicians of the opposing camps, or when a sovereign showed Catholic leanings, could the threat be considered a very serious one.

## DIVISIONS AMONG THE PROTESTANTS: PURITAN DISCONTENT

**The Anglicans.** The Anglicans—or Episcopalians, as they are called in America, from their system of church government by bishops (Greek, *episcopoi*)—were too much under the royal thumb to be able to pursue an independent policy of any consequence. Though the bishops of the Established Church were appointed for life, they might aspire to further promotion, as to the archbishopric of Canterbury, and that advancement depended, of course, entirely on the royal favor. Even if an Anglican leader abandoned hope of higher office and followed a course of his own choosing, he could not safely expect to do so unmolested. When one incumbent of the see of Canterbury, Archbishop Grindal, tried to resist the Queen's wishes on an ecclesiastical matter, Elizabeth suspended him from the exercise of his official duties and had them handled by more pliable underlings. In time many Englishmen came to be thoroughly devoted to the hybrid religion that the Tudor sovereigns had devised, and hence the Anglicans secured a measure of popular support. But in case of a difference of opinion as to the interpretation of the official creed the clergy followed the royal bidding rather than that of the laity.

**The Puritans: Protestant Clericals.** It was the Puritan faction that made the most serious challenge for political power, and one which later was temporarily successful. This group—sprung from the Tyndale school of reformers, and greatly influenced by Swiss thought, especially as formulated by the French reformer of Geneva, John Calvin—may be described, for the purposes of the constitutional historian, as Protestant clericals. They wished to dispense with what they considered superstition and corruption in the Catholic religion, but they saw no reason to give up the financial and political strength of the medieval Church. Their theory of the relation of spiritual and temporal arms was virtually the same as that of their medieval forebears, and they were not averse to persecuting those who differed with them on religious questions. Elders (in Greek *presbyteroi*) were substituted for priests and bishops in their scheme of church government, but the powers of these officials were much the same as those of their predecessors. "New presbyter is old priest writ large," said the poet Milton in this connection.

**Their Biblicism and Discipline.** The Puritans, like the Lollards, wished to substitute the Bible for the Church as the ultimate source of religious authority. As they interpreted this book, it forbade the retention of Catholic robes and ceremonies in the conduct of church services, enjoined a high standard of moral life—including an austere attitude toward amusements—and prescribed a strict discipline. This discipline was to be enforced by a constant supervision of individual contact, exercised by the ecclesiastical authorities.

**The Monarchy and the Puritans.** In many ways it will be seen that the Puritans were the logical successors of the medieval monks, and like them they soon obtained a great hold over the people of all classes. Self-discipline and devotion bore the same fruit in the sixteenth and seventeenth as in earlier centuries. From this base of popular support the Puritans launched a campaign to take over the established Anglican Church and make it a truly reformed one, as they understood the idea of reformation. In Convocation and Parliament they introduced measures to alter the organization and ceremonies of the official body. Elizabeth, however, jealous of her power, firmly blocked the way and successfully defeated all efforts of this sort. She realized that a semi-independent clericalism was not compatible with absolutism, and she also objected to certain democratic tendencies in the movement. The Stuart rulers took the same attitude. James said that the Puritan system agreed as well with monarchy as God with the devil. Charles, who had been brought up an Anglican and had never known any other kind of official religion, was firmly persuaded not only that his religion was the most convenient type for a monarchy, but also that theologically it was the only correct one. With a working majority in the House of Lords, ensured by the presence there of a sizable number of bishops, the rulers were able to defeat practically all the legislation the Puritans proposed. By their general control of the bishops, who in turn controlled the machinery of the church courts, they could and did greatly hamper the Puritan movement. Furthermore, by means of a new prerogative court for ecclesiastical affairs, called the High Commission (page 400), they were able to deprive especially troublesome Puritans of their positions in the Established Church.[3]

**The Puritan Split: The Presbyterians.** This implacable opposition from the crown resulted in a split in the Puritan ranks, somewhat like the one in the Catholic party. Different theories of church government were adopted, according to what the factions considered the best means of dealing with the situation. Originally the Puritans had not concerned themselves greatly with the problem of ecclesiastical government. They had been content with the assertion that whether bishops were employed or not, all preaching churchmen were a variety of New Testament elders and were to pay attention to duty accordingly. If it seemed more convenient to have one act as superintendent over his fellows, the Puritans at first had no objection so long as he preached and lived moderately. When the Anglican bishops began to use their powers more and more to suppress Puritanism at the royal behest, however, most of the party came to repudiate the episcopal system altogether. Instead they proposed to have

[3] Though the Puritans were opposed to the Anglicans, they had, as already suggested, no objection to the principle of an Established Church, but merely to the particular form of the Tudor one. Thus they took positions in it and tried to alter it by the means already mentioned and also by refusing to conform to its ceremonial rules. Hence they are sometimes called Nonconformists.

each local church governed by its preaching minister, or elder, together with several lay elders to help with the discipline—hence called ruling elders—and deacons to collect funds and look after the poor. The whole body of local church officials was called a session. All the churches of a given area were to send delegates from their sessions to form a committee called a presbytery.[4] These presbyteries in turn sent delegates to form a synod for a larger area, and eventually a national assembly. This system was known as the presbyterian one because of the importance in it of elders (presbyters) and presbyteries. It was the general pattern of church government used in Protestant Scotland, and it began to be seriously advocated in England about 1570.

**And Independents.** Such a complicated system could not, however, be put into practice until the national Church was definitely taken over. The more advanced Puritans, led by one Robert Browne, grew tired of waiting for that distant day, and so in the 1580's began to form churches with no more official machinery than the local session. Because these "gathered" bodies did not need to have any connection with other ecclesiastical bodies, they were called independent churches and those who advocated them, Independents. An alternative name is Congregationalist, because the individual congregation was the ultimate governing authority in this system.[5] Throughout the last years of Elizabeth and the period of the early Stuarts these two schools of Puritans—Presbyterian and Independent-Congregational—were quarreling with each other as well as with the government and

[4] Originally the session was known as a presbytery and the presbytery as a classis, but the later terms are here used in order to make clear the distinction between Presbyterian and Independent.

[5] Because many of these Puritans separated from the Established Church and refused to attend its communion service or have anything else to do with what they regarded as a non-Christian body, they are sometimes called Separatists. But not all the Independents advocated complete separation of this sort, and so a large part of them—including the founders of the Massachusetts Bay colony—are known as Non-Separatists, and the somewhat stricter Plymouth colonists are called only Semi-Separatists.

the Anglican authorities. By themselves they could not therefore expect to make much progress while in this divided condition. But they had powerful allies in the ranks of the secular opponents of the crown, to whom we now turn.

## GRIEVANCES OF THE GENTRY, MERCHANTS, AND LAWYERS

**The Country Gentry and the Commons.** The effect of the Tudor reluctance to create nobles, combined with the dissolution of the monasteries, was to increase the importance of the nontitled country gentry and of the House of Commons in which they were represented. The niggardly policy in the matter of distributing titles had in it the seeds of future difficulties, for powerful men who in preceding reigns would have been given titles and so brought into the House of Lords, where they would be forced to be somewhat circumspect in their activities (page 261), were now left to sit in the lower house and express their sentiments there. It is partly for this reason that in this period the initiative in parliamentary activities passes from the Lords to the Commons.

**Grievances of the Lower House: Taxation.** The feelings of the lower house—and the classes it represented—toward the monarchy were somewhat mixed. In Tudor times, as we have seen, the rulers generally managed to keep the Commons in good humor, but there were several points of disagreement, which first appeared in the sixteenth century and which under the Stuarts became very serious indeed. There was always a complaint about taxes, especially among the merchants. Actually the English taxes were very light compared to what Continental peoples were paying. England was extremely prosperous, as already noted. But things are never so good but what men think they might be better, especially when one kind of administration is in power year after year, as it was then. This meant that the grumbling opposition was never given the responsibility of governing, and a resulting sense of the difficulties any administration must face.[6] When James came to the throne, with his somewhat lavish ideas, he increased the expense of the government by nearly one-fifth, and the complaints mounted proportionately—or rather out of all proportion, for the country had been spoiled by Elizabeth's economy and was shocked at the expenditures of a no more than normally extravagant ruler.

**Monopolies.** Another grievance of the merchants was the royal method of controlling industry through the granting of monopoly rights to a few individuals. By these patents of monopoly, granted, like a modern patent, to those who had perfected some invention or were otherwise thought to be entitled to special rights in a certain field of operations, the absolute control of a particular type of business might be put in a few hands. For example, if one man were given the monopoly on the making of glass tumblers, everyone else engaged in this activity had either to suspend operations or pay the monopolist for the privilege of continuing, which meant that all rival manufacturers had to accept the monopolist's supervision and regulation. The merchants had not yet come to the point of believing in a laissez-faire system of economics, even for internal trade. They were willing to accept a reasonable regulation of wages, working-conditions, and marketing devices. They did not so much object to monopolies as such, as to the way in which they were administered. The merchants of the outports—ports other than London—objected that the workings of the system tended to concentrate business in the capital. All the merchants objected that courtiers—especially under the Stuarts—were too often given these privileges, to the exclusion of legitimate businessmen who had pioneered in an industry and might be presumed to know

[6] When at long last the opposition elements did gain control in the middle of the seventeenth century, the cost of their government was far more than that of the one about which they had been complaining (page 454).

best how to develop it. So intense was the feeling on this subject that in 1601 Elizabeth thought it advisable to consent to
the annulment of many of the more objectionable monopolies,
and in 1624 Parliament pushed through an act prohibiting the
giving of monopolies to anyone except inventors and the intro-
ducers of new processes.[7] The royal advisers, however, soon
worked out a method of evading this restriction by granting
monopolies to incorporated companies rather than individuals.
This naturally angered the merchants who had made the original protests.

**Political Grievances of the Gentry.** The country gentry, like
the merchants, objected to the financial policies of the Stuarts,
but a bigger factor than the economic grievance in alienating
their support from the crown was the political one. No doubt it
was well that the Tudors humbled the overmighty subjects. But
much humbling, long continued, did not soothe the feelings of
proud landed proprietors who had long been accustomed, in
their capacity of justices of the peace, to directing local affairs
in their particular counties. They resented sharp orders from
the Council,[8] and were also offended by a general indifference
on the part of the government to their opinions and desires. It
was monstrous, as one of them put it long afterwards, to suggest
that the gentlemen of England were fit only to give money and
did not know how an invasion was to be resisted. When James
tried to extend the monopoly practice to the licensing of inns
and taverns, which had long been a prerogative of the justices
of the peace, the wrath of the gentry became something to be
reckoned with.

**Attitude of the Common Lawyers.** Besides the gentry and the
merchants, a third social element may be observed in the secular

[7] S-M, No. 90D, pp. 434-35. The exemption of "corporations, companies, or
fellowships" (in spite of the phrase "bodies politic or corporate") is in Sec. IX
of this act, a part of which is not included in the excerpts given by Stephenson and Marcham.

[8] For a sample, see S-M, No. 83H, pp. 382-83.

opposition to the crown, and that is the professional class of the common lawyers. These men drew most of their fees from the other two, often came from the ranks of the gentry themselves, and had been educated at the inns of court along with many of the fortunate elder brothers who returned home to inherit the family estates and become justices of peace and members of Parliament. For these reasons the men of the common law were naturally drawn into the opposition camp. But they had a particular grievance also, in the encroachments of Chancery and the prerogative courts on what they regarded as their special preserves in the field of litigation. It is true that many of the common lawyers practiced before these other courts as well as their own. They had perforce to compete there, however, with men trained in the Roman civil law. They also objected to the strange and simple procedure of these tribunals, which tended to reduce the demand for the services of the common lawyers and hence lower their incomes.

**Puritan Sentiment Unites the Opposition.** Finally, these gentry, merchants, and lawyers were on the whole puritanically inclined, and hence they were also angered by the religious policy of the crown. They were the men who would be the lay elders in the Puritan religious establishment, and they objected to seeing the bishops do badly—as they thought—the things which they believed themselves capable of doing well. Aside from their offended self-esteem there was, of course, a very sincere religious feeling that the Anglican system was full of superstitions and inefficiencies that were endangering the welfare of many souls. So the secular opposition found little difficulty in making an alliance with the Puritan wing of the religious opposition. Together they could attack the existing system quite harmoniously, as long as they did not try to become too definite about the exact kind of arrangement to substitute for it. For on that question there were serious points of disagreement, which, as we shall see later (pages 432-9), would appear whenever the coalition of opposing forces should get the upper hand.

## THE POLITICAL THEORY OF THE TWO PARTIES

**The Divine Right of Kings.** Elizabeth, as already suggested (page 336), handled the opposition with finesse and tact. On the few occasions when it proved too strong for her, as in the case of the monopolies (page 358), she yielded gracefully in order not to attract too much attention to an inconvenient precedent. When she thought it best to employ strong measures, she was never explicit about her reasons, and thus left little room for argument. The pedantic James, on the other hand, loved to lecture his opponents in a father-knows-best strain. In justifying his claims he developed and expounded the theory, already to be found in the Bible and medieval literature, of the divine right of kings. According to this,

> Kings are by God appointed;
> And damned are those who do resist
> Or touch the Lord's anointed.

In other words, the king was king not because Parliament or any other group elected him, but by the decree of the Almighty. The ruling sovereign was therefore responsible to God, and to God only. If he did wrong, God would punish him severely—and this was an important part of the theory which must not be forgotten. Tyranny was not to be justified by this argument. But the question of what was tyranny had to be left to the king and his Almighty Overlord, for the subjects had no right to judge God's appointee—only the duty of absolute and unquestioning obedience.

**The Social Compact, or Contract.** Such talk was merely asking for trouble. Cool-headed lawyers took this royal brief home with them and calmly picked it to pieces as they worked out one to set against it. When Parliament met in 1614, Sir Edwin Sandys—prominent in the early history of the Virginia Company also—arose and suggested a rival theory of the social compact, which in a somewhat more developed form became the doctrine of the opposition. According to this line of reasoning, which can be traced back to the rationalizations of the medieval feudal contract, the ruler owed his position to an original consent of the ancestors of the ruled that the ruler's ancestor and his heirs should have such an office on certain conditions. These included ruling wisely, efficiently, and justly. If these conditions were not fulfilled—in the opinion of those being ruled—the original compact was broken. The king lost his position, or rather had already abandoned it by ceasing to be a proper king. His subjects might therefore go to work all over again to set up a new government of any sort that might please them. Such upheavals, however, were expected to be very rare occurrences.

**The Issue Drawn and the Stage Set.** By this elaboration of conflicting theories the clash of interests and constitutional outlooks was made clear and definite. It remained to be seen whether it could be resolved by any peaceful means. Two types of such efforts were made by the opposition, one in the courts and one in Parliament. An examination of the struggle in each sphere will show how the king kept control of the situation in spite of vigorous agitation.

## SIR EDWARD COKE AND THE STRUGGLE IN THE COURTS

**Insecurity of Judicial Tenure.** The key to understanding the conflict in the courts is the fact that up to this time judges were considered the king's personal agents (page 166). They were appointed by him and, in contrast to the bishops, could be dismissed by him at will. In consequence, the precarious tenure of their positions made the judges generally susceptible to royal pressure in spite of their professional desire to maintain the traditions of the common law. This was generally true in Elizabeth's time, though in her reign there were occasional instances of successful assertion of judicial independence. One of these had to do with the long-standing practice of the judges' controlling the appointment of clerks in their own courts. Elizabeth tried to force the selection of one of her nominees, but withdrew the request when the judges made a firm stand for the old custom.

**Attitude of the Common Law Judges under the Early Stuarts: Calvin's Case.** Under James the judges at first continued to favor the crown on most constitutional points, notably in the Calvin, or Colvill, case. This had to do with the English citizenship of Scottish subjects born after the union of the two crowns. James was very anxious to secure English rights for his Scottish subjects, as already noted (page 345), but Parliament had prevented their being conferred in the normal way. It occurred to the royal supporters to argue, however, that the *post-nati*—as those Scots were called who were born after the accession of James to the English throne in January, 1603—must be considered English citizens for purposes of landholding, since at birth they acquired a loyalty to the person who was King of England. In a collusive suit the majority of the common law judges, meeting in the Exchequer Chamber (page 397) in 1609, accepted this argument and ruled the infant Calvin, in whose name the suit was brought, eligible to hold land south of the border without naturalization.[9]

**The Great Exception: Sir Edward Coke.** One great judge, however, between 1606 and 1616 chose to oppose the King, partly as a matter of principle and partly out of a sense of his own importance. This was Sir Edward Coke (pronounced Cook), a Norfolk man and a great authority on the common law. By sheer ability he had worked his way up the legal ladder until

[9] S-M, No. 91C, pp. 438-41.

CARDINAL WOLSEY, 1475?-1530
Lord Chancellor, 1515-1529.

SIR EDWARD COKE, 1552-1634

OLIVER CROMWELL, 1599-1658

SIR FRANCIS BACON, 1561-1626

he had become Chief Justice of the Court of Common Pleas. After some years of controversy the King, who was loath to use the short, sharp method of removal as long as maneuvering and his beloved reasoning power might in time produce the same effect, thought to warn and shelve his adversary by "kicking him upstairs" to the Chief Justiceship of the King's Bench (1613). But there, too, Coke found means to keep his oar in the stream of constitutional matters. In our treatment of his cases we shall not consider them so much with regard to the time or the court in which they arose as to the principles with which they were concerned.

**The Doctrine of Judicial Review: Bonham's Case.** The basic case that best shows Coke's conception of the role of the courts in the constitution is Bonham's, in which Sir Edward laid down the doctrine of judicial review, which has played such an important part in American constitutional history. Henry VIII had granted a monopoly of medical practice in his capital to the College of Physicians. Its members were not only to enjoy the sole right to treat the sick, but to pass on the qualifications of all those desiring admittance to their number, in other words, those seeking a license for such practice. This grant had been confirmed by an act of Parliament in the same reign. According to the act those practicing without a license might be imprisoned and fined by the officers of the college. Bonham came from Cambridge with a medical degree, but the London College of Physicians, wishing to keep down the number of practitioners in their vicinity, refused him admission. He defied the college, and in spite of the refusal of the license did medical work. He was thereupon punished under the terms of the act, and retaliated promptly by bringing an action for false imprisonment against the officers of the college. The matter came before Coke, who found for the plaintiff by calmly ruling that Parliament had no right to pass the act of confirmation, since in giving the officers of the college the right to pocket the fines assessed, it went contrary to the principle of the common law that no man might be both judge and interested party in the same case. "When an act of Parliament is against common right and reason or repugnant or impossible to be performed the common law will control it and adjudge such act to be void," was his dictum. In other words, he held that there were principles of the common law, the fundamental law of the land, to which Parliament, and the king as well, were subordinate. In the light of these principles, he said, the actions of both legislature and executive might be reviewed by judges and overruled if found to be in conflict with the higher law.[10]

**Indirect Attacks on the Prerogative: Rival Jurisdictions.** With this conception of his role, Coke proceeded to play the overruling reviewer in a great number of cases. Some were primarily concerned with the jurisdictions of rival courts. Potentially these had an important effect in limiting the power of the king, since the crown found it easier to work its will through Chancery and the ecclesiastical and prerogative courts than through those of the common law. But because they have only an indirect bearing on our present story and are much more closely related to the subject of a later chapter, they will be dealt with in that connection (page 398).

**Direct Attacks.** Other cases involved direct assaults on the royal prerogative. In the case of Proclamations (1611) Coke ruled that a man could not be tried for building a London house in defiance of a royal proclamation designed to relieve congestion in the metropolis.[11] He held that the proclamation did not have the force of law (pages 329, 380), and that where there was no law, there was no offense. In the case of *Brownlow* v. *Cox and Michell* (1616) he and the other common law judges wrung

---

[10] This traditional interpretation of Bonham's case has been challenged—in my judgment unsuccessfully—by S. E. Thorne, "The Constitution and the Courts: Reexamination of the Famous Case of Dr. Bonham," in *The Constitution Reconsidered,* ed. by Conyers Read, Columbia University Press, 1938, pp. 15-24.

[11] S-M, No. 91D, pp. 441-42.

from James a recognition of those rights of appointing subordinates in their own courts which Elizabeth had conceded before
him (page 362). A more important case was that of Peacham,
which had come up in the preceding year. This man was a Puritan minister in Somerset, in the west. When the ecclesiastical
authorities deprived him of his clerical rank on a charge of
libeling his bishop, his study was searched. There notes were
found for a sermon in which the King and his ministers were
charged with misconduct and extravagance, and the possibility
of the ruler's sudden death was hinted at. James was furious
that such ideas should be spreading, and he insisted that Peacham
be tried for treason. Legally, however, this offense required the
commission of an overt (open) act (page 380). It was difficult to
say whether making notes for a sermon was such an act. Peacham
was to be tried before the assize judges on the western circuit.
James, in order to be sure that the judges he selected for that
tour would rule favorably, called in most of the eligibles, exclud-
ing Coke, and questioned them individually as to their opinion
on the disputed point. Coke found out about these proceedings
and made a heated protest against this taking of "auricular"
(private) opinions from the individual judges instead of consulting them in a body. For once, however, from the standpoint
of precedents he was on bad ground. James and his legal advisers, including Sir Francis Bacon, Coke's great rival, pointed
out that the sovereign had always been accustomed to receive
advice on legal affairs from individual judges as well as from
his own attorneys. Two friendly judges were thus secured and
Peacham was duly convicted, though he died in prison before
the sentence was carried out.

**The Royal Right to Delay Legal Proceedings: Neile's ("Com-
mendams") Case.** Neile's case was the last of this series, and the
most dramatic.[12] Neile was a clergyman who supported the royal

12 Also cited as *Colt and Glover* v. *the Bishop of Coventry.* S-M, No. 91F,
pp. 442-43.

cause, and in 1614 was accordingly appointed Bishop of Coventry and Lichfield. This see had, however, been so impoverished by the royal policy of spoliation already described (page 329) that the appointee secured the King's special permission to hold along with it two other ecclesiastical livings. Holding livings in this fashion was called holding them *in commendam* —hence the case is sometimes called the *commendams* case— and was forbidden by the medieval canon law on the theory that a bishop should not have besides his bishopric any position involving pastoral care (the cure of souls). The owners of one of the advowsons concerned, who felt cheated out of their rights of appointment, thereupon sued Neile for interfering with this right. In 1616 the case came before Coke and his fellow judges in the joint appellate body known as the Exchequer Chamber (page 397), and was being heard when Bacon discovered what was going on. He naturally requested a delay in order to file what we should call an intervening brief on the King's behalf, since it was obviously the royal action that was in question. This request was made in the form of a writ called *de non procedendo rege inconsulto* (concerning not proceeding since the king has not been consulted) from the fact that it alleged that a case involving the crown was being heard without the King's having been consulted. Coke felt that if a delay were granted, the royal pressure would be such that Neile would certainly win. He therefore persuaded his fellow judges to ignore Bacon's writ and proceed with the case. On hearing this James was furious. He called all the judges before him, read them a lecture, and then demanded whether in the future they would recognize the writ *de non procedendo rege inconsulto*. Eleven of them declared that they would, but all that could be extracted from Coke was the declaration that in such cases he would do "what it befitted an honest and just judge to do."

**Coke's Dismissal.** James then had recourse to his ultimate argument. Angered also by the contemporary assault of Coke on the Court of Chancery (page 398), he suspended him from office for a few months and told him to spend some of the time revising his published legal works (page 409).[13] In them there were comments generally considered hostile to the royal prerogative, but Coke insisted that they were reasonable enough if given proper interpretation. He refused to make any substantial alterations in his writings, though he offered to let the other judges pass on the moot points. On this showing of recalcitrance, in November, 1616, he was permanently removed from office.

**Later Judicial Subservience: Coke's Ultimate Influence.** The lesson of Coke's fall was not lost on the remaining judges. Thereafter James and Charles had little trouble with the courts. A judge named Crewe was removed in 1626 for refusing to endorse the forced loan (page 373) of that year as legal, and in 1629 the Chief Baron of the Exchequer was removed, apparently because he was not sufficiently "forward" in aiding the King against Eliot and his associates (page 375). But otherwise the judicial decisions were uniformly favorable to the crown, notably in the Eliot case and in the great issue of ship money (page 376). Though a sizable minority dissented in the latter case, it did so only after the majority had given its opinion and the victory of the crown was assured. The precedents set by Coke were not followed by his immediate successors, and their value at the time was chiefly one of propaganda for the opposition party. They served to enunciate, and focus attention upon, principles that would inspire men to the use of force and which might be adopted after a military victory. Coke's argument in Peacham's case, for example, though rejected when first made, set a standard for future relations of the executive and the judiciary that was adopted in England after the civil wars. It should be pointed out, however, that though his doctrine of judicial review was eventually adopted in the United States, it found little support in England and never became a permanent part of her constitution.

13 S-M, No. 91G, pp. 443-44.

## THE LONG STRUGGLE IN PARLIAMENT

**The Role of the House of Commons.** Very much the same generalization applies to the struggle in Parliament between the opposition and the sovereigns of this period. Great principles were enunciated in the course of it, but force was needed to make them effective. As already indicated (page 356), the House of Lords lost much of its importance during this period, while the lower house largely took over its role in the governmental system. This was due to the policy of Henry VIII and the succeeding sovereigns. Not as economical as his father, by his extravagance, especially in the matter of foreign wars, Henry was forced to return to the practice of having frequent sessions of Parliament. Since the nobility and the Church had been crushed, he perhaps felt, and not without reason, that the Commons could do him no harm. On the contrary, they could be a convenient source of revenue. He and his Council therefore resumed the policy of Edward I, of calling Parliaments on the theory that they could be easily browbeaten into giving the king money. This usually proved to be the case in Henry's time, especially when his minister Thomas Cromwell put a little—and sometimes more than a little—judicious pressure on the local officials and electing bodies. Under Edward VI and Mary similar efforts were made to pack the lower house. These efforts, however, did not always succeed quite so well, due in part to bad management and in part to the unpopularity of some of the policies which those in control of the government were endeavoring to force through Parliament. Elizabeth was more adroit in her tactics and also more popular; and so on the whole she succeeded in controlling the Commons quite effectively.

**Parliamentary Powers and Privileges under the Tudors.** This policy was, however, open to the same objections as that of the thirteenth-century rulers. Bodies frequently called to vote taxes or approve royal policies would readily acquire the notion that they were an important part of the government, and would be quick to assert their power whenever a weak ruler should appear. So under the Tudors the Commons were repeating the old claims of parliamentary privilege to which the rulers found it convenient to pay a kind of lip service. In 1512 Parliament successfully intervened to protect a member named Strode, who was prosecuted in the Stannary Court—the special court for the tin industry (page 183)—for introducing in the Commons a bill to which the tinners objected. In 1542 the Speaker included this privilege of free speech along with freedom from arrest and freedom of access to the ruler among the privileges requested of the sovereign at the opening of a session, and after 1572 this request was regularly made and regularly granted. The Commons also established a precedent in Mary's reign—and renewed it in the 1590's—to the effect that the House itself should pass on all cases of disputed elections, instead of leaving them to Chancery or some other royal court. This was designed to prevent the packing of Parliament by the crude practice of challenging the election of opposition members. Elizabeth found it expedient to make these formal concessions; at the same time she found ways of evading their effect.[14] In spite of the grant of freedom of speech, for example, by peremptory orders or by putting pressure on the Speaker she frequently prevented the House from discussing topics of state that she chose to reserve for her own consideration and decision, such as foreign affairs, her marriage, the succession, or religion. In serious cases she resorted to the practice of arresting and imprisoning for short terms those who ventured to speak in defiance of her known will. Such actions were tolerated by the House because of external dangers and the respect they bore their woman sovereign.

**And the Early Stuarts.** These considerations did not apply,

[14] For sample clashes between monarch and Commons, see S-M, No. 82F-J, L-M, pp. 363-70, 372-73.

however, in the early Stuart period. Then the struggle was bitterly fought out on the three issues of parliamentary privileges,
the right to impeach royal ministers, and the control of taxation. Since these three conflicts are inextricably intertwined at
several points, they are best described in roughly chronological
order rather than in a topical arrangement.

**Freedom from Arrest and Freedom of Election: The Shirley
and Goodwin Cases.** In James's very first Parliament, which he
did not bother to pack by the usual method of influencing elections, he found himself confronted with the issue of parliamentary privilege. The case of a member, one Thomas Shirley, arrested for a private debt revived the old claim of freedom from
arrest, and this the King readily conceded.[15] Buckinghamshire,
however, raised the question of control over elections by choosing as knight of the shire a certain Sir Francis Goodwin. Goodwin had been outlawed in the process of a civil suit (page 292),
and since the royal proclamation summoning Parliament had
barred such candidates, the Court of Chancery quashed the election and ordered a new one. In this the defeated candidate, Sir
John Fortescue, a Privy Councilor, was seated. When Parliament
assembled, the House asserted the Tudor precedent establishing
its right to rule on election disputes and claimed the right to seat
Goodwin. James chose to fight this case on the general issue of
privilege and, relying on the theory of the divine right of kings,
enunciated a doctrine that greatly offended the Commons. He
asserted that he was not bound by the actions of his predecessors,
and that the privileges which Parliament claimed were held by
grace, or charity, of the ruling monarch, and not as of right. In
other words, Parliament had no established rights, but only such
privileges as the all-powerful king chose to concede to it for the
moment. After a prolonged controversy James finally granted the
right of the Commons to settle these election disputes in the

[15] S-M, No. 89D, pp. 414-15; No. 90C, p. 433.

future, but obtained the concession of a new election in this particular case.[16]

**Impositions.** The House of Commons thus won two minor victories at the beginning of the reign. A long series of defeats followed. The Tudors had frequently levied customs duties in excess of those sanctioned by Parliament, and no great objections had been raised. Now a merchant named Bate, or Bates, chose to resist the collection of such impositions, as the excess duties were called. He was sued by the crown in the Court of the Exchequer and there the pliable royal judges handed down the very important decision that the king must have revenues and therefore could take them when in need. Specifically, it was maintained that because the king had the duty of defending the country he had absolute control of the coast and ports, and could determine the conditions on which men and goods went in and out.[17] The King did not venture to proceed openly on the first line of argument. He continued to ask Parliament for grants of direct taxes. But under the second he charged whatever impositions his advisers thought the traffic would bear.

**Other Expedients.** Had England's foreign trade been great enough, this practice alone might have rendered the crown financially independent of Parliament. As it was, however, when refused direct taxes—as James frequently was—he and his successor were forced to resort to a great variety of revenue-producing devices. All the tricks of Empson and Dudley were revived. Wealthy men were prosecuted under obsolete laws. Forced loans and benevolences—which were levied and collected as though they were regular parliamentary grants of subsidies (page 386) and tenths and fifteenths—were exacted in spite of the statute (page 279) to the contrary. Monopolies of the Elizabethan variety were granted right and left whenever it seemed that the court might profit. To them were added clever new schemes. Titles of nobility were sold to aspiring purchasers, and a new honor was

[16] S-M, No. 89C, pp. 410-14.     [17] S-M, No. 91A, pp. 435-37.

invented to satisfy the demand of those who could not afford to become lords. This was the title of baronet, which conferred a hereditary rank above that of knighthood but below that of baron, and so did not give membership in the House of Lords. It was offered to anyone who would contribute enough to keep a battalion of soldiers a year in Ulster. The Dutch cautionary towns—Dutch towns held in pawn by English garrisons as a pledge of the repayment of the expenses incurred by Elizabeth in aiding the revolt of the seven Netherland provinces—were sold back to the Dutch at a big discount. When the House of Commons in the first Parliament of Charles I tried the novel experiment of refusing to vote the King tunnage and poundage for the duration of his reign because it wished to put the monarch on a probationary year-to-year basis, his agents—acting on the principle enunciated in Bate's case—collected it anyway.

**Impeachment Efforts.** To stop these leaks in their financial dike the parliamentarians tried to impeach the royal ministers whom they held responsible for the royal actions. Here they found that the old parliamentary power of impeachment (page 257) was effective only when the king was willing that it should be. Officials of whom the Stuart monarchs, or their great favorite, George Villiers, Duke of Buckingham, were not too fond were sacrificed readily enough, but Buckingham himself could not be touched. For example, because Coke's rival Francis Bacon, then Lord Chancellor, had endorsed certain of the objectionable monopolies, the Parliament of 1620-21 turned on him and accused him of taking bribes from suitors in his court. James did not try to defend Bacon. Confronted by a mass of damaging evidence, Bacon confessed his fault. He was punished by a fine of £40,000 and exclusion from all future offices.[18] One or two other important royal agents were similarly eliminated. But the Parliaments of 1626 and 1628, led by a Cornish knight, Sir John Eliot, failed in all their efforts to impeach Buckingham. By proroguing (dis-

18 S-M, No. 911, pp. 444-46.

missing for the session without terminating its services) or permanently dissolving Parliament Charles was able to protect his favorite, and by similar tactics he obviously could protect any of his ministers from legal attack if he wished.

**Forced Loans and the Petition of Right.** The House of Commons scored one victory, however, in the 1628 session by forcing the King—impoverished by his wars with France—to accept the Petition of Right.[19] This statement of constitutional principles— put in the form of a petition—was designed to settle once for all the vexed question of forced loans and benevolences, and the means employed to collect them. In 1627 five knights, headed by Sir Thomas Darnell, had refused to pay the amounts levied upon them in the forced-loan proceedings of that year and had been imprisoned by order of the royal Council. They applied to the Court of King's Bench for a writ of *habeas corpus*,[20] which normally would have compelled the representatives of the crown to show legal cause for the prisoners' detention. In this case the writs were granted, but the warden of the Fleet Prison in which the five knights were detained merely reported that they were being held "by the special command of his majesty" and the judges accepted this as sufficient ground for the detention.[21] Now, in return for generous grants the King reluctantly agreed to abandon the practices of (1) taking "any gift, loan, benevolence, tax or such like charge" without the consent of Parliament, (2) imprisoning his subjects without definite cause shown, "to which they might make answer according to law," (3) billeting troops upon them, and (4) imposing martial law upon civilians in time of peace. This document is generally considered to rank along with the Great Charter and the later Bill of Rights

19 S-M, No. 92D-E, pp. 450-54.

20 So called from the opening words—"Have the body of the prisoner before us"; a judicial command to the custodian to produce the prisoner and show satisfactory reasons for depriving him of his liberty or answer such other questions as the court may wish to put.

21 S-M, No. 94A, pp. 457-58.

(page 449) as one of the three important constitutional documents limiting the power of the king. Though the Petition clearly defined practical rules of government and Charles promised to abide by them, in fact it had little effect on the distribution of power until supported by force of arms fifteen years later.

**The Eliot Resolutions.** For the moment Charles continued to rule much as he chose, as is demonstrated by the defeat of the attempt to impeach Buckingham in the same session. The favorite was assassinated shortly afterwards, but this served only to stiffen Charles's determination to master the opposition. He maintained—probably on sound legal principles—that tunnage and poundage were not included in the terms of the Petition of Right, and he continued to collect them. When the House of Commons, on resuming its sittings in 1629, protested against this and also against his religious policy, Charles decided to dissolve the obstreperous body. He ordered the Speaker to put the question of adjournment. Anxious to place its attitude clearly on record, the House refused to adjourn. When the royal nominee serving as Speaker—whose withdrawal would have ended the sitting—tried to leave the chair, some of the most determined of the King's opponents seized him and held him in his place. At the same time the doors were locked to exclude the royal messenger sent to ensure the end of the session by removing the symbol of parliamentary authority, the mace which always rested on the table of the House during its deliberations. During this excitement one of the parliamentary leaders put the question of adopting three resolutions that had been introduced by Sir John Eliot.[22] They declared that anyone bringing in a change in religion, advising the collection of tunnage and poundage, or voluntarily paying it, should be considered a capital enemy of the realm. These resolutions were carried tumultuously before the doors were opened to admit the royal messenger.

[22] S-M, No. 92F, pp. 454-55.

**The Claim of Freedom of Speech: Eliot's Imprisonment and Death.** Charles's answer to this was to arrest nine of the opposition leaders. They claimed parliamentary privilege for what they had done and said, and denied that they could be held to answer for it in any court outside of Parliament. This was a reassertion of the principle of free speech for which medieval and Tudor parliamentarians had contended with mixed success. In the Stuart period the opposition leaders in the House of Commons had already twice advanced this claim, once in an "Apology" presented to James in 1604,[23] and once in 1621, when in defiance of the royal wish to have no such meddling with matters of state they had tried to discuss the Spanish match.[24] On that occasion they had entered a solemn "Protestation" in their journal, setting forth their rights as they understood them, but James had come to the House, demanded the book, and torn out with his own hand the pages recording the offending statement. Charles was therefore not disposed to tolerate any such line of defense, and the judges reluctantly yielded to the royal pressure. Holding that the parliamentary session had ended with the arrival of the King's messenger, they allowed Eliot and his associates to be tried and convicted in the King's Bench on a charge of conspiracy. The parliamentarians were fined and sentenced to imprisonment until they should confess their fault and give surety of future good behavior. Six of them complied with these terms, but Eliot and two others remained in prison rather than surrender the principle of parliamentary privilege for which they were contending. In his cold, damp Tower cell Eliot came down with tuberculosis. Charles, however, would not release the man whom he considered morally guilty of the murder of Buckingham, since Sir John had led the agitation against the favorite. So in 1632 Eliot died as a martyr to the cause of parliamentary free speech, while his two colleagues remained in confinement.

[23] S-M, No. 89G, pp. 418-24.   [24] S-M, No. 89J-L, pp. 427-31.

## THE VICTORY OF THE KING

**The Personal Rule of Charles.** After the troublesome session of 1629 Charles resolved to rule without any further help or hindrance from Parliament, which he dissolved at once, as he had intended. The kings of France had similarly dispensed with their comparable Estates General fifteen years before, and the precedent was an inviting one. By skimping and saving and having recourse to all possible expedients Charles managed to struggle along without parliamentary grants. Ship money was the most important of the new sources of revenue. Traditionally, this was a levy imposed on port towns for the benefit of the royal navy in times of stress. It went back to a time when the navy was composed of merchant vessels loaned by these towns. Now, in 1635, the King maintained plausibly enough that since all the kingdom was protected by the navy, the inland areas should also contribute, and he ordered a general levy. The money so obtained was actually spent on the navy, but in the eyes of many of his subjects this procedure represented a violation of the Petition of Right and the death knell of Parliament. They protested that no emergency existed, and that if the King were allowed to decree one at pleasure no man's property was safe. Several leaders of the opposition therefore refused to pay. Charles appealed to his judges, and in 1637 a test case was made of a Buckinghamshire knight, Sir John Hampden, who had been assessed twenty shillings.[25] The first seven of the twelve judges to deliver their decision the next year in the Exchequer Chamber ruled in favor of the King, and the collection went steadily on.

**Failure of the Parliamentary Opposition.** Charles had thus successfully overcome all opposition from his English subjects. Parliament, their chief medium for expressing their political sentiments, had been suppressed, its most important claim of privilege

[25] S-M, No. 94B-C, pp. 458-62.

flouted, and its supposed rights to impeach royal ministers and to control the royal revenues set at naught. All the peaceful, legal means of advancing the claims of Parliament to a share in the government had failed of their immediate object. Only a certain clarification of issues had taken place, and some propaganda had been made. Documents such as the Petition of Right served as statements of the opposition program. Incidents such as Eliot's death roused the passions of his supporters. Vengeful Charles was so inept as not to realize this, and made the further mistake of refusing permission to the family to take the body back home to Cornwall for burial. But none the less the King was fully in control of the English situation in 1637.

**The Lower Classes Not Yet Politically Significant.** The opposition to the crown, which had been struggling for power during these years, was, as we have noted, an upper and upper-middle class one, composed mostly of landlords, wealthy merchants, lawyers, and Puritan clergy. Their point of view was well reflected in the argument in Hampden's case, which was based in large part on the theory of the sanctity of private property. The lower-middle and lower classes were not politically significant as yet. Once or twice in this period they stirred restlessly and opposed the government, as in 1549 when the illegal enclosure of open fields and common lands by the wealthy landlords provoked what is known as Kett's Rebellion in the east counties. But it was a short-lived affair, easily suppressed. It suggested the potential strength of these elements, but also their current lack of organization, leadership, and morale.

# 18. THE MACHINERY OF GOVERNMENT
## 1485-1637

**The Pliability of Constitutions.** At several points in our discussion of this period we have noticed that theoretical restrictions or paper regulations readily gave way before, or were adapted to, the wishes of the powerful and determined rulers who inaugurated the system of absolute monarchy and flourished under it. In no aspect of the constitutional story of the time is this domination of the personal factor over the legal and traditional one more strikingly demonstrated than in that which has to do with the governmental machinery itself. For here we shall observe very few important changes. The very same mechanical contrivances that served to implement the wishes of the comparatively numerous nobility in the fifteenth century proved readily responsive to the strong hand of the individual Tudor ruler when he took command of the situation. This pliability of constitutions—which permitted the Roman Empire to exist for centuries under virtually the same regulations originally drawn up for the Republic, and which enabled the government of the modern German Reich to set up its dictatorship in a fashion strictly legal according to the provisions of the Weimar Constitution—has led one prominent observer to assert with pardonable exaggeration that a constitution is merely a state of mind. That is to say, rules, traditions, and even institutions themselves mean little until we know the spirit in which they are interpreted and the ends to which they are directed.

## THE MONARCHY AND THE LAW OF TREASON

**The Monarchical System Virtually Unchanged.** The legal framework in which the institution of monarchy operated remained virtually unchanged in the Tudor-Stuart period. The rules and regulations under which the feeble Henry VI carried on his fumbling activities sufficed well enough for his two masterful namesakes. Since the individual rulers were so powerful, the tendency to distinguish the official from the personal elements of sovereignty (page 269) naturally made little progress during these years. But all the old powers (pages 33, 271) remained, and were exercised through substantially the same agencies.

**The Law of Treason.** Besides the great Act of Supremacy, already described (page 325), a few alterations in the law of treason gave almost the only indications—and these relatively slight —of the real change that was taking place. A statute of 1495 declared that obedience to a de facto king such as Henry VII was not treason, and should not render one liable to impeachment or attaint in Parliament.[1] That is, whoever happened to be king in fact (de facto) should be obeyed whether he was rightly (de jure) king or not. Should a change of monarch take place, those who had followed the earlier one could not be legally punished for this support. This act, of course, strengthened the power of the ruling monarch, since it removed the fear of future punishment that had deterred some Englishmen from supporting wholeheartedly the rapidly changing Lancastrian and Yorkist kings. By another statute of 1543-44 the definition of treason was broadened to include the imagining or attempting to deprive the king, queen, or his heirs of "their titles, styles, names, degrees, royal estate, or regal power." This virtually made the mere speaking of words or thinking of thoughts against the

[1] S-M, No. 74E, pp. 301-02.

king equivalent to treason, though the judges came to rule that the thoughts themselves were not triable but had to be established by overt acts.

**Other Variations Mostly Temporary.** Under Henry VIII, in fact, the legal position of the crown reached its height. The acts which empowered Henry to determine the succession to the throne (page 332) and gave his proclamations the force of law (page 329) constituted additional legal support for the royal greatness. These were exceptional acts, however, and their importance was of short duration. The one concerning proclamations was repealed in the first year of Edward's reign. The line of succession prescribed in Henry's will was followed only as far as Elizabeth, and Edward's attempt to will the crown (page 333) —without an act of Parliament in his case—was a failure. The sharpest features of the act concerning verbal treasons were removed under Edward VI and not enacted again until 1571. Even the Act of Supremacy was repealed under Mary (page 334). It was, however, restored by Elizabeth's first Parliament,[2] and along with the new legislation on treason must be considered the only striking alteration in the constitutional law of the kingdom needed to implement Tudor despotism.

## THE ROYAL ASSISTANTS AND ADVISERS

**The Household and Administrative Offices: The New Secretary.** Except for the addition of a new Secretary and a few trappings for the court in the form of royal guards, gentlemen pensioners, and a master of the horse, the royal household and administrative officers remained on paper much the same as before. As the country grew more prosperous it was possible to have more royal attendants for ceremonial purposes so that their gaudy uniforms might help to impress foreign ambassadors, but we need not dwell on them. The new Secretary was first added

2 S-M, No. 81A, pp. 344-46.

by Henry in 1540 after the removal of the previous incumbent, Cromwell, whom the King suspected of forming a party in opposition to the crown. By dividing the responsibilities of the office thereafter between two men of equal authority it was hoped to avoid a repetition of such troubles. Both officials were equally to be considered Principal Secretaries, with concurrent duties. In practice, however, one of the two Secretaries, such as Sir William Cecil (later Lord Burghley), very often had so much more personal influence than his colleague that the lesser was frequently known as the Second Secretary. But in any case the additional Secretary was needed because of the increased attention to foreign affairs growing out of the newly developed ease of communication and the corresponding growth of overseas trade.

**The Diplomatic Service.** Another governmental offshoot developed to meet the new circumstances in this field was the permanent ambassador, sent "to lie abroad for the benefit of his country," as Sir Henry Wotton, Elizabeth's representative at Venice, wittily put it. Previous to the sixteenth century embassies had been temporary ad hoc affairs, consisting of representatives sent to treat with a foreign court on one particular matter and to return home on the completion of that set of negotiations. Venice, with its great trade interests, first established permanent embassies. The Venetian home government's requirement of detailed reports on general economic and social conditions, as well as on the political situation in the country to which its ambassadors were accredited, set a standard to which the other competing European nations soon tried to attain.

**The Privy Council.** The machinery of the Council was not greatly altered in this period. That body was composed much as before, though the Tudors were perhaps a little more cautious than their predecessors in the matter of keeping its numbers small and thus preventing it from becoming unwieldy. The Tudor rulers also showed a tendency to choose as Councilors untitled men from the "new" and rising upper-middle class rather than representatives of the old nobility, but this apparent difference may be due mostly to the Tudor parsimony in the matter of conferring titles on their faithful followers (page 315). The Council met regularly, as it had done formerly, and it did much the same sort of work.[3] The chief change in its organization was that its committee system was more highly developed. The creation of branch councils with judicial powers we have already noted (page 317). In a way, the Star Chamber (pages 317, 400) might be considered the committee for judicial purposes of the central body. At first it was virtually a committee of the whole, but later more strictly a subcommittee with some co-opted legal members. In addition there were committees of the Council appointed to deal with various temporary problems, and standing committees for those of a more permanent nature—such as Calais, Scotland, and Ireland. But the real distinction between the Tudor Council and its predecessors was not in its organization but in the fact that it really worked at its job. With the sovereign keeping a strict watch and talking over the important problems with the Secretary and other prominent members, the Council became a most important cog in the government. Through four full-time clerks it sent out to local officials a bombardment of orders, threats, and demands for reports, which kept the machinery of state tuned up to a fairly high pitch. During the fight with the Armada an English boat that had captured a Spanish galleon loaded with stores returned to shore because its own food supply was running low and the English crew did not dare replenish it from the enemy's supplies. This incident has sometimes been cited as an illustration of Elizabeth's parsimony, but it also illustrates the efficiency of her governmental machinery which might thus be expected to keep track of every loaf of bread even in the midst of a desperate struggle for survival.

[3] For samples of its work, see S-M, No. 83, pp. 376-84.

## PARLIAMENT

**The Lords.** The chief change in the organization of Parliament was caused by the dissolution of the monasteries. This, of course, eliminated the abbots from the House of Lords and gave a definite numerical advantage to the lay members, which they never lost thereafter. The baronets (page 372), however, were not admitted, and only those few Scottish nobles who received English titles sat with the English lords, since Scotland remained a separate governmental unit. Lords spiritual, in the persons of the bishops, and lords temporal from the five ranks of English peers, continued to form the membership of the House, which was still presided over by the Lord Chancellor.

**The Commons: Its Structure.** In the Commons the counties of Wales and nearly a hundred new boroughs were given representation by the Tudor and early Stuart rulers, often with a view to facilitating the packing process (page 334). It is interesting to note that James, who believed that the intelligentsia should have a special voice in the government, also gave parliamentary representation to the universities as such, so that Oxford and Cambridge have ever since had seats in addition to those for their towns. But this gesture in the direction of setting up philosopher-kings, or at least of putting scholars into politics, has never been of great constitutional significance. In general, the method of determining the franchise and the means of election were virtually unchanged (page 262). In the newly created parliamentary boroughs, indeed, the rulers were very careful to limit the suffrage to some small group, such as the town council, so that royal pressure might be more easily exerted during elections.

**Location and Appearance of the Commons.** Perhaps some of these increases in membership were responsible for the Commons' moving during the reign of Edward VI from the Chapter House of Westminster Abbey to St. Stephen's Chapel, across the

384 THE TUDOR-STUART ABSOLUTISM

street. The new home had originally been used by a group of chantry priests, but with the dissolution of the chantries (page 328) it fell to the crown. Since it lay within the precincts of the royal palace, which already housed the Lords, it afforded a convenient meeting-place for the Commons. It was an oblong building, originally designed for antiphonal singing, with seats for the two groups of priests arranged facing each other across the long axis of the hall. This form has been preserved in the modern Houses of Parliament, built in 1834, and it is possible that it may have had some influence on the development of the two-party system (page 497). At one end sat the Speaker and before him was a table on which was laid a mace—the symbol of parliamentary authority—whenever the body was in session.

**Procedure.** An ordinary public bill was first drawn up on paper and presented to the House of Commons either by the proposer or by the clerk, to whom it might be entrusted.[4] Before passing it had to be read three times by the clerk and voted on by the House. The first reading served to notify the members of the nature of the bill, and there was seldom much discussion at that time. A bill could be rejected at the first reading, but this did not often happen. Two or three days were then usually allowed to elapse, so that the members might have time to consider the bill. Then came the second reading, after which the House might decide to have the bill engrossed (written out in a gross—large hand—on parchment) at once, but usually it was first referred to a committee. This committee was named by the members of the House, who shouted out the names until the clerk had "a convenient number." The Speaker then asked the House to designate a time and place of meeting. Usually the committee met in one of the inns of court, where many of the members lodged when in London. At these committee meetings the bill was thoroughly discussed, and often amended. It was

4 There were also private bills, concerning matters of lesser importance, which followed a somewhat different routine.

then brought back to the House for the conclusion of its second reading, when it was generally debated at some length. If it passed this reading, it was engrossed, and two or three days later was given its third reading, when it was again debated freely. If still successful, it was sent to the Lords.[5] Bills originating in the Lords also passed through three readings and the committee stage and went through the same process as in the Commons. In case the bill passed the two houses in two different forms a conference was held between representatives of the two bodies to arrange an acceptable compromise. Finally it was necessary to secure the royal approval, which if given was in the French phrase *"Le roi le vult"* ("The king wishes it"). In 1509 the Lords began to keep a journal of their proceedings, and in 1547 the Commons followed suit. These journals contained records of the bills introduced and the action taken upon them. For a brief interval the Commons included in their journal a summary of their debates, but this practice was soon discontinued.

**Control of the Commons.** In the Tudor period, as we have seen (page 360), the House of Commons was largely under the control of the crown. This control was commonly exercised through the Council. Members of this body were active in influencing elections (page 334), and care was taken to see that those Councilors who were not lords were themselves given seats in the lower house. They prepared bills and planned the whole legislative session in advance. Once the Commons convened, they nominated the Speaker, and after his election he looked to them for advice. To facilitate this working arrangement the Councilors commonly sat together close to the Speaker. As a royal agent, the Speaker could be very useful, since it was his privilege to determine almost entirely the order in which bills should be considered, and who should be recognized to speak on them. The Tudor Councilors also shaped the policy of the Commons by diligent attendance at committee meetings, where they were

[5] S-M, No. 82B, pp. 360-61.

frequently in the majority because of the carelessness of the rank and file. In the Stuart period, however, this situation changed. James and Charles enlarged the Council to such an extent that it became less efficient. At the same time these monarchs did not take pains to see that Councilors were elected to the House of Commons. Ordinary members attended committee meetings more assiduously, and the control of the Commons passed into the hands of the opposition.

**The Committee of the Whole.** Yet the prolonged struggle with the crown resulted in only one notable change in the procedure or organization of the House of Commons, the introduction of the institution of the Committee of the Whole. Since the Speaker was virtually a royal appointee, though formally elected by the House, and since he could exercise a great control over ordinary debates and frequently reported their substance to the king, the Commons sought to find a way of meeting under conditions of greater freedom. Because it had long been the custom to have parliamentary committees composed of some particular members and all others who wished to attend, it was not difficult to apply this system to the problem in hand. By referring the most serious questions to a committee composed of the House as a whole, the Speaker was removed from the chair, ordinary rules were suspended, and the matter in hand could be threshed out at leisure and in comparative secrecy.

## THE FINANCIAL SYSTEM AND THE CHURCH

**The Financial System.** Direct parliamentary grants continued to be in the form of land taxes. Tenths and fifteenths (page 143) were supplemented by subsidies that amounted roughly to £80,-000 each. In theory, these taxes involved a levy on personal as well as real property, but in practice the system of assessment and collection remained much as it had been in earlier centuries. Local committees made the original apportionment of the

county quota; the hundred constable and his subordinates collected it, and paid it into the Exchequer. The various extra-
parliamentary devices worked out by the Stuarts and their supporters have already been described (page 371). The system of
raising money for local governmental expenditures will be explained later (page 391).

**The Church.** Aside from the lopping off of the Roman curia
and the substitution of the sovereign for the pope as head of the
Church, the central government of the ecclesiastical establishment underwent surprisingly little change as a result of the
Reformation. Under the watchful eye of the monarch, the two
archbishops and their courts and Convocations continued to
transact most of the ecclesiastical business. One or two special
courts were created, of which we shall speak later (pages 397,
400), and for a short time under Henry VIII Thomas Cromwell
held the post of royal deputy for church affairs, with the title
of vicar-general. But this last was a short-lived experiment; it
did not survive the execution of Cromwell in 1540.

## LOCAL GOVERNMENT: THE COUNTY

**The Justices of the Peace.** At the county level the sheriffs and
justices of the peace—with minor assistance from the coroners—
still did most of the governmental work. But by the sixteenth
century the local justices had become far more important than
the sheriffs. These justices of the peace were still appointed by
the Lord Chancellor and were directed by orders from the Council. They were kept under control by the institution of the
quorum, and by the office of the *Custos Rotulorum* (Keeper of
the Rolls). In the original commission given to the justices of
the peace of a county a select group were named, of whom
(*quorum*) at least one must be present at every quarter session,
and a *Custos Rotulorum* was named as a president of the whole
body. Since most justices of the peace desired to attain to these

honors, they could be induced to work at their assignments by the prospect of eventual promotion. The justices were, in fact, so burdened with legal and administrative duties as to earn from later historians the title of Tudor maids of all work. Since their records were filled with the licensing of inns, the regulation of wages, the administration of justice, and a thousand and one other topics, the accounts of their meetings read like those of the royal Council, though naturally on a smaller scale.[6] Indeed it is not out of place to think of the justices of the peace as constituting a council for the county. In their professional work they were assisted and advised by a clerk who was normally a trained lawyer.

**The Sheriff.** The sheriff still presided over the county court, which did virtually nothing but elect knights of the shire to sit in Parliament. He also fulfilled his old duties of serving writs, making arrests, collecting obligations to the crown other than the major land tax, and generally acting as royal representative in the county. In this last vague capacity he was burdened with a great weight of hospitality, being obligated to entertain the sovereign and other distinguished visitors whenever they came within the county boundaries. By Stuart times this obligation was considered to involve the necessity of remaining within the shire boundaries during the year of office. Since one could not refuse to accept an appointment to this post, a particularly objectionable leader of the opposition could be kept away from Parliament for a session by being named sheriff. The assize judges commonly made recommendations and the Chancellor submitted a list of three names to the sovereign, who pricked a hole in the parchment opposite the name of his choice. In this fashion Coke and five other opposition leaders were "pricked" for sheriff in 1626 and thus kept away from the parliamentary session of that year.

[6] For samples of their records, see S-M, No. 86C, pp. 392-94; No. 99C-D, pp. 495-98.

**The Lord Lieutenants and the Military System.** The sheriff had, however, been relieved of most of his military functions. Separate officials—preferably nobles and therefore of a somewhat higher social class than the country gentry from whom the sheriffs were drawn—were being appointed to do this work. These were called lord lieutenants, because they were the royal representatives (lieutenants, literally, "place-holders") in their shires. The reason for this change was that with the breakdown of the feudal system and the abolition of private armies by the Statute of Livery the militia—the lineal descendant of the old fyrd—became the only military force in the country, and the sheriff could no longer carry the burden of supervising it. Each county was given a quota of trained men that it was to supply. The lord lieutenant, together with various deputies, arranged for spreading this out among the different villages. They also employed a muster master (drill captain—drill sergeant, we should call him) to train the men. This individual, usually a hard-bitten professional soldier and a veteran of the Continental wars, laid out a circuit through the county and once a month had the militiamen of each district meet him at a convenient village green for drill. These men received a small allowance for their services, but none for powder. The most important training—firing practice—was therefore dependent on the occasional generosity of some local magnate. Since the men were paid at the conclusion of each day's drill and no village green without a tavern was considered a convenient meeting-place, the assemblages were commonly more convivial than practical. The local trained bands, as they were called, provided much mirth for contemporary humorists.[7] Only because of the sea moat with which England was surrounded was such a happy-go-lucky system possible. Geography, as indicated earlier (page 6), played a great role in determining the constitutional development of England.

[7] For documents relating to the Tudor military system, see S-M, No. 87, pp. 396-400.

**The Vice-Admirals and the Navy.** In the coast counties problems of defense were taken a little more seriously, as might be expected. Each of these shires, in addition to its lord lieutenant, had a vice-admiral charged with the duty of looking after the local naval resources. In an emergency these vice-admirals were to take over merchant vessels and co-ordinate them with those of the regular royal navy. The serious development of this important branch of the English governmental system—the national war fleet—dates from the time of Henry VIII, one of whose biggest warships was called, appropriately enough, *The Great Harry*.

## THE HUNDRED AND THE PARISH

**The Hundred.** Below the county level the hundred preserved a shadowy existence as a military, financial, and police unit. The trained bands recently described were commonly organized by hundreds within the counties, and the main taxes were collected by the hundred constables, as we have also seen (page 387). These officials were appointed by the assize justices, and were usually of the gentry class, like the sheriffs. They were supposed to assist the sheriffs with their police duties if necessary. The hundred courts, as already mentioned (page 279), were largely moribund by this time.

**The Parish.** Below the hundred was a newly developed governmental organization, the parish. The decline of feudalism meant the decay of the manor. It was therefore necessary to devise some substitute for taking care of the problems of village government. Since the Church was now under royal control, its local units naturally provided a convenient basis for the new system. To the parish priest—still appointed by patrons under the advowson system—were added a number of secular officials to do the routine work of local government. Those about whose work the central government was especially concerned were appointed from above. The others were elected in an annual meeting of the parishioners called a vestry meeting, because it commonly met in that part of the church where the priest's vestments were kept. Church wardens were so elected, officials whose duty it was to look after the fabric of the church, act as trustees of its property, and if necessary raise funds for the parish by levying a rate (local tax) or by the somewhat more cheerful device of church ales—parish drinking-bouts held for the benefit of the good cause (*cf*. page 160). From Mary's reign date the overseers of the highway—roughly the equivalent of the highway commissioners in some American townships—whose duty it was to direct the parishioners in six days' work per year on the local roads. With this community system of amateur engineering it is not surprising that the Elizabethans found travel rather a gamble, or even a hazardous adventure. There were comparatively few roads that were so much as passable for wheeled vehicles the year round, and even in the best of weather much of the country was accessible only on horseback. Parish constables were commonly elected to do the local police work and supervise the activities of the village watch—a band of more or less valiant inhabitants who did police duty on moonless nights. Since keeping the peace was an important matter, however, the constables were sometimes named by the justices of the peace. Other officials appointed—in this case regularly—by the justices were the overseers of the poor.

## THE POOR LAW SYSTEM: TUDOR-STUART PATERNALISM

**Its Origins.** The mention of the overseers of the poor brings us to a description of the Tudor-Stuart poor law system, one of the most important innovations of the period. In the Middle Ages secular agencies had made some provision for the poor, as already suggested (page 51), but this was of a very casual sort, since most of this charitable work was left to the Church. Endowed institutions, such as monasteries, regularly distributed alms—following the Benedictine rule that in aiding any stranger the faithful might be entertaining Christ unawares. Private individuals also gained credit in heaven by similar acts of charity. "Would it not be great alms to give a thick, warm cloak to this man?" said Henry II to his Lord Chancellor Thomas Becket, in the days of their friendship, as they approached a poor wretch in a London street. "Certainly, my Lord, great alms, and you should have an eye and spirit of this sort," was the reply. "Indeed *you* shall have credit for this great charity," said the King, and, after a friendly tussle, he wrenched off Becket's magnificent cloak and flung it to the ragged man. This system of poor relief was, of course, most unscientific, and pauperized many who might otherwise have earned an honest living. But in its crude way it met a real social need. With the Reformation, however, came the dissolution of the monasteries and the disappearance of the doctrine of purgatory which taught that believers who did not do enough good works on earth might be subject to severe punishment after death before admittance to heaven. The doctrine of justification "by faith alone" involved no such compelling motive to altruism. Combined with this religious change, a widespread distrust of the careless medieval methods of almsgiving tended to dry up the springs of charity.

**Its Organization.** At the same time, as the enclosure movement forced whole families off the land, the roads were filled with homeless unemployed, and the relief problem became acute. In the middle of the century the government strove to handle the situation by appealing to the Protestants to make voluntary offerings at church. Experience soon showed, however, that this device would not meet the need. If the collection was taken at the close of the service, men slipped out by side doors. If attempted during the service, it either yielded too little or was accompanied by such arguments with recalcitrant donors as to disturb the congregation. More and more legislation had to be passed to make relief a governmental affair. Two great statutes of 1598 and 1601 finally codified these regulations in the form which they retained until the nineteenth century.[8] Three cardinal rules were laid down: (1) The able-bodied and unemployed destitute were to be "set on" work. (2) The "impotent," who were too old or infirm to work, were to be provided for freely. (3) The "sturdy rogues" were to be punished. These last were the men who refused to work and preferred to live by begging, which was now prohibited, or by other types of crime. Punishment for them usually meant a public whipping and an enforced return to the parish of the wanderer's residence.

**And Operation.** The overseers of the poor were charged with enforcing these laws in each parish. When no other work was available they were to purchase raw materials, such as wool, flax, or hemp, and set the able-bodied poor to work making cloth, rope, or some other salable commodity. To the impotent they distributed alms, and with the aid of the constable they drove the rogues and the beggars out of the parish. The funds for these activities they secured by calling on the wardens, who raised the required amount by the rates mentioned above. Since the administration of relief was thus in local hands and financed by a purely local tax, there was no need to worry about extravagance, but rather the contrary. To prevent the better-class citizens who uniformly served as overseers—and wardens as well—from "grinding the faces of the poor" the overseers who fixed the scale of poor relief were appointed by the justices of the peace, who were in turn subject to control from Westminster.

**Tudor-Stuart Paternalism.** The poor law system well illustrated the paternalism of the Tudor government, which was also shown in the similar fixing of rates of wages for all classes of laborers by the justices of the peace, under the Statute of Artificers passed in 1563.[9] This policy of paternalism, as enforced

8 S-M, No. 81H, pp. 356-58.
9 Sometimes known as the Statute of Apprentices; S-M, No. 81C, pp. 348-51.

by the vigilant Council, was so successful that competent critics have maintained that the relative economic position of the lower class was better in this period than it ever was again until the twentieth century. It is an argument for the monarchical system —as old as Aristotle—that when a country is ruled by one man the poor will fare better than when it is ruled by many. For the one man will be so rich that he will have no desire to line his pockets, as will the many, but, as the person on whom sole responsibility is fixed, he will strive for a good reputation as the father of his people and a friend of the underprivileged. The rulers of this period understood this theory perfectly, and James in particular was fond of preaching it. He warned his son against the greedy merchants who "think the whole commonweal ordained for making them up," and who, in his opinion, were accustomed to "enrich themselves upon the loss of the rest of the people." It was the duty of the monarch, in his judgment, to beat down these and all other "proud oppressors" of the poor. His paternalistic system showed little confidence in the ability of the common people to control their own affairs—as the royal method of appointing important local officials shows.

**Attitude of the Lower Classes.** Because they were politically inarticulate (page 377), it is very difficult to tell just how the common people responded to this treatment. But had a poll been taken of them, it is not unlikely that the results would have shown as much support for the king as for the parliamentarians in the great constitutional struggle that was then agitating England. On the issues of religion and political theory the lower classes probably inclined to the parliamentary side, but on social and economic questions they must have preferred the royalist approach. Not only was the system of poor relief comparatively well administered, as we have seen, but the government tried hard to protect the average worker against the ill effects of a rapidly expanding capitalistic system. Act after act was put on the books to slow down the enclosure movement, and both Council and Star Chamber worked hard to enforce them. The regulation of wages in the rural areas proved popular with the country laborers, since it guaranteed them a living wage (*cf.* page 477). In the towns the government sided with the old gilds against the entrepreneurs who wished to free themselves from the traditional restrictions. And as the gilds themselves came under oligarchic control (page 248) the authorities at Westminster undertook to protect the rank and file of the yeomanry. In several cases these small masters were at last permitted to break away and form separate companies or gilds of their own under the royal charter. Though often abused in practice, the much-maligned monopolies of the Tudors and Stuarts were frequently designed to give government regulation and supervision to an industry that would otherwise be ruined by lack of capital, by cutthroat competition, or by men who cornered the available supply of raw materials.

**The Tudor-Stuart Governmental System Similar to Modern Fascism.** In many of its features the Tudor-Stuart governmental system bears a striking resemblance to modern fascism. There was close supervision of local government, much attention to the needs of the lower classes, and strict regulation of business. Strikes were outlawed by an act passed in 1548, while the Statute of Artificers of 1563 (page 393) not only regulated wages but made provision for compulsory labor service in time of harvest, and in some cases even throughout the year. When we add, furthermore, that the press was strictly censored and freedom of speech severely limited even in Parliament, we can see that there is little new about current dictatorial methods of government.

# 19. THE LEGAL SYSTEM
## 1485-1637

**The Pliability of Legal Institutions.** The principle of the pliability of constitutions, stated at the beginning of the last chapter, applies also to the legal system in this period. Comparatively few changes were necessary to adapt the medieval legal pattern to the needs of the Tudor-Stuart regime. With the exception of the introduction of the prerogative courts—which themselves represented only the development of old agencies along slightly new lines—the monarchs made few alterations in the machinery of the courts. In the field of court jurisdiction the chief interest centers around the efforts of the opposition, led by Coke, to limit the scope of operations of those courts which did not use the common law (page 364). In the development of the details of legal procedure and the different fields of substantive law the chief interest attaches to the alterations making for efficiency and the adaptation of the law to changing economic conditions.

## CHANGES IN THE COURT SYSTEM: EXCHEQUER CHAMBER AND REQUESTS

**The Three Courts of Exchequer Chamber.** The organization and jurisdiction of the common law courts remained during this period substantially the same as they had been at the close of the Middle Ages. There were still the three great central courts, with the House of Lords hearing cases in error from the King's Bench. The assize judges continued to make their rounds and the justices of the peace held their quarter sessions and exercised summary jurisdiction in petty cases. The only noteworthy alterations were the steadily increasing burden of criminal cases put on the justices of the peace (page 286), the introduction of one new Court of Exchequer Chamber, and some regularization of the practices of another. Since 1357-58 appeals from the ordinary Court of the Exchequer had been heard by a tribunal consisting of the Lord Chancellor and a few assistants sitting in a room in Westminster Palace known as the Exchequer Chamber and consequently called the court of that chamber. Now in 1584 the same location was assigned to a semiappellate body created to hear cases in error from the King's Bench when Parliament (particularly the House of Lords) was not in session—as it frequently was not under the Tudors. This was composed of all the judges of Common Pleas and Exchequer, or any six of them. Still another court meeting in the same convenient place and bearing the same name had grown up rather more gradually, beginning as early as the thirteenth century. Originally it was merely an informal consultation of the judges of King's Bench and Common Pleas on especially difficult cases. After 1579 the Barons of the Exchequer joined in these discussions. As we have seen in our account of the contemporary constitutional struggles (pages 366, 376), this body gradually came to be considered a court whose rulings were binding on all the constituent courts.

**The Courts of Equity: Requests.** The Court of Chancery flourished greatly under the Tudors, whose desire for law and order encouraged their subjects to seek the help of a court of equity when the common law failed them. Another indication of this popularity was the development of a subordinate and more informal court, as the rules of Chancery gradually became more definite and its machinery more expensive to operate. This new body was called the Court of Requests, and like Chancery itself, it developed originally out of the parent Council. It was in charge of the Keeper of the Privy Seal and was designed to give justice to the poor who could not pay the fees required else-where. A suggestion of its work is conveyed by its nickname of the "alms basket of Chancery" and by a reference to a case of "the ragged, barefooted boy" that appears in its records.

## COKE'S ATTACK UPON CHANCERY, THE PREROGA-TIVE COURTS, AND THE ECCLESIASTICAL COURTS

**Courtney v. Glanvil.** This simple and sometimes arbitrary justice roused protests from the common lawyers, who made their complaints heard as early as the time of Wolsey (1529). Because Coke felt, furthermore, that the methods and rules of the courts of equity made them tools of the royal prerogative rather than of the general English conscience, he undertook in 1615 to im-plement this old feeling of the common lawyers by devising a means to restrict the jurisdiction of Chancery. The test case he chose illustrates both the devious workings of his shrewd legal mind and the moral weakness of his position on this issue. It was *Courtney* v. *Glanvil.* Glanvil was a swindler who in the practice of his art had sold to Courtney for £360 a jewel worth only £20. He had taken a down-payment in cash and Courtney's bond for the rest. Courtney discovered the fraud, however, and refused to pay the balance due. He was thereupon sued on his bond at common law, where he of course lost (page 289). He then had recourse to the Chancellor, Lord Ellesmere, who, as many an-other judge in equity before him had done in similar cases, en-joined the enforcement of the judgment on the bond. When Glanvil refused to abide by this decision and continued to press for payment, the swindler was imprisoned by the Court of Chancery. He thereupon applied to the Court of King's Bench for a writ of *habeas corpus* (page 373) returnable there. It was granted, and in the subsequent proceedings Coke ordered Glan-vil's release. Coke then endeavored to persuade the grand jury of the county of Middlesex to indict Courtney on two grounds:

(1) that he had violated the Statute of *Praemunire* of 1353 (page 253) and (2) that he had broken another medieval law passed in 1403 before the development of Chancery as a legal tribunal. This fifteenth-century statute was directed against quarrelsome litigiousness (barratry) and ordered parties who had had a case settled in one royal court to be at peace thereafter. In strict law there was some color of justification for this second charge, if the obsolete law was to be recognized. But most weight was put on the first one, and it was on this issue that the struggle was fought out. Coke argued that the Statute of *Praemunire* prohibited the taking of cases normally actionable in the royal courts to any other court. Everyone knew that originally the Roman curia was the only court aimed at by the statute, but, holding to the letter of the law, Coke argued that since the common law courts— especially King's Bench, of which he was then Chief Justice— were, according to custom, described as the king's courts, Chancery was not such a court. Therefore, he maintained, suitors taking cases there which might be tried at common law were subject to the heavy penalties of *Praemunire*. Naturally, this line of reasoning raised a storm of opposition. The supporters of equity protested against this effort to destroy the jurisdiction of a long-established court by means of obsolete statutes and hyperlegal reasoning. The grand jury refused to protect an obviously guilty swindler by indicting his victim, and Coke was thus prevented from carrying out his scheme completely. Ellesmere, not fully satisfied by this partial vindication, appealed to James, who appointed a committee to consider the problem of equitable jurisdiction. It was chosen with an eye to the interests of Chancery, and it reported in favor of the claims of equity. When Coke was dismissed a few weeks later (page 366), this was one of the "four P's" which it was said led to his downfall, pride, prohibitions (page 401), prerogative, and *Praemunire*. The attack on the jurisdiction of Chancery thus failed, and more and more cases were submitted to it. There were so many, in fact, that its ma-

chinery became clogged, and at the end of our period there
were said to be many thousands on its docket still undecided.

**The Prerogative Courts.** The ordinary prerogative courts and
their important political role we have already described. They
were usually manned by Councilors, select judges, and some
prominent lay members. Besides hearing cases involving riots,
conspiracy, maintenance, and other matters of state importance
they also handled many private actions involving slander and
petty personal quarrels, or even poaching and delinquent tailor
bills. Coke also undertook to limit their jurisdiction by ruling
that they were not entitled to make use of certain kinds of process to compel appearances before them. But other means were
found for reaching the same end and these courts continued
their work virtually unhampered.

**The Court of High Commission.** The subordination of the
Church to the secular arm of the state made little change in the
old ecclesiastical courts, but did mean the introduction of two
new ones. One was the relatively unimportant Court of Augmen-
tations, a kind of Exchequer court for cases involving the ecclesiastical revenues by which the crown was now augmenting its
income. The other, the Court of High Commission (page 354),
however, was of major importance, since it was a prerogative
court for cases involving ecclesiastical discipline. Theoretically
the bishops' courts were supposed to deal with such problems,
but with the support of the local gentry recalcitrant clergymen,
especially Puritans, were able to bring the old and creaking machinery of the episcopal tribunals almost to a stop. Only by
the issuing of special royal commissions to groups of clergy and
laity in each province and diocese—somewhat after the fashion of
the medieval commission to the itinerant justices—could the
royal will in ecclesiastical matters be enforced. This practice
began in the reign of Mary, and the temporary committees, or
commissions, were made permanent bodies during the prolonged
struggle of Elizabeth with the Puritans. The one for the province

of Canterbury, commonly called the Court of High Commission,[1] naturally enjoyed the widest jurisdiction, and is the only one ordinarily mentioned, though there were, in fact, many others. The Archbishop of Canterbury, some prominent bishop in his province, an ecclesiastical subordinate or two, and probably one or more lay lawyers practicing in the church courts made up this important tribunal. Such bodies, with the royal prerogative behind them, found ways of matching all the legal devices the Puritan lawyers could invent, and thus enforced at least a semblance of order on the clergy of the Established Church.

**Fuller's Case.** Coke naturally directed his attention to the problem of the jurisdiction of these ecclesiastical courts also. Since the Middle Ages it had been common practice for the royal courts, especially the King's Bench, to issue writs of prohibition on matters of disputed jurisdiction (page 169). Thus if an ecclesiastical and a secular tribunal both claimed control over a certain case, the matter could be submitted to the King's Bench, and if it decided against the church court, a writ was sent prohibiting the clergy from proceeding further with the case. By a judicious extension of this practice the common law judges might thus cripple the ecclesiastical courts. The question was raised early in James's reign by Fuller's case. Fuller was a lawyer of Puritan sympathies, who in defending two Puritan ministers before the Court of High Commission used language that the commissioners deemed insulting. They thereupon imprisoned him for contempt. He appealed to the King's Bench for a writ of prohibition, on the ground that the High Commission had no right to imprison for contempt. The writ was duly issued, but at the same time the judges referred the matter to the consultative Court of the Exchequer Chamber. Archbishop Bancroft seized the opportunity to appeal to the King against the practice of the secular courts' issuing such writs. Coke now entered

[1] For a sample of the commission issued to this court, see S-M, No. 84, pp. 384-87.

the fray and protested against the King's presuming to take
jurisdiction on such a matter, alleging that the sovereign must
be bound by the actions of his skilled judges in this technical
field. In his account of the interview he asserted that he told
the King to his face, quoting Bracton, that the monarch was
under God and the law.[2] Less biased accounts seem to indicate
that Coke was much more submissive on this occasion, and
fell on his knees before James. But the issue was as stated, and
after some hesitation James agreed with the judges of the Exchequer Chamber that the common law judges should continue
to issue writs of prohibition, with the understanding that these
must not be of too extreme a sort. Though Fuller himself was
not aided by this ruling—for the High Commissioners changed
the charge to blasphemy, over which they had undisputed jurisdiction, and kept him in prison until he made his peace with
them—it did serve to keep the jurisdiction of the High Commission within reasonable bounds. Later on Coke further weakened the power of the churchmen by ruling against their right
to imprison people charged with adultery, and also by laying
down the principle that in cases where the common law supplied a remedy the church courts should have no jurisdiction.
The lesser ecclesiastical courts, as already suggested, were having great difficulty in exercising any jurisdiction at all, and from
this time on gradually declined in efficiency and consequently
in the extent of their jurisdiction. The Puritans were anxious
for discipline, but not of the kind which the church courts as
then established would administer. The archdeacon's courts, for
example, made fewer and fewer efforts after the beginning of
the seventeenth century to enforce the old laws against drunkenness, defamation, blasphemy, and sexual immorality.

2 S-M, No. 91B, pp. 437-38; *cf.* page 203 of this volume.

## FURTHER DEVELOPMENT OF THE ORIGINAL WRITS

**Ejectment.** In the field of legal procedure the movement for greater efficiency resulted in a great development of the writ of trespass. From about 1500 a form of trespass *vi et armis* (by force and by arms), known as ejectment, was allowed to cover real actions and do the work of the writ of entry and the old assizes. Ejectment had been commonly used in the fifteenth century to protect leaseholders who, not being legally seised of their holdings, could not protect their rights by the possessory assizes. They were therefore allowed to allege this kind of trespass *vi et armis* and collect money damages for any interference with their term of years. By the time of Henry VII, however, the successful suitor under ejectment was allowed to recover actual possession, and it was the extension by the king's courts of this privilege to copyholders ejected contrary to the custom of their manors which so strengthened the legal position of that class (page 266). Since this form of action originally involved an allegation of violence, it was at first considered a semicriminal action and permitted the use of arrest at the process stage. Because so many essoins were possible under the older real actions, there was pressure from freeholders to allow the use of ejectment in their cases also. But since the law had already provided them with remedies of a sort, the legal mind was reluctant to grant this request in a straightforward fashion. By alleging a lease, however, this reluctance was overcome. Thereafter when A wished to contest B's title to real property, he alleged that he (A) had entered upon it and had granted a lease to one John Doe, who had been ejected by another man claiming a lease right, one Richard Roe (*cf.* page 582 n.), or some other conveniently fictitious name. The action was begun in the name of John Doe against the "casual ejector" Roe, who was then represented as not wishing to defend, but as notifying

B, the one who had given him his lease, in order that B might protect his rights if he so desired. In the early years of the action, B might contest the genuineness of the original entry, lease, and ouster, though for the sake of convenience in getting the case before the court he often chose not to do so. By the close of the period, however, the judges were beginning to refuse to permit the defendant to dispute the elaborate fiction of leases, ejectors, and "loving friends" in whose imaginary names the lawyers had drawn up the papers in formal style. If B could prove that his fictitious leaseholder had a right to eject A's fictitious leaseholder, he kept the property; otherwise not. Ejectment was thus made to serve the purposes of entry and the old assizes from about 1500 onward. The personal action, with its efficient process, had taken the place of the older but more complicated real ones.

**Special ("Indebitatus") "Assumpsit": Slade's Case.** At about the same time the nonviolent branch of trespass, case, was taking over most of the other personal actions. As we have seen (page 302), the form called *assumpsit* was being used to cover what we now call contract, the nonperformance (nonfeasance) as well as the misperformance (misfeasance) of promises for which a *quid pro quo* had been given. This distinction between case and its offspring, *assumpsit,* was probably clear by 1500. But there was a further pressure to extend *assumpsit,* this time to debt cases, because under the older forms of action—which antedated the time when trial by jury became the generally accepted method of trial—the defendant-debtor was permitted to wage his law by compurgation. In the middle of the sixteenth century the judges began to allow this extension of *assumpsit* if and when the debtor had made a second and specific promise to repay the money. In 1602, however, in a celebrated action known as Slade's case, the Court of Exchequer Chamber ruled that *assumpsit* should lie for all debt actions, since "every contract executory [to be fulfilled in the future] imports in itself an *assumpsit*, for when one agrees to pay money or deliver anything, thereby he assumes or promises to pay and deliver it." Thereafter this special form of *assumpsit* was known as *indebitatus* (indebted) *assumpsit*, and was commonly used in debt cases.

**Trover.** Simultaneously and for the same reason of avoiding wagers of law, case was developing another branch, called trover, to do the work of the older action of detinue (page 191). In this action involving goods wrongfully withheld rather than money owed, the fiction was that the owner wishing to recover had lost his goods and that the defendant had trespassed (or at least damaged the plaintiff) by finding (French *trouver*, find) and retaining them. The approximate date for the admission of this form of case is 1550.

THE DEVELOPMENT OF TRESPASS
(Simplified from F. W. Maitland, *Equity*, Macmillan, 1926, p. 348)

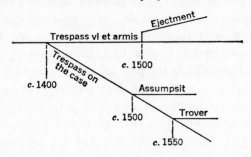

# OTHER DEVELOPMENTS IN PROCEDURE

**Initiating Steps in Criminal Cases: Pleading.** The first two procedural steps in civil cases—the original writ and process— were thus greatly changed by this development of trespass. Criminal actions were, however, begun by arrest and indictment (or occasionally appeal) in much the same way as before. Criminal procedure also differed from civil at the pleading stage where

criminal pleading remained oral while that in civil actions became almost entirely written (page 292).

**The Trial: Witnesses and the Jury.** At the trial stage the jury
—now almost the only method employed—was definitely separated from the witnesses. As maintenance ceased to be a problem, there was no longer any objection to having as many people appear to give evidence as might wish to do so. Indeed, this
came to be considered desirable, and in 1562-63 a statute was
passed providing methods for compelling the attendance of witnesses for the crown in cases to which the sovereign was a party.
That the criminal was still considered semiguilty from the moment of indictment, however, may be seen in the fact that witnesses for the defense were not allowed in treason cases.[3] As
the separate witnesses won their special place in the trial the
jury slowly divested itself of its character as a body of witnesses
and came to be considered a group of impartial judges of fact,
though as late as Coke's time jurymen were still contributing
their own evidence to aid in the decision of the case. Members
of the sworn body might be challenged, however, because of
their criminal record, known bias, or relationship to parties
interested in the suit. As the jury more and more took on a judicial character it seemed illogical to prosecute its members for
incorrect verdicts as though they had perjured themselves by
giving false testimony. The method of controlling the jury by
attaint thus died out. But the jury had not yet won complete
independence. The Star Chamber now looked into charges of
bribery and corruption (page 318). Jurors giving a verdict contrary to all the weight of the evidence might expect to be summoned before that body, or one of its branches, right down to
the end of our period.

**Later Steps.** The procedure in the steps of judgment, appeals
in error, and the execution of the judgment continued to be
conducted in this period much as it had in the previous one.

---

[3] Even after they were permitted in the next period, they could not be put
under oath until about 1700.

**Equity and Prerogative Court Procedure.** Equity procedure followed the lines already described, and that of the prerogative courts matched it on the criminal side. There most of the work was done by written complaints, questions, and answers. The parties concerned were infrequently before the court, though their counsel were commonly heard. The accused would therefore not have the opportunity to confront the witnesses against him, and did not have the protection from arbitrary executive actions afforded by jury trial. In serious matters he might be subjected to torture, not as a means of punishment or of compelling self-incrimination, but in order to ascertain whether a conspiracy existed and if so, who the accomplices might be. The sessions of the prerogative courts were not secret, as is sometimes supposed. Those of the Star Chamber were held regularly on Wednesdays and Fridays during the legal terms, and the public was admitted. There are accounts of lines forming at three o'clock in the morning before an important case.

## THE LEGAL PROFESSION

**Lawyers and Their Organization.** The legal profession was in a flourishing condition during this period. The inns of court were so crowded with the sons of gentlemen who considered a legal education the best preparation for life—as well as with aspiring sons of merchants and yeomen—that they attained almost the dignity of a third university. Gray's, the inn of the Bacons and Cecils, was especially popular with prominent county families during this period. The pressure for admittance to the inns, combined with their enhanced social standing, made it possible to exclude attorneys from membership in them. The members were not allowed to practice except as barristers. The attorneys, along with the growing numbers of solicitors, conveyancers, and other practitioners of minor legal arts, were left to get their training as best they might—usually by apprenticeship—and to make their own rules for the conduct of their professional activities. A comparatively small number of ecclesiastical and civil (Roman) lawyers—the services of the latter were occasionally in demand in the prerogative courts or where problems of international or foreign law were involved—also flourished during this period and maintained a kind of inn called Doctors' Commons.

**The Law Officers of the Crown.** Among the barristers the sergeants continued to be the select group, but the multiplication of law officers for the crown provided other paths to the highest judicial positions, and also a category which was in time to displace that of sergeant. With the increase of royal interest in law and order Henry VII named both an attorney and a solicitor to supplement the king's sergeants in what had previously been an unorganized body of legal advisers (page 299). Because the sergeants were traditionally confined to the Common Pleas court and were perhaps considered too thoroughly imbued with the common law tradition, during the sixteenth century the two new law officers of the crown gradually superseded the old king's sergeants (page 298). The royal attorney and solicitor, in spite of their titles, were actually distinguished barristers, and, like the two Principal Secretaries, had equal authority and interchangeable duties. From the position of Solicitor General, or Attorney General, as these royal advisers were called, one might hope to rise to a Chief Justiceship, as did Coke. In 1604 when neither of these posts was available James I, who wished to make room on his legal staff for Sir Francis Bacon, made official what in the previous reign had been a temporary and unusual assignment and created the new post of King's Counsel. When a place higher up was found for the philosopher-lawyer this office was retained, and more than one man was given this title.

## LEGAL LITERATURE

**The Reports and the Abridgments.** The literature of the law
during this period was enriched by the development of a system of reports that gradually displaced the *Year Books*.[4] Like
their predecessors, these reports began as private collections of
important cases, which the compilers later found it convenient
to publish. They were not confined to any one year, nor at first
to any one court. Edmund Plowden deserves to be remembered
as the first to publish such a report, in 1571. Sir James Dyer
was another prominent Elizabethan reporter, and Coke himself
was the greatest of the early compilers. In these reports the emphasis shifted from the pleadings—which were now written and
thus were defining the issue more clearly and simply, without
the elaborate jockeying in court that was such an important
part of the medieval law—to the decisions on dubious points of
law. Decisions by judges on demurrers rather than by juries on
issues of fact interested the reporters. In 1514 Sir Anthony Fitz-
herbert published *La Graunde Abridgement*—an abridgment or
summary of the *Year Books* which attempted to systematize the
whole of English law. About 1600 Thomas Ashe began the practice of using abridgments, or digests, of the reports, some of
which included material from the *Year Books* as well.

**Coke's Institutes.** Coke, who bestrode the legal field in his
time like the Colossus he was, not only compiled reports but
also prepared a comprehensive treatise on the English law called
the *Institutes*. This did what Glanvil and Bracton had done for
earlier generations in providing a survey of the entire field and
a guide by which students might learn the law. The first vol-

4 It is possible that the cessation of the *Year Books* is to be accounted for
by the decline at this time of the legal sergeants, who figure in them to the
exclusion of almost all other lawyers and who may have been the chief
patrons of the series. *Cf.* T. F. T. Plucknett, "The Place of the Legal Profession in the History of English Law," *Law Quarterly Review*, Vol. XLVIII
(1932), pp. 328-40.

ume contained an elaborate commentary on Littleton, which brought the subject of real property up to date. The second dealt with the Great Charter and virtually covered the remainder of the field of common pleas. A treatise on the criminal law and one on the court system completed the work. Due to the hostility of James and Charles, however, only the first volume could be published in Coke's lifetime. On his death in 1634 Charles ordered Coke's papers seized, and they were only surrendered for publication at the insistence of the Long Parliament in 1641.

**Selden's Works.** A younger contemporary of Coke was the learned John Selden, who wrote on a wide variety of subjects. His *Mare clausum* (*The Closed Sea*) was a treatise on international law occasioned by an English-Dutch controversy over the control of the English Channel and designed as a response to the *Mare liberum* (*The Free Sea*) of the great Dutch scholar Grotius. His *History of Tithes* attracted the unfavorable attention of James I because it attributed a human rather than divine origin to those important sources of ecclesiastical revenue. With treatises on the rights of the baronage, on Fortescue, and other medieval legal writers, he made a name for himself as a pioneer historian of the English law. His *Table Talk,* a record of his mealtime conversations compiled by his secretary Richard Milward, preserves for us a great many legal proverbs and aphorisms of the time, while also giving us some insight into the human side of seventeenth-century law.

**Rastell, Cowell, Spelman, Bacon.** Lesser names in the history of legal scholarship during this period are those of John Rastell, John Cowell, Sir Henry Spelman, and Sir Francis Bacon. Rastell published in 1527 a dictionary of legal terms that under the title of *Termes de la Ley* went through many editions. Cowell, trained in the civil law, tried by his *Institutiones juris Anglicani* (*Institutions of the English Law*), published in 1605, to show the similarities between English and Roman law and to induce the common lawyers to study the older code. Two years later he published a legal dictionary called the *Interpreter*, which gave offense because of the royalist tone of some of its definitions. Spelman, a great ecclesiastical as well as legal historian, also published a legal dictionary, the *Glossarium* (*Glossary*). In addition he wrote a treatise on knight service. Bacon, with the best mind of his generation, devoted it in part to obtaining political advancement by writing legal briefs for the crown, though philosophy was his first love. At one time he projected a scheme for the restatement of English law, and a tract that he wrote—*Maxims of the Law*—is a fragment of an unfinished work on this subject.

## SUBSTANTIVE LAW: REAL PROPERTY

**The Relation of Roman to Common Law.** The substantive law of the period was not as greatly affected by the doctrines of the Roman civil law as might have been expected in view of the popularity of this Continental code among the supporters of the crown, especially in the early Stuart period. There were some borrowings in Chancery and the prerogative courts, but these were counterbalanced by the influence of the common lawyers, who in practicing before these tribunals imported many ideas from their own sphere. While political considerations had some effect on the development of legal doctrines in this period, this influence did not always take the form of support for Roman principles, and in any case professional tradition and economic factors had at least as great an effect.

**The Statute of Uses.** This generalization is well illustrated by the major developments in the field of real property law. The Tudor sovereigns were anxious to limit the practice of creating equitable uses, since this device made possible the evasion of the feudal obligations of wardship and marriage, but their remedy did not take a particularly Roman form. A dying father saved the income from his property for his minor heir by the simple expedient of giving it to adults to hold in trust for his boy. The answer of Henry VIII to this was to force through Parliament in 1536 a Statute of Uses, which declared that thereafter in nearly all such trusts the beneficiary rather than the trustees should be considered to have the legal estate.[5] This executed the uses which it affected, in other words made them actionable at common law. Thereafter the minor heir had the legal estate in lands held in trust for him, and subsequent to this statute the king could enforce his claim to the returns from the land of his ward during the period of the minority.

**The Statutes of Wills and of Enrollments: Developments in Conveyancing.** This act also destroyed what was virtually a system of willing or devising land, since formerly it had been possible to set up a use to take effect on the death of the one establishing it. While the new statute effectively protected the king's interests, the resulting restriction on the devising of real property caused such an outcry that in 1540 Henry permitted the passage of the Statute of Wills. This legalized the willing of two-thirds of all lands held by military tenure and all those held in socage tenure, on condition that in such cases the crown should receive compensation equivalent to a good share of the lost feudal income. A minor appendage of the Statute of Uses was the Statute of Enrollments, which provided that no bargains and sales of estates of freehold or inheritance should be valid unless made in writing under seal and enrolled in one of the royal courts of record. Had the crown succeeded in obtaining the passage of a stronger version of the Act of Enrollments originally submitted, it might have made this method of transfer the standard one for all conveyancing, but in the form enacted this regulation was soon evaded by those who did not desire immediate publicity for their transactions. Instead, after one or two other experiments, conveyancers came to use the more con-

[5] S-M, No. 74H, pp. 312-13.

venient form of bargain and sale for a term coupled with a release. Under the medieval law landlords had occasionally passed title to land to their tenants by a system known as lease and release—that is, the land was first leased to the tenant, who then entered upon it, after which the landlord gave him a deed releasing him from all obligations to the landlord, in other words conveying all the landlord's rights to the tenant. Now, under the Statute of Uses it was possible to dispense with the necessity of entry under the lease, since by bargain and sale the vendor might become seised to the use of the purchaser for a term and the statute converted the use into actual possession without the purchaser's having to enter. This conveyance avoided any undesired publicity. By the seventeenth century it was accepted as the usual method of transferring legal titles to land.

**The Struggle over Perpetuities: Springing Uses.** In the old, old struggle over perpetuities the landed families and their lawyers scored a point by the introduction of a system of what were called springing uses. Under that arrangement the desired end was obtained by setting up a trust that was to come into operation when such and such an heir was born, *on condition* that on attaining his majority he should hold the lands in trust for his own heir, and so on. One use was said to spring from another in this system; hence the name. The common law judges, however, naturally resisted this movement, and sought means to check it. Before the end of the century they laid down the rule that if a future limitation could be construed as a remainder (which was legally destructible), it must be so construed. They also attempted to apply a similar rule to future interests that could not be construed as remainders. Early in the seventeenth century the family lawyers countered this latter move by appealing to Chancery, which was willing to give relief to persons whose interests were affected by the second of these rules. Accordingly, for a time the common law courts were forced to permit the creation of indestructible future interests by executory devises, that is to say, by wills, or even by deed (conveyance *inter vivos,* between the living). But in the next round in this long struggle (page 511) an effective limitation on this system was worked out.

## BUSINESS, FAMILY, AND CRIMINAL LAW

**Partnerships.** As might be expected, business law was greatly stimulated by the growth of English prosperity in this period. We have already noted the development of new forms of action to cover this type of activity (page 404). Partnership law was devised to care for the situation created by the popularity of joint business enterprises. The great principle there involved was that while partnerships reduced the risk of loss in trade to a great extent, they did not do so entirely. In case of the failure of a joint enterprise all the partners were individually liable for all its obligations, so that a single solvent partner might have to make good the entire deficit of the undertaking. The joint-stock companies, however, operated as corporations, that is, as fictitious persons after the manner of a town or medieval monastery. Here the general practice—though the issue was not often raised in this period—was that in the event of failure the investor's liability was limited to the amount of his investment. That is, he could not lose more than he had invested.

**Law of Husband and Wife: Divorce.** The most interesting development in family law was a tendency toward the permission of genuine divorces with the privilege of remarrying. The Protestants reacted against the subterfuges employed by the canon lawyers to secure the dissolution of marriages by annulments (pages 223, 323), and since they did not recognize marriage as a sacrament, they saw no insuperable religious objection to divorce. Because the Biblical teaching on the subject was somewhat confused, two different schools of Protestant thought developed on the Continent. The more conservative permitted

divorce only in cases of adultery and desertion; the liberal one
sanctioned it also in cases of cruelty, insanity, and some types of
disease. Since the English were very moderate in their Protestantism in the sixteenth century, only a part of the more conservative view was adopted. Men who were granted separations
*a mensa et thoro* (page 223 n.) by the church courts in cases of
adultery took second wives, and Parliament sanctioned this practice in the case of William Parr, Marquis of Northampton, in
1552. This precedent was frequently followed until the end of
the century, when the Anglican authorities, in their struggle
with the Puritans, began to frown on it as too Protestant a
procedure. In 1601-02 the Star Chamber forbade it in the case
of one Foljambe, and in Porter's case in 1636 the King's Bench
accepted this ruling. This conservative swing was, however, temporary, for we shall see in the next period that before the end
of the century private acts of Parliament were employed to grant
divorces with the privilege of remarrying (page 513).

**Criminal Law.** In the sphere of criminal law a new category
of offenses—misdemeanors—was definitely established in this
period. Though indictable offenses, they ranked below felonies
and did not involve capital punishment. Here at last we see
the final distinction between civil and criminal actions, for these
offenses had formerly been punishable only by the hybrid form
of action called trespass (page 192). Now no longer could a man
secure damages for himself and the punishment of the defendant
by the same action. Frauds, picking pockets, robbing orchards,
drunkenness, swearing, Sabbath-breaking, and perjury were some
of the misdemeanors established by statute in this period. It
will be noted that while some of them covered offenses formerly
punishable in the now moribund ecclesiastical courts, they also
served to fill gaps in the structure of the law as it had existed
in medieval times. Offenses, such as frauds, with which society
had formerly felt itself unable to cope were now brought within
the range of effective social displeasure.

# Oligarchic Liberalism

# 20. THE SETTING UP OF THE LIBERAL SYSTEM
## 1637-1714

**Oligarchic Liberalism and Its Establishment.** Between 1637 and 1714 England abandoned the Tudor constitutional system, which the early Stuarts had endeavored to operate, and substituted for it a species of that kind of government known as liberalism. Liberalism in European political thought is not necessarily connected with tendencies to socialism or communism, but may be defined as a system of government in which a large measure of the power is held by some or all of the classes below the nobility and the clergy. There may be oligarchic, or restricted, liberalism, in which the upper classes remain predominant, or there may be democratic liberalism, in which virtually every class enjoys an equal share in the suffrage. The type set up in England by the beginning of the eighteenth century was oligarchic liberalism. The story of the transition to this new system is the story of how (1) the power of the royal absolutism was broken, (2) the gentry and their upper-middle class allies gained the upper hand over their other associates in the opposition coalition, and (3) this position was consolidated. There is some overlapping in time between the first and second topics because, as in many another revolution, factional quarrels began before the main struggle was ended. But it will be convenient to consider these topics consecutively. We begin with the story of the destruction of the royal absolutism.

## THE DESTRUCTION OF THE ROYAL POWER: THE SCOTTISH TROUBLES

**Charles's Position in England.** We have seen that by 1637 Charles had gained the upper hand in England and might have retained it had the English been his only subjects. Peaceful methods had failed to break the royal control of the machinery of government. Force could be resorted to only in favorable circumstances and when emotions were aroused to a high pitch. Religion was the subject most heavily charged with emotional dynamite, and Charles, as one who had been brought up an Anglican in a country where that party was gaining strength, could be expected to ride out whatever storm his English opponents might stir up by themselves.

**Scottish Problems: The Nobility.** Charles, however, was also King of Scotland, and there the situation was quite different. James, who had grown up among his turbulent northern subjects, had learned how to master them, and had done it well (page 344). Charles knew little of their ways, and for that little he had only scorn. His second kingdom was to him merely a poor and backward land, and not until 1633—when his English opponents had been well disposed of—did he deign to visit it. By that time he had already offended most of the Scottish nobles by a high-minded but politically inadvisable attempt to recover from them the ecclesiastical property they had acquired during the Scottish spoliation of the Church in the preceding century. This spoliation had followed roughly the English pattern except that the crown had not profited, and now Charles wished to force the return of this ill-gotten wealth to the Church. A compromise was finally arranged on this issue, but not until a good deal of bad blood had been engendered. The situation was not eased during the royal visit by the demand of Charles's clerical friends for the leading places in the state processions. The Scottish Lord Chancellor, the "old cankered, goutish" Earl of Kinnoul, when asked to give precedence to Archbishop Spottiswood declared that while he was Chancellor, "Never a priest in Scotland should set a foot before him as long as his blood was hot"— a condition that, under the circumstances, bade fair to continue for some time.

**The Clergy and Scottish Nationalism.** It might be expected that the prospect of greater endowments would cause the very influential Scottish clergy to rally to Charles's support, but they were almost solidly Presbyterian and they felt sure that Charles intended to use the money to make the Church Anglican. These dark suspicions were strengthened by the marks of favor Charles bestowed on Scottish bishops, and were confirmed by the King's intrusion of "two English chaplains, clad in surplices," into the Sunday morning exercises at Edinburgh's St. Giles Cathedral, where they "acted their English service." Scottish sensibilities were deeply offended by this performance, and further outraged when the sounds of boisterous revelry in the near-by royal banqueting chamber prevented the holding of any afternoon service at all in the cathedral. Deaf to the mutterings of Scottish discontent, after his return to England Charles ordered the preparation of a service book on the Anglican model, under the supervision of his chief ecclesiastical adviser William Laud, Archbishop of Canterbury, and another English bishop. When the work was done, he coolly sent word that the book was to be employed in all Scottish churches. Since neither Scottish Council nor the national assembly of the Scottish Church had been so much as consulted in the matter, this was a gross affront to the Scottish national pride and dignity.

**The Tumult in St. Giles.** To ally the Scottish nobles, clergy, and national spirit against him almost simultaneously was an act of absentee madness on Charles's part. But he chose to ignore all protests against his arbitrary alteration of the traditional Scottish form of worship. Safely removed from the scene of the

troubles, he thought his command reasonable enough and ordered its enforcement. The Scottish response to such treatment
was duly made. James had dominated these people well enough,
but not for so long as to obscure the memory of the successful
uprisings against his mother and other predecessors. When on
the fateful Sunday morning, July 23, 1637, the Dean of Edinburgh began to read the required liturgy in St. Giles Cathedral,
he was met by angry buzzings from the common people, mostly
women, who customarily attended that service. When the Bishop
ascended the pulpit stairs to quiet the congregation, some unknown markswoman flung a footstool intended for him, though
it actually came closer to the Dean. This was the shot heard
round the British world. It precipitated a riot. "False thief, is
there no other part of the kirk (church) to say mass in but thou
must say it in my lug (ear)?" protested one irate worshiper as
she hurled her Bible in the face of a young man who was help-
ing with the Catholic-sounding responses. Troops had to be
called in to clear the church of the battling women before the
service could proceed, and then only to the tinkling of breaking glass as stones came through the window. Furthermore, when
at last the official exercises were duly concluded, it was pull-
devil pull-baker for the soldiers to get the clergy safely through
the crowd. Angry hands tore the clerical gowns from their
wearers' backs in the process. By afternoon the rioters had possession of the town.

**The Covenant.** Much as the better-class citizens of the community deprecated mob violence, they sympathized with the
rioters on the religious question. Rather than see the irresponsible elements take matters into their own hands without conservative leadership, prominent Scots decided to give these proceedings some semblance of legality. Back in the 1580's, when Catholic assassination plots had been rife in Protestant countries
and one against the Dutch William of Orange had succeeded,
the Scots had drawn up a Covenant, vowing to defend their

King and "the true reformed religion." This document was now resurrected, modified to suit the new circumstances, and submitted to nobles, clergy, and people, who with great emotion swore to keep the faith. The Covenanters, as they were now called, thus gave their movement the appearance of a traditional Scottish defense of both the welfare of the sovereign and the true religion—which to them meant Presbyterianism. According to their theory they were not rebelling against their King, but merely trying to protect him from bad advisers and to prevent any alteration of their long-established religion.

**The Bishops' Wars and the Short Parliament.** Charles now embarked on a long series of devious negotiations, threats, and broken promises that did nothing to help the situation. He did not know his Presbyterians, and could not grasp the seriousness of the problem. He felt confident that with a little delay tempers would cool and all would be forgotten. When he was disappointed in this hope, he attempted to use force, and in 1639 undertook the first of two campaigns, which are called, from the religious issues involved, the Bishops' Wars. For this campaign he raised what army he could afford without summoning the English Parliament, and marched north. But the impoverished Scots had long been eking out their incomes by acting as mercenaries in the Continental wars, and he was met on the border by an obviously superior force. After a little skirmishing he conceded the Scottish demands and withdrew; but only to look for further means of breaking his promises. In desperation he turned for advice to the Earl of Strafford (page 348), whose success in Ireland led the proud Lord Deputy to think that Parliaments could be managed. So in the spring of 1640 Charles summoned an English Parliament and demanded help against the Scottish rebels. The members of the House of Commons, remembering their last meeting and Eliot's fate, would provide no funds until grievances had been redressed. In three weeks Charles angrily dissolved this Short Parliament, as it was called.[1] Strafford had maintained that if worst came to worst and Parliament would not do its duty, the King would be justified in overriding the law (page 373) in the matter of parliamentary control of direct taxation. Charles therefore raised another army and tried to equip it by means of a forced loan. He even resorted to the expedient of reviving the old Great Council (page 274), and summoned the Lords to vote a tax without the presence of the Commons. But they would do no more than offer personal loans, and the King could not obtain sufficient funds for his needs by this means. Furthermore, his conscript army would not fight when it reached the border. In this Second Bishops' War the Scots did not stop on the border, but seized three of the northern English counties, exacted a promise of £850 a day indemnity, and demanded a parliamentary ratification of any future agreement.

## THE LONG PARLIAMENT AND CONSTITUTIONAL CHANGES

**The Long Parliament.** Strafford now returned to England, and relying on his personal assistance, Charles decided to brave an English Parliament again. This met on November 3, 1640. Since it was not finally dissolved until 1660, it is properly called, in contrast with its predecessor, the Long Parliament. Dark-browed Strafford, who by his masterful conduct of Irish affairs had won from his opponents the title of Black Tom the Tyrant, showed a strange lethargy in dealing with the English House of Commons. Though it was generally supposed that he intended to impeach the leaders of the lower house—particularly the most prominent, John Pym—they got their blow in first and impeached the Earl. Pym, like his Scottish counterparts, was an artist at playing on the mob, and by judicious words to Lon-

[1] For accounts of some of the stormy sessions of this body, see S-M, No. 95, pp. 471-75.

don merchants could fill the streets of Westminster with club-waving apprentices. These, combined with the Scottish army in the north, supplied a logic for his arguments more potent than any that could be found in legal precedents or put in parliamentary speeches. By thus menacing Charles and the Lords he pushed through Parliament several important measures.

**The Impeachment and Attainder of Strafford.** The first was the attainder of Strafford. No legal proofs could be discovered of actual misconduct on Strafford's part; so attainder was substituted for formal impeachment. This alternative procedure was an act of Parliament that simply decreed death for the victim without any proof of delinquency.[2] Charles had promised that Strafford should not suffer for any services rendered his master, but in the end he broke even this promise. Taking refuge behind his family, the King declared that for himself he feared no mob, but must protect his wife and children. So he signed the act of attainder. "Put not your trust in princes," quoted Strafford wryly on learning of his fate. On May 12, 1641, he was beheaded before a huge assemblage on Tower Hill, the rising slope just outside the Tower. Other royal ministers fled or were imprisoned. With force at its back, Parliament had at last found an effective way of controlling the royal officials.

**The Abolition of the Prerogative Courts and the Adoption of the Triennial Act.** The second achievement of the Long Parliament was the abolition of the prerogative courts—Star Chamber, High Commission, and the rest—including, unfortunately, the Court of Requests.[3] A minor act prohibited the collection of ship money and other royal exactions without parliamentary consent.[4] Furthermore, this revolutionary body protected the position of Parliament itself by a Triennial Act that provided for the assemblage of Parliament once every three years, whether the king summoned it or not.[5] Had it not been for the con-

2 S-M, No. 96B, pp. 477-78.     4 S-M, No. 96G, pp. 481-82.
3 S-M, No. 96E-F, pp. 479-81.     5 S-M, No. 96A, pp. 476-77.

troversial subject of religion, the Commons might have continued its reform program indefinitely.

**The Religious Question and the Militia Issue.** On the thorny religious question, however, no agreement could be reached. The Puritans wanted more or less sweeping reforms, depending on their particular party, while the Anglicans, led by a Cheshire gentleman named Sir Edward Hyde, wanted the ecclesiastical establishment to remain virtually unchanged. Charles was quick to take advantage of this opportunity to split the opposition. Ireland, also seizing its opportunity, had blazed out in revolt in October, 1641, and it was imperative that an English army should be raised to deal with the situation there. By all the precedents the King should have had the absolute command of such a force, but "King" Pym and his followers, naturally fearing that in such a circumstance it would first be turned against rebels nearer home, claimed control of it in the name of Parliament.[6] On this militia matter Charles could make a stand because of the discontent of Hyde and his followers with the program of religious reform that the Puritans were beginning to push through.

## THE FIRST CIVIL WAR: THE RISE OF CROMWELL

**The Outbreak of the First (English) Civil War.** The Puritans in Parliament aggravated the situation in December, 1641, by ordering the publication of the so-called Grand Remonstrance, a detailed attack on the royal policy. Charles retaliated in January, 1642, by a personal invasion of the House of Commons at the head of a file of soldiers in an attempt to arrest Pym and four other leaders. They had been warned in advance, however, and were safely down the river in the City of London, where the apprentices could be relied on to keep them out of

[6] For the ordinance on the subject finally passed by the House, see S-M, No. 96M, pp. 486-87.

harm's way. After this there was almost no hope of avoiding civil war. Feverish preparations alternated with fruitless negotiations during the next few months until August 22, 1642, when the King raised his standard on a hill near Nottingham, in the midlands, and called on all his loyal subjects to aid him against his enemies. With the Anglicans at his back Charles could now afford to challenge the show of force by means of which his opponents had been dictating to him. The English conflict, which in effect was already being conducted by violent means only partially concealed below the surface of events, was now transferred to the battlefield outright.

**Strength of the Two Sides.** In this First Civil War, as it came to be called to distinguish it from later troubles in England, the King had the support of a majority of the Lords and a large minority of the Commons. He was strong in the north and west, except for the seaports where trade and Puritanism went together. Best of all from his point of view, he had "birth and breeding," young gallants accustomed to riding and hunting, of whom his sister (page 346) Elizabeth's son Rupert, soon proved to be a most dashing cavalry leader. It was from these swashbuckling horsemen that the whole party received its title of Cavaliers. On their side the Parliamentarians had some thirty of the Lords to the king's eighty, the wealth of the south and east, including London, the support of the navy, and the grim determination that went with a belief in Calvinism. Because the Puritans of this faction tended to round (crop) their hair in short and sober fashion instead of following the Cavaliers' style of long locks, this party came to be known as Roundheads.

**First Years of the War.** At first military experience told. Parliament's conscripted army fared badly and Charles and Rupert fought their way almost to London. The capital was only saved by the efforts of its trained bands, almost the only efficient ones in the country. These militiamen, or rather militia boys—for most of them were the city apprentices temporarily released from their shops for this kind of military holiday—were an important factor in the war, for they constituted an emergency Parliamentary reserve that the King could not match. Establishing his capital at Oxford during the winter of 1642-43, the King planned a triple-headed drive on London for the next year. This came from the north, northwest, and west, and was only beaten by the stout resistance of the Puritan mercantile towns combined with the efforts of a Parliamentary cavalry leader who was developing into an able rival of Prince Rupert.

**Oliver Cromwell.** This was Oliver Cromwell, who dominated the scene for the next fifteen years. Pym died in 1643 and Hampden, of ship-money fame, was mortally wounded in a skirmish the same year, so new leaders had to be discovered. In any case the time for speeches and lawsuits was past, and a man of Cromwell's type was needed. He was a gentleman whose Welsh great-great-grandfather, Morgan Williams, was Thomas Cromwell's brother-in-law. Williams's son Richard, given a good slice of monastic property in Huntingdonshire by his uncle, had taken his patron's name. The seventeenth-century Cromwell had been a member of Parliament as early as 1628 but had not particularly distinguished himself in that body. On the battlefield, however, he found his proper milieu. After one of the early engagements he remarked to Hampden, who was his cousin, that nothing could be accomplished by such conscripts as the "old decayed serving men and tapsters." "You must get men of a spirit," he maintained. That winter he was busy in the east-county villages recruiting "such men as had the fear of God before them and made some conscience of what they did." By spring he had a cavalry regiment composed of suitably spirited men, and in the campaigning that followed they soon won for themselves the title of Ironsides. Though Cromwell was not made Commander in Chief of the Parliamentary forces until 1650, from this time on he was the chief factor in bringing victory to his side and as such was the dominant political leader of the army after 1647 at the latest.

**Scottish Intervention and the Victory of the Parliamentarians.** During the first two years of the English Civil War the Scots, who had made it possible in the first place, refused to participate, because the House of Commons, composed of Puritans of different shades of opinion, would not commit itself to a strictly Presbyterian position. In December, 1643, however, the serious military situation drove the English Parliamentarians to take the Covenant,[7] and the next year a Scottish army duly crossed the border. That summer, with its help the Parliamentarians won a very important victory at Marston Moor, near York, which gave them control of the north. In this action Cromwell's disciplined cavalry turned the tide. After an initial success on the wings, where cavalrymen regularly fought, the royalist cavalry commonly got out of hand—as they did on the opposite wing on this occasion—and pursued their fleeing rivals off the field. Cromwell was able to keep his Ironsides in control after the initial successful charge, however. Wheeling them around, he took the royalist infantry in the rear, and under the double

CROMWELL'S TACTICS

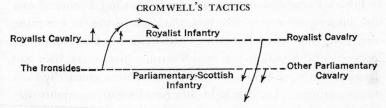

assault it soon broke. The following year, after a thorough reorganization on the Cromwellian pattern, the New Model Army, as it was called, gained a similar victory over Charles himself at Naseby, north of Oxford. In 1646 the university town surrendered. After a period as a wandering fugitive the King gave himself up to the Scots, and the First Civil War was over.

[7] S-M, No. 100, pp. 504-05.

## THE SECOND CIVIL WAR AND THE EXECUTION
## OF CHARLES I

**Negotiations and the Second Civil War.** Charles had chosen
to yield to the Scots because he felt that he could make better
terms with them than with the English. At first he was disappointed, for they rejected his offers, and on the payment of
the Scottish war expenses by the Parliamentarians his custodians
surrendered him to the English. But their southern allies did
not keep the agreement about the Covenant (page 429), and in
December of 1647 the Scots came to terms with the captive King,
who surrendered his convictions to the extent of consenting to a
three-year trial of Presbyterianism. This led to the Second Civil
War in 1648, in which the English Parliament—still opposed to
Charles's exaggerated demands for power—and the New Model
Army, now inclined to Independency, were opposed to the English royalists and the Scots. It was a short-lived affair in which
a large Scottish army caused considerable alarm but proved to
be no match for the New Model. Scattered revolts in Wales and
England came to even less.

**Pride's Purge and the Execution of the King.** Cromwell and
his military supporters now took the decisive step of executing
the King. The majority of the Puritans in the Commons were
opposed to this policy. Like the Scottish Covenanters, they had
begun the war with no intention of eliminating monarchy from
the constitution. They thought they could regain the rights they
claimed and share control of the state with a monarch properly
limited, somewhat after the medieval fashion. At first they waged
war ostensibly only on the royal advisers; not until the fighting
had gone on for months did some of them begin to accept the
theory of the absolute supremacy of Parliament, and then but
gradually. Cromwell dealt with this opposition majority among
the Commons by sending Colonel Pride with some soldiers to

exclude them from the House. After Pride's Purge, as this action was called, there remained only some ninety members in the sitting part of the Commons, now dubbed the Rump. These members were, of course, pliable enough and under Cromwell's direction set up a special court to try the King.[8] Cromwell reasoned that Charles was a troublemaker and a shedder of innocent blood, as the Second Civil War showed. Until "Charles Stuart, that man of blood" was brought "to justice" there would be no peace. "If we beat the king ninety and nine times yet he is king still," a shrewd observer on the Parliamentary side had remarked long before. Cromwell therefore had recourse to the principle—already applied to Strafford, and in 1645 to Laud— that stone-dead hath no fellow. According to existing law the penalties of treason could only be applied properly to offenses against the king, but under the new theory of popular—or at least parliamentary—sovereignty it was possible to accuse Charles of treason against the people of England. This was done. Charles, showing more dignity in his last hours than in his earlier career —"Nothing in his life so became him as the manner of his leaving it," said a poet—refused to recognize the jurisdiction of the court.[9] He went calmly to his death on January 30, 1649. As the executioner swung the ax no thunderbolt was hurled to save the head of the Lord's anointed. After that disillusionment the theory of the divine right of kings was discredited in the eyes of many.

**Final Defeat of the Royalist Party.** The death of Charles did not, however, mark the end of the royalist party. Taking up the cause of the dead King's son, who was now known to the faithful as Charles II, it struggled on in Ireland and Scotland. In the summer of 1649 Cromwell crushed it and the Roman Catholic cause simultaneously in the western island. This was done with a ferocity that has left a lasting stain on the General's memory, one only to be explained by the English Puritan's feeling that

[8] S-M, No. 104A, p. 516.          [9] S-M, No. 104B, pp. 517-18.

an Irish Catholic was not entitled to the same treatment as an Anglican royalist or a Scottish Presbyterian. In 1650 and 1651 the last signs of resistance were stamped out in Scotland and the north. A clever maneuver, which lured Charles into England, ended with his being a wandering fugitive after a disastrous defeat at Worcester, on the Severn not far from the border of Wales. After many further adventures, including a day spent in hiding in an oak tree while Cromwell's soldiers searched the neighborhood, the Stuart claimant was glad to escape to the Continent. Less than fifteen years from the day the footstool was thrown in St. Giles Cathedral the royal power was virtually eliminated as a factor in English politics and in the English constitution. It was to revive to some extent in the future, but it would never be what it had been before Charles I gave the opposition the fatal opening by arbitrarily altering the form of the Scottish church service.

## CONFLICTS WITHIN THE OPPOSITION COALITION

**The Opposition Coalition and Its Growth.** To destroy the absolute monarchy was one thing. To determine what should be put in its place was another. We have seen that the original opposition coalition consisted of Presbyterian and Independent Puritans and the secular elements represented in the House of Commons—country gentry, well-to-do merchants, and common lawyers. But when the controversy was taken to the battlefield these men could not do all the fighting themselves. There is an old proverb that a rich man's war is a poor man's fight. The work of such recruiting agents as Cromwell in appealing to the yeomen, and even to the laboring classes, naturally made these elements politically conscious and politically important—just as the original Parliament summoned to be a pliable money-granting body eventually became politically important in its own right. Years of hard campaigning and of discussions around the campfire in the evening—when the strict discipline of the New Model forbade chicken-stealing expeditions or other mundane soldierly diversions—sharpened this feeling of political importance. This was particularly true among the troopers, the cavalrymen, who were required to provide their own horses and were therefore commonly yeomen's sons who had volunteered. Before the Civil Wars were ended, therefore, other social elements had been added to the opposition, elements of whose political aspirations some account had to be taken. These were called Levellers and Diggers, the equivalent of the modern democratic liberals and communists.

**Organization of Our Story.** The tangled story of the fortunes of these many competing interests which altogether made up the victorious Parliamentary coalition can best be told by indicating how each of the unsuccessful ones in turn made its bid for power and was beaten, leaving the field to the alliance of gentry, merchants, and lawyers.

**The Presbyterians.** The Presbyterian Puritans—strongly Protestant clericals, with a long tradition and international standing that brought support from Scotland and the Calvinistic churches on the Continent—might have been expected to recover a measure of power similar to that which the Church had enjoyed in the Middle Ages. Their allies in Parliament did succeed in organizing some of their leaders into an advisory body on religious policy, called the Westminster Assembly, and for a time (1643-45) it looked as though they would be successful. But their long English tradition included a century's experience of looking to laymen, in the persons of the country gentry, for political leadership and legal protection, while their international standing—particularly their Scottish connections—did not endear them to the increasingly nationalistic English. Worst of all, they cared more for the niceties of a narrow factionalism than for the broad considerations of Protestant statesmanship. Accordingly they were never able to come to any agreement with the Independents, with whom they held so many major doctrines in common. Furthermore, the university-trained Presbyterian clergy found service as army chaplains too troublesome and left this field to their more enterprising Independent brethren, who soon controlled the religious policy of the army. Consequently, the Presbyterians in the Assembly could not secure effective support for the program they enunciated. Though they drew up a confession and catechisms that have since been standard equipment in most English-speaking Presbyterian churches, they could not obtain parliamentary endorsement for their most important constitutional demand. That was the right of the local churches, controlled by their ministers, to excommunicate whomever they chose. Without the free exercise of this powerful disciplinary weapon the Presbyterian clergy would have no effective authority. The Puritan laymen in Parliament had been greatly influenced by Tudor theory and practice in the matter of the supremacy of the secular power over the Church—a system commonly called Erastianism, from Erastus, a sixteenth-century theologian who championed one version of this teaching. After a great struggle in the spring of 1646 the Erastian element in the Long Parliament kept the power of excommunication in its own hands, and after that the clerical Presbyterian party ceased to have any great strength.

**The Levellers.** The spring of 1646 also marked the end of the First Civil War. During the interlude preceding the Second Civil War there were many negotiations and discussions on the future form of the state. Had the authorities of the Long Parliament paid most of the army in full and mustered it out, they could perhaps have kept the upper hand over that rising political power. With a folly equal to that of Charles in 1637, however, they tried to discharge the surplus regiments without making up their arrearages in pay. That highhanded project at once disclosed the strength of the Leveller movement. This movement was led by one John Lilburne, a former officer in the army, of

Independent religious views, who had honorably resigned rather than take the Presbyterian Covenant that was required of all officers under the terms of the Scottish treaty of 1643 (page 429). Though he had been a zealous Puritan, he had become disgusted by the factionalism of the clerical leaders and had turned to secular political agitation. He and his followers reasoned that if the war was being waged in the name of the people of England, as the Parliamentarians were maintaining, it was only fair that the common people—who were also doing most of the fighting—should be represented in Parliament. "The poorest he that is in England," said these early democrats, "hath a life to live as the greatest he. And therefore . . . every man that is to live under a government ought first by his own consent to put himself under that government." Consequently they began to advocate a democratic program, contained in a document called the Agreement of the People, which provided for universal manhood suffrage, frequent parliamentary elections, and electoral districts equal in population.[10] Their opponents, who believed that democracy eventually meant communism, accused them of preaching economic equality for all. Since communism was then supposed to involve the leveling of all classes and individuals, Lilburne's supporters were called Levellers, though actually they advocated only political equality, not economic.

**Their Opportunity and Their Failure.** Roused by the threat of dismissal without pay, the rank and file of the army, which had been greatly influenced by Lilburne's teaching, appointed representatives, called agitators, or agents, to an army council that was formed to present the case of the army to Parliament. Cromwell and the higher officers were also represented on the council, which undertook to formulate a governmental policy as well as to collect the money due the men. Though Cromwell did not sympathize with the democratic aspirations of his men,

10 For a later and somewhat more conservative version of this document, see S-M, No. 103, pp. 511-16.

he wished to retain their loyalty and so supported their refusal to be discharged without pay. In this stand they were successful. But when the worst of the crisis was passed, Cromwell and his son-in-law, General Ireton, who had formulated conservative arguments used against the Levellers in the debates of the army council, tried to suppress the Leveller movement by sending the agitators back to their regiments and diverting the attention of the army to other problems. Torn between their loyalty to their General and their devotion to Lilburne's principles, the soldiers wavered. For a time there was the threat of a serious mutiny, but Cromwell's personality carried the day. Though the discontented veterans had him at their mercy at one tumultuous mustering, they would not shoot the man who had led them to so many famous victories, and at length the General's orders were obeyed. Lilburne struggled on with his agitation, however, and after the Second Civil War the Levellers once more made a bid for power by insisting on the adoption of a version of the Agreement of the People as the price of their co-operation in the program culminating in Pride's Purge (page 430). Here again, however, Cromwell outmaneuvered them, and after another small mutiny the movement was effectively suppressed. Though the Levellers formulated virtually all the ideas of the American Constitution and nineteenth-century democracy, including the theory of a written constitution and reserved powers, these ideas were too new to win widespread support immediately. The shopkeepers and yeomen needed more education and more training in democratic thinking before they dared take the risk of asserting their real power.

**The Diggers.** Most extreme of all the competing movements was that of the Diggers, led by one Gerrard Winstanley. These people took the step which Lilburne refused to take, and asserted that the people who had fought to free England could not be genuinely free unless they were given some means of subsistence. Very often during the enclosure movement

> The village green that had got mislaid
> Turned up in the squire's back-yard.

These reformers insisted that the land of England was the heritage of Englishmen, and particularly that landless ("disinherited") men had a right and a duty to dig—hence the name—plant, and sow the old common lands. Current religious teaching they denounced as a mere cloak to conceal inequality, a pretty story designed to divert popular attention from the obvious injustices of this life. They thus spoke, as they thought, for the material interests of that inarticulate group of completely landless laboring men whose voice had not been raised before, even in the Peasants' Revolt. In 1649, after the Second Civil War, they endeavored to put their ideas into practice in a few scattered co-operative colonies established on the commons (land reserved for community use). But where the Levellers could not succeed there was little hope for these people. Soldiers were sent to drive them from their holdings. Much force was not commonly necessary, however, and the experiments were of comparatively short duration.

**The Independent Saints.** With the Presbyterians, the Levellers, and the Diggers eliminated as political factors by 1650, the field was left to the Independents and the landlord-merchant-lawyer group. Both elements had the advantage of numbering Cromwell among their sympathizers. While the General hesitated to choose between them, the issue was in doubt. During the next three years he was occupied with the Scottish wars and also a naval fray with the Dutch, but by 1653 he was ready to turn his attention to the internal problems of England. By this time the curse of individualistic factionalism was beginning to affect the religious party of the Independents, and this group was showing signs of splitting into still more subdivisions. Of these the most important politically was one called the Fifth Monarchists, who believed that Christ was about to return to the earth to set up His Kingdom and that it was the duty of the earthly saints to take over the English government and prepare the way for Him.[11] They were thus Protestant clericals somewhat on the Presbyterian model in desiring to dominate the state, though independent in their polity. Cromwell was not an avowed Fifth Monarchist himself, but in looking over the administration of the English government he saw so much bribery and corruption among the members of the Rump Parliament, particularly in the matter of confiscated estates of royalists, that he thought it might be well to experiment with the idea of government by saints.

**The Nominated Parliament.** Accordingly, in 1653 Cromwell asked the Rump to dissolve, and when the members refused he drove them out with his troops. In their place he called the Nominated Parliament, a body of one hundred and twenty members named by Independent clergymen. They were not all "saints," but a working majority were, and they at once instituted a reform program. Much of this was sound, but it took a religious line instead of beginning with the moral abuses that Cromwell had in mind. One of the major proposals was to abolish the tithe system so as not to require unbelievers to support the Church. But since many of the tithe rights had come into lay hands at the dissolution of the monasteries which had formerly held them, this seemed to Cromwell and his landlord friends like an attack on the institution of private property. Consultations were held; the soldiery appeared once more; and the saints were sent off home.

**The Triumph of Gentry, Merchants, and Lawyers: The New Secular Policy.** Thereafter Cromwell and his supporters turned to a secular policy. The merchants who were prospering as a result of the destruction of the monopoly system in domestic trade were anxious to secure more markets overseas. There was

[11] According to their interpretation of the Biblical prophecies in Daniel and Revelation, there had already been four earthly monarchies, Babylonia, Persia, Macedonia, and Rome, with the fifth and heavenly one yet to come. Hence the name.

a clamor for a return to the tactics of Hawkins and Drake. Under Cromwell's leadership England now allied herself with Catholic France and attacked Spain. Reviving some of the glories of Drake and Raleigh, and even Edward III, the English took Jamaica in the West Indies, blockaded the Spanish ports, waylaid the treasure fleet, and took Dunkirk, a Channel port in the Spanish Netherlands that was regarded as making up for the loss of Calais. It was a brilliant revival of English national power and a great stimulus to further advances along the road to world empire. But it was far removed from the religious policy Cromwell had advocated in those dark winter days of 1642-43 in the east-country villages. Henceforth, except for a few small risings of Fifth Monarchy men, Independency was politically dead.

## ATTEMPTS OF THE VICTORS TO CONSOLIDATE THEIR POSITION: THE COMMONWEALTH AND PROTECTORATE

**The Problem of Consolidation.** There remained the problem of consolidating the success of the gentry, prominent merchants, and lawyers who had thus eliminated their rivals. This problem proved to be a very difficult one indeed. With a military genius such as Cromwell to lead them their position was strong enough. They could

> decide all controversies by
> infallible artillery,

and few dared to dispute them. The difficulty was to devise a constitutional system that did not depend on having a military genius to keep in order the elements in society which had potential political strength—in other words, a system which commanded the voluntary support of these elements. Cromwell and his advisers tackled this problem early in his career, but as a constitution-framer he proved to be a good general and little more.

**The Commonwealth, 1649-53.** On the execution of the King in 1649, monarchy and the House of Lords were both abolished by acts of the Rump Parliament.[12] A Council of State, consisting of forty-one men—mostly members of Parliament, with a sprinkling of peers, and judges—was set up to aid the Rump in directing the government.[13] Though Cromwell was the dominating influence, theoretically there was no chief executive; and this system is therefore known as the Commonwealth, the seventeenth-century equivalent of Republic.

**The Protectorate, 1653-58.** After the dissolution of the Nominated Parliament, which had merely been substituted for the Rump in the Commonwealth system, England began her first—and thus far her last—experiment with a written constitution. In its original form this was called the Instrument of Government.[14] It provided for a Parliament—to be elected by men having a property qualification that kept control of the government in the hands of the classes now dominant, a Council of State, and an elected Lord Protector, Cromwell, to hold office for life. Because of this last feature the government of England during the period while it lasted (from 1653 to 1658) is known as the Protectorate. As Lord Protector, Cromwell was given nearly all the powers of the former monarch, and indeed the Protectorate under his rule is hard to distinguish from the Tudor monarchy. The likeness became even more striking toward the end of the Protectorate, after a supermilitaristic interlude. Cromwell quarreled with his first Parliament and ruled for a time through major generals who were given military command of different sections and enforced martial law on the areas under their control. Then in 1657 the Instrument of Government was modified by the Humble Petition and Advice.[15] This created a Second House—virtually the House of Lords under another title—and gave Cromwell the privilege of selecting the man to succeed him

[12] S-M, Nos. 106-07, pp. 521-22.      [14] S-M, No. 111, pp. 525-29.
[13] S-M, No. 105, pp. 519-21.           [15] S-M, No. 112, pp. 529-32.

as Protector. It was even suggested by his advisers who drew up the Petition that Cromwell take the title of king, but he refused to make such an obvious admission of the failure of the anti-monarchical movement. The Protectorate system creaked and groaned, but on the whole it worked not too badly as long as the great General lived, which was until September, 1658.

**The Period of Confusion, 1658-60.** No one else could operate such machinery, however. Oliver's oldest son Richard, named as successor by the father, had little to commend him as a ruler except the family name. In the spring of 1659 the leading army officers forced him to resign. They recalled the Rump Parliament to do their will, but when that unfortunate body proved intractable, it was expelled a second time. Public sentiment—which once more made itself felt in popular demonstrations in the capital—would tolerate military rule in none but an Oliver Cromwell, however, and soon the officers were compelled first to recall the Rump and then to add to it the surviving victims of Pride's Purge. This enlarged Long Parliament, being dominated by a majority of Erastian Presbyterians, was of course more conservative than the Rump.

## THE RESTORATION OF THE STUARTS

**Charles II (1660-85).** Gradually it became apparent that if the group which had been victorious in the major and minor struggles of the Civil Wars was to hold any great part of its gains, it must speedily find a ruler and a type of government that would be acceptable to the nation. Years of exile had rendered the fugitive Charles II tractable, and negotiations soon showed that he was the answer to the problem. Both the Parliamentarians and the Stuart claimant felt that half a loaf was better than none. By giving up most of the substance of power Charles could have a crown and a comfortable living. By conceding the monarch a few small points the oligarchic liberals could retain most of the gains made in the two preceding decades. A Parliamentary general named George Monck and the Parliamentary admiral, the Earl of Sandwich, arranged everything with Sir Edward Hyde, who was acting as Lord Chancellor for Charles. From Breda in the Netherlands, Charles issued a declaration promising—subject to parliamentary modification or approval—a general amnesty for all offenders, freedom of conscience in religious matters, security for property acquired during the recent troubles, and all the delinquent back pay for the army. A specially elected Parliament, called the Convention Parliament because it was not regularly summoned by a king, voted for the recall of the royal exile. In May, 1660, he returned in triumph. A new Parliament was elected, and undertook the work of giving effect to the compromise already arranged.

**The Restoration Settlement.** For the time, the country had had enough of formal constitutional documents, and no efforts were made to define in general terms the restrictions placed on the king. In theory Charles resumed the position occupied by his father. He was given the royal title, the royal property, and nominally the royal prerogative. None of the legislation passed by Parliament since 1642 without the royal assent was recognized as valid unless it was specially re-enacted. The King was voted annual revenues supposedly sufficient for his needs. But actually the Restoration was far from a real restoration of Charles Stuart. By declaring invalid only those acts of Parliament which had not received the royal approval, those passed under pressure in the two-year revolutionary period before August, 1642, were left on the books. The prerogative courts were therefore barred and the King was obligated to have a Parliament at least every three years, though later a weakened version of the Triennial Act [16] was substituted for the original one. Furthermore, Charles kept the promises incorporated in the Declaration of Breda. Very few

[16] S-M, No. 1140, p. 552.

of those who had rebelled against his father were executed.[17] Most of the lands which royalists had lost during the period of upheaval were retained by those who had acquired them. The religious settlement, particularly, shows the weakness of the King. As suggested at Breda, Charles, who had become sympathetic with the Roman Catholic position during his exile, desired to introduce measures of religious toleration. But in a violent reaction against Puritanism the new Parliament—known as the Cavalier Parliament, in part because of its loyalty to the old religion—insisted on passing legislation, called the Clarendon Code,[18] making Anglicanism the only legal religion once more. When Charles a few years later tried to nullify this legislation by issuing a Declaration of Indulgence [19]—a proclamation granting religious toleration under certain conditions—there was such a storm of opposition that he withdrew it. When his brother James once remonstrated with him for not taking a stronger line with Parliament, he dryly remarked that he was too old to go on his travels again. That statement sums up the whole spirit of the Restoration. On paper the governmental system was very much like that of 1637. Actually, though a Statute of Indemnity and Oblivion was adopted, ostensibly to enable everyone to forgive and forget the past, no number of such acts could have wiped out the memories and the effects of the years between. The theory of the divine right of kings could not survive the experience of the realities of the execution in 1649 and the flight in 1651.

**Later Restrictions on the Monarchy.** Charles was the Merry Monarch, the easy-going person already pictured above who

[17] Nine regicides (those directly responsible for the death of Charles I) and one other, Sir Henry Vane, whose abilities coupled with strong republican sympathies caused him to be considered especially dangerous, were executed.
[18] Named for Sir Edward Hyde, the King's chief minister, whom Charles created Earl of Clarendon. Actually Clarendon had little to do with the preparation and passage of these acts; S-M, No. 114J-K, P-Q, pp. 542-46, 553-55.
[19] S-M, No. 115, pp. 559-60.

liked his fun, thought Puritanism no religion for a gentleman, and acted accordingly. As he enjoyed himself, additional laws and precedents were slowly heaped up to confirm the new trend of the English constitution. By acts passed in 1665 and 1667 Parliament revived the old practice of appropriating funds for a specific cause and insisting on an auditing of the royal books afterward. In 1673 the so-called Test Act took away the freedom of the crown to name civil or military officers by providing that thereafter all appointees must pass the anti-Catholic test of repudiating the doctrine of transubstantiation.[20] Some years before, in 1667, the King's chief minister, the Earl of Clarendon, was impeached and forced to seek refuge in exile. In 1678-79 impeachment charges were brought against another minister who was then the King's right-hand man, the Earl of Danby.[21] When the King granted him a pardon, the Commons voted it illegal, and Danby remained in prison for nearly five years. In 1679 also an act was passed to make the writ of *habeas corpus* more effective. The right to these important writs which protected the citizen against arbitrary imprisonment had supposedly been guaranteed by the Petition of Right (page 373), but the royal agents had found means to evade this regulation. Now the law was so phrased as to defeat most of these devices. This reform act,[22] incidentally, was one in whose passage humor played a not inconsiderable part. Voting in Parliament is by the method of division, in which the opposing factions file out separate doors, where they are counted by tellers from each side. Through the "aye" door on this occasion filed a more than usually corpulent lord. The teller for the ayes, who was keeping the count orally, jestingly counted him as ten, but then, seeing that the opposition teller, "who was a man subject to vapors [and] not at all times attentive to what he was doing," had not caught the joke, allowed the addition to stand and went on counting from there.

20 S-M, No. 114R, pp. 555-56.        22 S-M, No. 114U, pp. 557-59.
21 S-M, No. 116F, pp. 572-76.

The bill was finally declared passed by less than the margin of affirmative votes thus created, and although the total number of votes cast was more than the number present according to the records. This teller's "error" has been called by a great historian, G. M. Trevelyan, "the best joke ever made in England." [23]

**The Exclusion Bills and the Revival of Royal Power.** On one matter, however, which arose toward the end of his reign, Charles felt deeply enough to assert himself and risk his throne. As a result, the compromise arrangement of 1660-62 was temporarily upset and for a time it appeared that there might be a genuine restoration of royal power. This important issue, which so roused Charles, was that of the succession. Soon after returning to England the King had married the Portuguese princess Catherine of Braganza, who brought him Bombay as her dowry. There was, however, no issue of this marriage. The next in line of succession, according to the accepted feudal theory, was Charles's brother James, the Duke of York—who, as an interested party in a war with the Dutch in 1664, had given his name to the captured port that is now the American metropolis. But James, bolder than the King, had openly professed the Roman Catholic religion. Englishmen, still brought up on Foxe and in some cases still fearing an effort to regain the old monastic lands, were strongly opposed to a Catholic ruler. From 1679 to 1681 three Exclusion Bills were proposed in Parliament, all designed in one way or another to bar the Duke of York from the throne. Nevertheless, Charles set himself resolutely to secure his brother's legal rights. In a prolonged struggle, which occupied the balance

[23] Godfrey Davies and Edith L. Klotz, in "The Habeas Corpus Act of 1679 in the House of Lords," *Huntington Library Quarterly*, Vol. III, 1939-40, pp. 469-70, are inclined to doubt this story because the minute book of the House of Lords, which has been relied on by other scholars for substantiation of the original historian's (Burnet's) account, can be shown to be not strictly accurate in reporting the total number of members present in the House of Lords at a given half-day session. But no discrepancy has been found great enough to account for the difference noted on the day in question, and in any case no evidence has been uncovered that contradicts, or even bears directly on, Burnet's account of the episode, which is a circumstantial one.

of his reign, he dissolved Parliament, defied the Triennial Act, as rephrased in 1664, by keeping the two houses from meeting for more than four years, and gained his point. This was made possible partly by Charles's own initiative and partly by the fading of memories of the forties and fifties, but largely by the fact that James's probable successor was a Protestant. His first wife, a daughter of Sir Edward Hyde, was a Protestant, and their two children, Mary and Anne, had been brought up in that faith. In 1677 Mary became the wife of the Protestant William of Orange, Stadtholder of Holland, while James had no children by his second marriage with the Italian Catholic Mary of Modena. Consequently, though some of Charles's politically influential subjects thought it worth while to assert the powers they had won in the preceding generation, others felt that in view of the probable short duration of Catholic rule it was more important to preserve the tradition of a hereditary monarchy as a symbol of orderly government.

## JAMES II AND THE REVOLUTION OF 1688

**The Succession and Reign of James II (1685-89).** Charles, therefore, was able to bring about an apparent revival of royal power, and on the succession in 1685 of James—now James II— the new King proceeded to take advantage of this fact. Deceived by the apparent docility of his subjects, he undertook to violate the Test Act by putting Catholic officers in the army. He set up a prerogative court for the Church, under the name of the Ecclesiastical Commission. He also issued another Declaration of Indulgence, which he ordered to be read in all churches. When seven bishops submitted a petition remonstrating against this requirement, he had them arrested and tried for treason. In the midst of these proceedings a son was born to the Catholic Queen. This shattered the hope of an orderly Protestant succession and made the opposition's waiting policy futile. The resulting change of tactics soon disclosed the real weakness of the King's position.

**The Invasion of William of Orange, 1688.** At James's accession the opposition had been divided. One faction supported the claim of Mary, but another, which objected to a woman ruler with a foreign husband, preferred as its candidate the Duke of Monmouth, an illegitimate son of Charles II. An ill-timed revolt of Monmouth's sympathizers in 1685 ended, however, in his capture. With characteristic political stupidity James had him executed. This served very nicely to unite the opposition, since there was no longer any alternative to the claim of Mary and the Stadtholder. After a tumultuous trial the seven bishops were acquitted by a Middlesex jury amid scenes of great enthusiasm. Thereupon men of nearly all shades of opinion joined in sending William an invitation to come and claim the throne. The Dutch statesman was not particularly interested in getting control of England for its own sake, but he was engaged in a desperate struggle with the Catholic Louis XIV of France, and could very well use English support in his Continental operations. He duly raised an army and waited for a "Protestant wind." It came, and blew William down the Channel to Torbay in Devonshire, obligingly shifting just in time to enable him to make the turn into the port before James's fleet could overtake him.

**The Glorious Revolution.** Once safely on land, William had only to wait for the fulfillment of the promises already given him. He made no haste to advance on the capital. James collected what army he could and moved west to meet his rival. But every day brought the unhappy monarch news of fresh desertions to the enemy. *"Est il possible?"* ("Is it possible?"), his bumbling son-in-law, George of Denmark, Anne's husband, kept repeating when such word was brought, until James began to use the French phrase for the Prince's nickname. Then one day the King's best general, John Churchill, was gone, and the next *Est il possible?* himself disappeared. James realized that resistance was useless. He abandoned his kingdom, carefully dropping the great seal in the Thames as he went, and after some adventures managed to escape to France in December, 1688. Because of the bloodless nature of this upheaval, the events of these months are commonly referred to as the Glorious Revolution. The next year James came back to claim his throne, landing and soon establishing himself in hospitable and Catholic south Ireland. But William, with the help of the Ulster Irish, who have been called Orangemen ever since, easily defeated him in 1690 at the battle of the Boyne, north of Dublin. James promptly scuttled off to France again, never to return.

## THE REVOLUTIONARY SETTLEMENT

**The Theory of the Social Compact Adopted.** Immediately after James's first flight a Parliament—again called a Convention Parliament, because without the great seal the King's name could not be used on the summonses—was called to arrange the new governmental settlement. When it met, the harmony among those who had invited William disappeared. They had been in agreement about their distaste for James, but, as in the earlier revolutionary period, the leaders who were successful in destroying the old system could not agree on a substitute. The conservative group, called Tories for reasons that will be explained later (page 493), did not wish to abandon the theory of a monarchy based on strict hereditary right and so wanted Mary to rule alone, on the pretext that James had abdicated by his flight and that the throne had automatically descended to her.[24] The more advanced party, however, called the Whigs (page 493), advocated the full theory of the social compact (page 360). According to them, James had ruled badly, broken the social contract,

[24] The superior hereditary claim of James's infant boy was explained away either by the fact that he too had left the country or by asserting that he was an adopted child, not truly born by the royal mother.

and so forfeited his position. The throne was therefore vacant. Parliament, in the name of the nation, might fill it with whomever they chose. And the Whigs preferred to name William and Mary as joint sovereigns. In the end William settled the quarrel in the Whigs' favor by letting it be known that he would refuse to be his wife's "gentleman usher." The Tories were forced to yield, and husband and wife were given the crown jointly, with the right of succession to either survivor.

**The Bill of Rights.** Besides making a definite ruling on this major issue of political theory, the Convention Parliament decided to put the conditions of the royal tenure in writing this time and leave less to the vague sphere of tacit understandings and gentlemen's agreements. There was talk of drawing up a formal statement of constitutional principles, somewhat after the order of the Instrument of Government. But when it was seen that a long time would be needed to reach an agreement on the terms of such a document, a shorter course was taken, the formulation of a statement of particular governmental abuses to be barred for the future. This was, of course, quite in the tradition of the Great Charter, to which the opposition had been constantly appealing during the seventeenth century. The result was a Declaration of Rights, which, when passed by Parliament in 1689, became the great Bill of Rights.[25] This listed most of the faults of which Parliament considered the Stuart monarchs guilty, and settled the crown on William and Mary on the understanding that these misdeeds were not to be repeated. In this bill were included final settlements of many questions of long standing, on which the opposition had obtained some kind of a favorable statutory or legal ruling before, but without being sure of their enforcement. Frequent Parliaments, control of taxation by that body, and freedom of speech in it were all secured. So were the rights of subjects to petition the crown, and to have juries fairly drawn. Cruel and unusual fines, excessive bail, the Ecclesiastical

25 S-M, No. 120A, pp. 599-605.

Commission, and the power of the crown to dispense with the enforcement of certain laws were all abolished. The prohibition of the maintenance of a standing army in time of peace without the consent of Parliament was a new principle, introduced to cope with an abuse unknown before the time of James II.

**Supplementary Acts.** A corollary to this last provision was a supplementary statute called the Mutiny Act, which permitted the raising of an army and the enforcement of martial law for a period of six months.[26] On the expiration of this period that act was renewed, as it was regularly later, usually for a year at a time. This helped to ensure frequent meetings of Parliament, though the financial needs of the government were a more compelling cause. Another supplementary statute, called the Act of Toleration, gave freedom of worship to all Christians except Catholics and those extremists who denied the doctrine of the Trinity.[27]

**Later Acts.** Even with these supplementary acts, however, some loopholes were left to the executive because of the haste with which the revolutionary settlement was arranged. These loopholes were stopped up by a succession of acts passed before William's death in 1702. By keeping in session for seventeen years a Parliament elected in circumstances unusually favorable to the crown, Charles II had to some extent prevented the true wishes of the electorate from being represented in Parliament in the late sixties and early seventies. A new Triennial Act of 1694 forbade this practice and provided for fresh elections at least every three years.[28] A Treasons Act of 1696 protected the interests of potential opponents of the king by requiring that anyone accused of treason must be allowed to see his indictment in advance, and have legal counsel, while proof of the act in

[26] S-M, No. 120B, pp. 605-06.
[27] S-M, No. 120D, pp. 607-08.
[28] S-M, No. 120E, pp. 608-09. The period was changed to seven years in 1716 (S-M, No. 123B, p. 618), and to five in the Parliament Act of 1911 (page 555).

question was to be supplied by two witnesses in open court.[29] At the same time censorship acts, which had given the royal authorities control over the press, were allowed to lapse.[30] Finally, in 1701 an Act of Settlement gathered up the remaining loose ends.[31] The act was made necessary by the death of the last surviving child of George and Anne. William and Mary—the latter had died in 1694—had no children, and it was thus evident that the line of the Protestant Stuarts was running out. In order to avoid a Catholic successor many individuals with better hereditary claims—such as the members of the Continental House of Savoy, who were descended from Charles the Second's sister Henrietta—were passed over, and the crown was settled on the Protestant Electress Sophia of Hanover and her issue. Sophia was a daughter of James the First's daughter Elizabeth, and her husband the Winter King of Bohemia. Their descendants thus at long last came into a kingdom far greater than the one lost in 1620. In arranging this settlement Parliament seized the opportunity to make a few more conditions. By one of them the action of Parliament in the Danby case (page 444) was confirmed. The king's pardon was not to be a bar to any future impeachment charge. Secondly, the precarious tenure of judicial office which put judges at the mercy of the crown (page 361) was abolished. Henceforth judges were to hold office for life, subject only to charges of misconduct proved in Parliament, instead of holding office at the royal pleasure as before.

## THE HANOVERIAN SUCCESSION

**Anne (1702-14), the Act of Union, and the Hanoverian Succession.** Parliament thus became, to all intents and purposes,

29 S-M, No. 120F, p. 609.
30 S-M, No. 123A, pp. 619-21. For samples of these rules in their earlier forms, see S-M, No. 85, pp. 387-89.
31 S-M, No. 120H, pp. 610-12.

theoretically sovereign in England, as it had been in practice since 1689 at the very latest. It had unmade and made kings, and had prescribed the conditions on which they were to hold office. It remained to be seen whether this new combination of laws, precedents, and the national temper would stand the test of an actual Hanoverian succession—whether those who held the real power would accept a German-speaking monarch, of whom they knew nothing, rather than acknowledge the incomparably superior hereditary claim of the son of James II, who after the death of his father in 1701 had continued to reside in France. William died in 1702—killed by a fall when his horse stumbled on a molehill—and his sister-in-law Anne succeeded him. At first she co-operated in the plan to pave the way for the Hanoverian succession, and in 1707 after prolonged negotiations Scotland and England—thereafter known as Great Britain—agreed upon an Act of Union by which they were united under one government, with a single Parliament sitting at Westminster.[32] In exchange for giving up their separate government the Scots were granted free trade with England and all the foreign trading rights of Englishmen. This Act of Union was largely designed to eliminate the possibility that the Scots—who had been none too cordial to William when he supplanted the direct line of the Scottish Stuarts—might refuse to accept the Hanoverian line when Anne should die. Gradually, however, the Queen, who personally preferred the Tory party, came under the influence of a minister named Henry St. John, Viscount Bolingbroke, whose devotion to the theory of hereditary monarchy was such that he planned to restore the Stuart claimant. To do so he needed a free hand in the government for a period of time before Anne's death long enough to make the proper arrangements. After months of careful preparation the Queen was persuaded to give him the all-important post of Lord Treasurer, but the

[32] S-M, No. 121A, pp. 612-15.

excitement of the political struggle killed her, and Bolingbroke was not given the six months' time he considered necessary for his scheme. "What a world this is, and how doth fortune banter us," he exclaimed when he realized that his opportunity—golden, as he thought—was slipping from his grasp. Whether, in any case, the country would once more have received a Catholic monarch, or have long retained him had it once done so, is doubtful. But as it happened the matter was not put to the test in the way Bolingbroke had hoped. Sophia had died a few months before Anne, but her son George peacefully succeeded to the English throne in 1714.

**Later Unsuccessful Jacobite Revolts: The '15 and the '45.** Still there was a vigorous group of Bolingbroke's followers who supported the claims of the Jameses, father and son, and so were called Jacobites—from the Latin name for James, *Jacobus*. Twice they troubled the Hanoverian government with revolts. In 1715 the son of James II, called James III by his faithful followers but the Pretender by the Hanoverians, claimed the ancestral throne, and there was a rising of his supporters. It was mostly confined to Scotland, and put down without great difficulty. Thirty years later there was another on behalf of the Pretender's son Charles, called the Young Pretender by the Hanoverians to distinguish him from his father, now dubbed the Old Pretender. England was then engaged in a war with France, the King George's War of American history, and "Bonnie Prince Charlie" had some help from abroad. He was able to occupy Edinburgh and invade England, but at length he was put to flight. His adventures during his wanderings and along the route of his ultimate escape to France were even more romantic than those of his grand-uncle and namesake, but his exile had no such happy ending. Eventually he drank himself to death, and with him the Stuart cause leaves the pages of history for those of song and story.[33] Oligarchic liberalism was definitely established in England.

**The Nature of the Resulting Liberalism.** Why we have called this liberalism oligarchic liberalism may be understood by recalling that parliamentary suffrage was still as limited as it was in the Middle Ages (page 262). Furthermore, by an act passed in 1710 membership in the House of Commons was restricted to men having an income of £600 a year from lands if they were county members, or £300 if burgesses. The legislation of this period naturally reflects the wishes of the elements that were in control of the government. In the Restoration settlement the old feudal dues (wardship, marriage, and so on), which had forced the landed class to pay a good share of the cost of the government, were quietly dropped.[34] Instead, Parliament perpetuated the excise (sales) tax introduced during the Civil War period, which bore most heavily upon the common people, since even the purchases of their food were taxed while the upper classes did not spend all of their income in ways subject to the excise. The method of administering existing governmental agencies also reflected the change in control of the machinery involved. The high standards to which the Tudor-Stuart councils had held the overseers of the poor were allowed to deteriorate in the troubled period of the Civil Wars. With the propertied classes dominating the government thereafter, these standards could never be restored. Poverty came to be regarded as virtually a crime, and the lot of the underprivileged, from this time until the present century, remained very bad, with emigration the best available remedy.

[33] "Sound the Pibroch," "The Skye Boat Song," "Charlie Was My Darling," "Will You No' Come Back Again?" "Carle, an the King Come," "Bonnie Charlie's Noo Awa'," and many others. The great Scottish poet Robert Burns, though a tax-collector for the Hanoverian government, was an inveterate writer of Jacobite songs.

[34] S-M, No. 114B, pp. 536-37.

# 21. GENERAL HISTORY
## 1714-1822

**The Eighteenth Century: Constitutional Conservatism and World Power.** During the eighteenth century England's interest shifted from constitutional conflicts to economic development and the expansion of the British Empire. Englishmen were tired of domestic upheaval and content with the governmental system as shaped by the struggle of the preceding century. Accordingly, few reforms were proposed and even fewer accepted. At the same time British industry and commerce flourished greatly. This development naturally led to competition with other powers for foreign markets, which in those days often meant overseas colonies as well. When this rivalry led to war, England was nearly always successful, and her victories naturally contributed further to the growing prosperity and strength of the island kingdom. After the defeat of Napoleon at the beginning of the nineteenth century England was unquestionably the world's leading nation.

## THE FIRST TWO GEORGES AND WALPOLE

**George I (1714-27).** While the ultimate political authority over the country was now firmly in the hands of the classes represented in Parliament, the monarchs were still very important as administrators (page 481), and therefore we must continue to take account of their personalities and policies. The Hanoverian who came to England in 1714 as George I was a fifty-four-year-old German who spoke no English and made no effort to learn it. He left his Queen on the Continent, shut up in prison on a charge of infidelity that was never fully proved. But he brought with him two German mistresses and a set of German friends. Quite evidently he thought more of his Continental homeland that he did of England. Partly for that reason and partly because his title to the throne depended on his acceptance of parliamentary supremacy, he accepted the newly developed limitations on the royal power and permitted his ministers to determine governmental policy on nearly all domestic matters. What influence he exerted was mostly in the sphere of foreign affairs, where he shaped English policy with an eye to advancing the interests of Hanover. This attitude, combined with a natural frigidity and reserve, quickly cost him whatever popularity he enjoyed at the beginning of his reign, and helped to bring on the Jacobite rising known as the '15 (page 453).

**Walpole.** Though in 1714 George had been primarily the Whig candidate for the throne, at first he tried to conciliate the Tories by including some of their number in his ministry. Many Tories, however, were implicated in the Stuart rebellion in the second year of his reign. This served to discredit the Tory cause and put the government entirely in the hands of the Whigs. They did not lose power until nearly fifty years later. In the early years of their ascendancy, however, the dominant element in the party disgraced itself by becoming involved in a gigantic speculation known as the South Sea Bubble. This centered around a company organized ostensibly to trade with South America, but actually used to manage the public debt in a fashion temporarily profitable to the company stockholders—and ultimately disastrous for all concerned. When the collapse came in 1720-21, a Whig leader from the minority faction, Sir Robert Walpole, was called to the rescue. He was hard-headed, and realistic to the point of cynicism, and while he would not take bribes himself, he had no scruples about bribing parliamentary electors to support his candidates, or against purchasing the votes of members already elected—practices not unknown before his time and which soon came to be accepted as routine political procedures. He had excellent financial sense and a gift for managing men as well as hiring them. He remained as chief minister until 1742. During his long tenure of office, in which the cabinet system was largely developed (page 492), he strove steadily to promote the prosperity of England. To that end he simplified the tax system as much as an unenlightened public opinion would permit, and within the same limits he kept his country out of war. His policy aroused no particular enthusiasm even in the ranks of his own party, but it made England strong. So efficient was Walpole that he could not be displaced in 1727 when George I died and was succeeded by his son.

**George II (1727-60).** The new ruler, George II, was very anxious to be rid of Walpole, because as Prince of Wales the younger George had been a center of opposition to his father, and his friends were practically all political opponents of Walpole. In the history of the House of Hanover we shall see many examples of this antipathy between the younger generation and the older, each in turn reacting against the traditions and ideals in which it was reared, after the manner of youth of all social classes. Though married to a German, Caroline of Anspach, the younger George had striven hard to adopt English ways and to have English friends, and although, unlike his father, he kept his Queen at court, in his early years he had several English mistresses. He was not so phlegmatic as his father, but he was pompous, irritable, and fussy about details. He thirsted for military glory, and with his natural interest in his native Hanover was eventually able to gratify this ambition—to the extent, at least, of being the last English king to lead his troops into battle. This he did in 1743 against the French at Dettingen in Germany. To understand the causes of the conflict with France which led to this battle we must go back to the close of the preceding century, when the lines of English foreign policy for the following hundred and twenty-five years were really determined.

## THE LONG DUEL WITH FRANCE

**The Early Wars.** Charles II and his brother, influenced by their religious outlook and by their political and financial weaknesses, had been content to take pensions from Louis XIV of France, and to follow his lead in attacking their Continental Protestant competitor for world markets, Holland (page 445). The Revolution of 1688 meant a reversal of this English foreign policy, however (page 447). William of Orange, uniting the Protestant sympathies and mercantile interests of his new subjects and linking them to his Continental program, devised the fundamental policy and the basic system that were eventually to bring England to world dominion a century and a quarter later. France was the great rival for world empire, and the long series of conflicts with her extending from the late seventeenth to the early nineteenth century is sometimes called the Second Hundred Years' War. By forming intricate networks of alliances and granting generous subsidies to Continental allies, England kept armies on the French frontier until that populous and wealthy power was worn down to the military size of its adversaries and eventually beaten. At first Louis XIV, the Grand Monarch who had dominated Europe during the reigns of Charles II and James II, was himself the victim of these tactics. Some of the destructive work was done in William's own lifetime in the War of the League of Augsburg (known in this country as King William's War), which ended with the Treaty of Ryswick in 1697. But much more was accomplished during the next reign in the War of the Spanish Succession (Queen Anne's War), which was terminated by the Treaty of Utrecht in 1713. By this treaty France ceded to England the Hudson Bay territory, Newfoundland, and Nova Scotia. From Spain, which was now connected with France by dynastic ties, England acquired Gibraltar, the island of Minorca in the Mediterranean, and also important trading rights in Spanish America. The general chiefly responsible for the military victories on the Continent which brought about this treaty was "Jack" Churchill of *Est-il-possible?* fame (page 447), who was created Duke of Marlborough for these later exploits.

**The Fall of Walpole and the Resumption of Hostilities.** Walpole, who was keenly aware of the immediate costs of military operations, did not approve of the war policy. Instead, he strove to keep on good terms with France and Spain and to develop England's internal economy and foreign trade by peaceful means. In 1739, however, English mercantile interests, wishing to expand British trade in Spanish America beyond the limits prescribed by the Treaty of Utrecht, forced Walpole to consent to a war with Spain. This was popularly known as the War of Jenkins' Ear, because one of the atrocity stories peddled by the merchants promoting it concerned a Captain Jenkins who was alleged to have had his ear cut off by a Spanish pirate. The Spanish conflict soon merged, however, into a larger war with France, known in European history as the War of the Austrian Succession and in this country as King George's War. This lasted from 1740 to 1748, though England's formal declaration of war on France did not come until 1744. As in many of her other wars, England did not fare very well in the early years of these hostilities, and in 1742 Walpole was forced to yield his place to other Whig leaders. After a short interlude the Duke of Newcastle and his brother Henry Pelham, also Whigs, gained control of the government. Pelham became the chief minister and held that position until his death in 1754. His administration was efficient, though undistinguished. In the remaining years of the War of the Austrian Succession King George took the field and won a victory at Dettingen (page 457), while two years later the young Stuart Pretender unsuccessfully invaded Scotland and England (page 453). The English successes in these operations were offset, however, by the French victory at Fontenoy in the Netherlands in 1745, and the peace of Aix-la-Chapelle, concluded in 1748, left England without either gains or losses.

**The Seven Years' War.** The next eight years were little more than a breathing-spell for the two adversaries. After some preliminary sparring in India and America, another great European conflict was begun in 1756. Because it did not end until 1763, it is known as the Seven Years' War, though we know our part of it as the French and Indian War. In this conflict England had as her ally Frederick the Great of Prussia, who had been on the French side in 1740-48. To keep the balance, Austria, England's former colleague, now fought on the French side. This shift of partners is known as the diplomatic revolution, and illustrates the ease with which countries might change sides in the prolonged duel. Incidentally, this frequent shifting of Continental powers from Britain's allies to Britain's enemies prevented any one of them from being as regularly on the winning side as was England, and so none of them profited as much from the eighteenth-century wars as did the island kingdom.

**The Elder Pitt.** Once more England fared very badly at the beginning of the war. Minorca was lost. There were defeats in America, India, and on the Continent. As a result the Duke of Newcastle, who had become Prime Minister on the death of his brother, was forced to give way to a brilliant young orator and statesman, William Pitt. Since George II did not like Pitt, the nominal power was left in other hands, but Pitt became the real leader of the government. It was as dark an hour as modern England was to know until "Jack" Churchill's descendant took office in 1940. Many competent and patriotic Englishmen thought their cause was hopeless, but Pitt proved equal to the emergency. He roused the nation, substituted young generals for old, and "organized victory." By 1761, with the help of the navy, which cut off French re-enforcements, the English under Clive had won India, and under Wolfe had broken the French power in Canada. When Spain came to the aid of France in 1762, Havana and

Manila were soon taken by the British. By the Treaty of Paris, signed in 1763, England recovered Minorca and the remainder of Canada and clear title to the North American continent as far west as the Mississippi. France was forbidden to fortify her holdings in Bengal, which meant the end of her power in India. In addition, she surrendered one of her African colonies and some West Indian islands. Thanks to Pitt, England was now definitely on the road to world empire.

## GEORGE III AND THE AMERICAN QUESTION

**George III (1760-1820).** Pitt was not in office when the peace was signed, however, for a new monarch had come to the throne during the course of the war, and Pitt did not fit in with his plans. The new king was George III, who was not the son, but the grandson, of George II. Frederick, the son of George II, who had opposed his father as vehemently as George II did his, had died in 1751, and left his German Princess, Augusta, to bring up the new heir apparent. She had come from a small German court and was imbued with Continental notions of the powers of royalty. "George, be a king," was her favorite injunction to her son. Since she also had him read the lectures of the great lawyer Blackstone (page 509), who emphasized the theoretical powers of the crown, it is not surprising that when he came to the throne in 1760 the new King was determined to rule for himself instead of leaving the chief responsibility to others. By discovering and playing upon differences of opinion within Pitt's cabinet, George soon managed to bring about the fall of the great war minister and to replace him with a succession of more pliable men who were willing to allow the monarch to exercise the real authority in the government. Nevertheless George was something more than the stubborn wrong-headed schemer so commonly portrayed in popular American histories. Besides being the first really English Hanoverian and an enthusiastic agriculturalist, he was a good family man and a hard-working ruler. When reading his private correspondence, filled with solicitous inquiries about the welfare of old family servants, it is hard to recognize the tyrannical oppressor described in our Declaration of Independence.

**The American Question: In Law.** As a matter of fact, it must be admitted that as far as the legalities of the matter were concerned George was in the right in his controversy with his American subjects. Politically he may have been mistaken, but the weight of constitutional precedents was nearly all on his side.[1] The colonists generally recognized the authority of the king as an executive, but denied that the British Parliament had any power over them. Yet as early as 1659 Parliament had asserted its right to legislate for the colonies, and had in fact frequently done so. Legally the American colonies were as much subject to Parliament as were the English municipal corporations. All the distinctions the colonists tried to draw between internal and external trade or between taxation for revenue and taxation as a means of regulating commerce were equally groundless. Legally, Parliament was quite within its rights in legislating on all of these matters.

**In Practice.** Nevertheless, for many years in the eighteenth century Parliament had not made use of its powers in any of these fields except trade regulation, and even there the administration of the laws had been very slack. In the colonies the authority of the mother country was chiefly represented by royal governors, who were, however, usually dependent for their salary on colonial legislatures. At home colonial affairs were the concern of no single official, but were bandied back and forth between the Board of Commissioners for Trade and Plantations (page 492), the Colonial Committee of the Privy Council, and

---

[1] This is the opinion of R. L. Schuyler, *Parliament and the British Empire*, Columbia University Press, 1929. For a contrary view see C. H. McIlwain, *The American Revolution*, Macmillan, 1923.

the Secretary of State for the Southern Department (page 498).[2] The result was that in practice the colonies got into the habit of handling most of their affairs to suit themselves. For example, though the Molasses Act of 1733, designed to preserve the mercantile system (page 314), laid a prohibitive duty on molasses and sugar imported into the mainland colonies from any of the West Indian islands except the British ones, colonial smugglers and the authorities alike generally ignored it. This was because the New England colonies had built up a profitable three-cornered trade, involving the exchange of lumber and fish in the West Indies for molasses and sugar, which in the form of New England-made rum could be used to obtain slaves in Africa for export to the West Indies again.

**And in Equity.** Since the demand for sugar and molasses on the American continent eventually came to exceed the supply in the British West Indies, it may be granted that there was some justice in the American claim that the original Molasses Act was unreasonable. There was also some equity in the colonial protest that taxation without representation was tyranny. The British reply to this was that many Englishmen who did not get to vote for members of Parliament were nevertheless taxed. The argument ran that they were theoretically and "virtually" represented in the tax-levying body by their more prosperous neighbors, and that the American colonists were to be considered in the same class with these Englishmen who did not enjoy franchise rights. But there was really a fundamental difference between these two groups of taxpayers who did not vote for members of Parliament, for the English ones had economic and political interests somewhat the same as those of the voting group, while the Americans did not.

2 S-M, No. 125, pp. 646-56.

## THE AMERICAN AND FRENCH REVOLUTIONS

**The Seven Years' War Precipitates the Struggle.** The Seven Years' War brought this dormant controversy to life. The conquest of Canada removed from colonial minds the fear of the French and made the colonists feel correspondingly less need of the tie with the mother country. On the other hand, the colonial gains registered in the Treaty of Paris aroused new interest in imperial affairs on the part of the home government, while the course of the war itself had revealed some of the inefficiencies of the colonial system as it then existed. Though in times of peace the colonies had been mostly responsible for their own defense, after the war broke out those not attacked had been slow to aid the others and to help with the various expeditions against the French in Canada. It had therefore been necessary to send troops from Great Britain. Furthermore, the entire cost of the naval protection for the colonies fell on the British taxpayers at home. Worst of all, throughout the war the American colonists had been guilty of trading with the enemy in the French West Indies, which otherwise must have been starved into surrender. Clearly there had to be some tightening-up of imperial ties and some spreading of responsibility if the newly enlarged British Empire was to survive.

**The Course of the Conflict.** The effort to make these readjustments, however, ran afoul of the growing spirit of American nationalism and of official ignorance at home—both perhaps inevitable results of the geographical factors involved. The American colonists, long accustomed to managing their own affairs and so far away from the homeland that they were rapidly developing an independent social and political outlook, naturally resented any interference from the authorities in London. The English in general and particularly George III and his ministers, on the other hand, were quite incapable of appreciating the bitterness of colonial feeling or of dealing with it effectively when it began to manifest itself. Hence the sad, familiar story of the attempt to enforce the Molasses Act, the passage and repeal of the Sugar and Stamp acts,[3] and the experiment with the Townshend Acts.[4] In the early years of this new policy George employed one minister after another, but in 1770 he settled on Lord North, a Tory, and shortly thereafter the home government took a firmer line. The Boston Tea Party (1773), the Coercive Acts ("the Intolerable Acts," 1774), the first Continental Congress (1774), Lexington, Concord, Bunker Hill, and the Declaration of Independence followed in rapid succession.

**The Revolutionary War.** In his efforts to suppress the colonial uprising George was supported by nearly all his subjects in the homeland. They could understand the legal arguments of the King and his ministers well enough, while the equitable reasoning of the colonists was lost on them. Furthermore, there was a sizable minority of Empire loyalists (Tories, as we call them) in the American colonies who wished to retain the political tie with the mother country, and commonly these were from the better social classes. Nevertheless, although the British were able to hire German mercenaries to aid them and also had a vastly superior navy, the revolt could not be put down. At first this was due largely to the ordinary difficulty of conquering any hostile country far from one's home base. But in the end French intervention was the decisive factor. When the colonists—after three years of fighting almost entirely on their own—managed to surround and capture Burgoyne's invading force in the Hudson Valley, the French decided to give them open aid against the common enemy. French regular troops were then sent to this country, and, even more important, a revived and strengthened French navy. While the French ships did not succeed in securing permanent control of American waters, for one brief and vital period they did prevent the British squadrons from

[3] S-M, No. 126A-B, pp. 658-60.     [4] S-M, No. 126C, pp. 660-61.

bringing aid to the beleaguered Cornwallis at Yorktown. Thus they brought about the surrender that virtually ended the war. By the Treaty of Paris signed in 1783 Great Britain confirmed the independence of the United States. In the parallel Treaty of Versailles she ceded Minorca and Florida to Spain, which had joined France and the American colonists in 1779. These treaties marked the only real setbacks for the British in a long succession of imperial wars.

**The Younger Pitt.** The failure of the King's colonial policy brought about the resignation of Lord North in 1782. But the Whigs who took over the government quarreled among themselves, and by the end of the next year the King was able to put in another Tory Prime Minister. This time it was William Pitt, the second son of the great war leader of the preceding generation. Though the younger Pitt was only twenty-five when called to office, the extreme contentiousness of the Whigs and a general feeling that they were mostly concerned with feathering their own nests—combined with a generous expenditure of funds by George III in the purchase of votes—made it possible for him to wear down the opposition and to win a general election in 1784.[5] He remained in office continuously for eighteen years. In the first half of this period he was conspicuously successful in introducing some very badly needed reforms into the governmental system. By his India Act of 1784 the British East India Company, which had been the rather irresponsible representative of British interests in India, was forced to share its authority with the British government itself. A Board of Control of six men, including a Secretary of State and the Chancellor of the Exchequer, was set up to supervise all the political acts of the India Company directors. On the domestic front the objectionable practice of bribing members of Parliament (page 456) was suppressed, though, as we have seen, Pitt himself had profited by such tactics. The financial machinery of the gov-

[5] S-M, No. 1281, pp. 699-704.

ernment was overhauled, and very much simplified (page 499).
Furthermore, under the influence of Adam Smith's theories of
laissez-faire economics (page 523), a beginning was made on the
long process of reducing customs duties. In 1786, in spite of
protests from the mercantilists, a treaty with France provided
for such reductions on both sides. The event justified Pitt's policy, for English industry and commerce developed greatly in
the years that followed.

**The French Revolution.** After 1789 the younger Pitt's task
was greatly complicated by the French Revolution, which began
in that year. The leaders of this great upheaval not only undertook to do for France what the seventeenth-century revolution
had done for England in the way of limiting the power of the
crown, but also to put the control of the government in the
hands of the people themselves—in other words, to institute genuine democratic liberalism instead of the oligarchic variety still
in existence in England. Since the English had just been cele-
brating the hundredth anniversary of their Glorious Revolution, many of them at first tended to welcome the changes across
the Channel. But as the French disturbances became more and
more violent and the movement was seen to be going beyond
the limits the British had set to their own revolution, a reaction
set in. A great Whig leader and political theorist, Edmund Burke,
did much to turn English thinking into the conservative channel by his *Reflections on the French Revolution,* published in
1790. Although the controversialist Thomas Paine, who had contributed *Common Sense* to the American cause in the earlier
troubles, answered Burke in his *Rights of Man,* the conservative reaction was soon in full swing. Movements for further reform in England were speedily suppressed, and Great Britain
began to look for an opportunity to stamp out the spreading
fire across the Channel.

**War with France Again.** An excuse to go to war was soon
forthcoming, for early in 1792 Austria and Prussia undertook

to check the French menace,[6] only to have the revolutionists promptly overrun the Austrian Netherlands (the modern Belgium). The English considered this a threat to their interests, particularly because the French opened to navigation the Scheldt River, which had been closed ever since the Treaty of Westphalia in 1648. This meant that Antwerp, now in the hands of a great power, might on the open river become a trading-center and naval base so strong as to threaten Great Britain's position on the Channel. In February, 1793, therefore, the two countries resumed their old struggle. This time they fought for twenty-two years with only minor interruptions. England's policy was much the same as it had always been—to blockade France from the sea, and to secure as many Continental allies as she could. When one coalition broke down, another was formed as soon as possible, until France was finally beaten.

## THE STRUGGLE AGAINST NAPOLEON

**The First Coalition and Napoleon.** In the first attempt Austria, Prussia, Holland, Sardinia, and Spain were persuaded to join, and Russia promised to aid with her fleet. In 1793 the French were driven from the Low Countries and forced inside their own boundaries. But the next year their government became somewhat more conservative and stable, and under the stimulus of foreign invasion it introduced conscription and raised a large popular army. The allies quarreled among themselves, and in 1795 the French occupied the Austrian Netherlands once more, and this time also Holland, which under a revolutionary government soon became allied with France. Shortly afterward Prussia and Spain made peace with France and the First Coalition broke up. In the same year (1795) the French set up a body of five men, called the Directory, to hold the executive authority

---

[6] As in the case of England, however, the formal declaration of war first came from the French side.

in their government, but this committee was soon overshadowed by the rising Corsican general Napoleon Bonaparte. He managed to obtain the command of the French army in Italy, and in 1796-97 he defeated the Austrians and Sardinians so decisively that they withdrew from the war. Thus England was left to fight on alone. Her navy saved her, even though the French were able to add the Dutch and Spanish ships to their own. Forced to give up his plan to invade England directly, Napoleon tried to destroy her empire by seizing Egypt, the connecting link with India and the East. Once more the British fleet, now under the command of Lord Nelson, thwarted his plan, this time by destroying a French fleet in Aboukir Bay off the coast of Egypt (the battle of the Nile), thus cutting Napoleon's line of communication with his home base.

**The Second Coalition.** Napoleon himself managed to escape to France, however, and there he soon took over the government in his own name, in 1799 as First Consul and in 1804 as Emperor. He found himself confronted by a Second Coalition in which England, Austria, and Russia were the major factors. Of this he made short work. Russia soon withdrew because of friction with Austria, and in two different battles in 1800 the armies of the luckless Continental power that remained were crushed by the master strategist. But he could not invade England without a fleet, while England could not conquer him without Continental allies. A treaty of peace was therefore signed at Amiens in 1802. This gave the English Ceylon (formerly Dutch) and Trinidad (formerly Spanish), but left the French in Belgium, and so strong on the Continent generally as to be damaging to English trading interests. Few people were surprised when the arrangement proved to be only temporary.

**The Irish Troubles and the Fall of Pitt.** In the course of the war the French had not failed to take advantage of the widespread discontent with British rule in Ireland. That unhappy island had been treated very harshly after the battle of the Boyne (page 448). To protect Englishmen from Irish competition, ruinous restrictions were put on the export of Irish meat and wool. At the same time, in spite of the tolerant terms of the Treaty of Limerick which ended the war, the Roman Catholics, who were in the great majority in Ireland, were subjected to a long series of persecuting acts. They could not sit in Parliament or hold office, will their lands, teach school, or even own a horse worth more than £5. Naturally these degrading laws produced a great deal of bitterness, with which England had to reckon whenever she was weakened by more powerful enemies. "England's extremity is Ireland's opportunity," ran the proverb. Thus in 1780, during the war with the American colonies and France, England was forced to abolish some of the restrictions on Irish trade. Two years later (after Yorktown) she felt obliged to repeal the hated Poynings Act, which made the Irish Parliament almost a puppet of the English council (page 345). In April, 1793, shortly after the war with France was resumed, England conceded Catholics the right to vote, though not to sit in Parliament. In 1798 the French fomented a revolt in Ireland, which the English easily suppressed.[7] But Pitt then decided that in the interests of unity the Irish Parliament, like the Scottish (page 452), must be merged in the one in Westminster. The result was the Act of Union (1800), which was forced through the Irish Parliament by a generous mixture of bribes, peerages, offices, and promises, including one of Catholic emancipation, that is, a grant of the right of Catholics to sit in the Westminster Parliament.[8] But George III, who was strongly Protestant in sympathy, refused to support the bill that Pitt brought forward to give effect to his promise, and the Prime Minister accordingly resigned in 1801. Pitt's general line of policy was, however, followed by his successor, and Pitt himself resumed office in 1804 and held it until 1806. During the nine years after Pitt's second term of office a series of leaders con-

[7] S-M, No. 129G-H, pp. 716-18.	[8] S-M, No. 126N, pp. 671-73.

tinued the war policy, the last being Lord Liverpool, who took office in 1812 and held it after the defeat of Napoleon until 1827.

**The Third Coalition and the Fall of Napoleon.** The war with France was resumed in 1803, with Russia and Austria on the British side once more. Again Napoleon's plan to invade England was thwarted by the vigilance of the British navy, which in 1805 under Nelson won a crushing victory over the combined French and Spanish fleet at Trafalgar off the coast of Spain. Again Austria was crushed on the battlefield, this time at Austerlitz. When Prussia took up the quarrel, she was beaten the next year at Jena, and Russia's turn came in 1807. By the Treaty of Tilsit of that year Russia dropped out of the coalition, and Napoleon seemed supreme on the Continent. But without a navy Napoleon could not conquer England unless he could shut off all her Continental trade. He therefore undertook to do so by a series of embargoes known as the Continental system. This alienated the Russians and also gave the British an opening in the Iberian peninsula, which Napoleon attempted to occupy in order to enforce his anti-British trade policy. The Spanish and Portuguese revolted, and British troops under General Wellesley (later Duke of Wellington) were sent to aid them. In a series of hard-fought campaigns known as the Peninsular War the French were finally driven back across the Pyrenees. Meanwhile, in 1812 Napoleon's attempt to conquer Russia failed disastrously, and in 1813 he was beaten by a combination of Russian, Austrian, and Prussian armies at Leipzig in Germany. Early the next year the allies invaded France and captured Paris. Napoleon was forced to abdicate, but was allowed to retain the island of Elba in the Mediterranean as an independent principality. A brother of the former Bourbon King of France whom the revolutionists had executed was put on the throne of the conquered country with the title of Louis XVIII. But his reactionary rule alienated so many of his subjects that Napoleon, encouraged also by quarrels among the victorious allies over the

terms of the peace treaty, returned from Elba the next year.
He was enthusiastically welcomed by many of the French, and
soon regained control of the government, as Louis fled the country. The allies, however, reunited by the renewed danger, massed
their troops in the Low Countries and on the Upper Rhine
under the command of Wellington and the Prussian general
Blücher. When Napoleon attempted to attack and disperse these
armies, he scored some minor successes, but eventually was decisively defeated at the battle of Waterloo, not far from Brussels.
He abdicated his imperial title a second time, and finally surrendered to the British, who held him prisoner on the island
of St. Helena, in the South Atlantic, until his death in 1821.

**The War of 1812.** In the history of England during these exciting years the war with the United States that we know as
the War of 1812 was merely an annoying incident, precipitated
by the failure of the young western republic to recognize the
"necessity" of the blockade that England set up against the countries under Napoleon's control. Though American ships scored
some notable individual victories, British naval superiority soon
asserted itself, and the chief ports in the United States were also
tightly blockaded. Stout Canadian resistance prevented our armies
from overrunning our northern neighbor, though the invading
forces did once manage to burn the provincial capitol at York
(the modern Toronto) and thus provide a precedent for the burning of the White House a few months later. In general the Anglo-
American conflict was an indecisive one, and with the fall of
Napoleon both sides were glad to conclude an equally indecisive
peace.

**The Peace of Vienna.** The peace terms for the main war,
drawn up at Vienna, restored France practically to her 1789
boundaries, and gave Great Britain Malta (a Mediterranean
island previously held by a crusading order called the Knights
of St. John), Ceylon (page 469), the Cape of Good Hope (like
Ceylon, also formerly Dutch), and other minor territorial gains.

More important, it left England undisputedly the foremost power
in the world, able to continue her policy of taking almost any
undeveloped overseas territory that might seem worth having.
In that way Australia had been occupied for use as a prison colony in 1787, and other prizes were later to be acquired almost
as easily. So open to England was the world oyster and so casual
was the British occupation of certain territories—taken for reasons which were soon forgotten or were never clear in the first
place—that it has been said that the British Empire was acquired
in a fit of absence of mind. But a magnificent empire it was
nevertheless, a collection of trophies among which little Calais,
the salvage from the first Hundred Years' War, would scarcely
have been noticed. The little sea-moated island in the North
Sea, which had seemed poor and mean to homesick Romans and
decidedly backward to most medieval visitors even after the
Norman Conquest, was now—in an age of new discoveries and
of improved offensive methods of warfare, when protection was
at a premium—astride the paths of world trade with her virtually
kingless people taking the best fruits themselves and well able
to collect heavy toll from all others who passed by.

## POSTWAR POLICY AND THE SUCCESSION
## OF GEORGE IV

**Britain's Conservative Policy, 1815-22.** To safeguard the privileged position thus won, England was willing to join with Russia, Austria, and Prussia in a Quadruple Alliance, also arranged
at Vienna, by which the contracting parties agreed to take steps
against any revolution or usurpation that might threaten the
tranquillity of any of them. This was primarily the policy of
Metternich, the Austrian Minister of Foreign Affairs, but for
a time England was glad to co-operate. At home also the fright
occasioned by the French Revolution and Napoleon took some
time to wear off. In the postwar depression that followed the

suspension of activity in the various war industries the government did little to alleviate the distress of the working class, and took sharp measures against those who tried to protest. When crowds assembled in St. Peter's Fields, Manchester, in 1819 to demonstrate for representation in Parliament, which that new and rapidly growing borough did not then enjoy, soldiers were ordered to charge the crowd, and five or six citizens were killed and fifty wounded. This incident came to be known as the Peterloo Massacre from the scene of the trouble. It led to further repressive measures by the government,[9] including one that forbade meetings in corporate towns unless the gatherings were summoned by the mayor. By 1822, however, a measure of prosperity had returned, the troubles with France were becoming a memory, and a shift in Lord Liverpool's Cabinet brought in as Foreign Minister and the most dominant influence in the government George Canning, who was willing to sponsor a more liberal policy. That year therefore marks the end of the generally static period in Britain's constitutional history, which began with the Hanoverian succession in 1714.

**The Regency and the Succession of George IV.** Meanwhile England had acquired a new sovereign. Beginning in 1788, George III suffered recurrent attacks of insanity, and after 1810 he was both blind and demented. His oldest son George was accordingly appointed Regent in 1811, and the period from that time to the father's death in 1820 is known as the Regency. The advent of a new ruler made no fundamental change in governmental policy, however, for the Tory Cabinet continued to hold office as before. Likewise, when the son became legally king as George IV in 1820, there was no marked change in British policy. For that reason we prefer to take for the terminal date of this section the year 1822, when there was a pronounced shift in governmental attitude, as was explained in the preceding paragraph.

[9] S-M, No. 129I, pp. 718-19.

## THE INDUSTRIAL AND AGRICULTURAL REVOLUTIONS

**The Industrial Revolution.** Throughout the eighteenth century, with peace and security at home—whatever might be the case abroad—and a good share of the world's markets open to her products, Great Britain prospered enormously. Foreign trade, as reflected in the figures of ships engaged and financial returns, sometimes doubled in the space of a few years—particularly when Continental wars and blockades kept rivals from markets to which British merchants found easy access behind the "wooden walls" of their fleet. To meet the greatly increased demand for exportable goods, improved methods of production were introduced. Shrewd inventors contributed ideas for everything from mechanical means of spinning wool to "unpickable" locks behind which to keep the profits. The factory system gradually displaced the domestic one. Hand and horse power were supplanted by water and steam. This great change in manufacturing methods is commonly known as the Industrial Revolution, though actually the transformation was not such a sudden one as that label would imply. We now know that the process of introducing these new processes began as early as the sixteenth century and lasted well into the nineteenth, or even the twentieth. The term, however, is well established, and doubtless will continue in use.

**The Agricultural Revolution.** To the end of the Napoleonic Wars, at least, agriculture, though occupying a steadily diminishing proportion of the nation's population and capital, kept in some kind of step with industry and trade. It was conducted at a good profit and by steadily improving methods. Mechanical drills were devised that made possible more efficient sowing of the crops than was possible by the old broadcast method. The introduction of forage and root crops, such as clover and turnips, and the development of more intelligent systems of using fertilizers and rotating the crops, enabled farmers to keep up the fertility of the soil without the necessity of allowing for fallow years, and thus more and more domestic animals could be carried through the winter. At the same time breeding experiments greatly improved the available strains of sheep and cattle. As a result, the average Englishman had more fresh meat to eat in the winter and a better-balanced diet generally.

**The Enclosure Movement and the Decline of the Yeoman Class.** Against these great gains must be set the loss of the yeoman class and the social problems arising from the introduction of factory life. With the brake of royal opposition removed, the landed class pushed ahead with its long-standing policy of enclosing the open fields. While this made for greater efficiency of agricultural production by eliminating all paths dividing the old strips and facilitating the introduction of improved methods, its social effects were bad. Most of the enclosures were legalized by acts of Parliament in which the country squires, as the gentry were now coming to be called, had the controlling influence. Though efforts were made to provide yeomen and copyholders with equivalent holdings under the new arrangement or give them financial compensation for their losses, the actual result was to put the old fields and even the commons in the hands of the squires. They rented the lands in large blocks to farmers who now worked them with hired laborers. Bitter comments there were in plenty:

> The law locks up the man or woman
> Who steals a goose from off the common,
> But leaves the greater felon loose,
> Who steals the common from the goose.

It had been settled in Cromwell's time, however, that the gentry were to rule England for generations to come, and there was no satisfactory solution of the yeoman's problem, short of emigrating or else changing his calling and trying his fortune in the new manufacturing towns.

> And Birmingham grew so big, so big,
> And Stratford stayed so small.

The English yeomen, who had been one of the strongest elements in the nation from Crécy to Naseby, thus slowly dwindled away before the aristocratic tendencies of the countryside.

**Difficulties Created by the Factory System.** While the factory system made possible the production of a much greater quantity of goods than ever before, it raised certain serious social problems. Not only were large numbers of workers crowded together in unhealthy town slums, but they ceased to have such close contact with their employers as they had previously enjoyed. This led to much inhuman treatment, which was aggravated by the unhealthy environment in which the factory workers found themselves. Long hours of work over a loom in a country cottage could be endured much better than the same length of time in the regimented conditions of the factory. Furthermore, the employees were forbidden to strike. A clause in the Elizabethan Statute of Artificers (Apprentices; page 393) prohibited the laborer from leaving his work before it was finished, and the courts interpreted this as barring joint refusals to work in the effort to get better wages. To make matters sure, in 1799 and 1800, during the conservative reaction caused by events in France, Parliament passed laws, known as the Combination Acts, specifically outlawing strikes.[10] In 1814 employers scored another success when, over the protests of the workers, they secured the repeal of that section of the Statute of Artificers which empowered justices of the peace to fix minimum wages for workers of all classes. This action left the laboring class almost at the mercy of the factory-owners who controlled the means of production, since the workers were not allowed to strike against the owners'

10 S-M, No. 126P, pp. 674-75.

wage scale, however low. On the other hand, Parliament did pass some Factory Acts regulating sanitary conditions in the factories, the education and housing of apprentices, and the hours of child labor—which were set at twelve per day in the act of 1802.[11]

## RELIGIOUS LIFE

**The Weakening of Religious Forces.** The triumph of Erastian principles in the seventeenth century (page 434) had a disastrous effect on the Church. Two thousand Puritan clergy—over a fifth of the whole number in the country—resigned their livings in 1662 rather than accept the Anglican Act of Uniformity, which was part of the Clarendon Code (page 443). A similarly conscientious group of Anglicans, who had been teaching their flocks the theory of the divine right of kings, became nonjurors at the accession of William and Mary. That is, they refused to take the oath of allegiance to these man-made rulers, and lost their positions as a result. Other lesser purges of scrupulous clergymen took place until by the beginning of the eighteenth century the Established Church was left with pliable leaders who, like the famous Vicar of Bray, were not averse to shifting their theological sails with every new political wind.

> When royal James possess'd the crown,
>   And Popery grew in fashion,
> The penal laws I hooted down,
>   And read the Declaration.
> The Church of Rome I found would fit
>   Full well my constitution;
> And had become a Jesuit
>   But for the Revolution.
>
> And this is law that I'll maintain
>   Until my dying day, sir:
> That whatsoever king shall reign,
>   I'll be the Vicar of Bray, sir.

[11] For the one of 1802, see S-M, No. 126Q, pp. 675-76.

When William was our King declared
   To ease the nation's grievance,
With this new wind about I steer'd
   And swore to him allegiance.
Old principles I did revoke,
   Set conscience at a distance;
Passive obedience was a joke,
   A jest was non-resistance.

     And this is law, etc.

.   .   .   .   .   .   .

Th' illustrious House of Hanover
   And Protestant succession,
TO THEM I DO ALLEGIANCE SWEAR—
   (While they can keep possession);
And in my faith and loyalty
   I never more will falter,
AND GEORGE MY LAWFUL KING SHALL BE—
   (Until the times do alter).

Though some conscientious churchmen were left, the country clergyman frequently turned sporting parson, joining the squire in the local hunt and in the deep drinking that followed, while his congregation were supplied with whatever scanty spiritual fare happened to be handy when it came time for service.

**The Dissenters and the Methodists.** The Dissenting bodies— whose public worship was permitted after the passage of the Act of Toleration in 1689—the Presbyterians, Independents, Baptists, and Quakers—provided a few gleams in the darkness, but they appealed almost exclusively to the lower middle class.[12] While they were free to have their public services, their members were not considered the political equals of the adherents of the Established Church and could not hold any important office without taking communion publicly after the Anglican fashion. Prominent citizens therefore drifted into the state

12 The Baptists were a sect that, like the Quakers (Friends), developed during the Cromwellian period, though its English origins can be traced to the early part of the century.

Church, and the dissenting groups suffered from this steady
draining-off of their most able members. Toward the middle of
the century Anglican and Dissenter circles alike were stirred by
the Methodist movement, which, under the leadership of John
and Charles Wesley, revived interest in pietistic, evangelical religion. This was virtually a revival of the old popular Puritan
movement, and did much to keep the common people contented
with their lot during the latter part of the century. But it did
not readily commend itself to the Anglican authorities. An Evangelical wing developed within the established body, but most
of the Methodists were finally compelled to form their own separate Nonconformist organization.

# 22. THE DISTRIBUTION OF POWER
## 1714-1822

**Oligarchic Liberalism.** The Hanoverian succession in 1714, as already indicated, marked the triumph of the coalition of the country landlords, merchants, and lawyers. Through the medium of Parliament, which they could dominate, they were able to control the general course of the government. This is the constitutional system which we have described as oligarchic liberalism. And as likewise suggested previously (page 455), England's attention during the eighteenth century was so fixed on foreign expansion and economic development that there was comparative little disposition to alter this arrangement. Accordingly not much need be said on the subject of the distribution of power in this period.

## THE CROWN AND THE CHURCH

**The Crown.** While the chief power in the state was now in other hands, the monarchs were far from negligible quantities. As the chief administrators of the state, even the first two Georges had great power in routine matters, such as the making of appointments. To some extent this power extended even into the sphere of policy-making, for the monarchs had a good deal to say about who should be in the ministry. For example, in spite of Walpole's great abilities and political strength he had to exercise all his arts to retain his position at the change of monarchs in 1727 (page 457). And George II, as we have seen (page 460), prevented Pitt from having the title of Prime Minister, though he could not withhold the real power from him. In matters having to do with foreign policy the first two Hanoverians were also quite influential, and there was frequent complaint that England's interests were being sacrificed to those of Hanover because of the royal interest in the homeland. George III, as we have seen, made a determined effort to rule as well as reign. His methods, however, were not those of the Stuarts. He did not attempt to govern without Parliament or in defiance of it. He undertook to influence elections and virtually to be his own Prime Minister, in other words, to rule through Parliament in a manner that suggests a pale reflection of the Tudor system. Like earlier Prime Ministers in his own century, he used his financial and patronage powers in the way most calculated to strengthen his political powers. In fact, George was not above doing a bit of electioneering himself. When there was a close election in the borough adjacent to the royal palace of Windsor Castle, where he was trying to defeat the sitting member, Admiral Keppel, he went to the shop of a silk dealer who was supporting the Admiral, and said in his usual hurried way, "The Queen wants a gown, wants a gown. No Keppel, no Keppel." These methods were indeed feeble compared to the Tudor use of the headman's ax, but for forty years during a period of keen party rivalries they enabled the King to hold the balance of power. Recent research has shown that while the King retained his sanity he continued to dominate the younger Pitt and the other Tory cabinet leaders much as he had Lord North during the American Revolution.[1]

**The Established Church.** The churchmen and the nobles, though greatly weakened by the events of the preceding century, also continued after 1714 to exert an influence out of all proportion to their numbers. The archbishops and bishops remained in the House of Lords. Their numbers did not grow as

[1] See Donald G. Barnes, *George III and William Pitt, 1783-1806*, Stanford University Press, 1939.

did those of the secular lords—who soon swamped the handful
of clerics in the upper house—and often they were purely political appointees of the government in power.[2] When this government was Whig, as it was under the first two Georges, the bishops
often found themselves wholly out of sympathy with the rank
and file of the clergy, who were Tories. Nevertheless, they retained a position of moral influence that made them a power
to be reckoned with, even in the worst of the eighteenth-century
decadence.

**Dissenters.** The Dissenters, as already indicated (page 479),
continued to be at a political disadvantage in this period. The
Act of Toleration did not repeal the laws against Nonconformity,
but merely suspended them for those who would swear allegiance
to the new rulers and subscribe to a declaration against transubstantiation. By the terms of the Corporation and Test acts Dissenters were barred from holding public office unless they would
take the sacrament after the manner of the Church of England.[3]
Beginning in 1727, annual indemnity acts were passed which
protected from punishment those who took office without fulfilling this requirement. But since these acts only applied where the
failure to observe the rule was due to "ignorance of the law,
absence, or unavoidable accident," they did not afford conscientious Dissenters any remedy. Not until 1767 in the case of *Har-
rison* v. *Evans* did the courts decide that Nonconformity was no
longer a crime in England. If orthodox nonconforming Protestants fared so badly, it can readily be understood that people
whose beliefs were at greater variance with the creed of the state
Church fared much worse. Catholics and those who did not
accept the Christian doctrine of the Trinity (that is, Jews, Uni-

[2] New dioceses have been set up in modern times, but the number of
bishops allowed to sit in the House of Lords has not been increased by these
new creations. At the present time there are twenty-six lords spiritual, the
Archbishops of Canterbury and York, the Bishops of London, Durham, and
Winchester, and twenty-one other bishops chosen according to seniority.
[3] The Corporation Act was a section of the Clarendon Code (page 443).

tarians, and skeptics) were expressly excluded from the provisions of the Act of Toleration, and by such laws as the Test and Corporation acts they were barred from membership in Parliament and from other civil and military offices.

## THE LANDED ARISTOCRACY AND PARLIAMENT

**The Nobility.** Although it is correct, as a general rule, to say that by 1714 the initiative in Parliament had passed to the Commons, there are so many exceptions to this rule in the eighteenth century that their effect must be carefully noted. Titles were distributed so plentifully in the late seventeenth and early eighteenth centuries that many of the political leaders of the time advanced into the House of Lords. Since these leaders, such as Newcastle and other great Whig dukes, were often extremely wealthy, they were able to devote all their time to politics and to play upon the comparatively small number of voters by bribes and otherwise until they built up considerable "interests" in the Parliaments of the time. These groups of followers—mostly in the lower house—could usually be counted to do their noble lord's bidding, and at times the parliamentary scene resembled that of fifteenth-century England, with actions nominally starting in the Commons, but with the actors prompted from behind the scenes by the nobles.

**Practical Indifference of Those with Theoretical Power.** In other words, the small country landlords and town merchants—who had the great bulk of the votes in any parliamentary election and thus could have controlled the course of political events had they so wished—in fact were willing to let the monarch, the Whig dukes, and a few untitled leaders such as Walpole actually manage affairs. Throughout the static eighteenth century propertied Englishmen, tired of upheaval and agitation, tended to accept the political status quo in which they enjoyed security for their property and comparatively little governmental interference with their business and professional activities. They felt that they had had their revolution and needed no other. Cromwell, who had done so much to produce the revolution and bring the Whig squirearchy to the happy state in which it found itself, was looked upon as a man of blood who had produced nothing but disturbance and tyranny. The "peaceful" parliamentary moves of 1641-42 and 1688-89 were supposed to have been responsible for all the blessings of the later age. So the temper of the ruling class was for law and order, though at the expense of failing to exercise its own rights.

**Inequalities in Parliamentary Representation and Suffrage Rights.** The voting groups even held to this attitude long after the old distribution of parliamentary seats had ceased to represent their own class fairly. Populous counties like Yorkhire still sent the same number of members (two) as tiny Rutland. In the boroughs the situation was still worse. Because there had been no redistribution of seats since the early seventeenth century, big new manufacturing towns, such as Manchester, were unrepresented while tiny vestiges of medieval boroughs were still sending burgesses. These towns, having decayed, were known as rotten boroughs, or sometimes as pocket boroughs, since some local dignitary had control of their electoral machinery and could produce a place in Parliament at will, as though from his pocket. The site of one Lincolnshire borough had long since slipped into the sea, but the neighboring landlord went on sending his sons and friends to Parliament to represent it. Old Sarum in Gloucester existed only as grassy mounds in a meadow, but served the same purpose as its counterpart off the Lincolnshire coast. Even where a populous borough had representation, the suffrage usually, as always in the shires (page 454), remained in the hands of the propertied class.

## THE MOVEMENT FOR SUFFRAGE EXTENSION

**Theoretical Basis.** Against this concentration of power in the hands of a few, protests gradually mounted after the middle of the eighteenth century. Some came from the ranks of the Methodists, those eighteenth-century Puritans who valued every soul alike and thought the common people worth educating.[4] More came from liberals who were inspired by the thought of John Locke and his French philosophical followers. Locke had been secretary to the great Whig leader Shaftesbury (page 492) in the late seventeenth century, and after the Revolution of 1688 had undertaken to formulate the Whig political theory by way of justification of the *fait accompli* (accomplished fact). In his *Two Treatises on Government* he therefore stated the theory of the social compact and supported it, not from the Bible or history, but by the theory of natural right. According to this line of reasoning—not dissimilar to Lilburne's (page 435) —every citizen acquires at birth certain inalienable rights, such as those to life, liberty, and property. By making property-holding a natural right Locke offered some defense for existing inequalities, but in the hands of his followers the theory of natural right tended to become even broader, with "the pursuit of happiness" substituted for property-holding as a natural right. On any such basis it was hard to explain why all men were not entitled to the franchise. The voice of the Leveller was again heard in the land.

**Efforts to Put These Theories into Practice: The Wilkes Affair.** There were several different kinds of attempts to make these ideas politically significant and effective. Early in the reign of George III a member of Parliament named John Wilkes dared to publish an attack on the governmental policy reflected in the peace of 1763. When the King and his supporters secured the

[4] John Wesley himself, however, was a stanch political conservative, and vigorously denounced the American colonists for "rebelling" in 1775.

expulsion of Wilkes from the Parliament then sitting, London mobs rallied to his support. After a prolonged struggle in which he was several times elected and as many times expelled, the Parliament of 1774 was finally forced to accept him,[5] and in 1782 he succeeded in carrying a motion expunging from the journal the record of his incapacity made in 1769 when the Commons had ruled him ineligible to become a member of Parliament. This incidentally established the constitutional principle that while Parliament was a judge of the validity of elections, it could not by mere resolution of either house incapacitate a man for standing for membership in a future contest. But much more important was the fact that the popular will had made itself felt as it had in 1640-42, even though the members of the mobs did not themselves as yet have the right to vote.

**Political Societies.** One of the measures taken to support Wilkes in his struggle was the formation in 1769 of the Society of the Supporters of the Bill of Rights, which championed electoral reform as well as the cause of the popular hero and "martyr." An offshoot of this group was the Constitutional Society, which had similar objectives. Later (1780) came the Society for Promoting Constitutional Information. In 1788 the centennial celebration of the Glorious Revolution of 1688 furthered the activities of these societies and led to the organization of still another, the Revolution Society.

**Proposals in Parliament.** As a result of all of this agitation, suggestions for suffrage reform naturally began to be made in Parliament. In 1770 the elder Pitt, then Lord Chatham, proposed to counterbalance the rotten boroughs by adding a third member for each county. In 1776 Wilkes urged the disfranchisement of the rotten boroughs, the granting of representation to the new manufacturing boroughs, and the allotment of additional members to London and the more populous counties. In 1780 the Duke of Richmond proposed to introduce universal

[5] S-M, No. 128A, C; 129A, pp. 679-81, 682-85, 704-05.

suffrage and equal electoral districts. These schemes attracted little support, however. More practical was the moderate proposal of the younger Pitt, who in 1785 tried to secure the adoption of a bill depriving the worst of the rotten boroughs of their representatives and redistributing them among the more populous counties and towns.[6] He also proposed to admit copyholders (as well as freeholders) to the franchise. But though he was Prime Minister at the time, he could not secure the support necessary to enact this measure, and thereafter lost interest in the reform movement.

**The Effect of the French Revolution.** Then came the French Revolution. At first this, like the celebration of the 1688 centennial the year before, helped to further the cause of reform in England, for English sympathizers with the Continental revolutionary movement were stimulated to draw together in new organizations to agitate for electoral and other changes. In 1792 moderate English reformers established the Friends of the People; the more radical element set up the London Corresponding Society and similar groups in other towns. But with the coming of the horrors of the Terror, which shocked the average Englishman, the conservative forces found a convenient and effective excuse for resisting the suffrage agitation. The right of the citizen to the writ of *habeas corpus* (page 444) was suspended by act of Parliament in 1794.[7] In the next year other acts were passed sharply restricting reform agitation,[8] and in the fright of the vested interests at the prospect of change and resulting disorders in England savage repressive measures were undertaken. In Edinburgh the local liberal movement was suppressed by means that savored more of hysterical panic than of legality. "Come awa', Maaster Horner," whispered the presiding judge, Lord Braxfield, to an acquaintance on the jury hearing an early

[6] For a similar proposal made by Pitt in 1783, see S-M, No. 128G, pp. 692-96.
[7] S-M, No. 126J, pp. 667-68.          [8] S-M, No. 126K-L, pp. 668-70.

case, "and help us to hang ane o' thae damned scoundrels."
When a defendant in a later trial reminded the court that the
Founder of Christianity had been a reformer in His time, he
received the judicial response, "Mickle (much) He made o' that.
He was hanget."

**Surviving Traces of the Reform Movement.** The reform movement was thus effectively crushed for the time being, but there
were occasional indications that the movement was not completely dead. In 1797 a moderate bill, somewhat on the order
of Pitt's proposals twelve years before, was introduced in Parliament by Charles Grey, who as Earl Grey was many years later
(page 546) to succeed in putting through the long-desired measure. In 1797, however, Pitt opposed the Grey bill and it was
defeated by 252 to 91. In 1810 a member of Parliament named
Sir Francis Burdett gained a short-lived popularity of the Wilkes
variety by resisting arrest for protesting against the imprisonment of a president of a debating society that had published
criticisms of actions of the House of Commons. In the same
year a publisher named William Cobbett who in his *Cobbett's
Weekly Register* was agitating for electoral reform was tried,
convicted, and sentenced to two years' imprisonment for criti-
cizing the policy of the government. These incidents show that
there was some public interest in the reform movement even
during the heat of the war period. But the cause made little
headway, and for the most part lived on in semisecret (page
546) among the few who still dared to think along this line.
In general, as was said at the beginning of the chapter, the distribution of power in the English governmental system remained
at the end of the eighteenth century much the same as it was
at the beginning.

# 23. THE MACHINERY OF GOVERNMENT
## 1637-1822

**General Characteristics.** The chief alteration in the machinery of government during the period when oligarchic liberalism supplanted absolute monarchy was—as might be expected—the addition of devices by which the will of the new masters could make itself felt. These devices were political parties and the Cabinet system. Otherwise the routine work of governing England went on much as before, with only such minor alterations as the changing circumstances demanded.

## MONARCH, HOUSEHOLD, AND COUNCIL

**The Monarchy.** Whether the king exercised the real power in the government, or whether he was forced to share it with his ministers and therefore ruled only on sufferance and merely so far as the force of his personality permitted, the monarch went through much the same motions. He met with his Council, issued proclamations, and filled vacancies in governmental offices. He called Parliament, opened it in state with an address from the throne, and passed final judgment on its work. A superficial observer ignorant of the historical background might not have noticed that he no longer met with his Council so frequently, or that no bill passed by Parliament was ever vetoed after 1707, when Queen Anne rejected a proposal concerning the militia. For the pomp and circumstance was much the same as ever. What changes were made in the legal status of the monarch were comparatively minor ones, and not all of them reduced his powers. It is true that in 1760 an arrangement was made by which the proceeds from the royal estates and most other sources of royal revenue were turned into the Exchequer for the credit of the general fund in return for an augmentation of the civil list. The civil list was a fixed sum, which since 1697 had been appropriated for the support of the civil side of the government, as distinct from the very expensive armed forces, but which eventually came to cover only the upkeep of the royal family, its household, charities, and dependencies. But if the bargain of 1760 somewhat reduced the king's control over his hereditary sources of income, he obtained power of another sort when, in 1772—at the request of George III, who rightly anticipated the usual Hanoverian difficulty with children who would not conform to the parental pattern—Parliament passed a statute providing that no descendant of George II could legally marry without receiving the royal assent or else waiting three years and then securing the approval of Parliament. On the other hand, in 1788 and again in 1811 the monarch's illness necessitated the passing of regency acts that vested his official powers in his eldest son. These acts of course served to strengthen the "official" theory of kingship as against the personal one (page 269), since they permitted the monarch's work to be done by someone other than the royal personage himself.

**The Household and the Council.** Both the royal household and the Privy Council continued to exist as official bodies in the eighteenth century. With one or two exceptions, however, they had lost all their governmental importance. The household —now completely divorced from the great administrative offices— consisted merely of the monarch's personal attendants. Some of them retained considerable social importance because of the ceremonial nature of their duties, but they had little or nothing to do with the work of administering the kingdom. Similarly, the Privy Council was important rather for show than for real governmental work. Special committees, particularly the Colonial Committee (page 462), the Board of Commissioners for Trade and Plantations, and the Judicial Committee (page 576), occasionally did real work, but the parent body left more and more of the burden to that most special committee of itself, the Cabinet. Since the history of the Cabinet is inextricably connected with that of the party system, we must deal with the two together.

## THE CABINET AND PARTY SYSTEMS

**The Early History of Political Parties.** From the earliest time in remote antiquity when more than one person became politically important at the same time there have been political parties in the sense of unorganized political factions. Not until power was being avowedly transferred to a sizable group outside the immediate royal circle, however, did the necessity for organized political parties arise in England. A group numbering thousands or more cannot make its will effective without some suitable machinery. John Lilburne grasped this point readily enough, and in his Leveller movement he made provision for propaganda, organized groups of local sympathizers, and regular dues. In the early part of the reign of Charles II Clarendon's supporters were known as the Court party and his opponents as the Country party—names originally used to designate the contending political factions in the 1620's. The real founder of the modern system, however, was Anthony Ashley Cooper, the Earl of Shaftesbury (page 486) who, after serving Charles as a minister, lost favor in 1673.[1] Soon he was busying himself in collecting as many supporters as he could, using for his headquarters a London tavern known as The King's Head. His followers took a green ribbon as their emblem, and were soon known as the Green Ribbon Club.

[1] He probably obtained most of his ideas from Pym, but he was the first to put them into practice in a time of comparative peace.

**Whigs and Tories.** It was this last group which agitated for the passage of the Exclusion Bill (page 445). When in 1679 this struggle grew heated and Charles dismissed Parliament, backers of the Green Ribbon Club in the country sent many petitions praying that Parliament might be recalled to enact the bill. The supporters of the crown, led by Thomas Osborne, Earl of Danby (page 444), got up counterpetitions whose subscribers expressed themselves as abhorring the very idea of any attempt to encroach on the royal prerogative in the matter of summoning Parliament. The two parties thus came to be known as the Petitioners and the Abhorrers. These names were, however, too sedate to fit well into the rough-and-tumble of the violent political exchanges of those days. Each side, following a tendency—not unknown today—to smear all of one's political opponents with the traits of their most objectionable allies or supporters, looked around for such seventeenth-century equivalents of communists or fascists. In Scotland there were bands of extreme Presbyterian opponents of the crown who were being hunted from cave to cave and were not above stealing cattle to maintain "the Lord's cause." They were popularly known as Whigs, and so the Abhorrers fastened this cattle-stealing title on all Shaftesbury's group. It was not difficult to return the compliment, for there were similar bands of Roman Catholic outlaws in Ireland, known as Tories, and so "Tory" was soon substituted for "Abhorrer" as a designation for supporters of the royal policy. Later, in the nineteenth century (page 519), "Liberal" and "Conservative" gradually supplanted the older appellations.[2]

**The Function of the Cabinet.** Even with organized parties, however, the large groups that were coming of age politically found difficulty in actually keeping control of the government. Impeachment of offending ministers was a slow and cumber-

[2] For a time toward the end of the nineteenth century and into the early twentieth century, during the struggle over a project for Irish Home Rule, the Conservatives were called Unionists because they opposed this division of governmental authority in the British Isles.

some process. A more direct tie between parliamentary party and administrative officials was needed. After some preliminary hesitation this was at last discovered in the Cabinet system.

**The Cabinet Committee of the Council.** Like the parliamentary system itself, with which it was to be so intimately associated, the Cabinet idea was originally a royal one designed only to benefit the monarch. The early Stuarts were so openhanded with their distribution of honors that the Privy Council, which the Tudors had kept conveniently small (page 381), was soon inconveniently large. Worse still, it included a good many members whose sympathies lay rather with the opposition than with the crown. Not wishing to intensify ill feeling by dropping these men from the Council, the Stuarts bethought themselves of a device for allowing these Councilors to retain their membership without thereby acquiring knowledge of the secrets of royal policy. The rulers found this in the committee system of the Council (page 382), which enabled them to create an inner circle within the formal body. By appointing only the king's special friends on the committee that was for the time being the most important—say the one on Spain during the negotiations for the Spanish match (page 347) or later a committee for foreign affairs in general—a big step could be taken in the desired direction. A supplementary device was the reference to this special committee of things that did not directly concern it but which might be informally discussed by its select members. In this fashion a new group of secret advisers was created without unduly offending the official Privy Councilors. Because this particular committee met in great secrecy, it came to be known as the Cabinet (closet) Committee.

**The Cabinet Survives the Triumph of Parliament.** Throughout the later years of the seventeenth century there was great opposition in Parliament to this device, because in the hands of the king it obviously served to strengthen his power. Protests against it were frequent, and in 1701 the Act of Settlement (page

451) even prohibited any more such secret committees, requiring that all governmental counseling be done in sessions of the Privy Council and that the Councilors should sign the resolutions they approved. It was soon found impossible, however, to run a government satisfactorily without some such body. And as the restrictions placed on the power of the crown by the Bill of Rights and the various supplementary acts were seen to be effective, Cabinet committees ceased to be considered dangerous, and the section of the Act of Settlement directed against them was repealed in 1706. Under Anne the leading ministers continued to meet, with or without the Queen, in a small informal body, sometimes called the Committee of the Council and sometimes—apparently when the Queen was present—the Cabinet Committee. The practice was continued in the reign of George I, but because of the language difficulty and perhaps because, with his autocratic background, George thought it unseemly for a king to be present while ministers debated matters of royal policy, he soon ceased to attend except in unusual circumstances. In the absence of the sovereign, as a general rule, these committee sessions began to assume the aspect of a modern Cabinet meeting.

**Cabinet Connected with Party: The Developed System.** It was the middle of the eighteenth century, however, before the institution of the Cabinet was fully developed and properly related to the party system. In the experimental stage under William and Anne, members of both parties sometimes sat in the Cabinet, which still depended largely for its composition on the judgment of the monarch. But under the early Hanoverians, the great Whig minister Sir Robert Walpole worked out a system by which the Cabinet became what it is today, the executive committee of the party in power. Its deliberations were to be secret and no record of them was to be published. Its conclusions, though reached by a majority vote only, were treated afterwards as unanimous. That is, all members of the Cabinet were required to support them on the floors of their respective houses or else resign, though this stage of development was not definitely reached until 1792. The Cabinet stood or fell as a unit. If a measure presented by one minister was defeated in Parliament, all the Cabinet ministers accepted joint responsibility and normally either resigned or called for a new general election to test the reaction of the country.

**The Prime Minister.** This unanimity was largely the product of the system of leadership that Walpole introduced. Though he repudiated the title with its suggestions of Continental favoritism, he did create the role of the modern Prime Minister. He chose his Cabinet by suggesting to the King the names of his colleagues, and if any of them differed from the Prime Minister, they must either be silent about it or else resign their Cabinet posts and hope that by a public agitation in Parliament they could drive him from power. The Prime Minister thus became the chief executive of the English government, and would be a real dictator were it not for the necessity of retaining the support of Parliament. To do this he must so conduct the affairs of state as to persuade a majority of the members of Parliament to vote his "government" (group of ministers) the funds necessary to carry on its work.

**The Lack of Definite Organization of This System.** Throughout the remainder of this period there was a good deal of vagueness about matters of party and Cabinet organization, for these institutions were not recognized by any statutes whatever. In practice there was similar uncertainty. In spite of the prevalence of bribery in the eighteenth century, there was no effective method of party discipline, and the two great parties were often little more than collections of personal cliques representing the interests of their various leaders. The great number of permutations and combinations these circumstances permitted made for frequent changes of Cabinets and not infrequent transfers of allegiance from one party to the other. The composition of the Cabinet was similarly vague. From among the many ministers of the crown whom the Prime Minister nominated he chose only some to sit in the Cabinet. The others, like the Assistant Secretaries in the American system, were excluded from these secret consultations. While certain officials, such as the Lord Chancellor and the Chancellor of the Exchequer, were commonly included in the Cabinet, there was no certainty about the matter, as in the United States. The average number included seems to have been around fifteen during most of this period, though the usual attendance was much smaller.

**The Tendency to Two Parties.** In spite of this prevailing vagueness, however, certain general traits of the party-Cabinet system can be made out. One of these is the tendency to limit the number of political parties to two. The English did not develop a great number of separately organized parties, as did the French and other Continentals when they came to adopt liberal methods of government. Possibly the looseness of the early English party organization had something to do with this characteristic—since different factions could exist in a party at the same time without feeling under the necessity of separation. Another influential factor was doubtless the peculiar arrangement of seats in the meeting-place of the House of Commons (page 384).[3]

## ADMINISTRATIVE AGENCIES AND GOVERNMENTAL FINANCE

**New Administrative Posts.** During this period there was a steady expansion in the number of administrative agencies of the government. In 1640, as the result of a differentiation of interest that had been growing up for some time, the two Prin-

---

[3] When St. Stephen's Chapel was destroyed in 1834 by a fire started to consume some old Exchequer tallies (page 138), new Houses of Parliament were built, but the seating arrangements remained essentially the same.

cipal Secretaries—now known as Secretaries of State—divided their functions, one taking the Baltic area for his province and the other the Mediterranean. Thereafter they were known as the Northern and Southern Secretaries respectively. In 1782 a new arrangement was made by which one of the Secretaries took over all foreign relations and became known as the Foreign Secretary, while his colleague turned his attention to domestic and colonial affairs and became the Home Secretary. A Secretaryship of State for War was established in 1794, and in 1801 colonial affairs were transferred to this office from that of the Home Secretary, who thereafter concerned himself largely with the administration of the police and the prison systems of the country.[4] After the development of opposition to James II, who before the passing of the Test Act was Lord Admiral, that position was considered too important to give to any one man. The practice therefore developed of putting it in commission. That is, a committee, usually consisting of three (though later of five) men, called Lords of the Admiralty, was set up and charged with the responsibility of doing the work of the Lord Admiral. Of these Lords of the Admiralty the First Lord was the chairman and the most important.[5] Since 1708, except for one short interval, the Admiralty has remained in commission.

**The Public Debt, Death Duties, and the Income Tax.** The financial system of the central government underwent three great changes in this period besides the substitution, already referred to (page 454), of the excise tax for the feudal dues. The first was the establishment of a permanent public debt, which under

---

[4] At intervals between 1709 and 1746 there was an additional Secretaryship of State for Scottish affairs and between 1768 and the reform of 1782 there was one for the colonies. There was also a Secretary at War from the time of the Restoration to 1863, but he did not rank as a Secretary of State. His office developed out of the private secretaryship to the Commander in Chief of Cromwellian times and was chiefly concerned with the finances of the army.

[5] While the lesser Lordships of the Admiralty still exist, the First Lord is the head of the department and directly responsible to Parliament.

the able management of the semiofficial Bank of England (founded in 1694) became a source of strength rather than weakness to the government. People who had lent money on the public credit were naturally anxious that this credit should stay sound. Particularly, this had the effect in the early days of discouraging attempts at revolution in favor of the Stuarts. The comparatively wide distribution of consols (bonds forming part of the consolidated debt) has ever since been a pillar of strength to the English government, in spite of the fact that the debt is steadily growing. Old debts are taken care of by new borrowings, so that actually Britain has never paid off the obligations contracted in financing the Seven Years' War of 1756-63. The second important innovation was the introduction of death duties (taxes on legacies) in 1796. This was one of the younger Pitt's devices for meeting the expense of the war with France. Though in the early years the rates of assessment were moderate, eventually this tax was to bear very heavily on the larger British fortunes (page 565). The third great change was the institution of the income tax. This new type of tax was first employed in 1797, also to meet the financial strain of the war with France. At that time the government virtually abandoned the assessments on land that had been instituted, on the Cromwellian model, in the reign of William III, to take the place of the tenth and fifteenth and subsidy (page 386) by that time unproductive and hopelessly inequitable, after the manner of all English land taxes grown old.[6] The income tax is generally considered the fairest of all types of tax, since it adjusts the burden to the capacity to pay. At the conclusion of the war in 1816, the income tax was abandoned, but the precedent was not

---

[6] The assessments on land were transformed into a fixed charge, on the basis of the old rate of assessment, to yield £2,000,000 a year. Since this was a comparatively small amount and since provisions were made for individual owners' redeeming their land from the tax by a lump-sum payment at the existing valuation, this type of levy ceased to be of much consequence in the national financial picture. Local rates on real estate (page 391) remained, however.

forgotten, and later it bore important fruit, as we shall see (page 564). The collection of these various taxes was generally entrusted to commissioners appointed for the purpose, though as late as 1769 some of the taxes were still being farmed—that is, the right to collect them was sold to private individuals for a lump sum or fixed percentage, so that part of the return from the tax was left in private hands to cover the cost of collection.

## THE ARMY AND THE CHURCH

**The Standing Army and the Militia.** In spite of the popular English prejudice against militarism, which dated from the time of Cromwell and James II, the necessities of England's expanding empire forced the retention of the hated standing army after both 1660 and 1689. Regular troops, serving long-time enlistments, now attended to most of Great Britain's military needs, and the proudest of the regiments in England's modern army trace their history back to the latter half of the seventeenth century. This development naturally caused a decline in the importance of the lord lieutenants and the old militia (trained-band) system. In 1757, however, at the beginning of the Seven Years' War, an attempt was made to reorganize the militia system. A parliamentary act of that year provided that a fixed number of men, totaling 31,600, were to be selected by lot from each county in England and Wales and given twenty-eight days' training every year for three years. They were to be subject to the Mutiny Act (page 450) while in training, but were not to be deprived of life or limb by the sentence of a court-martial during that time. The act provided that the king should notify Parliament whenever he called the militia to active service, and it also established a property qualification for the militia officers. Since the succession of temporary Mutiny Acts already kept the regular troops under the thumb of Parliament, it can be seen that Parliament and the classes it represented were constantly on the alert to keep control of the armed forces and to suppress any tendency to use the army for political purposes, as it had been used in the preceding century.

**Suppression of Convocation.** In the ecclesiastical sphere the chief change in this period was the suppression of the Convocation of the province of Canterbury, the chief legislative branch of the Established Church.[7] This body consisted of an upper house of bishops and a lower house made up of representatives from the lower clergy. While the bishops were commonly subject to the prevailing political pressure, as we have seen, the lower house was uniformly royalist in the seventeenth century and Tory in the eighteenth. Convocation as a whole therefore aroused parliamentary opposition when it claimed to legislate without regard to the wishes of the secular body, as it did in passing some anti-Puritan canons in 1640. In 1664 the clergy were forced to surrender their ancient right of voting their own tax contributions (page 117). Thereafter they were virtually powerless, since legislative independence commonly depends on financial power. In 1717, after repeated quarrels, the Whig government of that day prorogued (page 372) Convocation before any business could be transacted, with one minor exception. This precedent was followed for the remainder of the period, and Convocation thus ceased to have any constitutional importance.

**Changes in the Poor Law and Its Administration.** In an age of general indifference, if not hostility, to reform, the machinery of local government was little altered. Only in the field of poor law administration was there significant change. Beginning in 1662, "laws of settlement" made the lot of the poor harder than it had been in the period of Tudor-Stuart paternalism. These acts forbade paupers to leave their home parishes in search of work, lest they become a burden elsewhere. Because the parish unit proved to be too small for effective relief work, however, during the course of the eighteenth century the justices

---

7 The Convocation of the province of York suffered a similar fate.

of the peace assumed most of this responsibility. By the early part of the nineteenth century the poor law rates had become very high in some parts of the country, owing in part to what is known as the Speenhamland policy, from the place in Berkshire where the justices first put it into practice. This was a plan of supplementing wages with relief funds in necessitous cases, but it seems only to have encouraged employers to pay lower and lower wages and to depend on public assistance to keep their laborers alive. The result was to pauperize many of the agricultural laborers of southern England, where this policy was followed.

# 24. THE LEGAL SYSTEM
## 1637-1822

**General Characteristics.** Just as most of the general governmental machinery that had done service in the period of absolutism continued to be used in the system of liberal oligarchy, so there were few striking modifications of former practice in the legal field. Only the effort to adapt the law to the great upsurge of British manufacture and trade produced any striking change in the pattern with which we are already familiar. For the rest, the conservative tendencies of the professional lawyers served to defeat all efforts to introduce the fundamental reforms needed to bring the English legal system abreast of the times.

## MOVEMENTS FOR LEGAL REFORM

**Theories of the Extremists.** Legal reform was in the air during the Cromwellian period. To the leaders of the more advanced groups in the opposition coalition (pages 435, 437) the abolition of the prerogative courts was merely a good beginning. Chancery was to go next, for the rules of equity had hardened, and in the former home of plain and speedy justice thirty thousand cases were said to be held up. Then was to come a general simplification and reform of the common law system. There was a widespread feeling that the technicalities on which the lawyers fattened were—like the strong monarchy itself—a kind of foreign slavery imported by the Normans, from which the original Anglo-Saxon Englishmen had been free. The governmental and legal systems were to be reconstructed on their primitive English basis. The Fifth Monarchy enthusiasts went even further. They were devastating in their attacks on the legal profession, comparing its different types of practitioners to the various kinds of locusts that were predicted in the Bible as the plagues to come upon the earth. When they set up their Nominated Parliament of saints, they interpreted the membership qualification as automatically barring lawyers. They felt that if the law of the Old Testament had once been sufficient for God's people it should be still, and wished to adopt it as the only law of the land. Some even went so far as to propose the abolition of all statutes and precedents and to substitute for them the single code of the Ten Commandments.

**Even Moderate Reform Projects Defeated.** The projects of the Fifth Monarchists died with the political failure of their movement in 1653. The less extreme proposals survived the defeats of the Levellers, who had strongly championed them, for these suggestions commanded a good deal of support among the merchants and country gentry, including Cromwell himself. A less popular but very trenchant critic of the established legal system who was writing during this period was the royalist philosopher and political theorist Thomas Hobbes. Committees were appointed from time to time in the different Parliaments, and various projects were drawn up. But other matters were frequently more pressing, and the professional lawyers, who had done their bit for the Parliamentary cause,[1] were solidly and obstinately opposed to these plans. In part, this was probably due to the natural conservatism of professional practitioners who had been trained to follow established precedents, but it may also have been due to a fear that a simplified system would render their calling less profitable. In the end, the lawyers were conceded their wish in this matter. Just as the merchants had

---

[1] See page 358. A special company had been raised in the inns of court at the beginning of the First Civil War, and many of its members had risen to military prominence. Many others educated there, like Ireton, had achieved distinction on the battlefield and had become important political leaders.

secured an increased freedom of internal trade and the gentry freedom from feudal exactions (pages 438, 454), so the lawyers won freedom from legal reform as their share of the spoils of victory.

**Bentham.** For the next century and more the law remained in its generally static condition. It was almost entirely unaffected by the Revolution of 1688, and the ultraconservatives who had blocked earlier attempts at reform found the stagnation that overtook the whole governmental system in the eighteenth century very much to their liking. Not until the reforming strictures of the critics of the law were taken up by one who could speak as a member of the legal profession himself was progress made, and then by painful steps and slow. This "renegade" was Jeremy Bentham. The son of a wealthy solicitor, he was educated at Oxford in the 1760's and later called to the bar as a member of Lincoln's Inn. Freed by his inherited wealth from the necessity of practicing his profession, he was able to view it with detachment, and soon he was publishing works on its obsolescences and absurdities. These criticisms were coldly received at first, however, and their effect was not really felt until after they were taken up and pressed by vigorous followers of Bentham, toward the end of this period (page 571).

## CHANGES IN THE COURT SYSTEM

**The Effect of the Abolition of the Prerogative Courts.** The only important change in the organization of the courts to be noted between 1637 and 1822 is the abolition of the prerogative courts, already mentioned (page 425). While the elimination of these tribunals undoubtedly was a great step in the direction of political liberty, it must be remembered that only a small minority of the cases heard before them were of a political nature and that they had performed many other important functions, such as handling special types of cases and giving cheap, speedy, and effective justice. The courts of common law and equity broadened their jurisdictions to take up some of the slack thus created, in the field of libel, for example. But the British legal system remained the poorer for the lack of such a body as the Court of Requests (page 397). Not until the nineteenth century was a determined effort made to put justice within the reach of the poor man again.

**The Victory of Common Law Courts over the Admiralty in the Struggle for Civil Jurisdiction.** Though theoretically the organization and jurisdiction of the other courts remained unchanged after the Restoration, in fact the Cromwellian era marked a very definite decline in the prestige of the Court of Admiralty and the loss of a great part of its most important areas of jurisdiction. As early as the time of Elizabeth the common law courts had cast jealous eyes on the lucrative commercial cases heard in the Admiralty. Although the common law rules of venue barred them from hearing cases concerning contracts made abroad, they began to permit suitors to allege that Bordeaux or Amsterdam was part of London, and thus to bring their cases into the common law courts. When the Admiralty judges continued to hear such cases, they were confronted with writs of prohibition (page 169). In 1575 a division of the available business was agreed upon, but when Coke was raised to the Common Pleas bench in 1606 he renewed the attack with great vigor. He denied that the Admiralty was a court of record (page 174), that it had the necessary powers of process or of enforcing its decisions, and he challenged nearly all of its jurisdictional claims. In 1632, after his fall, another compromise was arranged, but the victory of the common lawyers in the revolutionary struggles that followed left them very largely in possession of the field. Nearly all cases connected with shipping or foreign trade were thereafter tried at common law, and when the diarist Pepys visited the Admiralty court shortly after the Restoration he overheard the judges scheming "how to proceed with the most solemnity and spend time, there being only two businesses to do." The immediate effect of this victory of the common law courts was to set back the development of commercial law in England by at least half a century, for principles that had already been adopted in the Court of Admiralty were threshed out all over again at common law. But eventually, under Lord Mansfield (page 512), this consolidation had the beneficial effect of permitting a unification of English law and practice in this field that otherwise would probably not have been possible. Principles of the law merchant originally worked out abroad had a great effect on the development of the common law as applied to commercial transactions, but the English common law judges claimed and exercised the right to reject any elements they considered unreasonable. Consequently, English commercial law became essentially English rather than international or Roman in character. In this way, for example, the status of slavery, which was sanctioned by mercantile custom, was refused recognition in English law.

## PROCEDURE AND A STATIC PROFESSION

**Procedure.** Throughout this period legal procedure, already badly in need of reform in 1637, naturally grew more antiquated year by year after the reform efforts of the Cromwellian era were thwarted. Parliament could only be induced to correct the most barbarous practices or the most obviously absurd abuses. Thus in 1772 it was provided that in the future a person standing mute and refusing to plead to a criminal charge should be considered to have pleaded not guilty, and the inhuman institution of *peine forte et dure* (page 199) was thereby abolished. In 1818 occurred the scandalous case of *Ashton* v. *Thornton,* in which Thornton successfully resisted a charge of murder, of which Ashton had appealed him, by demanding the trial by battle to which he was legally entitled under the appeal procedure. Consequently, by a parliamentary act of 1819 trial by battle was at last abolished as a legal means of settling disputed questions of fact. But otherwise little in the way of reform was accomplished in this neglected field of procedure.

**The Decline of the Inns of Court.** Having secured their preeminent position in the legal field, the common lawyers proceeded to enjoy it. They refused to worry about such matters as legal education, and in the eighteenth century the inns of court became centers of idleness and vested interests rather than instruction. Members who were elected readers (page 297) used their legal ingenuity to escape the burden of the obligation. For example, they read one or two lectures in a perfunctory fashion and then stopped, maintaining that they had duly "read lectures" as required and therefore had fulfilled their assignment. The other members of the inns did not bother to protest, and beginning barristers were left to learn their trade however they could—usually by reading in the chambers of some older lawyer. A bright spot in the gloom, however, was the work of Charles Viner. Before his death in 1756 he had produced a twenty-three volume revision of an *Abridgment* (page 409) of English law by Henry Rolle, Chief Justice of the Court of King's Bench, originally published in 1668. But more important than this was the fact that in his will Viner provided for the establishment and endowment of a professorship of English law at Oxford University. Hitherto the English universities had taught only canon and civil (Roman) law. Thereafter they were never without some students of the law of their own land.

**The Solicitors.** With the increasing technicalities of equity (page 516) and the resulting similarity between many aspects of equity and the common law, the ranks of the solicitors and the attorneys began to merge about 1700. Thereafter the practitioners of the joint arts were known simply as solicitors. They became established as family legal advisers, much like family doctors in the medical profession. They did the routine work of

SIR WILLIAM BLACKSTONE, 1723-1780

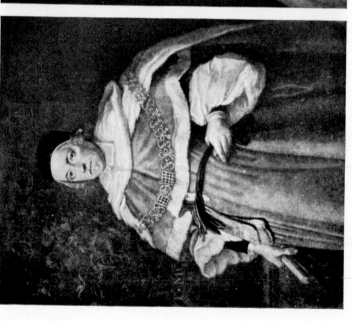

SIR MATTHEW HALE, 1609-1676

looking after estates, drawing up legal papers, and beginning
lawsuits. Only if no satisfactory compromise could be arranged
and an actual trial was necessary did they call in the barrister—
the trial specialist.

**Hale and Blackstone.** The prevailing gloom of the early part
of the modern period was relieved not only by Viner's work but
in two further areas by legal lights of the first class, Sir Matthew
Hale and Sir William Blackstone. The former was a judge of
the Court of King's Bench in the Restoration period, who wrote
a volume on the *Pleas of the Crown* and another on the *History
of the Common Law*. The first did for the criminal law of Hale's
time what Littleton and Coke had done for that of real property
in theirs. The second was a much more comprehensive undertaking than anything that Selden had written in the field of
legal history, and it furnished the general pattern for all later
surveys of the sort. In his *Commentaries* Blackstone, Vinerian
professor of law at Oxford, presented the eighteenth-century
equivalent of Coke's *Institutes,* an inclusive survey of the whole
contemporary legal system. It was designed for students of the
law, and it remained the chief source of legal instruction until
the rise of English and American university law schools in the
succeeding century. Even today there are few students who could
not profit by its perusal. For it is not only a clear statement of
the law of Blackstone's time, but it is written in English. This
shift of language reflects the transition, at long last, from the
use of Latin and law French as the languages of the profession
to the simpler modern practice. At one time it was confidently
maintained that the close, logical ideas of the law could not be
properly expressed in English. Blackstone demonstrated the fal-
lacy of that theory. Nevertheless, this famous legal writer was
extremely conservative on most points, and his smug satisfaction
with the law of England as it then stood marks the height
of professional complacency as to the matter of legal reform.
Though he recognized some weaknesses in the established system,

he was, as the historian Gibbon remarked, a very respectful critic.

**The Principle of "Stare Decisis."** To the general conservatism of the eighteenth century, and to Blackstone in particular, must be attributed a marked increase in respect for precedents during this period. Though previous decisions had long been influential in establishing the law on a given point, judges had commonly overruled them if reason or their conception of justice seemed to dictate otherwise. As the common lawyers became more and more powerful, a tendency developed to regard precedents as absolutely determining the nature of the decision in a similar case arising later. This attitude was expressed in the proverbial rule *stare decisis et non quieta movere* (to stand by the decisions and not disturb established principles [quiet things]). Blackstone declared that at common law it was "an established rule to abide by former precedents," and this dictum had great influence on later courts. But even Blackstone allowed that precedents are not to be followed if they are "flatly absurd or unjust," and it was not until the next century (1898) that the House of Lords ruled that precedents must be followed and that the highest court in England could not reverse itself if the earlier tradition was clear.[2]

## SUBSTANTIVE LAW: REAL PROPERTY AND BUSINESS LAW

**The Struggle over Perpetuities.** In the sphere of substantive law proper, pride of place must still be assigned to real property —an incidental reminder of the enduring importance in the island economy of agriculture, which even after the Industrial

---

[2] In practice, however, the Law Lords (page 576) have shown themselves very ingenious at drawing distinctions between present cases and past precedents so as to avoid the effect of this rule. It may be added that this rule has not been followed in the United States, where courts may reverse themselves and so keep the law abreast of changing social conditions. See Max Radin, *Handbook of Anglo-American Legal History*, West Publishing Co., 1936, pp. 352-58.

Revolution remained England's largest single industry. In this field the old struggle over perpetuities went on. It will be remembered (page 413) that in the reign of James I the common law courts had been forced by Chancery rulings to admit that indestructible future interests could be created by executory devises (page 414). But in a case centering around a will left by the Duke of Norfolk (1682) Nottingham, the Lord Chancellor, reversed the earlier tendency of his court and laid down the rule that future interests created by executory devise were valid only if the date at which they would vest (and so become destructible) was not too remote. He did not fix upon an exact outside limit of permissible time (which was settled later, page 583), but the principle he established then has remained in force ever since.

**The Statute of Frauds.** If agriculture remained the largest single industry, all branches of manufacture and trade combined were nevertheless growing to the point where they produced the major share of the national wealth by 1800 (page 475), and the law inevitably developed to keep pace with this expansion. During the period of the Stuart Restoration the law of contract was systematized and clarified by the great Statute of Frauds (1677). This required that for the future many kinds of contracts be in writing if they were to be enforceable at law, and prescribed the forms to be used. For all this caution, however, business flourished to the point of wild speculation by the beginning of the Hanoverian period.

**The Bubble Act and Eighteenth-Century Business Companies.** After the disastrous collapse in 1720-21 of the nebulous enterprise known as the South Sea Bubble (page 456) a Company Act was passed. This was not repealed until 1825, so that for over a century business operated under regulations made in a moment of extreme pessimism. The act itself was loosely drawn, but in general it was directed at the current abuses arising out of the existence of large blocks of transferable stock issued by companies not subject to strict supervision. Pains and penalties were provided for any group "presuming to act as a corporation," and the act also led the governmental officials in charge of incorporating companies to be extremely cautious about granting charters to those who applied. When charters were granted, they often contained severely restrictive clauses. Thus business was necessarily conducted under legal handicaps. Nevertheless some progress was made. In 1768 a decision finally assured to stockholders in incorporated companies the limited liability for the companies' losses that they were already commonly enjoying in practice (page 414). Unincorporated companies worked out various legal devices for conducting business as companies, though without charters. The most common of these devices was to put the affairs of the interested group into the hands of trustees. Though under this arrangement it was difficult to carry on lawsuits or transfer individual shares of stock, the trustee device had the great advantage of making possible an alteration in the scheme of operation without having to ask Parliament to sanction a change in the charter.[3] In consequence, many companies carried on business for years without making much—if any—effort to secure a charter.

**The Development of Common Law in the Field of Business: Lord Mansfield.** If the law was not to be an absolute dead weight around the neck of business, however, it was necessary that the judges of the common law courts should pay some attention to the needs of merchants and financiers and make an effort to incorporate into their decisions some of the convenient principles of the old law merchant and of current business practice. During the latter half of the eighteenth century Lord Mansfield, Chief Justice of the Court of King's Bench, made a special effort to meet this need. He cultivated the acquaintance of businessmen and had special juries of experts in the world of trade

---

[3] The difficulty as to lawsuits was because the common law required that in such cases all suits be maintained in the names of all the proprietors. On this whole topic see A. B. DuBois, *The English Business Company after the Bubble Act, 1720-1800*, Oxford Press, 1938.

LORD MANSFIELD, 1705-1793

before whom particularly complicated technical cases were heard. In this way precedents were established which adapted the common law to the needs of the growing world of industry and commerce.

## FAMILY AND CRIMINAL LAW

**Family Law.** The basic law of family relations remained substantially unchanged during this period, except in the matter of divorce. The conservative Anglican policy of permitting no divorces with the privilege of remarrying (page 415) could not long survive the victory of the secular upper class in the Cromwellian period. In 1670, after securing from an ecclesiastical court a divorce *a mensa et thoro* Lord Roos, a son of the Earl of Rutland, obtained the passage by Parliament (in its capacity of the highest court of the land) of a bill permitting him to remarry, although the act did not explicitly dissolve the earlier contract of marriage. This formal dissolution was, however, pronounced in the case of the Earl of Macclesfield, who obtained permission from Parliament to remarry in 1698, and also in the case of the Duke of Norfolk two years later. But in these instances there were no preliminary proceedings in the ecclesiastical courts. In the eighteenth century, however, it became customary to obtain a divorce *a mensa et thoro* from the church courts before approaching the House of Lords, where the parliamentary measure was regularly introduced. Thereafter the parliamentary act formally dissolved the earlier contract, though absurdly enough the petitioner could not secure the necessary preliminary decree from the church courts unless he gave a pledge (later broken in most cases) that he would not remarry. In 1798 the House of Lords, by a formal order, required the taking of the preliminary action in the ecclesiastical courts. Soon thereafter it also became the custom to insist that before coming to Parliament the plaintiff must obtain damages in a civil suit against the party guilty of adultery with the defendant in the main action. All this procedure was very expensive, commonly costing at least £500. Less than two hundred parliamentary divorces were granted in the century and a half during which this system was employed. Furthermore, it is noteworthy that the divorce acts passed by the Lords were almost always in favor of husbands rather than wives. No woman obtained a divorce under this system until 1801, and there were only three others granted to women before the Divorce Reform Act of 1857 (page 574).

**Criminal Law: The Old Theories and Practices.** Throughout this period the theory underlying criminal law continued to be the medieval one that by employing it society could take revenge on the criminal for his offense. It was also thought that to deter others from following in the criminal's footsteps punishments should be very severe. During the eighteenth century there were one hundred and sixty felonies that carried the death penalty. For example, it was a capital offense to steal a sheep worth over a shilling. Though the purpose of this severity was to terrify prospective criminals, actually it had a very bad effect. Men would as soon be hung for a sheep as a lamb. If any appreciable offense meant death, there was no premium on abstaining from the most serious crimes after the initial delinquency. Therefore possible witnesses might be murdered to cover up lesser misdeeds. On the other hand, juries often refused to convict at all in cases of ordinary theft, since they did not wish to inflict the death penalty on the accused. This also had the effect of encouraging crime.

**New Theories of Criminology.** A great eighteenth-century Italian reformer named Beccaria argued that the prevention of crime was more important than the punishment of it, and that the certainty and not the severity of punishment was the surest deterrent from crime. In England Bentham was greatly influenced by Beccaria's ideas and expanded on them. It was better, he said, to lighten the sentences so that convictions could be obtained regularly. He also pointed out that by reserving capital punishment for the most serious cases the incentive for petty offenders to commit crimes of violence would be taken away. This doctrine took root in England at the beginning of the nineteenth century, and Sir Samuel Romilly, who had previously been Solicitor General, made a devastating attack on the current administration of criminal law in a speech delivered in Parliament in 1808. This led to the abolition of capital punishment for the offense of pocket-picking, but major reforms in this field were not obtained until after 1822 (page 586).

**The Riot Act.** One important improvement in the field of criminal law during this period was the introduction of a more effective means of dealing with riotous assemblies. Before the accession of George I, if rioters were intending to effect an object of public nature, such as to break open prisons, they were considered guilty of treason. Otherwise rioting was only a misdemeanor. The punishment for the first type of offense was considered too heavy and that for the other too light. Consequently, to preserve public order in the troublesome times following the coming of the first Hanoverian ruler, Parliament passed an act, commonly called the Riot Act, which provided that if twelve or more persons assembled "to the disturbance of the public peace" and did not disperse within an hour after a proclamation ordering them to do so had been read by a mayor, sheriff, or justice of the peace they should be guilty of felony. In spite of this act, however, there was much serious public disorder in eighteenth-century England, for the mistaken opinion prevailed for many years that firearms could not be used on a mob unless the proclamation was read, though under the common law the magistrates had long been empowered to use such drastic means to keep the peace.

**Transportation.** A method of punishing criminals that first became common after the Restoration was transportation. In medieval times persons had sometimes been exiled after being indicted or convicted of crimes (page 197). After England acquired overseas colonies, convicts were sometimes given a royal pardon on condition that they go to one of the "plantations" to work for at least five years. The *Habeas Corpus* Act of 1679 (page 444) recognized this practice as legal. In 1717 another act of Parliament established transportation as a definite punishment for certain types of felony. Later this method of disposing of criminals became very popular with legislators and magistrates. It is not always safe for the American with colonial ancestry to be curious about the causes of the original migration.

**Equity.** Two great names in the history of equity during this period are those of Lord Hardwicke and Lord Eldon. The former (born Philip Yorke), who was Lord Chancellor from 1737 to 1756, did much to keep the doctrines of equity abreast of the times and also to maintain amicable relations with the common law courts. So far as possible he tried to keep the rules of equity in harmony with those of the common law, though of course they were often projected into fields that the rival rules did not touch. John Scott, Lord Eldon, who held office from 1801 to 1806 and again from 1807 to 1827, defined, clarified, and expanded the rules of equity relating to bankruptcy and mortgages, as well as those in many other fields. Both men, however, were so conservative in their general views that equity procedure was allowed to remain slow, expensive, and inefficient. Clerks charged large fees for making unnecessary copies of documents, and years often elapsed between the filing of a bill and the first hearing on it.

# The Trend to Democratic Liberalism

# 25. GENERAL HISTORY
## 1822-1941

**The Last Century: Reform and World Pre-eminence.** We start the last chronological section of England's constitutional and legal history with 1822, because that date marks the beginning of a series of governmental reforms that we shall consider more at length in the succeeding chapters. But the last century of England's history is also noteworthy for the pre-eminence Great Britain achieved as a world power before her position was seriously threatened toward its close. Besides her political and economic successes, England's moral and religious development in this period must also be included in our presentation of the historical background for recent constitutional and legal changes.

## PARTIES IN POWER AND THE SUCCESSION TO THE THRONE, 1822-1866

**The Parties in Power.** As might be expected, the reform movement soon brought the Whigs to power. While the Tories under the virtual leadership of the moderate George Canning yielded to the demand for constitutional and legal change and began the introduction of reform measures in 1822, they were soon carried away by the tide. In 1830 the sixty-year period of Tory domination came to an end with the advent of Lord Grey as a Whig Prime Minister. Under him was passed the Reform Bill (page 547), and thereafter his party remained in power (with a few short interludes) until 1866. In this new age the new names Liberal and Conservative replaced the old party labels Whig and Tory.

**The Succession to the Throne: George IV, 1820-30; William III, 1830-37; Victoria, 1837-1901.** Soon after the Whigs came into power the crown passed to a new sovereign. Appropriately enough, the new ruler was far better attuned to the spirit of the new age than her predecessors had been. Stout and gouty George IV had died without legitimate issue in 1830. In 1837 his brother, William IV, also died without leaving a direct heir, though like George he had for years before his accession enjoyed family life of a sort with a mistress whom he could not legally marry because of the Royal Marriage Act of 1772 (page 491). During his short reign his endlessly dull speeches earned him the nickname of Silly Billy. Victoria, who succeeded him, was a niece of her predecessors. Her father had been of their sort, but like most of the other Hanoverians she reacted against the standards of the previous generation. The reaction in Victoria's case may be explained in part by a very Evangelical upbringing supplied by her mother, a German princess, and her governess, the daughter of a German Lutheran clergyman. When she succeeded to the throne at the age of eighteen, the country had had quite enough of the "nasty old men," as one historian has dubbed her father and uncles.

**Victorianism.** Victoria's subjects promptly took her and her decorum to their hearts. The fright produced by the French Revolution had already led many members of the upper classes to take a serious interest in religion once more, and under the royal patronage Evangelicalism became a real force in public life. This movement also stimulated a revival of interest in the Dissenting sects as well in the Established Church, and the Methodists, Baptists, and Independents (Congregationalists) flourished along with the Anglicans. In 1840 Victoria married Prince Albert of Saxe-Coburg-Gotha, her first cousin, and until the death of Albert in 1861 the two set an example to the nation of a quiet and conservative family life. This combination of religious interest, respectability, and domesticity is generally known as Victorianism.

Another strong, though different, religious force was that represented by the Oxford (High Church) Movement, which began to develop in the 1830's. This emphasized the Catholic tradition of the English Church and its adherents opposed the prevailing Erastian tendency, that is, the tendency to subject the Church to the State and to settle religious questions by political means.

## FOREIGN AND IMPERIAL AFFAIRS

**Foreign Affairs.** During the first half of Queen Victoria's long reign England retained her position of world supremacy virtually unchallenged. France was too occupied with internal problems to give the English much cause for thought, and Germany and Italy were so divided politically (during most of this period) as to be called mere geographical expressions. Czarist Russia was stirring uneasily, however, looking for a port that would be open to world commerce and ice-free the year round. The bear that walked like a man was thirsty for warm water, as Kipling put it. In the Crimean War of 1854-56, fought in southern Russia, England secured the help of France, Turkey, and Sardinia—the nucleus of the modern Italy—in thwarting the Russian ambition to control the Dardanelles, the gateway to the Black Sea. Great Britain thus succeeded in keeping a powerful rival out of Constantinople and the "life line of the Empire," the Mediterranean route to India. During the American Civil War of 1861-65 the British government, though controlled by the Liberals, tended to favor the cause of the aristocratic South. This was partly because the Liberal leaders, headed by Lord Palmerston, were aristocrats themselves, and partly because some of them hoped to weaken a potentially dangerous rival by encouraging the seceders, in accordance with the age-old formula of divide and rule. By skillful diplomacy on the part of President Lincoln, however, Great Britain was prevented from committing herself too far, and an open clash was averted.

**The Empire, 1822-66.** For some time after the loss of the American colonies in 1783 many Englishmen doubted whether the political ties with any of their English-speaking colonies would stand the strain of developing nationalism and economic jealousy in the overseas settlements. They would all fall away like ripe fruit from the tree, said the pessimists. But one school of colonial statesmen, headed by an ingenious writer named Gibbon Wakefield, maintained that the loyalty of the colonists could be retained if they were given a greater degree of self-government than the thirteen American colonies had received. In 1839, in a report on the situation in Canada Lord Durham, who had adopted Wakefield's views, recommended that discontent in those provinces be allayed by the grant of self-government in all matters except those directly affecting relations with the mother country.[1] Though these recommendations were not immediately accepted, the Durham Report became the basis of the new British Empire. By 1848 its main principles were put into practice in Canada,[2] and shortly afterward similar grants of self-government were made to the provinces of Australia and to New Zealand, which had been annexed in 1839. Regions with large non-European populations were not granted self-government, however. Though nearly all of India had been brought under British control by the middle of the nineteenth century, it remained under the joint rule of the East India Company and the Westminster Parliament, or else under native princes who took "advice" from British Residents, accredited, like ambassadors, to their courts. A serious native uprising, known as the Indian Mutiny, broke out in 1857 and was not completely suppressed until 1859. One result of the Indian Mutiny was the final transfer of all East India Company powers to the English crown. Though some natives were afterward included in the various governmental councils, the real power remained in the hands

[1] S-M, No. 133A, pp. 776-79.
[2] S-M, No. 133B-J, pp. 779-92, particularly No. 133H, p. 790.

of the English Governor General (Viceroy) and his British assistants.

**Economic Prosperity and Free Trade, 1822-66.** At home, in spite of occasional temporary setbacks the country's economic activities expanded rapidly after recovery from the depression that followed the Napoleonic Wars. Because England had a long head start over other countries in the industrial race and could easily meet nearly any foreign competition, her manufacturers were anxious to eliminate as many barriers to trade as possible. As a result they readily adopted the arguments for free trade that had been put out by the great eighteenth-century Scottish economist Adam Smith. Under pressure from them import duties on manufactured articles and raw materials were steadily reduced. The landed interests, which feared competition from agricultural countries overseas, had long been protected by tariff acts known as Corn Laws, which imposed duties on imported foodstuffs. They were therefore opposed to the idea of free trade. But the Liberal leaders formed a national organization known as the Anti-Corn Law League, which kept up a continual agitation for the repeal of these acts. A great famine in Ireland helped the cause of this league by demonstrating the desirability of cheap food, and in 1846 the Corn Laws were repealed. In 1849 the Navigation Acts (page 247) were repealed,[3] and after the middle of the century England was virtually a free-trade country, with her markets open to the goods of the world. This made food cheap and therefore enabled English manufacturers to keep wages low and production costs down, which aided them in meeting foreign competition. At the same time the abolition of tariffs helped foreign buyers to pay for their purchases, since they could ship in raw materials or various kinds of luxury goods without having to pay duty on them. Industry, commerce, and even agriculture—after a temporary slump—prospered so remark-

[3] S-M, No. 131C, p. 735.

ably during the twenty years following this shift in economic policy that those who had opposed the change soon dropped the issue.

## THE SECOND HALF OF VICTORIA'S REIGN

**Parties in Power, 1866-1901.** After the death of her husband Victoria remained in seclusion for some years "enjoying" her widowhood as some people are supposed to "enjoy" ill health. But her government was ably carried on by the Conservative and Liberal leaders, of whom Benjamin Disraeli and William E. Gladstone were the most important. These men exchanged places every few years and took turns in shaping the national policies. In general the Conservatives were more vigorous in their foreign program, while the Liberals emphasized domestic reform. But both parties were sufficiently in agreement on major issues, so that the changes of ministries did not fundamentally affect the course of events.

**Imperial Expansion and Foreign Affairs, 1866-1901.** The latter half of Victoria's reign marks the height of Great Britain's power. Though Germany and Italy became unified in 1870, their challenge to British supremacy was not considered serious enough to necessitate any important diplomatic shift. England remained without any alliances, feeling confident of her ability to deal with Russia, who was still regarded as her chief rival. In the general rush for overseas colonies that marked the 1880's and 1890's some concessions were made in France, Germany, and Italy, but Great Britain still took the lion's share. Between 1875 and 1882 England obtained virtual control of the Suez Canal and of Egypt. In 1886 the conquest of Burma was completed. Eight years later Great Britain took over Uganda in Central Africa, which had already been occupied by a British company in 1888. In 1899 Nigeria in West Africa was acquired in similar fashion, and in the same year the Sudan was subjugated, to mention only some of the most important prizes in 1887. In order to strengthen the ties of the Empire, in 1876 Disraeli persuaded Victoria to take the title of Empress of India. In 1887 and in 1897, on the fiftieth and sixtieth anniversaries of Victoria's accession, imperial jubilees were celebrated in London, which made the British people more and more conscious of the greatness of their Empire. The one really unpleasant incident in the long series of triumphs was the Boer War (1899-1902), which the British fought to secure undisputed control of South Africa. After the occupation of Cape Colony during the Napoleonic Wars, many of the Boers, the descendants of the original Dutch settlers, moved inland and founded two independent states of their own, the Orange Free State and the Transvaal South African Republic. There was a good deal of friction between these states and the British all through the remainder of the century, but after the discovery of gold in the Transvaal in 1884 matters gradually came to a head. Cecil Rhodes, a wealthy mine operator and the Premier of Cape Colony, was the leader of the movement to bring all of South Africa under British control. Backed by Conservative governments in London, he pursued a vigorous policy that eventually brought on the war, though Rhodes himself was not in office at the time. The English anticipated an easy victory, but the Boer farmers held out for three long years against all the forces the widespread British Empire could bring against them. By the time they were overcome many Englishmen, particularly the Liberals, who were traditionally cool on the matter of imperial expansion, were questioning the value of such expensive additions to the Empire.

> For our chiefs said "Done," and I did not deem it;
> Our seers said "Peace," and it was not peace;
> Earth will grow worse till men redeem it
> And wars more evil, ere all wars cease.

**The Dominions.** With the colonial areas to which self-government had already been conceded (page 522), however, the mother country continued to show herself generous. In 1867 the British North America Act consolidated the provinces of Nova Scotia, New Brunswick, and Upper and Lower Canada (Quebec and Ontario) into a single Dominion of Canada, with a federal constitution and provision for the admission of new provinces as the western lands should be settled.[4] Though providing for a federal system, the Canadian plan of government differs in various ways from that of the United States. Instead of having a separation of powers between the legislative, executive, and judicial branches of the government, it follows the English pattern of responsible cabinet government, already described. The Governor General, who represents the English monarch, takes the advice of his Canadian ministers just as his royal master follows the lead of his English ones.[5] Furthermore, instead of the provinces' delegating certain powers to the federal government, as our states do, the chief power is in the hands of the Dominion government, with certain specific powers assigned to the provinces by the 1867 act. In 1900 the Commonwealth of Australia Act set up a similar federal government for Tasmania and the provinces of Australia.[6]

**Economic Trends.** In the economic sphere England was the undisputed leader of the world during the early part of the period from 1866 to 1901, but toward the end was beginning to feel the effects of challenges from aspiring rivals. Until 1873 the country enjoyed that remarkable prosperity which followed the adoption of free trade. But then came a depression. British agriculture began to suffer from the competition of cheap land overseas. Improved methods of production and transportation made it possible to import wheat and meat from America, Australia,

[4] S-M, No. 131G, pp. 738-44.
[5] Because Canada has a written constitution that is considered the supreme law of the land, however, it does employ the doctrine of judicial review and permit its judges to declare unconstitutional acts of provincial or Dominion Parliaments conflicting with it.
[6] S-M, No. 135F, pp. 811-17.

New Zealand, and Argentina at prices the home producers could not meet. Some British farmers turned to dairying and truck gardening, but no fully satisfactory solution of their problem was found. British industry also suffered in the same depression. American factories were winning some of the markets formerly supplied from England, and after the unification of Germany in 1870 German manufacturers also became keen competitors. In the 80's and 90's British industry made something of a recovery, and in 1900 England's exports still exceeded in value those of any other country. But she was no longer the undisputed "workshop of the world," as she had once been.

**Religious Trends, 1866-1901.** The age of England's prosperity was one of religious decline. The publication of Darwin's *Origin of Species* in 1859 undermined the foundations of Evangelicalism without providing any satisfactory substitute. Men and women lost in admiration of imperialistic successes and material progress were slow to appreciate the loss. Here and there a warning voice was raised, like Kipling's after Victoria's second imperial jubilee:

> The tumult and the shouting dies;
> The Captains and the Kings depart:
> Still stands Thine ancient sacrifice,
> An humble and a contrite heart.
> Lord God of Hosts, be with us yet,
> Lest we forget—lest we forget!

But the average citizen, totaling up his profits, paid little attention.

## THE TWENTIETH CENTURY: THE SUCCESSION AND PARTIES IN POWER

**The Royal Succession, 1901-41.** Victoria did not live to see the end of the Boer War. She died in January, 1901, at the age of eighty-one and was succeeded by her eldest son Edward VII. Edward had followed the Hanoverian pattern of reacting against the parental ways and his tastes were not at all Victorian.[7] But he was nearly sixty when he came to the throne, and as he reigned only nine years, he did not upset the tradition of monarchical decorum that George III had begun and which Victoria had done so much to establish. His son George V, who followed him in 1910, faithfully conformed to the Victorian tradition, and by the time of his death in 1936 had become very popular with his subjects. Like his grandmother, he developed into a kind of symbol of all that his people wished themselves to be. As might be expected, however, his oldest son and successor was a throw-back to Edward VII. Though still a bachelor when he succeeded to the throne at the age of forty-one, before the end of the year he announced his intention of marrying an American woman named Mrs. Simpson, who had been twice married and was about to secure her second divorce. This made his position untenable, not because he was proposing to do anything illegal, but merely because in doing what one of his more obscure subjects would be permitted to do he was failing to measure up to the moral ideal that, rightly or wrongly, the British have set for their mon-archs since Victoria's time. The pressure of public opinion forced him to abdicate on December 10, 1936.[8] He was succeeded by his brother Albert, who took the title of George VI in the effort to suggest a continuation of his father's popular regime.[9] The new King, a properly domestic husband and father, threw him-self into the traditional constitutional monarch's work of making public appearances and setting social standards with such con-scientious devotion that he soon acquired something of the posi-tion his father had occupied in the hearts of his subjects. During the war that began in 1939 his willingness to share the dangers of the London bombings with his subjects and his refusal to send

[7] The name "Hanoverian" is still loosely applied to the reigning house, though on Victoria's marriage to her cousin Albert its name legally became Saxe-Coburg-Gotha, or Wettin, which was changed to Windsor during the World War of 1914-18.

[8] S-M, No. 142, pp. 885-91.    [9] S-M, No. 143, p. 891.

his own children out of the country further strengthened his popularity.

**Parties in Power, 1901-41.** Though a new party, Labor, began to appear on the political scene, Conservatives and Liberals continued to alternate in power until 1916. Then the stress of the First World War forced the adoption of a coalition Cabinet that united representation of all parties in a government under the leadership of the Liberal David Lloyd George. This coalition arrangement lasted until 1922, when the old system of party Cabinets was resumed, with the Conservatives in control. At the general election held in 1923, however, Labor proved so strong that no one party secured a majority, and a Labor-Liberal coalition Cabinet was formed, headed by the Labor leader Ramsay MacDonald. He alternated with Stanley Baldwin, the Conservative leader, until 1931. In that year a serious economic crisis led the country to resort once more to a national government, with a Cabinet made up of representatives of all parties, though the majority of the Laborites refused to co-operate, and it was in effect a Conservative government. This national government headed in turn by MacDonald, Baldwin, and Neville Chamberlain was still in power when the Second World War broke out in 1939. In that emergency an agreement was made to adjourn political activity for the duration of the war and to leave each party in possession of what seats in Parliament it already held. But after British reverses in the spring of 1940 Winston Churchill succeeded Neville Chamberlain as Prime Minister, and more representatives of Labor were taken into the Cabinet.

## FOREIGN AFFAIRS

**The Triple Entente.** After the conclusion of the Boer War in 1902 Great Britain at last abandoned the policy of isolation to which she had clung throughout the nineteenth century. In that year she contracted an alliance with Japan to ensure the protection of her interests in the Far East, but the chief problem was the European one. Germany already had an alliance with Austria-Hungary and Italy. Her army was the best in Europe. Her competition for world trade was increasingly serious. In Kaiser Wilhelm II she had an aggressive ruler, and in the late 1890's she embarked on an ambitious program of building up her navy. In these circumstances England's difficulties in overcoming the Boers, plus the fact that she received scant sympathy from any European power during the struggle, convinced the British government that it must henceforth have working agreements with Germany's main rivals on the Continent. Consequently, outstanding differences with France and Russia were hastily patched up, and by 1907 the Triple Alliance of Germany, Austria-Hungary, and Italy was confronted by a Triple Entente (Triple Understanding) of England, France, and Russia. In arranging this Entente Edward VII, who had spent considerable time in France and was popular there, did rather more than might normally be expected of a "constitutional" monarch. His personal relations with Wilhelm, his sister's son, also had something to do with storing up fuel for the approaching conflagration. For the Kaiser—who already had developed something of an inferiority complex from a withered arm that he, not without reason, attributed to his mother's blind faith in the universal superiority of English doctors—was goaded to fury by the patronizing lectures of his self-satisfied uncle. Edward, however, escaped the holocaust by dying in 1910. His son George V was reigning in 1914 when the spark was supplied by the assassination of the Austrian Archduke Francis Ferdinand at Serajevo, a political murder growing out of the rising nationalism of the Balkan peoples and the rivalry of Slav and Teuton in that area.

**The First World War and the Versailles Treaty.** Instead of fighting with her original allies, Italy remained neutral at first, and later entered the war on the British side. Japan remained

true to her alliance with England, and eventually the United
States also fought on Britain's side. Yet, even so, England and
her Empire were saved only after four years of bitter struggle.
In that time Great Britain lost nearly a million men and was
very nearly starved out by the German submarine blockade. Consequently, while many Englishmen agreed with President Wilson
in trying to write into the peace treaty provisions that would
help to eliminate the cause of such conflicts, others co-operated
with the French Premier Clemenceau in undermining this effort. The Treaty of Versailles was therefore neither a peace of
vengeance and maximum Allied security nor one of generosity
and justice, but something in between. It set up a League of
Nations, designed to modify unjust provisions of the treaty, but
the immediate terms were so contrary to the spirit of the Fourteen Points—the American peace program—that the United States,
rightly or wrongly, refused to join the League. Thereafter England wavered between the two policies, at times standing by
France in her effort to prevent a recovery of Germany's military
strength and at other times conniving in German violation of
the restrictive clauses of the treaty. In following the latter course
the British seem to have been actuated largely by a desire to
use Germany to counterbalance the French power on the Continent.

## IMPERIAL PROBLEMS

**Ireland and Egypt.** Since the First World War stimulated nationalistic sentiment throughout the world, it greatly complicated the already difficult problem of holding the British Empire
together. For forty years before the outbreak of the war Ireland had been struggling to obtain home rule, that is, the repeal
of the Act of Union of 1800 and the establishment of her own
autonomous government. In 1916, following the old slogan that
England's extremity is Ireland's opportunity, the leaders of an
extremist party called Sinn Fein endeavored to set up an Irish

republic. They succeeded in occupying the general post office
and some other government buildings in Dublin, but the revolt
was soon suppressed by English soldiers. The agitation continued, however, and by 1921 guerrilla warfare finally wrung
from the British a concession of autonomy for Roman Catholic
south Ireland, then called the Irish Free State and now Eire.[10]
According to the constitution of the new state it was to have
Dominion status on the Canadian model. Protestant Northern
Ireland (Ulster) was separated from the Roman Catholic section
and given its own government also. Egypt—nominally an independent kingdom—likewise succeeded in gaining a large measure of practical independence under a treaty concluded in 1936.

**India and Palestine.** Elsewhere the British were less generous.
In order to secure native co-operation during the war the British
government stated that it intended to increase the share of In-
dians in their own government gradually until self-government
should ultimately be realized. After the war the principle of dy-
archy (dual rule) was introduced into the government of India.
By it certain services, such as education and health, were put
under native control. But others, such as justice and police,
were reserved for British control, and under the native Hindu
leader Gandhi widespread discontent made itself felt in the form
of boycotts of British goods and passive resistance against British
authority. By the India Act of 1935 the British made a further
concession. Provinces were to be entirely under native control
except in cases where peace or the rights of minorities were at
stake. The national assembly—where the native states as well
as British provinces were to be represented—was to have a responsible ministry by whom the British Governor General was
to be guided. But problems of defense, foreign relations, and
religion were left in British hands, and native nationalist sentiment is still far from satisfied. In Palestine the problem was
even more complicated, for in the war emergency the British

10 S-M, No. 137I, pp. 833-35.

had practically promised the same territory to both Arabs and Jews. After the war the area became a British mandate under the League of Nations, and the Arabs at first welcomed the Jewish Zionist immigrants and their foreign money. But as the flood of Jewish settlers continued, hostilities broke out between the two peoples. In desperation the British proposed to divide the country between the contending factors, but no agreement had been reached when the major difficulties of 1939 forced the Palestinian troubles into the background.

**The Dominions.** More peaceful, but equally dangerous to the established concept of empire, were the changes that occurred in the relations between the mother country and Canada, Australia, New Zealand, and South Africa.[11] Under the Treaty of Versailles these Dominions were allowed separate representation in the League of Nations Assembly, and they did not always see eye to eye with Great Britain on problems of foreign relations. Penetrated by the spirit of nationalism and anxious to foster their own infant industries, they also put protective tariffs on manufactured goods coming from abroad, including even those from the homeland. In 1931 they obtained from the British Parliament the Statute of Westminster by which each Dominion was recognized as fully self-governing.[12] The Colonial Laws Validity Act of 1865, which previously had invalidated any act of a colonial legislature that was repugnant to an act of the British Parliament affecting the colony, was now voided as far as the Dominions were concerned.[13] Thereafter the Parlia-

[11] Cape Colony, Natal, and the two conquered Boer republics were organized into the Union of South Africa and given Dominion status in 1910; S-M, No. 136B, pp. 817-22. The statute was dated 1909, but did not go into effect until the following year.

[12] S.M, No. 137M, pp. 839-41. *Cf.* No. 140, pp. 878-83. It was provided, however, that this power should not extend to alterations of the British North America Acts or the Constitutional Acts of Australia and New Zealand. But the Irish Free State was left free to alter its constitution and did so in 1933 by eliminating the oath of allegiance to the British king and barring appeals from the decisions of Irish courts to the Judicial Committee of the Privy Council; S-M, No. 139F, pp. 875-78.

[13] S-M, No. 131F, pp. 737-38.

ment of the mother country could not legislate for the Dominions without their consent, and without similar permission no English court could invalidate the acts of Dominion legislatures or rule on Dominion cases. Furthermore, it was provided that "any alteration in the law touching the succession to the throne . . . shall hereafter require the assent . . . of all the Dominions." The Dominions thus became virtually independent countries, bound to the homeland only by the fact that they owed allegiance to a common sovereign. The sentimental tie remained strong, however, and at the Imperial Conference of representatives from Great Britain, the self-governing Dominions, and India held at Ottawa in 1932 some progress was made in the direction of granting preferential tariffs to goods produced within the empire. Dominion support for the mother country in the present war is a further illustration of this connection, which is stronger than the mere letter of the law.

## ECONOMIC AND RELIGIOUS CONDITIONS

**Economic Trends, 1901-41.** In the twentieth century England has found little relief from the foreign competition that began to affect her economy toward the end of Victoria's reign. Although the total volume of British trade increased temporarily between 1900 and 1907, there was a depression in the two following years and there were disastrous strikes in 1911 and 1912. The military defeat of Germany did not end the economic rivalry between the two powers. In fact, the inflation of the German currency that followed her collapse in 1918 made it possible for her to undersell Britain in many of the world markets. Furthermore, the United States and Japan had both profited by England's preoccupation during the early years of the war, and the peace found them supplying many of Great Britain's former customers. In addition, the growing industrialization of Canada, Australia, and many other hitherto agrarian countries made it increasingly difficult to find overseas outlets for Britain's manufactured goods. In addition to the steady maturing of her rivals in the industrial race, Great Britain was also hampered in the postwar period by changing technical conditions. Her coal trade, which had been an important part of her economy in the nineteenth century, declined as the widest seams were exhausted and the narrow ones remaining became more and more expensive to work. Competition from oil was another big factor in this decline, and no pools could be discovered in the British Isles. As a result England's "heavy" industries—coal, iron, shipbuilding, and textiles—were in a state of almost constant depression between the two world wars. The problem was somewhat alleviated by the development of certain new "light" industries, such as the manufacture of radios and prepared foods, but this trend was never sufficient to fill the gaps left by the shrinkage of the demand for the older types of goods. Consequently England had constantly to deal with a serious problem of unemployment. The number of men and women out of work was always over one million and rarely under two million, out of a total working population of sixteen or seventeen million. Some areas in Wales and in the north were chronically "depressed," and nearly a whole generation of men in those localities grew up with little to look forward to but government relief. In these circumstances it is not to be wondered at that Great Britain lost her favorable balance of trade. No longer was there a great surplus of capital to export. On the contrary, since 1931 she has resorted to a policy of protective tariffs to safeguard the home market for her formerly dominant industries. Population trends are reflecting the changed economic circumstances. The birth rate has dropped sharply, and in spite of the almost complete refusal of America and most of the Empire to take any more emigrants, only the success of the medical profession in extending the average life span is preventing—temporarily, according to the statisticians—an absolute decline in the population of the British Isles.

**Religious and Moral Trends.** In the face of problems of such magnitude it might have been expected that the country would re-examine the principles on which its society was founded. But in spite of insistent campaigns by the labor interests, little could be accomplished. The classes in control preferred to sit tight, enjoying their privileged position as long as they could, and were not inclined to consider any sweeping social reforms. Housing-conditions for the lower classes remained very bad in both town and country. The best education and the best positions continued to be very nearly the closed preserves of the privileged groups. As in the eighteenth century, religion ceased to have much vitality and materialism became very largely the order of the day. It is true that the leaders of the Established Church showed some strength when they co-operated with other conservative moral elements in forcing the abdication of Edward VIII. But the Church was unable to resist the demand for a more liberal divorce law that grew out of this incident (page 586). A somewhat hopeful sign, however, is the spirit Britain has shown in the present war. In the crisis class lines have tended to break down, and homes, schools, and positions previously restricted to members of the upper classes are now open to all. Beyond and below the grim determination to take whatever emergency measures may be necessary to preserve Britain's national existence there apparently lies some realization that the social order must be changed to afford more opportunity in the future for able and ambitious members of the hitherto under-privileged classes. For this necessary work of reconstruction England has spiritual reserves in the form of inherited traditions stretching back to the time of Athelstan (page 51). Whether the military situation will permit her to make use of them remains to be seen.

## THE SECOND WORLD WAR

**Renewed Pressure from the Dissatisfied Powers.** The League of Nations, set up by the Treaty of Versailles, was designed to enforce peace as well as to provide a means of revising treaties (page 531). But because the United States did not lend her support and because the English and French co-operated very imperfectly, it was unequal to the task. Japan, Italy, and Germany all left the peace conference bitterly dissatisfied. Italy felt that the promises of considerable territorial gains, which had brought her into the war, had not been kept. Japan felt that she was not given a sufficiently free hand in China. Germany not only had been forced to accept the loser's role but was bitter because she had not obtained the Fourteen Point peace (page 531) that she had been led to expect. In the 1920's Japan and Italy—which became a fascist state under the leadership of Benito Mussolini in 1922—could do little to improve their position. In fact, Japan was forced to accept further restrictions on her naval building program and her territorial ambitions in China as a result of the Washington Conference of 1921-22. But as the western world slipped into the depths of the great economic depression that followed the American stock-market crash of 1929, the picture changed. Japan found pretexts for taking over Mongolia and then invading China proper. Italy seized Ethiopia, a member state of the League of Nations, in spite of the economic sanctions which that body sought to impose. Most serious of all, under the National Socialist regime that came to power in 1933 Germany recovered her strength rather more rapidly than England had anticipated. During the Ethiopian crisis she reoccupied the demilitarized Rhineland, in defiance of the Treaty of Versailles. France protested, but England refused to take any punitive measures. In 1936 Italy and Germany instigated a revolt by fascist elements against the liberal "Popular Front" govern-

ment of Spain. Though Soviet Russia aided the loyalist government, the Italians and the Germans supported their side
much more vigorously, and England and France stood aloof
while the fascist cause prevailed at the end of a struggle of two
and a half years. In the spring of 1938 Germany absorbed Austria, and in the Munich settlement of September secured the
German-speaking sections of Czechoslovakia. In March of 1939
she took the Czechish area also, the first non-German territory
to be seized by the resurgent German state. Thoroughly alarmed
by this departure from Chancellor Hitler's announced program
of taking only German peoples into the Third Reich, England,
relying on what she considered assured Russian support, now
joined France in guaranteeing the independence and territorial
integrity of Poland, Rumania, and Greece. But under the Versailles Treaty Poland included a corridor (strip of territory)
reaching to the German-speaking port and Free City of Danzig,
which cut off East Prussia from the remainder of Germany.
Chancellor Hitler was determined to eliminate this corridor, and
in August managed to arrange a nonaggression pact with Soviet
Russia which gave him a free hand in that area. On September 1
he invaded Poland. The Poles immediately asked their allies for
help, and two days later, after some hesitation, England and
France kept their pledge by declaring war on Germany.

**The Course of the War, 1939-41.** The western allies could not
send aid directly to Poland, and they hesitated to attack the
heavily fortified western frontier of Germany. Poland alone was
no match for the invader and was overrun in three weeks. England and France relied on the great French fortifications of the
Maginot line to protect them while their combined naval forces
slowly wore down German strength by means of an economic
blockade. They therefore settled down to a winter of watchful
waiting. Their hopes were disappointed in April, 1940, however, when the Germans suddenly seized Denmark and Norway,
thus gaining considerable supplies of food and assuring their

access to the Swedish iron mines. Although given strong naval
support, a combined British-French expeditionary force proved
quite incapable of dislodging the Germans from Norway. A
month later the Nazis struck again, this time through neutral
Holland and Belgium. A week after the campaign began Holland had been conquered, Brussels occupied, and the Allies even
forced to abandon Antwerp. Farther south the main Maginot
line was outflanked and the weaker northern continuation of
the great fortifications along the Belgian frontier was pierced.
Half of the Allied army, including virtually all of the Continental British expeditionary force, was soon surrounded. On
May 28 the Belgians capitulated, and only with the greatest
difficulty did the British navy and merchant fleet succeed in
evacuating most of the British and some of the French troops
through the Channel port of Dunkirk in the four days preceding June 4. The victorious Germans then advanced on Paris, and
after a sharp struggle along the Aisne River took it on June 14.
Italy, which had remained neutral at first, entered the war on
the German side on June 10. On June 16 Marshal Pétain became Premier of France, and immediately sued for peace. On
June 22 the French accepted the German terms for an armistice
and so withdrew from the war.

**The War in 1940-41.** England was thus left to fight on virtually alone. But though London and her industrial towns were
severely bombed, the Channel, the British navy, and the Royal
Air Force proved sufficient to ward off a threatened invasion during the next anxious months. Her enemies then turned to attack
Egypt and Greece, another of Britain's allies in the Mediterranean. The Italians invaded Egypt from Libya in September,
and when that drive fell short of its goal, the Suez Canal, they
moved against Greece in late October, 1940. These campaigns
proved disastrous for Mussolini's forces. With some help from
the British air force the Greeks put up a stout resistance to the
invasion effort, and fought back so successfully that by the end

of the year they were masters of approximately one-fourth of the Italian dependency of Albania on their northwestern border. In Egypt a British counterattack launched in December drove the invaders from Egyptian soil with heavy losses and put them on the defensive in their own Libyan territory. Much of this was occupied early in the following year by Australian troops, who bore the brunt of the campaigning in that sector. After a two months' campaign in the winter and early spring British imperial forces also occupied Italian East Africa and captured most of the Italian army there, which had been cut off from the homeland by the British control of the Suez Canal. But meanwhile Hungary, Rumania, and Bulgaria had admitted German troops, and on April 6, 1941, Chancellor Hitler's Balkan armies moved against Yugoslavia and Greece. By the end of the month both these countries were occupied. Troops from Britain, Australia, and New Zealand sent to aid them were forced to withdraw. Simultaneously German and Italian forces regained practically all of Libya, and the next month German air-borne forces succeeded in driving the British from Crete. The Suez Canal was thus threatened from both the west and the north. In June, however, the Germans attacked Russia, and while their armies made great gains in that vast country, these operations served for the time to relieve the pressure on the British, who were being aided by the United States with supplies and equipment. Though battered by aerial bombardment and suffering heavy shipping losses, England was still uninvaded and fighting on as the second year of the war drew to a close.

# 26. THE DISTRIBUTION OF POWER

**The Democratization of Liberalism.** The last century has witnessed the transformation of the British government from a system of oligarchic liberalism to one of democratic liberalism. The power that was once avowedly in the hands of the upper class is now—legally at least—held by the people as a whole. In constitutional theory there are only a few minor exceptions to this generalization, but we shall see that in practice the popular control is far from perfect. The practical difficulties encountered by the theoretically attractive system of democratic liberalism have led in the last half-century to the development of rival principles of governmental organization, which today both challenge and menace the supremacy of the liberal ideal.

## DECLINE OF THE POWER OF CROWN, CHURCH, AND NOBILITY

**The Monarchy.** Although, as we have seen (page 481), the crown retained considerable influence over the government of England during the eighteenth century, the insanity of George III and the dissolute incompetence of his sons weakened the institution of the British monarchy so seriously that it has never been able to recover much of its former political importance. Not only did the full political power slip into the hands of the Cabinet between 1810 and 1837, but the character and activities of George IV and his brother William so alienated their subjects that when these monarchs did try to interfere in matters of state they were often forced to give way before the opposition of their ministers. From such a defeat of William IV in 1834 over the question of the composition of a new Cabinet may be dated the establishment of a definite precedent that the monarch should not interfere in matters that are the subject of political controversy. Victoria, it is true, regained much of the lost popularity of the royal house, and in 1839 did succeed in preventing the fall of a ministry headed by her favorite statesman, Lord Melbourne. The particular issue here was whether the Queen should be required to accept new ladies in waiting drawn from the families of the party controlling the Cabinet, and hence this affair is known as the Bedchamber Crisis. But after Victoria's marriage to her German cousin Albert she accepted good advice from her husband on the duties and limitations of her position as a constitutional monarch, and under his careful coaching she may be said to have created the modern English role for that part. Even so, behind the scenes she exerted some influence when discussing ministerial changes with her various Prime Ministers, who disliked to cross her imperious will any more than necessary. The part of Edward VII in foreign affairs has already been suggested (page 530). In the reign of George V party lines became somewhat muddled because of the rise of a third party (Labor, page 552) and the economic crisis. In his capacity as summoner and adviser of ministers when a new "government" (Cabinet, set of ministers, page 560) was to be formed, it is generally supposed that, like his Hanoverian forebears, George exercised considerable influence. He is thought to have been particularly responsible for the formation of the national government in 1931, although the historian must wait for the publication of the memoirs of those concerned before he can speak with confidence. In any case, there is no doubt that though the monarch is so weak in his own domestic sphere that, like Edward VIII, he cannot even do things which are legal for his subjects (page 528), the modern English sovereign who keeps a good personal reputation can still quietly exert, on occasion, an important political influence.

**The Established Church.** As the reform movement progressed and control of the government passed into the hands of the people as a whole, the special privileges of particular groups were gradually diminished, though not always completely abolished. In the case of the Established Church most of the old endowments were retained, but the rights of taxation and the political restrictions imposed on the adherents of other faiths were taken away, except in the case of the royal family and the Lord Chancellor.[1] In 1828 Parliament repealed the Test and Corporation acts (page 483) and thereby threw practically all political offices open to Dissenters.[2] Roman Catholics, however, were still barred by the necessity of taking an antipapal oath prescribed by the Bill of Rights (page 449). Agitation in Ireland on the part of a Catholic Association headed by Daniel O'Connell forced the British government to pass the so-called Roman Catholic Emancipation Act in the following year.[3] This abolished all anti-Catholic tests for officeholding and put Roman Catholics on terms of equality with Protestants, politically speaking.[4] In 1857 the ecclesiastical courts of the Established Church lost all their important secular jurisdiction (page 573). In 1858 the Commons abolished a clause in its qualifying oath requiring members to swear on the true faith of a Christian. Eight years later the Lords did the same. This admitted Jews to Parliament. In 1888, after a prolonged controversy over the admission of a professed Atheist, Charles Bradlaugh, members-elect were allowed to substitute an affirmation for the oath which contained the words "So help me God." [5] Thus Atheists also became eligible for membership in

[1] The king is still required to be a communicant member of the Church of England, and he may not marry a Catholic. Catholics were barred from the position of Lord Chancellor by the Catholic Emancipation Act of 1829.
[2] S-M, No. 127B, pp. 677-78.  [3] S-M, No. 127C, pp. 678-79.
[4] Marriages performed by Catholic priests, however, were not recognized as valid until 1838.
[5] S-M, No. 139A, pp. 857-61.

Parliament. By a parallel series of statutes the right of the Established Church to collect tithes (page 43) and similar taxes for its support was restricted, and finally eliminated altogether. In 1869 Parliament passed a bill completely disestablishing the Church in Ireland. By this the Anglicans in Ireland lost not only their tax rights and public endowments dating from before 1660, but also their ecclesiastical court jurisdiction and the memberships of their bishops in the House of Lords at Westminster. As a result of this act the Church of Ireland became a purely voluntary organization, retaining only its former buildings and private endowments received since 1660. In 1920, after a long struggle, the Church was similarly disestablished in Wales, whose population was overwhelmingly Protestant but Nonconformist. Finally in 1936 arrangements were made by statute for the government to buy up and discontinue all ecclesiastical tithe rights in the remainder of Great Britain. In spite of these losses, however, the Established Churches of England and Scotland (in the latter case Presbyterian) still retained their public endowments, and the English Church held its twenty-six seats in the House of Lords. Consequently, Anglican bishops continued to speak with more political authority than other ecclesiastical leaders. One of them, the Bishop of Bradford, began the public agitation against Edward VIII which culminated in his abdication (page 528).

**The Nobility.** During the last century the political influence of the nobility has declined greatly. Governmental leaders have found it increasingly desirable to remain in the powerful House of Commons rather than take the higher social rank enjoyed by the politically weak Lords. The constitutional steps by which the powers of the House of Lords were weakened are so closely connected with the movement for extending the suffrage that we may describe them along with the story of that reform later in the chapter.

**Nineteenth-Century Predominance of the Mercantile Element in the House of Commons.** Within the group that dominated the lower house we must note a shift in the center of political gravity. The lawyers had always been a bad third to the gentry and merchants. They were naturally the professional servants of these classes and so they remained—effective mouthpieces, but rarely formulating a policy of their own on any really important matter. During most of the eighteenth century the landed class was easily superior to the mercantile one, just as it had been since the Middle Ages, when one knight or squire was socially and politically equal to at least two burgesses. But by the beginning of the nineteenth century the enormous development of English trade enabled the manufacturers and merchants to hold their own with their country cousins. By the middle of the century they had so far outstripped them as to be able to force the repeal of the Corn Laws (page 523) which were regarded as the chief defense of agricultural England. The junior partner had thus exchanged places with his senior colleague, though socially the country is still preferred to the town, and the wealthy merchant commonly acquires a landed estate as a symbol of his success.[6] Ask an Englishman where he is from, and instead of naming the large city nearest his home, as the American tends to do, he names his county, suggesting a rural setting even though if he says Lancashire it may mean that he comes from the heart of Liverpool or Manchester.

## THE SUFFRAGE REFORM BILLS

**The Reform Bill of 1832.** An even more fundamental change in the distribution of political power was brought about by

---

[6] It has been estimated that of all the economic interests represented in the House of Commons in 1832 "land" accounted for 66% as against 34% for the industrial, commercial, and finance groups. By 1865 these figures had become 44% and 56% respectively. See J. A. Thomas, *The House of Commons, 1832-1901: A Study of Its Economic and Functional Character,* Cardiff, Wales, 1939, p. 9.

the success during this period of the movement for suffrage reform. During the dark days that followed the suppression of the movement during the 1790's (page 488) the reform ideal was largely kept alive by the devotion and ability of a London tailor named Francis Place, who successfully catered to gentlemen's trade in the front of his shop while in his back room running a propaganda mill for revising the political and social system. As tempers cooled and war hysteria diminished after the defeat of Napoleon, the reform movement slowly gained headway. The repeal of the Test and Corporation acts and the passage of the Catholic Emancipation Act in the following year encouraged the reformers and increased the agitation for a broadening of the suffrage base on which the government rested. In the election of 1830 that followed the death of George IV some of the leaders of the Whigs, who had long been out of power, championed general suffrage reform. The comparatively peaceful revolution in France, which set up a liberal monarchy in July of that year, helped the cause of progressive liberalism in England by demonstrating that constitutional change did not necessarily mean bloodshed. The Whigs won a majority in the new House of Commons, and under the leadership of Lord Grey began to press for reform. The Tory leader, the Duke of Wellington, Napoleon's conqueror, infuriated his opponents by describing the existing system as more nearly perfect than any which could at that time be designed to take its place, since "the nature of man was incapable of reaching such excellence at once." The angry Whigs drew up a plan for changes that would give the ballot to the middle class in general, but this was more than some of their number would support and it could not be pushed through the House of Commons. A new election was held in which the Whig slogan was "The bill, the whole bill, and nothing but the bill." Public opinion supported the Whigs, and the new House passed the bill. The Lords, however, rejected it.[7]

[7] S-M, No. 132A, pp. 755-62.

Popular excitement was very great. Bishops who had opposed the bill did not dare venture out on the street. One was sent a purse with thirty pieces of silver to suggest that he was a traitor to the best of causes. Place tried to bring pressure on the government by starting a run on its financial bulwark, the Bank of England. "To stop the Duke, go for gold," read the sign in his window. But the threat of force supplied the really effective argument. Mobs filled the streets in a manner reminiscent of the seventeenth century, and men prepared for civil war. William IV thereupon overcame his original reluctance and promised, if necessary, to pack the House of Lords by creating enough new peers in sympathy with the bill to ensure its passage.[8] Rather than have their titles thus debased, the reluctant Lords bethought themselves of such important engagements as fishing trips when the bill was next to come up, and in a comparatively deserted House it was passed without the necessity of any new creations.

**Its Provisions.** The bill provided for: (1) Some redistribution of seats by which both seats of the rottenest of the rotten boroughs and one from the others were transferred to the populous new towns or inadequately represented counties. (2) The extension of the county franchise from the forty shilling freeholders to men holding land of the annual value of £10 by other tenures or by long leasehold, and to tenants at will and short-term leaseholders whose lands were worth £50 per year. (3) A similar reform in the borough suffrage by which those occupying houses worth £10 a year in rent and fulfilling a few other minor requirements were enfranchised.[9] The total effect was to give the vote to about one person in thirty in the population, that is, to the middle class but not to the working class. Universal manhood suffrage would have enfranchised some seven times as many.

[8] This device had been used once before in the reign of Anne when a small number of peers were created to secure the passage of a bill that the government deemed an essential piece of legislation.
[9] S-M, No. 130A, pp. 723-25.

**Further Extensions of the Suffrage.** There followed thirty peaceful and exceedingly prosperous years, undisturbed by any of the dire calamities that Wellington and the Tories had asserted would follow an extension of the franchise. It was therefore possible for the working classes to press their demands for the ballot. This they did in the Chartist movement, so called because the demand for universal manhood suffrage was incorporated in a document drawn up in 1838, called the People's Charter, which they hoped Parliament would adopt. The wealthier classes, however, used the Anti-Corn Law agitation to distract attention from the Chartist movement, and the People's Charter was not adopted when it was presented to Parliament in 1848. But twenty years later the result of the American Civil War showed that a democratic government might be more efficient than had formerly been supposed, and that the laboring class which had supported the North might be as potentially wise politically as the upper classes. The time was therefore ripe for another extension of the suffrage, and in 1867 the aspiring Conservative leader Benjamin Disraeli contrived to secure the credit for granting the ballot to town laborers. By the act of that year nearly half the adult males in the population became voters, and some readjustments were made in the distribution of seats.[10] As the democratic tide swept on acts of 1884 and 1885 extended the ballot to the laboring class in rural areas, and also rearranged the entire system of distributing seats.[11] Instead of having borough and county representation thereafter, England was divided into districts roughly corresponding to congressional districts in the United States, usually with approximately equal population and sending a single member to Parliament.

**Woman Suffrage.** Throughout the nineteenth century there was occasional agitation for woman suffrage, and in the early years of the twentieth century there was great pressure for it. The

[10] S-M, No. 131H, pp. 744-46.
[11] S-M, No. 135A, p. 805; No. 135B, pp. 805-06.

chief argument against it was that women, not being fighters, should not be given the power to involve the country in war. By slashing pictures, pouring acid in mailboxes, and throwing bombs certain militant suffragettes, under the leadership of Mrs. Emmeline Pankhurst and her daughter Christabel, undertook to disprove this assertion. The coming of the war, in which women of all shades of political opinion nursed, farmed, organized labor corps, and otherwise did their bit, gave an opportunity for a somewhat more acceptable rebuttal of the male arguments. In 1918, as a reward for their valuable wartime services, women were enfranchised.[12] At the same time men—such as servants and unmarried males living with their parents—whose lack of occupancy of separate quarters had previously prevented their qualifying for the ballot were also given the vote. Since, however, there was some fear of a women's party which might dominate a country that had lost a million men in the war, to keep the balance between the sexes the age limit for women voters was set at thirty, and the property qualifications required for voters in local governmental elections was imposed. Only those who occupied houses or other property worth £5 a year or whose husbands occupied such property were permitted to vote. But after ten years' experience it was seen that women's political views were influenced much more strongly by their economic interests than by their sex, and that consequently women merely affiliated with the established parties instead of forming one of their own. Accordingly, the property qualifications for them were abolished and their age qualification was reduced to twenty-one by an act passed in 1928, which was popularly known as the Flapper Bill because of the age of the women enfranchised by it.[13] Since that date England has had universal adult suffrage.

12 S-M, No. 137D, pp. 827-29.    13 S-M, No. 137K, p. 837.

## REMAINING INEQUALITIES AND THE LABOR MOVEMENT

**Remaining Inequalities.** Suffrage reform did not make the English constitution fully democratic, however. In the elections for the House of Commons there was not absolute equality, for some citizens still enjoyed the privilege of a second vote. These were the occupiers of business premises worth £10 a year and the holders of university degrees.[14] In other words, businessmen and the intelligentsia were given a double voice in the government. Much more serious, however, than this unequal suffrage were other undemocratic features of the British system of the late nineteenth and early twentieth centuries. These were the lack of political machinery for expressing the will of the lower classes, the expense of being a member of Parliament, and the constitution and powers of the House of Lords. Most of these obvious handicaps have been overcome in the last half-century, but behind them lay an accumulated mass of economic and social distinctions that survived the formal constitutional changes. Right down to the outbreak of the present war, at least, they still reflected something of the old class attitudes of feudal times, and thus they prevent our describing the constitution of the country as a completely democratic one.

**Popular Education.** There was no use in having the ballot if the enfranchised classes had no leaders who could properly reflect their point of view. Lack of proper educational facilities handicapped the working classes at first. The Puritans had agitated for universal education at the time of the reformation. This system was established in Presbyterian Scotland and has ever since been one of the glories of that country. But in England, until 1833 there were only a comparatively few "charity"

[14] See page 383. According to the terms of the Parliament Act of 1911 those qualified in both of these ways could exercise only one of their supplementary privileges.

schools; the rest were supported entirely or in large part by tuition fees.[15] From the time of the Reform Bill the government began to grant some subsidies to education, but the system remained very inadequate, reaching less than half the children of school age. With the extension of the suffrage, even the well-to-do elements in society became sympathetic with popular education, on the theory that "it is necessary to educate our new masters," as one of their representatives put it. By an act passed in 1870 local authorities were required to provide elementary schools in all areas where there was demand for them.[16] At first fees could be charged and attendance was not uniformly compulsory, but these deficiencies were remedied by subsequent legislation, so that after 1891 all English children were required by law to be kept in school (without fees) until the age of thirteen.[17]

**The Trade-Union Movement.** As the electorate grew literate and educated leaders became available, the laboring classes decided to form their own political party. This decision was the result of the development of two forces, the trade-union movement and socialism. After 1822, when Parliament was once more willing to give serious consideration to reforming measures, it was recognized that some compensation must be made to the workers for the abolition in 1814 of the Elizabethan minimum-wage legislation (page 477). The restrictions on trade-unions were accordingly modified to some extent by legislation in 1824-25,[18] but unions did not begin to flourish until after 1875, when they secured their so-called Charter of Liberties, an act legalizing collective bargaining, peaceful picketing, and all acts

15 The best of these were the boarding schools, which were known as public schools because their educational facilities were open to any member of the public who wished to pay the fees, in contrast with the private tutors whom many of the better class maintained in their homes. An English public school is therefore what Americans would call a private school.
16 S-M, No. 131I, pp. 747-49.
17 Raised to fourteen in 1918 and in 1938 to fifteen.
18 S-M, No. 127A, pp. 676-77.

done by a group in a trade dispute that were legal when done by an individual. Workers in the more highly skilled trades were the first to take advantage of this legislation, but after a successful strike of London dock workers in 1889 unskilled urban labor began to organize also. By 1900 there were two million members of trade-unions in England.[19]

**The Socialist Movement and the Labor Party.** Socialist thought in England is at least as old as the Digger movement (page 436). A manufacturer named Robert Owen advocated and tried to put into practice a system of co-operative enterprise in the early nineteenth century. But the great impetus to the movement came from the "scientific" theories of the German exile Karl Marx, who made a thoroughgoing analysis of the contemporary economic system and worked out a detailed plan for a communistic society.[20] His work *Das Kapital* was published in 1867, and by the 1880's socialism had a considerable following among the English intelligentsia. The Fabian Society, organized in 1884, though not strictly Marxian, contributed much to the spread of socialist doctrines.[21] Some radical unionists, led by a Scottish miner named Keir Hardie, were attracted to the socialist point of view, and in 1892 formed an Independent Labor party. Previous to this time representatives of labor had commonly been members of the Liberal party. Because Marx's reform program was a much more drastic one than that of the ordinary trade-union leaders, who were usually content with moderate improvements in wages and conditions of labor, it

[19] There were over eight million in 1920, but less than five million in 1935. In the Taff Vale case, decided in 1901, the House of Lords (the Law Lords) held that unions were financially liable for losses to employers (in this case the Taff Vale Railway Co.) for losses sustained as a result of strikes. The Trades Disputes Act of 1906 reversed this decision, but in 1927, after a general strike in the preceding year, Parliament outlawed all general and sympathetic strikes.

[20] Called "scientific" in contrast to the milder theories of Robert Owen and his contemporaries, which the Marxists dubbed "Utopian."

[21] "Fabian" for the Roman general Fabius Cunctator, who won his vic- tories by a policy of cautious delay.

was not possible to attract the bulk of the trade-unionists into the new socialist movement. A working agreement for independent political action in conjunction with the conservative trade-union elements was concluded, however, in 1899, and in 1906 the Labor party, as the joint undertaking came to be called, elected twenty-nine members to Parliament.

**Salaries for Members of Parliament.** Since membership in Parliament had ceased to be a burden and had become a coveted honor, the medieval financial arrangements for members had become obsolete. Far from arranging for compensation for its members, Parliament, as already noted (page 454), had required that they be men of substance. This was a requirement obviously unsuited to the new age, and it was abolished in 1858. Since no salaries were provided for members of Parliament, however, there remained the problem of making membership possible for men without financial resources of their own. After the rise of the Labor party the trade-unions made a practice of paying their M.P.'s. In 1909 this was declared illegal by the House of Lords (the Law Lords) in passing judgment in a case brought by W. V. Osborne. Because this greatly handicapped the Labor party, and since in any case it was clearly unfair to expect the laboring class to compensate its representatives for their loss of wages, provision was made by a statute of 1911 for an annual salary of £400 for all members of Parliament.

## THE PARLIAMENT ACT OF 1911

**Social-Security Legislation and the Opposition of the Lords.** To satisfy the demands of the newly enfranchised classes and also to "kill Socialism with kindness," the Liberal party, which came into power in 1906, pushed through a great deal of social-security legislation. This provided for government employment agencies, old-age pensions, and sickness and unemployment insurance,[22] which virtually constituted a reform of the old poor law. After the acts were passed many Englishmen recalled the comment made by the Liberal statesman Sir William Harcourt after the Reform Acts of 1884 and 1885—"We are all Socialists now." Before this program was completed the House of Lords, which was strongly conservative in its outlook, undertook to block it by refusing in 1909 to pass the annual budget bill. This bill had been introduced by the Chancellor of the Exchequer, David Lloyd George, who had been active in championing the reforms it was designed to finance. Consequently, the financial scheme of taxation it proposed was known as the Lloyd George budget.

**The Attack on the Lords.** The rejection of the budget raised the question of the power of the House of Lords.[23] For some time this body had been considered by the Liberals a worse than useless appendage to the government, an assembly that was best occupied, if at all, in doing nothing.

> When Wellington whipped Bonaparte,
>     As every child can tell,
> The House of Lords, throughout the war,
> Did nothing in particular,
>     And did it very well.

Yet as the constitution then stood the Lords had the clear right to reject the Lloyd George budget. The Liberal party, backed by the small Labor party, undertook to alter the constitution by limiting the power of the Lords to reject bills passed by the Commons.[24] A general election was held, which gave the Liberal-Labor group enough of a majority to induce the Lords to pass the budget. But although the Lords granted that some reform was necessary, they rejected the Commons bill limiting their powers.[25] A new election was fought on this issue alone in December of 1910—the second in the same year—and the result confirmed the verdict of the first. George V, who had succeeded

22 S-M, No. 137B, pp. 824-26.    24 S-M, No. 138B, pp. 846-50.
23 S-M, No. 138A, pp. 841-46.    25 S-M, No. 130C, pp. 850-51.

to the throne in May, thereupon promised, at the request of the Liberal Prime Minister, Herbert Asquith, to name any number of new peers that might be necessary to pass the bill. After being informed of this threat, which had already proved effective in the struggle for the Reform Bill (page 547), the Lords yielded and the bill became law.

**The Parliament Act of 1911.** The act provided: (1) that all money bills passed by the Commons should, after a month's time, go to the king for his assent, whether the Lords had passed them or not; (2) that if there was any question as to the nature of a bill, the Speaker of the House of Commons was to decide; and (3) that any other bill, if rejected in the Lords, was nevertheless to go to the king for his assent if passed in three successive sessions of the Commons, provided two years had elapsed since its original introduction.[26] Thereafter the Lords had only a suspensory veto over legislation. They could delay it, but could not finally defeat the popular will as expressed in the House of Commons.

## LATER DEVELOPMENTS

**Growth of the Labor Party.** This was a big step forward on the democratic road. The success of the Labor party after the war shows the results of the changes that had been going on, during the past half-century in particular. In the election of 1923 it secured more seats than the Liberal party, and with Liberal support took office in 1924. The fact that most of the new ministers were sons of workingmen and had been workmen themselves before becoming trade-union officials or party leaders affords a striking illustration of the degree to which the English constitution had changed since medieval times, or even since the eighteenth century.

**The Situation in 1939.** This was, however, a minority government and short-lived (January-December, 1924), as was the sec-

[26] S-M, No. 137A, pp. 822-24.

ond Labor government of 1929-31. In the so-called national, or coalition, government that succeeded it a small branch of the Labor party was nominally represented, as was a section of the Liberals, but the Conservative party had the great majority of the seats. This situation suggests well enough the distribution of power in England at the outbreak of the present war, when formal political activity was suspended. Though the middle and lower classes have almost as much voting strength in proportion to their population as do the other elements of society, it is doubtful whether in time of peace their combined power is equal to that of the upper class. Their financial weakness puts them at a disadvantage in many ways. Very few of their number, particularly from the working class, can secure a university education. They cannot afford to give time to campaigning activities, and their views are inadequately represented in the press. By the Trade Disputes Act of 1927 trade-union funds cannot be used for political purposes unless the individual contributors give a special authorization in writing. Social attitudes of long standing also help to explain this inferiority. Respect for the institutions of the monarchy, the royal family, the titled nobility, and even the surviving lords of the manor are deeply rooted. As yet no successful union of agricultural laborers has been formed, and this large section of the community is represented politically by spokesmen from another class. Doubtless the draining-off by emigration during the past century of much of the stock from which leadership might have come has had something to do with this phenomenon. On balance, it is perhaps best to say that during the past two centuries the English government, which is in form a liberal monarchy, has become in fact an aristocratic democracy.

# 27. THE MACHINERY OF GOVERNMENT

**Further Evidence of the Pliability of Constitutions.** In beginning the last section of our study of the development of English governmental machinery we must remind ourselves once more of the principle (pages 378, 396) that changes in the distribution of power do not necessarily mean comparable changes in the framework of government, since new forces can operate through old apparatus. In the last century of English constitutional history we find many changes in details, mostly dictated by a desire for greater governmental efficiency. But there are few striking changes caused by the transition from oligarchic to democratic liberalism. Power, which was seeking an ever lower center of gravity and a correspondingly lower level in the body politic, was applied from new directions and in differing proportions to different parts of the old machinery, but the traditional framework remained. For example, even today men are still appointed to high office by letters patent under the great seal—with the old-fashioned stamped wax still dangling from the parchment ribbons—though the impetus comes from a popular agitation instead of the royal whim.

## MONARCH, HOUSEHOLD, AND COUNCIL

**The Monarchy.** The real powers of the crown suffered a sharp decline in this and the preceding period, as we have already seen (pages 449, 541). Nevertheless the modern monarch continues to go through much the same motions as his predecessors, and his position in his country's constitution can only be understood by reminding ourselves of the important distinction between the royal person and the royal office (pages 269, 490). The old feudal laws of parentelic inheritance still determine the succession to the crown, subject only to the possibility of parliamentary interference, and theoretically there has been none of this since 1701; for legally the abdication of Edward VIII was a purely voluntary act. The new ruler, succeeding by hereditary right, is proclaimed by heralds in medieval fashion, and in the normal course of events is anointed and crowned by churchmen in the traditional way. He takes the coronation oath and sits in the royal chair made, in part, of the stone of Scone—the Scottish coronation seat—that Edward I brought from the north at the time of his supposed conquest of Balliol's kingdom. Once legally king—a status still independent of coronation rites (page 133)—the monarch commissions his ministers and army officers, approves laws,[1] and generally does all the things his predecessors have ever done. Legally, it is a matter of no consequence that

> . . . his will is not his own
> For he himself is subject to his birth;
> He may not, as unvalued persons do,
> Carve for himself; for on his choice depends
> The safety and the health of the whole state.

Indeed the office of the modern monarch is even more powerful than that of earlier sovereigns. For example, due to the efforts of George III to control his family (page 491), it still wields a dictatorial power over the marriages of all descendants of George II, including the most distant connections of the king. This is typical of a multitude of minor perquisites vested in the crown. More important constitutionally is the fact that by the Statute of Westminster of 1931 (page 533) Parliament gave up virtually all control over the Dominions, and the office of the monarch

---

[1] Theoretically he may still veto them, though this privilege has not been exercised since the time of Queen Anne (page 490).

remains almost the only constitutional tie that holds the British Empire together. Since this has resulted in the king's being bound by the wishes of a number of different sets of ministers whom he cannot possibly consult face to face, his personal influence has been greatly diminished by this change, although his official importance is magnified.

**The Household and the Privy Council.** Two historic elements of the British constitution are still in existence, though they have lost nearly all of their political significance. The king is still surrounded by an impressive retinue of household officials, but all of the posts are of minor importance and only five of them change hands with a change of government. There is still a Privy Council, but except for the Judicial Committee (page 576) its functions are almost entirely honorary. It includes all who have ever been Cabinet ministers, and many other distinguished citizens besides. It solemnly meets to hear the news of the accession of a new sovereign, and at least two of its members are summoned to constitute a quorum and assist in the installation of a new Privy Councilor. Members of this body are distinguished from the ordinary "Honorable" members of Parliament by the title of "Right Honorable," and the body enjoys the further dignity of a semimilitary uniform. Draped around the scarcely military figures of modern British politicians, it brightens many a royal garden party. The power enjoyed by the Council in Tudor days has departed, but the glory lingers on.

## CABINET AND PARLIAMENT

**The Prime Minister and the Cabinet.** Throughout the nineteenth century the Cabinet system continued to operate on its informal and extralegal basis. In 1937, however, the position of Prime Minister was recognized by statute and a definite salary was attached to it. During the past forty years the Cabinet has become somewhat better organized than it was in earlier years.

Since 1916 it has had a paid secretary who keeps its minutes, though the traditional secrecy is preserved and these are rarely made public. Agenda lists are circulated before meetings, and subcommittees are employed where necessary. The principle of unanimity is also retained. An exception was made, however, in the case of the national government that reversed the country's free-trade policy after August, 1931. Then certain Liberal members were permitted to dissent publicly from the official stand without giving up their posts.[2] But this arrangement proved impracticable, and they resigned in 1932. Cabinet ministers, as well as other ministers, are not necessarily required to be members of Parliament, but in practice they almost always are, because of the desirability of their being able to defend their actions before the body to which they are responsible.[3] The number of ministers in the Cabinet has tended to increase to twenty or more, though during the wartime emergencies of 1914-18 and 1939-41 it was reduced in each case in the interests of efficiency to less than ten. Most of the important ministers sit in the House of Commons, for the reasons already indicated (page 544), but frequently they have a representative in the form of a parliamentary undersecretary to speak for them in the other house. The choice of ministers and their inclusion in the Cabinet is still largely a matter of the Prime Minister's choice, though in practice he must be guided by political considerations; for if he does not please enough of the influential members of his party to keep his majority in Parliament, he will be forced out of his position.

**Unitary Parliamentary Control: Lack of Checks and Balances.** In this close relationship of Prime Minister, Cabinet, and Parliament lies one of the most distinctive features of the modern British constitution, for it gives the country an extremely flex-

[2] S-M, No. 138D, pp. 851-57.
[3] Ramsay MacDonald and his son Malcolm were members of the Cabinet for a time in 1935-36 when they were without seats in either house.

ible government under the control of a single authority instead of a government with checks and balances such as ours. That is to say, the British have in reality no separation of executive, legislative, and judicial powers in their government, but a concentration of all of them in the hands of the one body, Parliament. The executive branch of the government (the Prime Minister plus the Cabinet) holds power only as long as it retains the confidence of Parliament, and may be changed at any moment when it loses this necessary support. Similarly, there is in England no doctrine of judicial review that gives judges the right to declare acts of Parliament unconstitutional (page 367). On the contrary, the judges are bound by the statutes, and if they interpret one in a way of which Parliament disapproves that body need only state its will clearly in a new statute and the courts must then enforce the law as determined in Parliament. In other words, since the constitutional monarch never uses the veto power (page 558 n.), Parliament is all-powerful in the sphere of government. It can do anything—as the saying is—except change a man into a woman. The American student should notice carefully that the English have thus found it possible to run a most efficient democracy without having recourse to any of the checks and balances with which we are so familiar. With them the government can, and usually does, respond immediately to changes in public sentiment. There are no delays caused by quarrels between the executive and the legislature, or by judges who have the power to thwart the expressed will of both. This flexibility comes from the fact that in England the legislature has absolute control over the executive and the judges, and consequently there can be no rivalry between these different elements.

## ADMINISTRATIVE AGENCIES AND THE CIVIL SERVICE

**Administrative Agencies.** The number of important administrative positions in the government was greatly increased during this period by the expansion of the British Empire, and by the extension of governmental activity into new fields at home during the last half-century. In 1854, because of the pressure of business connected with the Crimean War, the office of the Secretary of State for War and the Colonies was divided and an additional Secretary of State was created to take charge of colonial affairs. In 1858 still another such Secretaryship was established, this time for India as a result of the Mutiny and the subsequent reorganization of the government of that important part of the Empire (page 522). In the last twenty-five years additional Secretaryships have been set up for the Air Force (1917), the Dominions (1925), and Scotland (1926). At home the laissez-faire attitude was so strong that it was difficult to secure the establishment of adequate administrative agencies to supplement the work of the Home Secretary in dealing with domestic problems. But in 1826 the President of the Board of Trade and Plantations (page 492) was made a salaried official. After 1853 the board itself ceased to meet and in 1867, when the office of vice-president was abolished, the President became the head of an ordinary executive department with functions similar to those of our Department of Commerce. His title was changed to President of the Board of Trade in 1862. The similar office of the President of the Board of Education was created in 1899. It grew up as a result of the Education Act of 1870 and supplanted an earlier Education Committee of the Privy Council. Other boards have now formally given way to ministries. The Poor Law Amendment Act of 1834 established commissioners to supervise the administration of poor relief. In 1847 these commissioners were superseded by a Poor Law Board. In 1871 this was transformed into a Local Government Board, which was also charged with exercising the functions of an earlier Board of Health. In 1916 ministries were established for Labor and Pensions. In 1919 a Ministry of Health supplanted the Local Government Board. Because the Minister of Health manages a large part of the system of grants-in-aid to local government authorities (page 570), his power is much greater than his title might seem to indicate. In 1919 also a Minister of Agriculture took over the duties of a Board of Agriculture, set up in 1889. In the same year additional ministries were established for Transportation and Mines. The Postmaster General, whose office goes back to Tudor times, and the First Commissioner of Works—charged with the care of public buildings, parks, and royal palaces—whose office dates from 1851, are minor administrative officials.

**The Civil Service.** Down to 1855 the lower offices in these administrative agencies were filled by a haphazard system of political nepotism and sale of clerkships similar to that already described as existing in the courts (page 283). While this frequently produced some much more capable administrators than might be supposed, on the whole it was highly unsatisfactory. As the governmental machinery became more and more complicated, the situation became intolerable. In 1855, thanks to the efforts of Sir George Otto Trevelyan and his brother-in-law the historian Macaulay, both of whom had had administrative experience with a civil-service system in India, such a system was instituted in Great Britain. Before the end of the century practically all ordinary governmental posts were brought under it. Positions were classified, and filled only by those who had successfully passed qualifying examinations. For the highest category university training was required, and age limits were so fixed as to make civil-service work a definite career in itself instead of something to fall back on in case of failure in some other line of work. That is, one might not take the qualifying examination after passing the age of twenty-four. Furthermore, the salaries, promotions, pensions, and prospective knighthoods for the most able were so arranged as to attract a good proportion of the best men finishing the universities in a given year. In nearly every ministry there was created a permanent undersecretaryship, or its equivalent, as head of the permanent civil-service side of the department. The holders of these posts gave advice on the routine work of their offices to their changing political heads. In theory the Cabinet ministers and their political associates determined all matters of policy, and the permanent undersecretaries merely supplied them with information and carried out their decisions. In practice, however, it is safe to assume that the permanent undersecretaries exercised and still do exercise a considerable influence on the shaping of governmental policy. In this left-handed manner it is possible that the intelligentsia are regaining some of the power lost by the decline of their old medium of expression, the Church.

## FINANCIAL AND PARTY MACHINERY

**Government Finance.** To compensate for the loss of revenue caused by the general abandonment of customs duties in the middle of the century, the income tax (page 499) was again introduced. This device, which had served the country's needs so well during the Napoleonic Wars, soon became the core of the British tax structure. The rates of assessment, which have been very heavy since the war of 1914-18, are adjusted to meet current needs.[4] There are also heavy excise taxes on liquor and tobacco and such simple luxuries as sugar and tea, taxes that bear heavily on the common people. But the upper classes do not escape either. In 1894 the budget of the Liberal Chancellor of the Exchequer, Sir William Harcourt, greatly increased the century-old

---

[4] It was estimated in 1938 that the average Briton paid approximately twice as large a percentage of his income in taxes of all sorts as did the average American citizen.

death duties (legacy taxes; page 499). Under the provisions of the Budget Act of that year real property, which had previously been assessed for death duties only at its worth to the recipient in terms of annual income, was thereafter taxed according to its selling value in the open market, and the rate of duty was graduated according to the size of the estate. Since that time these assessments have become so heavy that if a wealthy father and son die within a short time of each other the family fortune is seriously affected. Under these circumstances many of the old families can no longer afford to maintain their imposing but unprofitable country estates. Landholders are not required to pay any appreciable direct tax on real property, however. An attempt, originally included in the Lloyd George budget of 1909, to augment the governmental revenues by reviving that obsolescent tax (page 499) was defeated at the time and also when the effort was renewed after the First World War.

**Party Machinery.** As the organization of the governmental ministries was gradually made more definite, so that of the political parties was clarified during the same period. In the latter half of the nineteenth century central and local committees were established. These raised campaign funds and supervised annual summer conferences at which party policies were discussed and proposed lines of action determined. Members of the party in Parliament were regularly notified of the party's wishes by officials appropriately known as whips. The whips, like the managers of packs of hounds in the hunting field, kept their fellow party members in line, though here the compulsion was the threat of withholding financial and political support in the next campaign. If a member refused the whip, that is, declined to accept the orders sent by the whips, he might expect to find his local committee endorsing a rival candidate at the next election.

## ROYAL COMMISSIONS, MILITARY FORCES, AND THE CHURCH

**Royal Commissions.** Another feature of the central government that should be noted is the institution of the royal commission. This is an investigating body, composed of any persons whom the Prime Minister may care to choose—in or out of Parliament. These royal commissions, whose roots may be found as far back as medieval times, came into prominence in the nineteenth century, when they began to be extensively used for the purpose of doing the spadework for—and incidentally educating public opinion to accept—future legislation, usually of a fundamental nature. By appointing men and women who were not active in political life but either broadly trained, public-spirited citizens or experts in their fields, the government found it possible to bring the best brain power of the country to bear on legislative problems in a nonpartisan way. The commissioners gathered evidence by means of paid investigators, questionnaires, or other requests for written testimony, and also by oral questioning of witnesses at public hearings. After the evidence had been obtained it was weighed by the commissioners, and specific recommendations were made in a final report. The recommendations of these commissions paved the way for many of the great reform acts of the nineteenth and early twentieth centuries. Royal commissions are still appointed from time to time, though the present tendency is to rely more and more on advisory committees or specially constituted boards connected with a single governmental department already established.[5]

**Naval and Military Forces.** England's chief defense in this period, as in all others, was her navy, which was always maintained in first-class condition. The backbone of her military

[5] See Hugh McDowell Clokie and J. William Robinson, *Royal Commissions of Inquiry*, Stanford University Press, 1937.

force, as in the preceding century and a half, was the standing army, still kept under tight parliamentary control by the annual disciplinary acts (called Army Acts after 1881). The problem of providing reserves of adequately trained men was a perennial one. After 1829 the system of drafting quotas from each county for the militia was suspended, and voluntary recruiting took its place. In 1907, under the influence of an able Secretary of State for War named Lord Haldane, most of the reserves were organized into a Territorial Force (renamed Territorial Army in 1921), which was designed to supply an expeditionary army in time of need and also to fit more effectively into the regular army organization and provide for rapid expansion in the event of war. From 1916 to 1919, during the First World War, England was forced to resort to conscription to maintain the strength of her armed forces. Again in the spring of 1939 as the war clouds darkened once more, conscription was introduced to provide for a trained reserve of sufficient size, and it is now being employed to provide men for active service in the present war. The important place that aviation occupies in modern warfare was recognized in 1917 by the creation of a separate air force, which has its own Cabinet minister (page 562) and is now considered one of the three arms of the service, along with the army and the navy.

**Church Government.** While Parliament continued to keep a very tight control of the Established Church, in 1852 it did permit the Convocation of the Province of Canterbury (page 501) to reassemble and transact business. In 1855 debates were also permitted. Six years later the York Convocation was similarly revived. In the present century there has been a marked trend toward increasing the influence of lay communicants in church government. The year 1919 saw the establishment of a national assembly of three houses, bishops, lower clergy and laymen. This body was empowered to legislate on church affairs, though it was required to secure parliamentary endorsement of all actions before they could take effect.[6] The laity were also given a greater voice in the ecclesiastical affairs of their own parishes by the institution in 1921 of church councils, composed largely of laymen. These serve as advisory bodies with which the local clergy may consult before making any important alterations in the forms of worship, hours of service, or other matters of interest to the parishioners concerned.

## LOCAL GOVERNMENT

**County Government.** In the sphere of local government, at the county level the system of sheriffs and lord lieutenants has continued virtually unchanged since the seventeenth century and that of the justices of the peace was not greatly altered until 1888. The lord lieutenants have, however, declined in military importance because of the development of the standing army (pages 500, 567). The county militia—Territorials, as they are now called—have also passed largely out of the hands of the lord lieutenants and under the control of the regular army, to whose units they have been attached more and more closely by a succession of acts extending from 1871 to 1907. The administrative duties of the justices of the peace were taken away by the Local Government Act of 1888 and given to the councils of new counties established by the act.[7] These councils were elective bodies set up for some sixty-two new administrative areas, labeled counties by the authorities, though many were really subdivisions of the older areas which went by that name.

**The Boroughs.** The boroughs were reformed by an act of 1835 called the Municipal Corporations Act.[8] By it the old oligarchic constitutions of most of the towns (page 262) were abolished, and the resident ratepayers were authorized to elect councils serving for limited, but "staggered" (overlapping) terms. In this

6 S-M, No. 137G, pp. 830-32.    8 S-M, No. 130F, pp. 729-33.
7 S-M, No. 135D, pp. 808-10.

way provision was made for a responsible body that would always contain some experienced members. It elected the aldermen and mayor, and had control of all publicly owned utilities. By the Local Government Act of 1888 the boroughs were divided into two classes. Continuing certain ancient grants of privileges, the statute constituted some with a population of 50,000 or more as county boroughs, and made them equal in authority to the county government, and independent of it.[9] The others were called municipal boroughs, and received only partial autonomy.

**Urban and Rural District Councils.** Further changes in the sphere of local government deprived the parish of most of its importance. In 1834 a Poor Law Amendment Act revised the whole system of poor relief.[10] This act set up local districts (unions of parishes) whose poor law guardians were to administer the system for their entire area. A central supervisory commission was also established (page 562). Furthermore, the instructions given by the first commissioners established by the act provided that no more outrelief—that is, assistance to people not residing in poorhouses—should be given to able-bodied applicants. While the prohibition of outrelief was gradually abandoned during the late nineteenth century, the principles of central supervision—now exercised through the Ministry of Health (page 570)—and administration through local areas larger than parishes have been retained.[11] The institution in 1872 of urban and rural districts,[12] with councils on the pattern of the borough, provided means of enforcing health regulations for the populous areas without borough status and also for the sparsely settled areas smaller than the administrative counties but larger than the parishes. This system was regularized and extended by acts of

[9] S-M, No. 135D, p. 810.
[10] S-M, No. 130E, pp. 728-29.
[11] In 1929 the poor-relief districts were abolished and the responsibility for the administration of the poor law was transferred to the even larger areas of the administrative counties.
[12] Originally called sanitary districts.

1888, 1893, and 1929 which broadened the scope of the councils' activities to include all of the functions of local government. This naturally made for a further decline of the parishes.

**The High Quality of English Local Government: The Grants-in-Aid.** All English local government is kept on a high level of honesty and efficiency by a combination of circumstances. The great homogeneity of the population of England keeps the racial element out of politics and out of the law courts when politicians or local officials are tried for criminal offenses. Since the introduction of a national civil service, corruption has ceased to be a feature of national political life, and the standards of the offices in the capital are reflected in those of the smaller units. Civil-service arrangements have been introduced in local as well as central government, though the process here is still far from complete. More specifically and cogently, high standards are enforced by the system of grants-in-aid under the supervision of the Minister of Health. This is an arrangement by which the funds of local governmental authorities are supplied in part from local rates and in part by grants from the national treasury. The original reason for instituting this system was that it was manifestly unfair, as well as impossible in an industrial age, to expect the small areas in which social problems were most acute to raise the funds necessary for their relief when the employing class, which drew its wealth from the labor of these underprivileged citizens, might live in another rating unit whose relief problem was small. But besides meeting this difficulty, the grant-in-aid system has also served to keep standards up and corruption down in the field of local government. By threatening to withhold the grant-in-aid until its conditions are met the central government can nearly always enforce its will on the smaller units.

# 28. THE LEGAL SYSTEM

## SUCCESS OF THE REFORM MOVEMENT

**A Period of Notable Reforms.** Though the United States Supreme Court is supposed to be above politics, the humorist Finley Peter Dunne ("Mr. Dooley") once remarked that it certainly followed the election returns. English lawyers have been similarly able to discern the ebbs and flows of the political tides. Therefore it is not surprising that when the great reform movement set in after 1822 the legal system soon reflected the new trend. What had seemed quite satisfactory to Blackstone fifty years before was now suddenly recognized as being hopelessly out of date. The dubious channels of justice, long since clogged with antiquated and absurd growths of various sorts, were straightened and cleared out. Modern ideas of economics, sociology, and psychology were introduced into the theory of the law itself, and the whole English legal system was raised to a level that has made it the admiration and the envy of the rest of the world.

**The Utilitarians and Dickens.** Much of the immediate credit for getting this movement under way belongs to the disciples of Jeremy Bentham (page 505). This distinguished reformer lived to see a few of his ideas adopted before he died in 1832, but had younger men not been willing to fight for his principles in his later years and after his death, the alterations in the English legal system might have taken quite different forms. His two chief followers were the Mills, father and son (James and John Stuart), who were active in publishing a quarterly called the *Westminster Review* that expounded the reformers' theories. Because

571

these thinkers appealed so constantly to the principle that institutions are to be judged by their utility (usefulness), instead of by their antiquity, social respectability, or any other criterion, these reformers were called Utilitarians. By hammering away on this doctrine they did much to persuade the English people and their Parliament to revise and simplify the law of the land. The novelist Charles Dickens also made a great contribution to this end. Although not as philosophically inclined as the Mills, he had a facile pen and a ready sense of humor, which soon won him a large reading public. Since he had been a court reporter and was therefore well acquainted with the workings of the law, he was able to satirize the absurdities and injustices of the contemporary legal world in a way that demanded action, and frequently got it.

## CHANGES IN THE ORGANIZATION AND JURISDICTION OF THE COURTS

**The County Courts.** The first addition to the old court system was the institution, in 1846, of civil courts that made their type of justice as quickly and cheaply available as the justices of the peace had made the criminal sort. Since the decline of the old county courts, except in some of the large towns there had been no tribunals below the slow and expensive assize level where disputes over small debts, for example, could be settled. Now, under the immediate sponsorship of a Whig leader named Lord Brougham,[1] it was provided that courts for some five hundred districts organized into fifty-nine circuits should be established, with their judges to be appointed by the Lord Chancellor. In them, cases up to the value of £20 were to be heard. If the total sum was under £5, a jury was only employed at the discretion of the judge; otherwise it could be requested by either party, but was not deemed necessary. When it was employed, its num-

[1] For whom the old-fashioned carriage, which he popularized, is named.

ber was limited to five. By a stroke of legislative perversity these tribunals were named county courts, though the circuits did not correspond to the county areas, and none of the administrative duties of the old county courts were put upon their modern namesakes.[2] They proved to be very popular from the start, and the scope of their jurisdiction has been steadily widened, until now they may hear cases to the value of £500, or even more in special circumstances.

**The Divorce and Probate Courts.** Reform of the central court system was a more difficult problem, but a beginning was made in 1857 by the secularization of the probate and divorce jurisdiction of the church courts. The extremely complicated and expensive system of parliamentary divorce established at the close of the seventeenth century (page 513) obviously made divorce a luxury beyond the reach of the average Englishman. In 1845 it was ridiculed by a Justice Maule in the Warwick assizes at the trial of a poor man for bigamy. The defendant had pleaded that when he remarried he had in reality no wife, for his former wife had first robbed and then deserted him and was then living with another man. In passing sentence the judge said:

Prisoner at the bar, you have committed a grave offence in taking the law into your own hands and marrying again. I will now tell you what you should have done. You should have brought an action into the civil court, and obtained damages, which the other side would probably have been unable to pay, and you would have had to pay your own costs—perhaps £100 or £150. You should then have gone to the ecclesiastical court and obtained a divorce *a mensa et thoro,* and then to the House of Lords, where having proved that these preliminaries had been complied with, you would have been enabled to marry again. The expenses amount to £500 or £600, or perhaps £1000. You

2 These circuits, unhappily, do not correspond with the administrative counties created in 1888 (page 568). The reader must notice, therefore, that the term "county" is used in three different senses in modern England. In earlier times some towns were also known as counties (page 569) for administrative purposes. Hence London, which was not affected by the Municipal Corporation Act of 1835, still has its sheriffs.

say you are a poor man and you probably do not possess as many pence. But, prisoner, you must know that in England there is not one law for the rich and another for the poor. The sentence of the court upon you therefore is that you be imprisoned for one day, which period has already been exceeded, as you have been in custody since the commencement of the assizes.

In the comparatively short space of twelve years a reform act was pushed through Parliament—finally by the insistence of Viscount Palmerston, the Prime Minister, who threatened in the event of prolonged opposition to keep the House in session after the August grouse-shooting season began, an unheard-of encroachment on the natural rights of English gentlemen. The act provided for the establishment of a secular divorce court with power to grant separations and, in cases of adultery, absolute divorces without the previous expensive preliminaries. At the same time the testamentary jurisdiction of the ecclesiastical courts was taken away and given to a separate and secular Probate Court.

**The Judicature Acts.** In 1873 a general reorganization of the central courts was at last begun. Under the terms of an act of that year and supplementary legislation of 1876 and 1884, a Supreme Court of Judicature was established, in which most of the existing central courts were absorbed.[3] Its main branch, called the High Court of Justice, took over the courts of (1) Chancery, (2) King's Bench, Common Pleas, and Exchequer, (3) Probate, Divorce, and Admiralty. For convenience' sake the old jurisdictions of these courts were grouped in divisions as indicated by the numerals. But the judges of any one division might serve in the other, and it was specifically provided that the law of any one division might be applied in the others when the case seemed to demand it. Whenever there was a conflict between the rules of equity and law in a given case, the rule of equity was to prevail.

**The Court of Appeal and the House of Lords.** Above the High Court of Justice was placed a Court of Appeal, to be

[3] S-M, No. 131K, pp. 750-53; No. 131L, pp. 753-54.

## LINCOLN'S INN HALL

This engraving shows the lord chancellor's court holding a session in the hall of Lincoln's Inn during the early nineteenth century. This is not a moot court for students but a real session of chancery, which in modern times sought more convenient quarters than the noisy, open Westminster Hall (page 287). Later in the nineteenth century a Law Courts building was erected near the inns, and there the sessions of all branches of the Supreme Court of Judicature (page 574) are now held.

Notice the wigs and robes which the lawyers are wearing. The robe has come down from medieval times. The wig became fashionable for all gentlemen in the eighteenth century and the lawyers who adopted it then (*cf.* the pictures of Blackstone and Mansfield, pages 509, 512) have since retained it along with the robe and the white neckbands (which are a survival of the wide white falling collar of the seventeenth century) as part of their professional costume.

THE MODERN ENGLISH COURT SYSTEM

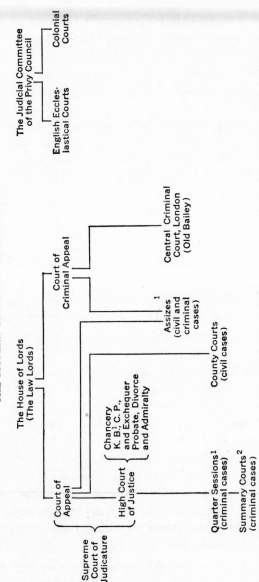

1. In the King's Bench division of the High Court and in the assizes both civil and criminal cases are heard. Criminal appeals from the King's Bench division go to the Criminal Court of Appeals. Some appeals from Quarter Sessions go directly to the Criminal Court of Appeal.
2. When two unpaid justices of the peace or one stipendiary magistrate hear a case the sessions of these courts are called petty sessions.

Adapted from the charts in R. M. Jackson, *The Machinery of Justice in England*, Cambridge, Eng., 1940, pp. 24, 104.

staffed by senior judges. This was originally designed to take over the appellate jurisdiction of the House of Lords (page 283), but when the Lords protested, it was arranged that their lordships should continue to be a court of last resort for all cases heard in the Supreme Court of Judicature in England and similar courts in Scotland and Ireland. Since, however, it was obviously absurd for a body of some six hundred untrained laymen to presume to reverse the Court of Appeal, two (later increased to four and again to six, and finally to seven) skilled judges were appointed Law Lords. They were considered members of the upper house for the term of their own lives, but were given no hereditary title to transmit to their heirs. Thereafter, when appeals came to the House of Lords the Lord Chancellor and the Law Lords heard them, and the ordinary members of the House, by a gentlemen's agreement, refrained from participating in these matters. The rank and file in the upper house did, however, retain an old jurisdiction as a court of first instance for the trial of lords accused of treason or felony. Thus a lord was assured of trial by his peers in such cases, according to the rule laid down by the Great Charter.

**The Judicial Committee of the Privy Council.** Parallel to the House of Lords as an appellate court of last resort was the Judicial Committee of the Privy Council, which had jurisdiction over English appeals in ecclesiastical cases and also in appeals in all types of cases arising in the colonies—in other words, in all cases arising outside the jurisdiction of the old English common law, equity, and admiralty and the corresponding Scottish and Irish (now North Irish) laws. As the direct representatives of the crown the Privy Council took this jurisdiction and exercised it—as the Lords did theirs—through specially appointed judges, who constituted its Judicial Committee. Since, in practice, the most important members of this committee are the same individuals who serve as Law Lords, there is in effect one highest court for the British Empire.

**The Court of Criminal Appeal.** One gap was left in the judicial structure after the passage of the acts of 1873 and succeeding years, and that was the lack of a court of appeal for criminal cases. Only civil actions were reconsidered by the machinery already described. English criminal justice preserved its reputation for expeditiousness at the expense of making no provision for rehearings. In the early years of this century the conviction for the second time of one Adolf Beck, an innocent man who was discovered to be a double of the person really guilty of the crime of which Beck was accused, called attention to the fact that no remedy was available in such cases except that of a royal pardon, customarily recommended by the Home Secretary. In 1907 a Court of Criminal Appeal was set up to make good this deficiency. It consisted of the Chief Justice of the King's Bench division of the High Court of Justice and eight of his colleagues, of whom three were necessary for a quorum. When in the first nine months of service the new court quashed eighteen sentences, there was some speculation as to how many legally innocent victims the law might have claimed in the years before the institution of this tribunal.

**Local Criminal Jurisdiction.** At the lowest level of criminal jurisdiction the unpaid justices of the peace (assisted by their professional clerks) continued to carry the brunt of the work throughout this period. Under the terms of the Municipal Corporations Act of 1835, however, some towns have stipendiary (paid) magistrates who exercise a summary jurisdiction equal to that of the justices of the peace below the level of quarter sessions.[4] And a growing criticism of such unprofessional methods

---

4 Ordinary criminal jurisdiction for the metropolitan area of London is exercised by a special Central Criminal Court—dear to devotees of detective stories under its popular name the Old Bailey, from the site of its meeting-place, which was just inside the bailey (outer wall) of the old City of London. In it sits a professional judge from the High Court of Justice (as well as three judges paid by the city), but he is commonly accompanied on the bench by an alderman of the City of London who is, in theory, as much a judge of the court as his professional colleague. The old tradition that the City enjoys special judicial rights is thus preserved.

as those of the amateur justice who regularly asked the suspects tried before him, "Have you anything to say before the jury finds you guilty?" has led most boards of justices to elect a legally qualified chairman.[5] But the tradition of voluntary service in this important capacity is still a strong one, and it is not unreasonable to suggest that in time of peace it has been one of the most important pillars of British society. By showing the spirit of noblesse oblige in both peace and war the privileged class has done much to justify and retain its privileged position. Once more, power is a function of service.

## PROCEDURAL REFORMS AND RESULTING SIMPLICITY

**Procedural Reform.** The story of the reform of legal procedure closely parallels that of the organization of the courts. After 1822 parliamentary commission after commission investigated the workings of the different courts and brought in proposals for their amendment. Not all of these suggestions were sound, but by trial and error the job was eventually done. The original writs, already long since obsolete—though they still linger on in some American jurisdictions—were abolished by statute in 1833. In their place was put a single blanket writ of summons with which any civil action might be commenced. Compurgation as a method of trial was removed from the arsenal of legal tricks in the same year. In 1837 defendants accused of felony were at last allowed to have professional counsel. The Hilary rules of pleading—so called from the term of court in 1824 when they went into effect—were not so successful, because they tended to increase the amount of special (page 292) rather than general pleading, and had to be supplemented by the Common Law

---

[5] Some of the professionally trained men at this level were not above criticism. After asking the prisoner how he pleaded and receiving the reply, "Not guilty," one clerk is said to have made it his practice to remark grimly, "We shall see about that."

Procedure Act of 1852. The latter statute also gave to the common law courts the right, hitherto enjoyed only by Chancery, to compel the production of documentary evidence in the hands of parties to actions before them. At the same time Chancery was given the right to employ a jury and hear oral evidence in its capacity as a court of equity. Finally, under the terms of the legislation of 1873 and succeeding years the Supreme Court of Judicature was given the right to fix its own rules of procedure, much as the American federal courts have been by an act of Congress passed in 1938. With this authorization an entirely new and modern set of rules was drawn up that completed the elimination from modern usage of legal museum pieces which had long cluttered up the law courts.

**Resulting Simplicity.** As a result, in modern English courts the time of the jury is not so often wasted or the judge's freedom of action so much impaired as is commonly the case in the United States. The English judge takes part in the questioning of witnesses, offers advice to counsel in the framing of their questions, and makes careful notes on the case. These, together with the full transcript, become part of the official record. Furthermore, the English judge may comment fully on the evidence presented, without running the risk of having the higher court order a new trial. "Listen closely, members of the jury," he has been known to say, "for I believe that in answering this question the witness is about to perjure himself." Under this system the cult of the missing comma has almost disappeared from English legal practice. It is an eye-opener to the American visitor to see a criminal case begin in an English court. It is presumed that an honest sheriff has chosen an impartial jury, which duly files into the box. The defendant in the dock is asked to look at the jury and state any objection he may have to any member of it. He rarely has any to make, and the case begins at once, without the endless preliminary questioning and challenging that consume so much time in American practice. In most civil cases, in fact, the use of the jury has been greatly restricted since the Judicature Act of 1873, and particularly since the Administration of Justice Act of 1933. It may only be used by special application in cases of libel, slander, malicious prosecution, breach of promise of marriage, and certain types of fraud. Even then the judge may refuse the request if the trial involves prolonged examination of documents or scientific material. Less than 10 per cent of civil cases in Great Britain are now tried before juries.[6]

## THE LEGAL PROFESSION, LEGAL EDUCATION AND SCHOLARSHIP

**Barristers.** The legal profession and the cause of legal education have also felt the beneficial effects of the reform movement. In 1852 there was formed the Council of Legal Education, which since 1872 has administered a joint bar examination for the four inns and maintained a comparatively high qualifying standard. Another consequence of the revival of interest in legal training was that lectures were once more offered at the inns, though the student continued to obtain most of his instruction elsewhere. This might be in special tutorial schools or in the universities, which followed the precedent set by Viner and Blackstone (page 509) and began the teaching of the common law as a serious discipline in the nineteenth century. Today residence at the inns is still computed in terms of dinners eaten, and students who are keeping terms at the universities are given a reduction in the number of these meals required. Since Oxford and Cambridge reckon residence in terms of nights slept in the university precincts and the train service between London and those towns is good, it is possible to keep the two different kinds of residence simultaneously and so qualify for the bar shortly after finishing one's university career.

[6] *Cf.* page 588 n. on the virtual abolition of the grand jury.

**The Solicitors.** In 1825 the solicitors organized a Law Institution, which in 1891 became the Law Society. This body early assumed the responsibility for administering qualifying examinations for those wishing to enter this part of the profession. While many solicitors still secure much of their preliminary training by being articled (apprenticed) as a clerk to a practicing solicitor, a year of law-school work is required. This may be obtained in a law school conducted by the Law Society itself or in a university.

**Legal Scholarship.** The nineteenth century also saw the institution of a comprehensive system of law reports, with a series devoted to each of the important courts. They were prepared under the supervision of the Law Reporting Council, organized in 1865. This system of reports rapidly displaced the old one of individual efforts, and has made information on judicial rulings in particular courts easily accessible to the precedent-hunter. A great flood of digests, encyclopedias, and guides issued by enterprising individuals has also contributed to the same end. Lastly, the student of legal history must be referred to the works of Professor F. W. Maitland and Sir William Holdsworth. Maitland, in conjunction with Sir Frederick Pollock, composed a masterly *History of the English Law before the Time of Edward I* (2 vols., 2d ed., Cambridge, Eng., 1923), and before his untimely death in 1906 was the leading spirit in the Selden Society. This is an organization named for the great seventeenth-century scholar (page 410), which exists for the purpose of publishing documents of importance for the history of English law down to 1600. The introductions to the various volumes are often in themselves standard treatises on the topics to which the documents relate. Sir William Holdsworth, Vinerian professor of English law (page 508) at Oxford University, is the author of an unfinished comprehensive treatment of English legal history that already includes twelve stout volumes.

## SUBSTANTIVE LAW: REAL PROPERTY

**Early Reforms.** To a limited extent the field of real property felt the effects of the general movement for legal reform in the years following 1822. Commissioners were appointed to investigate the law of real property, and between 1829 and 1833 they issued four reports. As a result some reforms were made in the fields of conveyancing and procedure. "Old abuses fell like leaves in autumn. Fines were not saved by their antiquity nor recoveries by their absurdity, nor real actions by their costliness. Our sense of historical continuity was not enough to save the 'causal ejector' or the 'common vouchee.' A decent oblivion was provided for John Doe and Richard Roe" (pages 403-4).[7]

[7] F. W. Maitland, *Collected Papers*, ed. H. A. L. Fisher, 3 vols., Putnam, 1911, Vol. I, pp. 198-99. Later a kindly mourner (George Hayes) penned these lines "To the Memory of John Doe and Richard Roe (lately deceased)":

Should Doe and Roe be e'er forgot,
    And never brought to mind:
Should John and Richard go to pot
    And not a mourner find?
For auld lang syne, my friends,
    For auld lang syne;
We'll chant a dirge for Doe and Roe
    For auld lang syne. . . .

When quarrels rose about the right
    To houses or to lands
Then John and Richard took the fight
    Entirely in their hands
And Richard, ever rash and brave,
    To enter did incline,
And turn'd John out "with stick and stave"
    For auld lang syne.

Then, sad to say, Doe sued poor Roe,
    For this his valiant part,
But Richard would not ward the blow,
    It almost broke his heart.
A letter of advice he penn'd
    In most pathetic line,
And signed himself "Your loving friend,"
    For auld lang syne.
        —W. S. Holdsworth, *History of English Law*, 12 vols., Little, Brown, 1923-1937, Vol. IX, pp. 432-33.

**Primogeniture and Perpetuities.** The landed gentry were still influential, however, and the old rules of primogeniture and inheritance, cornerstones of the oligarchic social system, were only slightly affected. One of the principles which the French Revolution established across the Channel was the rule that all children should have an equal share in most of the lands which their parents might leave. But England had not become as democratic as that, and since landed families were generally still anxious to assure as far as possible the continuity of the family holdings, the lawyers were under constant pressure to devise ways of keeping family estates intact in spite of judicial rulings dictated by the contrary policy (page 511). In 1832 the courts finally determined upon the maximum length of time during which an estate could be tied up so as to make it inalienable. This was set at twenty-one years plus a life or lives in being, roughly the equivalent, in the social policy involved, of the ninety-nine-year period that is the limit of leases in some American jurisdictions.

**The Strict Family Settlement.** This remains the law, and theoretically the English law knows no such thing as a perpetuity for private purposes. By the operation of an ingenious device known as the strict family settlement, however, something approaching it is obtained. Under this arrangement the father holds the family lands in trust. The conditions of the trust provide him with a life interest, and his widow, should she survive him, with a rent charge (annuity). Provisions may also be made for younger children, but the chief interest is given to the tail male, with remainder to the tail general (female heirs) and reversion to the settlor. When the eldest son (next in line in the tail male) comes of age, he is offered a generous allowance if he will consent to a resettlement. Under the terms of this resettlement the son guarantees the succession right of any male heir he may have, and in return his allowance is made a primary rent charge on the land, that is, one which takes precedence over any others. If the son refuses to be a party to such a resettlement, he is left without means for the time being and without any certain interest in the land, since he may die before his father and thus never come into the land at all. Without better security it is difficult for him to borrow money, and therefore he usually consents to the desired arrangement. The tradition of primogeniture is thus perpetuated. Indeed, until 1925 the law provided that if the parent should hold the lands in fee simple and die intestate, they should go to his eldest son. In this way the great family estates have been quite generally kept intact during the last century. In the course of time, however, the cumulative effect on them of the heavy death duties now in force (page 565) may well be to break them up. The new law of intestacy, which assimilates the rule of inheritance of real property to that for personal property—according to which all the children fare alike—will of course also contribute to that end.

**The Property Acts of 1925.** Throughout its long history English law as a whole has never been codified. It remains a body of separate decisions and statutes instead of a single organized code—such as Justinian's collection of Roman civil law or the Napoleonic one in Continental Europe—which, with the addition of periodic amending acts, brings all the law up to date. The English arrangement has the disadvantage of allowing the accumulation on the statute books of a great deal of obsolete legislation that is legally still in force. To remedy this difficulty in part, the law in certain fields has been revised by statute. That is to say, a single statute has been passed embodying virtually a new code for that particular portion of the law. After many abortive proposals this objective was finally attained in the field of real property by the Property Acts of 1922 to 1925, sometimes called the Birkenhead Code because the Earl of Birkenhead, Lord Chancellor in 1922, was influential in securing the passage of the parent act in that year. By the operation of these acts new practices were introduced in nearly all aspects of real property law. The most important of these fall under two general heads. First, the law once worked out for the great was made the law for all. In other words, the law was simplified in such a way as to make available to the small landholders nearly all the large powers that the law had conferred on the great landlords. Though many old types of estates, tenures, and customs, such as the estate for life, copyhold, and borough English (page 219), were abolished, the law provided that nearly all the old objectives could be attained, if desired, by the simple device of an equitable interest, that is, by allowing the creation of different kinds of trusts. The second general type of reform was the assimilation of the rules for holding real and personal property. Not only were the rules of inheritance made substantially the same (page 181) but conveyancing practice in the field of real property was simplified to correspond as far as possible to that relating to dealings in stocks and bonds. On the other hand, it became possible to entail personal property, and the rule against perpetuities (page 583) was applied to that type of arrangement also.

## BUSINESS AND FAMILY LAW

**Business Law.** The general spirit of reform at last made it possible for businessmen to secure the passage of statutes regularizing and continuing the progress made in the field of company organization during the century since the passage of the severely restrictive Bubble Act (page 511). In 1852 and 1856 Parliament made the privilege of incorporation available on easy terms. The acts of those years also provided statutory authority for the principle of limited liability, which had hitherto depended solely on the judicial ruling of 1768 (page 512). These new laws greatly facilitated the conduct of British business, and contributed not a little to the remarkable prosperity of the country in the years that followed.

**Marriage and Divorce Law.** In the sphere of marriage and divorce law the grip of the Established Church, with its conservative tradition, is being slowly broken. In 1836 Nonconformist ministers were given permission to perform legal marriages. The change in the divorce law in 1857 has already been mentioned (page 574). Women, who under the 1857 law were obligated to prove not only infidelity but some such "aggravating conduct" as cruelty in order to secure a divorce, were given the same rights as men in 1923. Affinity as a bar to marriage (page 223) was abolished by a succession of acts before and after the First World War. In 1936 the events centering around the abdication of Edward VIII (page 528) focused attention on the unsavory practice of obtaining divorces by collusive suits. In the following year a reform statute known as the Herbert Act was adopted. By the terms of this act the permissible grounds for absolute divorce were extended to include desertion, insanity, and extreme cruelty.

## REFORM OF THE CRIMINAL LAW

**The Acceptance of the Ideas of Beccaria and Bentham.** With a reference to the development of criminal law in modern England we may well end this outline sketch. For the changes in this field typify very well the spirit of the modern English constitution. When Parliament became willing to listen to suggestions of reforms, those concerning criminal law were among the first considered. An important act of 1827 abolished benefit of clergy,[8] the heritage of Becket (page 112), and at the same time began the process of moderating the severity of the punishment prescribed on conviction for nearly all felonies. In theory this had been death, though, as already noted, benefit of clergy (which was available to all who could read) and provisions for transportation as an alternative penalty had in practice considerably modified this principle. Now transportation was substituted for the extreme penalty in all cases formerly covered by benefit

---

[8] The right of sanctuary connected with some ecclesiastical premises (page 242) had been abolished in 1623.

of clergy, and in a succession of statutes extending down to 1861 capital punishment was abolished for all but four types of offenses: treason, murder, piracy with violence, and arson involving government dockyards and arsenals. Statutes passed between 1854 and 1863 abolished the punishment of transportation, leaving penal servitude or imprisonment, with or without hard labor, as the sentence ordinarily imposed, though whipping is sometimes added in cases involving crimes of violence and for juvenile offenders. In 1870 Parliament abolished the penalty of forfeiture of real and personal property formerly connected with conviction of treason or felony (page 199). Short terms of imprisonment, fines, or (in rare instances) whippings remained the usual punishments for misdemeanors.

**Modern Means of Law Enforcement.** With the institution of these reforms England became a much more law-abiding place. When a professional police force was introduced in London and other large towns after 1828, its members were armed only with wooden truncheons.[9] Consequently the small criminal class does not carry guns, knowing as it does that the police will not shoot on sight, as in certain other parts of the world, and that the offender's punishment will be much more severe if he is found to be armed. An incidental result of this situation is a somewhat higher expectancy of life among that long-suffering class of innocent bystanders which so often bears the brunt of police activities elsewhere. Yet the police—helped, it is true, by the smallness of the country, the homogeneity of the population (page 570), and past emigration trends, which have eliminated much of the more troublesome stock—generally succeed in apprehending those whom they wish to arrest. The cases are then prepared for trial without efforts to extract confessions by beating or otherwise torturing prisoners. If the evidence is considered sufficiently

---

[9] The members are popularly called "bobbies," after the Home Secretary Sir Robert Peel, who was responsible for the original organization and establishment of the system in 1828.

strong by the coroner, justice, or judge to whom it is presented,[10] the prisoner is held for trial in the appropriate criminal court, where he soon receives fair and simple justice, largely free from technicalities. In this efficient police work, combined with the just and speedy legal proceedings that follow, are reflected many of the finest developments of the constitution we have been studying. A free people, hitherto blessed by military security and economic opportunity, has learned to govern itself quietly and efficiently without forgetting those rights of the individual upon which any society worthy of the name is based.

[10] With a few minor exceptions in certain types of cases, the method of indictment by grand jury was abolished in 1933.

# APPENDIX

## THE KINGS OF ENGLAND, 802-1941

| | | | |
|---|---|---|---|
| Egbert | 802-839 | Edward III | 1327-1377 |
| Ethelwulf | 839-858 | Richard II | 1377-1399 |
| Ethelbald | 858-860 | Henry IV | 1399-1413 |
| Ethelbert | 860-866 | Henry V | 1413-1422 |
| Ethelred I | 866-871 | Henry VI | 1422-1461 |
| Alfred | 871-899 | Edward IV | 1461-1483 |
| Edward the Elder | 899-924 | Edward V | 1483 |
| Athelstan | 924-939 | Richard III | 1483-1485 |
| Edmund I | 939-946 | Henry VII | 1485-1509 |
| Edred | 946-955 | Henry VIII | 1509-1547 |
| Edwy | 955-959 | Edward VI | 1547-1553 |
| Edgar | 959-975 | Mary | 1553-1558 |
| Edward the Martyr | 975-978 | Elizabeth | 1558-1603 |
| Ethelred the Unready | 978-1016 | James I | 1603-1625 |
| Edmund Ironside | 1016 | Charles I | 1625-1649 |
| Canute | 1017-1035 | Charles II | 1660-1685 |
| Harold I | 1035-1040 | James II | 1685-1688 |
| Hardicanute | 1040-1042 | William III and | |
| Edward | | Mary | 1689-1702 |
| the Confessor | 1042-1066 | Anne | 1702-1714 |
| Harold II | 1066 | George I | 1714-1727 |
| William I | 1066-1087 | George II | 1727-1760 |
| William II | 1087-1100 | George III | 1760-1820 |
| Henry I | 1100-1135 | George IV | 1820-1830 |
| Stephen | 1135-1154 | William IV | 1830-1837 |
| Henry II | 1154-1189 | Victoria | 1837-1901 |
| Richard I | 1189-1199 | Edward VII | 1901-1910 |
| John | 1199-1216 | George V | 1910-1936 |
| Henry III | 1216-1272 | Edward VIII | 1936 |
| Edward I | 1272-1307 | George VI | 1936 |
| Edward II | 1307-1327 | | |

# INDEX

(See also endpaper chart of chapters and subtopics)